THE KANGCHENJUNGA ADVENTURE

THE KANGCHENJUNGA ADVENTURE

BY

F. S. SMYTHE

GYAN

Published by

GYAN

Gyan Publishing House
5, Ansari Road
Daryaganj, New Delhi-110002
Phone: 011-47034999, 9811692060
E-mail: books@gyanbooks.com

Distribution Network
gyanbooks.com
India, USA, Canada, UK, Australia, France

ISBN : 978-81-212-9996-1 (PB)
First Published, 1930

2nd Impression 2021

Printed at: Gyan Press, Delhi.

The
Kangchenjunga Adventure
Author: F. S. Smythe

THE
KANGCHENJUNGA ADVENTURE

by

F. S. SMYTHE

LONDON
VICTOR GOLLANCZ LTD
14 Henrietta Street Covent Garden
1930

ICE FRETWORK ON THE LHONAK GLACIER: IN THE BACKGROUND IS THE DODANG PEAK

CONTENTS

LIST OF ILLUSTRATIONS

PREFACE

This book is a personal account of the attempt made in 1930 to climb Kangchenjunga, 28,156 feet, and the successful ascent of the Jonsong Peak, 24,344 feet, and other great peaks of the Eastern Himalayas, by a party of mountaineers from four nations, Germany, Austria, Switzerland and Great Britain, under the leadership of Professor G. Dyhrenfurth. I have endeavoured to record my own personal impressions of what was primarily an adventure. It is now no longer necessary to disguise adventure shamefacedly under the cloak of science. The scientific side of the expedition was well attended to, and interesting and important data has been gained. We went, however, to Kangchenjunga in response not to the dictates of science, but in obedience to that indefinable urge men call adventure, an urge which, in spite of easy living and "Safety First," still has its roots deep in the human race.

I should like to take this opportunity of expressing my appreciation of the interest, sympathy and help so freely offered by *The Times*, and especially Mr. R. Deakin, the Foreign News Editor, and Mr. U. V. Bogaerde, the Art Editor ; also to Mr. Alfred Watson, the Editor of the *Statesman*, Calcutta, who was responsible for the transmission of dispatches and who helped the expedition in many ways. I should like also on behalf of the expedition to tender grateful thanks to the Indian Government for allowing the expedition's goods into India free of Customs duty. Among the many kind friends in England and abroad who helped, thanks are due to Brigadier-General the Hon. C. G. Bruce, M.V.O., Lieutenant-Colonel E. L. Strutt, C.B.E., D.S.O., Mr. Sydney Spencer, Mr. T. H. Somervell and Mr. G. Seligman for valuable advice and help, and to Colonel Bonn, the proprietor of the Suvrettahaus Hotel, St. Moritz, for his kind hospitality to the expedition. In India, thanks are due to Field-Marshal Sir William Birdwood, Bart., Commander in Chief in India, for the loan of a Gurkha N.C.O., to Mr. Howell, the Foreign Secretary at Delhi, and to Colonel Dawkes, C.I.E., the British Envoy at Khatmandu, Nepal, for their advice regarding the entry of the expedition into Nepal; to Mr. W. J. Kydd of Darjeeling, for his efficient work with the expedition's mails; to His Highness the Maharajah of Nepal, for his kindness in allowing the expedition to enter Nepal, and for his great hospitality and help when it was in Nepalese territory, and to His Highness the Maharajah of Sikkim.

Without the help of the Himalayan Club it is safe to say that the expedition would never have reached the Base Camp, and it is, therefore, not out of place to express appreciation and gratitude of the invaluable work rendered to the expedition by Lieutenant-Colonel H. W. Tobin, D.S.O., O.B.E., Mr. G. W. Wood Johnson and Mr. J. S. Hannah, who accompanied the expedition, and of those who did not accompany it, to Mr. G. Mackworth Young, the Hon. Secretary, and Mr. G. B. Gourlay, the Hon. Local Secretary in Calcutta.

The expedition is extremely grateful to the Meteorological and Broadcasting Departments of Calcutta for combining to send out daily weather reports. The fact that the receiving apparatus was smashed beyond repair makes no difference to our gratitude.

I am extremely grateful to Mr. H. Ruttledge for permission to use a photograph of Chettan.

Many firms assisted the expedition, and I take this opportunity of expressing grateful thanks to the Imperial Tobacco Company at Calcutta, for the gift of over 100,000 cigarettes, and a large quantity of tobacco ; to the Hurricane Smock Company, Liverpool ; Messrs. Jaeger, Ltd., and Mr. W. Bill, of London, for woollies, and to Messrs. Sands, Hunter, Ltd., and Agfa, Ltd., for photographic apparatus and materials ; and last, but not least, the thanks of the expedition are due to the proprietor of the Mount Everest Hotel, Darjeeling, and the Lloyd Triestino Navigation Company, for a substantial reduction of charges and steamship fares.

CHAPTER I

AMBITIONS AND DREAMS

In the geography class at school we knew, on paper, three kinds of mountain ranges. There was the mountain range represented by a long line supported on either side by little legs which straggled pathetically across the page of our freehand geography drawing books, like some starved Mediæval dragon. This method of mountain delineation is technically known as hachuring, but our Geography Master generally referred to mountain ranges drawn thus contemptuously as " centipedes " and awarded but a low mark to home-made maps drawn in, as he rightly considered, such a slovenly fashion. Then there was the shading method. The idea of this was in imagining the sun to be shining on one side only of the range, the other side being in funereal shadow. Well done it is quite effective, and as there are few schoolboys who can resist rubbing a pencil lead up and down a piece of paper, it was universally popular. Yet, if giving some vague impression of form and relief, the mountain ranges we drew were grim sad affairs as desolate and unattractive as the airless vistas of the moon. And lastly, there was the contour method. This was popular among few owing to the time and labour involved, for unless approximate accuracy was achieved, a map drawn thus was sure to incur the wrath of the Geography Master.

Personally, I found much satisfaction in laboriously

drawing out and colouring any mountain range portion of the map, sometimes to the exclusion of all else on the map and other items of homework. Geography, was, indeed, one of the few subjects in which I took any interest whatever at school, and had it been the only subject necessary to qualify for promotion I *might* have reached the "Sixth." As it was, I was relegated for the remainder of my natural school life to the "Fifth Modern," a polite term for "Remove," the pupils of which were taught handicrafts on the apparent assumption that their mental equipment was such as to render it impossible for them to make their living otherwise than with their hands.

The green lowlands of the map had little fascination for me. Mentally, I was ever seeking escape from the plains of commerce into those regions which by virtue of their height, their inaccessibility and their distance from the centres of civilisation were marked, "Barren Regions Incapable of Commercial Development." My gods were Scott, Shackleton, and Edward Whymper.

There was one portion of the Earth's surface at which I would gaze more often than at any other, the indeterminate masses of reds and browns in the map which sprawl over Central Asia. For hours I would pore over the names of ranges, deserts and cities until they were at my finger-tips. By comparison with distances I knew—the distance to the seaside, or to London—I tried to gain some idea of a mountain range the length of which is measured in thousands of miles, the Himalayas.

In imagination I would start from the green plains, and follow the straggling line of a river up through the light browns of the map to the dark browns, to halt finally on one of the white bits that represented the snowy summits of the highest peaks. There I would stop and dream, trying to picture great mountain ranges lifting far above the world : the dull walls of the schoolroom would recede, and vanish, great peaks of dazzling white surrounded me, the airs of heaven caressed me, the blizzards lashed me. And so I would dream until the harsh voice of the Geography Master broke in with its threats and promises of punishment for slackness and gross inattention. If he had known, perhaps he would have left me there on my dream summits, for he was an understanding soul.

If I had learnt as much about other branches of geography as I knew about mountains I should, indeed, have been a paragon. As it was, the knowledge gained from every book on the subject on which I could lay my hands had its drawbacks, and I have a distinct recollection of being sent to the bottom of the form for daring to argue that the Dom, and not Mont Blanc was the highest mountain entirely in Switzerland.[1]

Three Himalayan names stood out before everything else, Mount Everest, Mount Godwin Austin (now called K 2) and Kangchenjunga. Once the knowledge that Everest was 29,002 feet high, instead of a mere 29,000 feet, resulted in my promotion to the top of the form, where for a short time I remained, basking in the sun of the Geography Master's approval (for he was a discriminating man) before sinking steadily to my own level, which was seldom far from the bottom.

For years my ambitions were centred about the hills and

[1] The peak of Mont Blanc is equally portioned between France and Italy. Only the extreme eastern end of the Mont Blanc *range* being in Switzerland.

crags of Britain ; the Alps followed naturally. They were satisfying, if not supremely satisfying, for they enabled me to erect a more solid castle of imagination upon the foundations of my early dreams. On their peaks I learnt the art and craft of mountaineering, and the brotherhood of the hillside. To some the British hills are an end in themselves, and to others the Alps, but the "Journey's End" of the mountaineer is the summit of Mount Everest.

Is mountaineering worth while? ask many. Not to them, but to others. Adventure has its roots deep in the heart of man. Had man not been imbued with it from the beginning of his existence, he could not have survived, for he could never have subdued his environment, and were that spirit ever to die out, the human race would retrogress. By " adventure " I do not necessarily mean the taking of physical risks. Every new thought, or new invention of the mind is adventure. But the highest form of adventure is the blending of the mental with the physical. It may be a mental adventure to sit in a chair, and think out some new invention, but the perfect adventure is that in which the measure of achievement is so great that life itself must be risked. A life so risked is not risked uselessly, and sacrifice is not to be measured in terms of lucre.

Mental alertness is dependent on physical virility, and an inscrutable Nature decrees that man shall ever war against the elemental powers of her Universe. If man were to acknowledge defeat, he would descend in the scale of life and sink once more to the animal. But there has been given to him that " something " which is called the " Spirit of Adventure." It was this spirit that sustained Captain Scott and his companions, and Mallory and

Irvine. Even in their last harsh moments, the crew of the R.101 knew that they did not perish uselessly. Mr. G. Winthrop Young wrote, " Will the impulse to adventure—which has coincided so happily for a time with that 'feeling' for mountains—die with its opportunity? Or will new outlets be found during yet another stage in our conquest of the elements? " I think they will, when man has conquered the Earth, he will turn his eyes to the stars.

CHAPTER II

KANGCHENJUNGA: ITS NATURE AND HISTORY

Roughly speaking, there are two types of mountains. There is the mountain which forms a point projecting from a range, ridge, or glacier system, and there is the mountain which stands apart from other ridges or ranges, and possesses its own glacier system. A good example of the former type is afforded by the peaks of the Bernese Oberland. Magnificent though they are individually, especially when seen from Mürren or the Wengern Alp, they are in reality but elevated points above an interlinking system of snowy plateaux and glaciers. Another good example is the great Himalayan peak, K 2. Though in many respects one of the most wonderful peaks in the world, it is, properly speaking, but a solitary spire of rock and ice rising above the glaciers and snow-fields of the Karakoram Range.

Of independent mountains, there is no finer example than Kangchenjunga. It is a mountain great enough to possess its own glaciers radiating from its several summits, and though surrounded by many vassal peaks, which add their quota to the ice rivers radiating from the main massif, the glaciers which flow far down to the fringe of the tropical forests cloaking the lower valleys are the undisputed possession of the Monarch. Of the world's first half dozen peaks, Kangchenjunga is the only one that displays its glories to the world at large. Only those who can afford the time and expense necessary to penetrate the remote fastnesses from which they spring can view the glories of Everest or the Karakorams, but Kangchenjunga is to be seen by anyone who cares to visit the hill town of Darjeeling, or climb one of the lower foot-hills. Thus man is able to turn his tired eyes towards the snows, and reflect that there are still worlds unconquered towards which he can gaze for inspiration and hope.

Whether or not Kangchenjunga is the second or the third highest mountain in the world is not yet certain, for its height is approximately equal to that of K 2, and it is still a matter of argument as to which should take pride of place. As determined by the Survey of India K 2 is 28,250 feet high, 194 feet higher than Kangchenjunga. These heights have been estimated by the most accurate trigonometrical processes possible. So many slight errors are, however, liable to creep into the most elaborate calculations that they can be regarded as approximate only. Sir Thomas Holditch, one of the greatest of survey authorities, held that there are bound to be errors owing to refraction. For instance, the rays of the sun passing through rarified air over snow-covered areas are liable to cause an error of refraction. Another difficulty is the attractive forces exercised by such a great mountain range as the Himalayas. It is well known that in the vicinity of the range there is a slight dip in the surface of water. It can hardly be doubted, therefore, that instrumental levels are affected.

With these factors taken into account, the heights of the three highest peaks in the world were worked out by Colonel S. G. Burrard, Superintendent of the Trigonometrical Survey of India, who arrived at the following :

Mount Everest, 29,141 feet ; Kangchenjunga, 28,225 feet ; K 2, 28,191 feet. Thus Kangchenjunga is made 34 feet higher than K 2. This slight difference is scarcely worthy of note and taking into account fluctuations of height due to seasonal snowfall on the summits, it may be assumed that there is a dead heat for second place.

Kangchenjunga is situated to the north-east of Nepal, an

By courtesy of *The Times*

independent state, and to the north-west of Sikkim, a state under British mandate. Its main ridges which run from N.N.E. to S.S.W. form a natural boundary between these two states, as well as a watershed to several important rivers. Twelve miles north of Kangchenjunga is the Thibetan frontier. This runs along what is strictly speaking the main watershed of the Himalayas, which separates the arid plateaux of Thibet on the north from the more fertile and rain washed country on the south. On this watershed, however, there are no elevations to rival Kangchenjunga, so that the mountain and its satellite peaks form a huge mountain massif pushed southwards from the main Himalayan Range.

Generally speaking, the more isolated a mountain or mountain group, the greater are its fluctuations of climate. Kangchenjunga is large enough not only to make its own weather, but to catch the full force of ready-made weather in addition. Only low foot-hills separate it from the Plain of Bengal, and these are not high enough to afford it protection from the south-west monsoon. The result of this is an annual precipitation of snow that is probably greater than that of any other peak in the Himalayas. Because of this Kangchenjunga boasts some of the most magnificent snow and ice scenery in the world.

Kangchenjunga not only breaks the force of the monsoon, but protects the main watershed to the north from its onslaught to a great extent. The result of this is an extraordinary variation of scenery and climate within a small area. The dry, almost dusty hills at the head of the Lhonak Valley, the Dodang Nyima range, and the plateaux of Thibet beyond are in striking contrast to the valleys radiating southwards from Kangchenjunga, for here is a dry reddish brown country with a snow level appreciably higher and glaciers considerably smaller than those of Kangchenjunga, and its immediate neighbours.

The huge annual precipitation of snow on Kangchenjunga is, from the mountaineer's point of view, a disadvantage, for it plasters itself on the mountain, and fills every hollow with clinging masses of ice. Owing to this quantity of snow, that is ever building up, plus the tug of gravity, these icy masses move downwards to join the main glaciers which they feed. Frequently, they are perched high up on the mountainside, and are unable to flow down the steep, rock precipices beneath, so they break off in chunks hundreds of feet thick, which fall thousands of feet to the glaciers beneath in terrible ice avalanches. These ice avalanches are Kangchenjunga's deadliest weapon.

There is probably no other mountain where the mountaineer is exposed to greater dangers than he is on Kangchenjunga, for not only has he ice avalanches to contend with, but uncertain weather as well, weather incalculable both in cause and effect.

With such a mountain before their eyes, it is perhaps small wonder that the peoples inhabiting the valleys round Kangchenjunga have become impregnated with the grandeur and mystery of the great mountain. To them its five summits are the "Five Treasures of the Snow," and on them rests the throne of an all powerful god. Their prosperity, and even their lives, depend on the good humour of this god, for he is able to blast their crops with his storms, or destroy their villages with his floods and avalanches. There are even dark tales of human sacrifices to this powerful deity handed down from the remote past.

Roughly speaking, there are four main lines of approach to Kangchenjunga, up the valley of the Tamar River in Nepal, passing Khunza and Kangbachen, up the Yalung Valley in Nepal, up the valley of the Teesta River in Sikkim, and up the Talung Valley also in Sikkim. Between the Yalung and Talung Valleys there is also the Rangit River, which has its sources in the glaciers of Kabru, 24,002 feet, one of Kangchenjunga's outpost peaks to the

KANGCHENJUNGA AT DAWN FROM DARJEELING

south. But compared to the first two, this is but a subsidiary valley, and does not form a main line of approach.

The first European to undertake serious exploration in the neighbourhood of Kangchenjunga was the famous botanist and explorer, Sir Joseph Hooker. Eighty years ago the valleys round Kangchenjunga were unknown and unexplored.[1] Dense, trackless jungle covered them, through which trails had to be cut, whilst transportation was very difficult. In 1848, Hooker traversed the Tamar Valley, and visited the Walung and Yangma Passes which lead from North-eastern Nepal into Thibet, north of Mount Nango. He then passed through Kangbachen and back to Darjeeling, via the Yalung Valley and the Singalila Ridge. In January, 1849, he reached Dzongri via the Rathong Valley, but was unable to go farther owing to snow. In April he ascended the Teesta Valley to Lachen, and made several attempts to climb Lamgebo Peak, 19,250 feet. Thence, he ascended the Poki River, and after bridging it near its junction with the Tumrachen River, tried to reach the Zemu Glacier. Failing to do this, he explored the Lachen and Lachung Valleys, and made attempts on Kangchenjau and the Pauhunri, 22,700 feet and 23,180 feet respectively.

Unsuccessful though these attempts were, they deserve something more than passing notice. At this date mountaineering had scarcely begun even in the Alps, and it was not until sixteen years later that the Matterhorn was climbed, yet here was an explorer attempting peaks 8,000 feet higher than the Zermatt giant. As it was, Hooker

[1] Mr. Douglas Freshfield in his book, *Round Kangchenjunga*, included an interesting chapter on the early history of Kangchenjunga. The subject was also dealt with more recently in Vol. II of the *Himalayan Journal* by Lieutenant-Colonel H. W. Tobin.

ascended to the Cholamo Lake at the head of the Lachen Valley, whence he ascended a small peak, and crossed the Dongkya La, 18,130 feet, into the head of the Lachung Valley.

Hooker, and Dr. Campbell, Superintendent of Darjeeling, who accompanied him, were seized and imprisoned at Tumlong on their way back to Darjeeling, at the orders of Namgay, Prime Minister of Sikkim, and it was some time before they were released. As retribution for this outrage, a portion of Sikkim, south of the Great Rangit Valley, was annexed by the British Government. This district had once belonged to Nepal, but after the Gurkha war of 1817, it was restored to the Sikkim Government, who in the same year ceded to us Darjeeling. It is now covered in valuable tea plantations.

Hooker made a small scale map of Sikkim to illustrate his wanderings, but this remained untouched until 1861, when Lieutenant Carter made a reconnaissance survey between Darjeeling and Tumlong during the march of Colonel Gawler's force. It was not until 1878 that the survey of Sikkim was resumed by Captain H. J. Harman, R.E., of the Survey of India. Harman made several journeys, which included an attempt to reach the Monastery of Tulung, but he was forced to return owing to the hostility of the inhabitants. He tried to reach the foot of Kangchenjunga, but his health suffered in the tropical valleys, and he was forced to return. Colonel H. C. V. Tanner undertook the continuance of the survey. It is thought that he was responsible for the survey training of the three Indian surveyors, " Pandits," signing themselves S. C. D., U. G., and R. N., who performed such valuable work in this district. The actual triangulation was undertaken by Tanner and his assistant, Robert, whilst the "Pandits" added topographical details.

In 1879, S. C. D. (Babu Sarat Chandra Das), the best known of the "Pandits," crossed the Kang La, 16,373 feet, from Sikkim into Nepal, passed up the valley of Kangbachen, traversed the Jonsong La, 20,200 feet, and the Choten Nyima La to Tashi Lhunpo in Thibet. This is certainly one of the boldest journeys on record in that part of the world, and the crossing of the Jonsong La, a high glacier pass, was a great feat. Two years later, in 1881, he crossed the Nango La, north of Kangbachen, and continued to Lhasa. In 1883, another bold journey was undertaken by a native, Lama Ugyen Gyatso of Pemayangtse Monastery, who travelled to Lhasa by the Teesta and Lachung Valleys, and over the Dongkya La, making valuable sketches *en route.*

In October to December of the same year, the survey of the more accessible parts of Sikkim was completed by Robert and his assistant, Rinzin Namgyal (Rinsing of Mr. Freshfield's *Round Kangchenjunga*) who explored the Talung Valley to the Tulung Monastery. In October, 1884, he crossed the Kang La into Nepal, explored the Yalung Glacier, and followed Sarat Chandra Das's route over the Jonsong La. But instead of crossing the Choten Nyima La, he descended the Lhonak Valley to its junction with the Lachen Valley, returning to Darjeeling on January 31, 1885.

I mentioned these preliminary explorations in the neighbourhood of Kangchenjunga if only to show how little was known but a short time ago of the approaches to the mountain. Had this preliminary exploration work not been carried out, and the way cleared for future mountaineers, one of the most beautiful and interesting climbing districts in the world might still be accessible only with great difficulty. It would be as well, therefore, for future parties, who may attempt Kangchenjunga, to remember that no route on the mountain can be considered as a *preserve* for any one party.

What may be called the first purely mountaineering party made its appearance in 1883, in which year Mr. W. W. Graham began his ascents in Sikkim. He first visited Dzongri at the beginning of April, and climbed a peak of about 18,000 feet on the Singalila Ridge. After a week he was forced to return to Darjeeling on April 12. Later in October, he ascended Jubonu, 19,350 feet, a peak in the Kabru Range that he gave as about 20,000 feet, and a peak west of the Kang La, which he gave as 19,000 feet. Finally came his climb of Kabru, 24,002 feet, the summit of which he claimed to have reached. This ascent has been the subject of much controversy, and whether or not he actually climbed Kabru is still doubtful. Possibly, he may have mistaken it for the Forked Peak.

Graham made one interesting remark: he said that May was the avalanche month. Furthermore, it should be noted that nearly all the big climbs in Sikkim have been done during or after the monsoon.

The most valuable mountain exploration ever carried out in the Sikkim Himalayas was that of Mr. Freshfield's party in 1899. Leaving Darjeeling on September 5, the party ascended the Teesta Valley and Zemu Glacier, crossed into the head of the Lhonak Valley, and traversed the Jonsong La. Owing to a heavy snow-fall, they were greatly hampered in their plans, and descended to Kangbachen without having attempted Kangchenjunga or one of its neighbours as had been their original intention. But though unable to do any climbing, Mr. Freshfield made many valuable speculations and observations as to the possibility of peaks, whilst Signor Vittoria Sella, who accompanied him, took many beautiful and instructive photographs.

Mr. Freshfield was the first mountaineer ever to examine the great western face of Kangchenjunga, rising from the Kangchenjunga Glacier. Speaking of this glacier he writes : " It has its origin in a snow-plateau, or rather terrace, lying under the highest peak at an elevation of about 27,000 feet, that is only some 1,200 feet below the top, the final rock-ridges leading to which look very accessible. Below this terrace, however, stretches a most formidable horseshoe of precipices, or what at least the ordinary traveller would describe às precipices. Since, however, this glacier affords what is in my opinion the only direct route to Kangchenjunga, which is not impracticable, I must qualify the word." He goes on to say, " But—and it is a ' but ' I desire to emphasise—the routes I can discern by careful study of my companions' photographs are more or less exposed to the worst, because the least avoidable by human skill, of all mountain risks. Steep places will have to be surmounted by a series of slopes, in which the crevasses and séracs have been filled or beaten down by avalanches from hanging ice-cliffs above, and when the peril of this staircase has been run, a way must be found along a shelf similarly exposed."

After passing through Khunza, Mr. Freshfield crossed the Mirgin La and the Kang La to Dzongri and Darjeeling. He describes his experiences in his classic book *Round Kangchenjunga*, a book which is unfortunately out of print.[1] During this expedition, one of Mr. Freshfield's companions, Professor E. Garwood, constructed a map of Kangchenjunga and its environs, which still remains of great value. It is, indeed, an extraordinarily accurate work, considering the difficult conditions under which it was made.

Between the years 1889 and 1902, the late Mr. Claude White, Political Officer in Sikkim, made various explorations, of which he has unfortunately left but few details. He was the first to investigate the gorges between the Pandim and Simvu Mountains, and in 1890 crossed the Guicha La, and ascended the Talung and Teesta Valleys. He ascended the Zemu Glacier to about 17,500 feet, and crossed the Tangchang La and the The La into the Lhonak Valley.

Of all mountaineering pioneers in the Kangchenjunga district, and for that matter in the Himalayas, Dr. A. M. Kellas's name will stand pre-eminent. He was perhaps the first mountaineer to regard the Himalayas in the same way that the modern mountaineer regards the Alps—as a playground. Topographical and scientific considerations, while being important to him, were nevertheless of secondary importance as compared to mountaineering, yet, in the course of a number of purely climbing expeditions into North-eastern and North-western Sikkim, he

[1] *Round Kangchenjunga* was published in 1903 by Edward Arnold, but owing to a disastrous fire, all copies in stock were subsequently burnt.

could not fail to acquire much valuable topographical knowledge which will be of much value to mountaineers in the future when Sikkim has been opened up, as it is bound to be one day, as the "Playground" of the Himalayas.

Kellas's climbs are too many to mention in detail, but among the many peaks and passes of 20,000 to 23,000 feet that he ascended or attempted in the immediate neighbourhood of Kangchenjunga, must be mentioned the Nepal Gap, 21,000 feet, separating the Zemu and Kangchenjunga glaciers, which he attempted four times from the former glacier, nearly reaching the crest of the pass; Simvu, 22,360 feet, which he attempted three times with European guides in 1907, but failed, owing to bad weather and snow conditions, to reach the summit; the Simvu Saddle, 17,700 feet, and the Zemu Gap, 19,300 feet, which he ascended from the Zemu Glacier in May, 1910; the Langpo Peak, 22,800 feet, ascended in September, 1909; the Sentinel Peak, 21,240 (or 21,700 feet), east of the Choten Nyima La, ascended in May, 1910, and the Jonsong Peak, 24,344 feet, on which he was beaten by bad weather after ascending in December, 1909, to 21,000 feet on the North-west Ridge.

Kellas's last expedition prior to his death on the first Everest Expedition was made in 1921, when he conquered Narsingh, 19,130 feet. His mountaineering has had far-reaching effects. He was the first systematically to employ and train Sherpa and Bhutia porters. On one occasion only, in 1907, was he accompanied by Europeans, at other times natives climbed with him. That he was able from such raw material as untrained natives to train men who subsequently worked and climbed so splendidly on Everest and Kangchenjunga expeditions shows how great a mountaineer he was. As one who has humbly followed in his footsteps on the Jonsong Peak, I can safely say that from the technical point of view of route-finding and mountaineering Dr. Kellas will stand out as the greatest pioneer of Himalayan mountaineering. Apart from climbing, he contributed to various scientific journals valuable papers on the physiological and physical aspects of high mountaineering. If in place of his occasional scanty notes and articles, he had written a detailed account of his climbs, posterity and the literature of mountaineering would have been the richer.

One more ascent must be mentioned before turning to the attempts on Kangchenjunga itself, and that was the attempt made in October, 1907, by two Norwegians, Messrs. C. W. Rubenson and Monrad Aas on Kabru, 24,002 feet. They tackled the mountain via the Kabru Glacier, which is broken into a great ice-fall, and had to cut their way for five days through a complicated maze of ice pinnacles and crevasses. These difficulties came to an end at about 21,500 feet, and they camped on the plateau above the ice-fall between the two peaks, which is so plainly visible from Darjeeling. From there they attempted to reach the eastern summit. Their first attempt was beaten by lack of time due to a late start. They advanced their camp to 22,000 feet on October 20, and tried again. Owing to intense cold they were not able to start until 8.30 a.m. At 6 p.m. they were only about 200 feet below the summit, although separated from it by a considerable distance horizontally. Here they were exposed to the full force of the terrible west wind, against which advance was almost impossible. At sundown the cold became so intense, that to save themselves from frostbite they were forced to retreat.

The descent was marred by a bad slip on the part of Rubenson, who was last man down. Monrad Aas held him on the rope, but the shock was so great that four of its five strands actually parted. When at last they reached camp, Monrad Aas's feet were frostbitten.

Thus ended a most plucky attempt, especially plucky in view of the fact that Rubenson had never been on a mountain prior to the expedition. The party, though failing to reach the top, made the valuable discovery that it was possible for men to spend a considerable time (in this case twelve days) at an altitude above 20,000 feet, and there to eat well and sleep well and generally keep fit and acclimatise without noticeable physical deterioration.

The Previous Attempts on Kangchenjunga

With the exploration of the lower valleys and peaks round Kangchenjunga it was only a matter of time before an attempt was made on the mountain. The first attempt was made in August, 1905, by a party consisting of three Swiss, Dr. Jacot-Guillarmod, M. Reymond, and Lieutenant Pache, who put themselves under the leadership of an Englishman, Mr. Aleister Crowley, who had been one of the companions of Dr. Jacot-Guillarmod during an expedition to the Karakorams in 1892. To help with commissariat arrangements, an Italian hotel-keeper from Darjeeling named De Righi was added to the expedition.

Leaving Darjeeling, the expedition proceeded by the Singalila Ridge and the Chumbab La Pass to the Yalung Valley, and having ascended the Yalung Glacier, attacked the south-western face of Kangchenjunga. This face is exceedingly steep, and consists for the most part of granite precipices. At one point, however, there is a snowy shelf, conspicuous from Darjeeling, which leads up to the ridge, falling in a westerly direction from the third highest summit of Kangchenjunga. This appears to be the only breach in the great curtain of precipices hemming in the head of the Yalung Glacier. Even supposing this face to be climbed, it would still be necessary for the mountaineer to traverse a long distance from the third highest summit to the highest summit, a distance which, in the opinion of all who have seen the intervening ridge and noted its exposure to the west wind, is too great. The snowy shelf looks, and probably is, desperately dangerous owing to falling stones and avalanches, and its dangers must be considerably increased by its southern and consequently warm aspect.

The party established a camp at 20,343 feet, and some of them appeared to have climbed 1,000 feet higher. Disaster overtook them on September 1. On that day the party was assembled at mid-day at the highest camp. In the afternoon Dr. Guillarmod, Lieutenant Pache, and De Righi with three porters decided to descend to a lower camp, leaving Crowley and Reymond at the higher. The danger of descending steep snow slopes in the heat of the day should have been obvious, and Crowley states that he warned them of the danger that they were incurring by doing so. While traversing a snow slope, two of the porters who were in the middle, slipped, dragging with them Pache and the third porter who were behind, and Guillarmod and De Righi who were in front. This slip in itself might not have proved fatal, had it not started a large avalanche of snow. Guillarmod and De Righi escaped with a severe shaking, but their four companions, Pache and the three porters, were buried and suffocated by the avalanche.

The cries of the survivors soon summoned Reymond, who, apparently, found no difficulty in descending alone from the upper camp. Crowley remained in his tent, and on the same evening wrote a letter printed in *The Pioneer* on September 11, 1905, from which the following is an extract : " As it was I could do nothing more than send out Reymond on the forlorn hope. Not that I was over anxious in the circumstances to render help. A mountain 'accident' of this sort is one of the things for which I have no sympathy whatever. . . . To-morrow I hope to go down and find out how things stand." In another letter, written three days later, and published on September 15, he explains that it would have taken him ten minutes to dress, and that he had told Reymond to call him if more help was wanted, which he did not do.

The first search for the bodies was in vain, and they were not found until three days later (after Crowley had left the party) buried under ten feet of snow. Thus ended a truly lamentable affair.

From such an expedition it is not easy to draw conclusions as to the dangers and difficulties of an ascent of Kangchenjunga from the Yalung Glacier. Yet, these dangers, even so far as they are revealed by telescope at Darjeeling, are great, and though the Yalung Glacier is well worth investigating both from the point of view of the magnificent scenery at its head and other routes up the great peaks bounding it, there would seem little justification for a further attempt on Kangchenjunga from it.

Kangchenjunga remained untouched until eleven years after the war. British mountaineers had devoted their energies to overcoming Everest, and it was left to other nations to attempt Kangchenjunga. The Everest expeditions produced far-reaching effects. They showed that men could stand, without extraneous aid in the form of oxygen, an altitude as great as 28,000 feet. The lessons learned in transport organisation and climbing equipment were invaluable, and perhaps what is most important of all, they proved that high Himalayan climbing depends on having the right mentality as well as the right physique.

The second attempt on Kangchenjunga was made, like the first, from the Yalung Glacier, and like the first, it ended in tragedy. Early in May, 1929, an American, Mr. E. F. Farmer, of New York, left Darjeeling. He was accompanied by native porters, his sirdar being Lobsang, whose work was to be so invaluable to our expedition. Farmer's climbing experience was limited to the Rockies, and he had never before visited the Himalayas. He told no one of his plans, and having obtained a pass to enable him to go into Sikkim, and signing an undertaking that he would enter neither Thibet nor Nepal, he left on May 6, with reliable Sherpa and Bhutia porters. He did not return. The porters' story, which has been carefully probed and tested in every particular, is as follows :

He first of all visited the Guicha La ; then crossed the Kang La into Nepal. In order not to arouse suspicion, he avoided the little village of Tseram in the Yalung Valley by traversing the rhododendron-clad slopes on the eastern side of the valley. He camped on the same site as the late Mr. Harold Raeburn and Mr. C. G. Crawford, who prospected this district in 1920.[1] Farmer's party found graves which must have been those of the victims of the first attempt on Kangchenjunga.

On May 26, Farmer and three ex-Everest porters started up towards the Talung Saddle. Farmer was warmly clad and wearing crampons, but the porters were poorly shod, and had no crampons. In view of this Lobsang advised turning back, and it was agreed to do this at noon. Climbing became difficult, and the porters found it impossible to proceed in their poor quality boots. Accordingly, Farmer ordered them to halt, while he continued a little higher for photographic purposes. The porters did their best to dissuade him, but, apparently, oblivious of all risk, he climbed up and up, through drifting mists. Now and again when the mists cleared he appeared, and the porters waved to him to descend. At 5 p.m. he was still seen to be climbing, then the mist came down and he was seen no more. The porters remained where they had halted until dusk, then they descended to the camp, and waited in vain for his return. They signalled at intervals during the night with an electric torch and Meta fuel, but to no

[1] Mr. Raeburn made two visits to the southern walls of Kangchenjunga. The first, on which he was accompanied by Lieutenant-Colonel H. W. Tobin, was made in order to investigate the south-east outlying peaks of Kangchenjunga and possible routes up the south-east face of Kangchenjunga itself, and to explore the Talung Glacier. Later Raeburn and Crawford ascended the Yalung Glacier and examined the Talung Saddle, which lies on the ridge between Kabru and Kangchenjunga, separating the Yalung and Talung Glaciers. According to Raeburn, it looked "vicious in the extreme, defended everywhere by overhanging masses of ice." Failing in this object, they descended to Upper Tseram, were able to cross the ridge just south of Little Kabru, and thus descended the Rathong Valley.

purpose. The next morning they climbed up to a point from which his route was visible, and caught a glimpse of him soon after dawn far up on a steep snow slope. He seemed to be moving jerkily, with arms outstretched. Of course, this may have been imagination on the part of the porters, but if true, it may well have been due to snow blindness. They kept up their vigil throughout the day, and it was not until the morning of May 28 that hunger forced them down to Tseram.

In order that any suspicion as to foul play should be eliminated from the score of possible contingencies, the narrative of each porter was taken down and checked. Investigation and minute cross-examination convinced those that enquired into this sad disaster that the whole truth was told, and that no blame whatever attached to the porters, whose conduct had been of an unimpeachable character throughout.

Kangchenjunga had scored heavily. Two attempts had been repulsed with merciless severity, but it must be confessed that the attempts were of so weak a nature that the great mountain had no need to call in its real weapons of defence, storm and altitude. Serene and untroubled, it had not even attempted to kill its attackers ; it had let them kill themselves. But its complacency was to be rudely shaken in the autumn of the same year, 1929, in which Farmer met his death.

In view of the fact that no published account has appeared in this country of this attempt which was made by Munich mountaineers, I make no apology for giving a detailed description of one of the most brilliantly resourceful and courageous attempts in mountaineering history, an attempt which has been described by the Editor of the *Alpine Journal* as " a feat without parallel, perhaps, in all the annals of mountaineering."

As all mountaineers know, Munich is the home of one of the most enterprising schools of young mountaineers there is. The men who attempted Kangchenjunga were the pick of this school. The leader was Dr. Paul Bauer and his companions were Herren E. Allwein, one of the conquerors of Mount Kaufmann in the Pamirs, Peter Aufschnaiter, E. Beigel, Julius Brenner, W. Fendt, Karl von Kraus, Joachim Leupold, and Alexander Thoenes. The expedition on arriving at Darjeeling were helped in their transport arrangements by Colonel Tobin, the Darjeeling Secretary of the Himalayan Club, and Mr. E. O. Shebbeare, Transport Officer of the 1924 Everest Expedition. So well planned were their transport arrangements, that three days after their arrival, the first half of the expedition was able to leave Darjeeling. The second half followed two days later, together with Colonel Tobin. Eighty-six porters were employed. Eight days later they reached Lachen, and ten days later, August 18, established their Base Camp (Camp Three[1]) on Green Lake Plain at a height of 14,126 feet.

Exploration of the north-east side of Kangchenjunga was immediately begun. One party ascended to the Simvu Saddle, whence an attempt, beaten by bad weather, was made on the Simvu Peak, 22,760 feet. The other party explored the possibilities of reaching the East Ridge of Kangchenjunga. As the terrific precipices leading upwards

[1] Permanent camps were established from Yaktang at the end of the Zemu Valley and numbered from that point.

to the lowest point in the North Ridge between Kangchenjunga and the Twins were quite hopeless, they decided to attack a spur, or ridge which leads up to the North Ridge, and joins it at the point where a conspicuous snowy terrace runs across the north-west face of Kangchenjunga about 1,500 feet below the summit. This ridge is heavily armoured in ice and its knife-like crest is broken up into towers and spires of pure ice. Great masses hang precariously from it and huge precipices fall on either side to the glacier, down which thunder great avalanches. No such formidable route had ever been tackled by any other party on any other peak in the world.

Owing to the weather, the snowfall, the great variations of temperature, and the quality of the ice, these ice ridges of Kangchenjunga are completely different from those encountered in the Alps. Mr. Freshfield had seen this ridge too, and there is an excellent photograph in *Round Kangchenjunga*, but he did not mention it as a possible route to the summit of Kangchenjunga, and small wonder. All one can say is that though the technique of icemanship may not have advanced far since pre-war days, the will of man to conquer the greater summits of the Himalayas has developed beyond all expectation. The Munich attempt on Kangchenjunga proves this.

Actually, the ice ridge has one advantage over the main ridges, and in particular the North Ridge of Kangchenjunga: it is sheltered from the prevailing western winds which blow with such paralysing force. If the upper part of this ice ridge could be gained, the party thought that they would have a chance of reaching the summit. But to do so, many and terrible difficulties had to be overcome. Yet, as Dr. Bauer wrote, "With mountaineers, it is the one remaining possibility of access to Kangchenjunga."

On August 24 and 25 the party had assembled at the Base Camp, and were ready to make the attempt. The porters had proved themselves worthy of the confidence that was to be reposed in them, and the party had become well acclimatised to altitude. The only drawback was the weather, which was stormy. But considering that the monsoon season had not yet finished, that was only to be expected.

The first difficulty was a 700 feet high ice-fall which had to be surmounted in order to reach the base of the ice ridge. From Camp Six, 18,696 feet, the party endeavoured to storm the 2,800 feet wall leading to the crest of the ice ridge. The way proved very dangerous ; falling boulders a cubic yard in size swept the route, compelling a sharp look-out. They had nearly attained the crest of the ridge when bad weather necessitated return. The following day a stronger party, four Germans and three porters equipped with bivouac necessities and food, returned to the attack in better weather. The slopes leading to the ridge were ribbed with ice flutings common to the Himalayas, between which rose sharp, serrated, and cornice crowned edges of rock. The party was spread-eagled one above the other on the smooth ice slopes without security, and the fall of one would have meant disaster to all. Also, there was a grave danger of stone falls. Once more they were forced to retreat.

On the following day, Allwein and Thoenes reached the ridge by climbing a steep ice gully. This gully was so difficult, however, that it was a question whether porters could be got up it. Indeed, so great were the difficulties proving, that it was nearly decided then and there to abandon the attack in favour of the East Ridge from the Zemu Gap, but this ridge is so long, and the obstacles so many, that there seems little chance of reaching the summit of Kangchenjunga by it. Incidentally, it does not even lead directly to the highest summit, but to the second highest summit, 27,820 feet, between which and the highest summit stretches a formidable ridge. But before abandoning the ice ridge, one more attempt was decided upon. Camp was pitched 900 feet higher up the wall. The following day dawned sulkily, and the weather was none too good, yet it was decided to make one last effort to hew a breach in the snow bosses, and force a way to the crest of the ice ridge.

The difficulties were immense. They slowly hacked away at the ice curtain ; everything that could be utilised as a help to the sorely-tried party was employed and even icicles as thick as a man's arm were used to hitch a rope round. Height was gained ; hope replaced despair ; the party turned back rejoicing at the thought that they had discovered the necessary ice-technique for making a formidable slope possible for laden porters.

But Kangchenjunga prepared to resist the onslaught. A snowfall compelled a retreat to Camp Six. Another attempt to reach the ridge was made, but another snowfall occurred, and avalanches drove the party down again. Camp Seven was rendered unsafe by these avalanches, and all the equipment had to be carried down through deep new snow to Camp Six.

On September 13, the weather cleared, and the assault was renewed. Two days of strenuous step-cutting brought the party to the crest of the ridge. A scene of incomparable splendour opened out before their eyes. "Nearly vertically below lay the Twins Glacier, while slopes of 60 degrees led downwards, on the farther side, to the Zemu Glacier. Icy and shining pinnacles led upwards for 6,500 feet. In a wide cirque above us towered the ice slopes of the Tent Peak, the Twins, Kangchenjunga, Simvu, above the two mighty glacier basins. Avalanches thundered in continuous icy cascades down these faces. Behind us swept endless glacier shapes into the dim and cloudy distance."[1]

Three great towers interposed, barring their advance. For two days they toiled and struggled in conquering them. Beyond these towers the ice ridge rose in a precipitous step. They had hoped to reach a snowy ledge on the step, and establish Camp Eight, but they were overtaken by night before they had reached this level. "Bivouac material and provisions were dumped where we stood. The porters belayed to a well-buried axe watched us with astonishment scooping out a place for the camp in a cornice on the dizzy ridge. Then Aufschnaiter and Kraus descended with them to Camp Seven, while Beigel and Dr. Bauer settled down in our tiny tent. The spot was not altogether trustworthy since in one place, where the axe had been deeply driven, we could look down through a hole on to the Twins Glacier. We slept well, but at dawn great care was necessary in distributing our stiffened limbs properly while wriggling gingerly out of the insecurely pitched tent.

[1] From Dr. Paul Bauer's account in the *Alpine Journal*, translated into English by Lieutenant-Colonel E. L. Strutt, the Editor.

Hardly had the sun begun to thaw us than we started on the first gendarme hacking out layer after layer of ice from its flanks, till we could force a way past it on the left and attain a névé slope at an angle of fully 70 degrees. Two hours later this also lay below and we had cut a good deep zigzag track through it connecting each icy boss with the next. A hundred feet below us lay the little tent, above us rose more ice pinnacles. A little ice crevice, enlarged by us into a chimney, brought us some twenty feet higher up the steepest part of the névé, much hampered here by many cornices. By the early afternoon we stood at length at the base of the last pinnacle separating us from the first platform in the spur. We saw the 'shock troops,' Nos. 2 and 3 parties, approaching from below with their porters; quickly we levelled out a space on the terrace for our friends' camp, and then turned downwards as the spur now lay in shadow. Soon it grew so cold that danger of frostbite became threatening. We met the other contingent, Allwein and Thoenes, with the porters Chettan and Lewa, just as they attained the terrace."

Above Camp Eight there were more pinnacles, or perhaps it would be more correct to say perpendicular steps or pitches in the ridge. These had to be stormed by the crest. The first was not so difficult. An overhanging crack filled with powdery snow led diagonally upwards to the left. The second pinnacle was harder. A short, nearly vertical ice runnel had to be negotiated, followed by a traverse to the left of it. A steep ascent to the right brought them to the crest. The next pinnacle hung over the ridge like an enormous mushroom some 120 feet high. "On the Twins side rose a wall formed of wind-blown powdery snow above the overhanging bulge. It was dreadful work crawling up on the treacherous powdery mass poised above the nearly perpendicular Twins Glacier slope."

The pinnacle above this gave them the longest work of all. Allwein's report reads as follows : " On reaching the fourth tower on September 23, we were at first completely at a loss, the crest appeared vertical or even overhanging, so was the slope falling towards the Twins Glacier, and so indeed was the left flank as well. Yet on this latter flank depended our only hopes, for a tiny ledge led upwards in the face crowned with a huge cornice furnished with a deep recess hollowed out of the ice in its centre. Higher up the ledge soon ended under impossible ice overhangs, leaving no other alternative but from the said recess to burrow a shaft perpendicularly upwards through the wide, stretching cornice. We worked away the whole day at this tunnel, but on returning to camp at 4 p.m. the work lay still unfinished."

On the following days they were able to improve this route, until finally this originally difficult and dangerous pinnacle became the easiest of all.

Such hard work as this has never before been accomplished at such an altitude. Its technique opens out an entirely new method of overcoming these terrific Himalayan ice ridges, though only time will show whether routes of this difficulty will ever lead to victory on the greater peaks of the Himalayas.

On September 25, they traversed along the edge of a dizzy snow rib corniced on both sides to the bottom of a long-dreaded 200 feet gap. So soft was the snow and so narrow the rib, which was not more than two feet wide, that no proper route could be made, and they could only beg the porters to follow exactly in their footsteps. Beyond the gap rose another great tower. The lower part of this was comparatively easy, but necessitated very hard work. Above rose a steep snow runnel, on which it was a severe struggle clearing away the soft snow and cutting steps in the underlying firm ice. The party forgathered on a little shoulder half way up. A hundred feet of more difficult work led to the foot of a wall of fearful steepness, crowned by a huge cornice. The base of this was masked by masses of rock and snow, and it was difficult to fashion reliable foot-holds from which the cornice could be flogged down, but at last a way was forced through the eaves of over-hanging snow, and the party stood on the crest of the ridge.

The great tower had been conquered ; slowly, but surely, the gallant party were winning their way up this terrific ice ridge. The fight was a fair one until Kang-chenjunga called in its ally, the weather. Snow began to fall nearly every day, and on the following morning after the conquest of the tower, lay fully a foot deep. The most difficult part of the route had been done, but it had cost two valuable weeks. Fresh obstacles were always cropping up ; disappointments had been many, and until the conquest of the gap and the great tower was accomplished, it had seemed problematical whether progress was possible at all. Now, however, the party were sufficiently far advanced to push hard for the summit.

In lieu of tents, ice caves were carved in the solid ice at Camps Eight and Nine, large enough to hold six to eight persons. The entrance to these was as small as possible, and the temperature inside rarely sank below 26° to 28°F., whilst outside it was usually about 14°F. by day and 10° to

25° below zero Fahrenheit by night. Future Everest expeditions would do well to investigate the technique of ice cave making. Ice caves properly constructed below and on the North Col of Everest would most likely prove more efficient than tents. Above the North Col only tents could be used, for the climbing lies entirely over rocks.

Above Camp Nine, 21,646 feet, the difficulties dwindled. Two easier ice towers were soon stormed. Snow slab avalanches broke away under the leader, but it was always possible to secure him so that he could not slip far. One snow slope entailed caution, but once firm steps had been made it became safe. Camp Ten, 22,288 feet, was pitched on easy and open snow. Here, as below, an ice cave was scooped out. Preparations were made for the final assault, communication was established between all camps, and food and equipment sent up with the utmost speed.

Theoretically, October should bring settled weather, practically, the weather was doubtful, it was not exactly stormy, but aggravated by continual snow flurries. On October 3, Allwein and Kraus set out to reconnoitre and track out the route above Camp Ten for the next stage on the following day. The snow was not good, and they often sank in knee-deep, but they were able in an hour to ascend about 350 feet, which was very fair going. They turned back at about 24,272 feet. As a result of their exploration, they considered that no more difficulties were to be expected, but that owing to the soft, powdery snow, two more camps would have to be pitched. Was this optimism justified in the light of previous Himalayan experience ? I think not.

This was the highest point reached. That night hopes

ran high in the ice cave. What they had hardly dared to expect, the summit, seemed to lie within their grasp.

October 14 dawned evilly. The sky was cloud covered; a cold wind was blowing and light snow falling. The snow thickened; by 8 a.m. it was coming down hard. Plans had to be altered, and preparations for a siege made. Kraus and Thoenes with two porters, Lewa and Chettan, left, and descended in order to save food, and help with the transport. The snow continued; by the evening of October 15 things looked black. "We began to realise with heavy hearts that the ascent of Kangchenjunga was now hardly possible. Only a deliberate abandonment of our hitherto 'safety-first' tactics for a desperate assault might result in success. This would entail a complete break-up of our lines of communication and result in 'every man for himself.' The 'summit' party could no longer, as hitherto, be supported by a reserve party ready to 'leap-frog' in case of necessity. Even with instant improvement of the weather it would take days for a relief party to fight its way through from below to our support."

As the weather appeared too bad for an attempt on the summit, they decided at least to make an attempt to reach the North Ridge and gaze down the unknown north-west side of the mountain. Even this proved impossible. After two hours' hard work they had risen not more than 250 feet. The wind-blown, crusted slopes of snow continually collapsed beneath them, letting them sink in thigh-deep. Abandoning their loads, they struggled upwards for an hour and a half. They reached a height of about 24,000 feet and then decided to retreat.

As they sat again by their ice cave, they were startled

by the extraordinary appearance of the sky to the south. A huge cloud bank over 30,000 feet high was forming, whilst above it the sky was of an extraordinary sea-green colour, " a most threatening and terrible sight."[1]

The following day they awoke to find the cave entrance completely blocked with snow. The snowfall continued, and many times during the day they had to sweep the entrance clear. By nightfall no less than seven feet of snow had fallen, and it was still snowing. "A cataclysm of nature seemed to foreshadow our doom." There was now no thought of advance. Communications had been cut off, they did not know what was happening below, and those below did not know what was the fate of those above. It was a terrible position to be in. To stay meant starvation. " The Storm God was still piling snow on us, yet, on the following morning, trusting to our powers and experience, we determined to 'Wrestle one more fall.' The descent appeared humanly impossible, but an attempt had to be made."

So deep was the snow that they fought their way down leaving behind a furrow a man's height in depth. A slightly *ascending* bit not 150 feet high took them over two hours. The porters behaved magnificently, though laden with some eighty pounds each. They had frequently to be jerked from the holes into which they sank, but they continued to struggle gallantly on.

Steeper slopes peeled off in avalanches as the leader,

[1] In *Round Kangchenjunga*, p. 114, Mr. Freshfield describes a similar strange atmospheric appearance, which heralded the great storm of September, 1899, during which no less than 27 inches of rain fell in 28 hours in Darjeeling, occasioning considerable loss of life and damage to property. See also my own description in my book *Climbs and Ski Runs*, p. 70, of the green ray sunrise which preceded a terrible storm on the Schreckhorn.

tightly held on a rope, stepped on them. The most dangerous slope had fortunately already avalanched. They descended in the actual groove made by the avalanche, thus saving a good two hours. Disaster nearly overtook them when another slope with Allwein and two porters on it avalanched, and only a desperate effort on the part of Dr. Bauer saved them. So great an effort was it for all concerned, that for ten minutes or more they lay motionless and exhausted before they could resume the fight.

On their arrival at Camp Nine they had to clear the ice cave entrance from beneath seven feet of snow. They lay there all night, recovering their strength for the tussle with the most difficult portion of the descent.

The next day things went wrong. The porters, not unnaturally, were nervous. To face such difficulties with heavy loads was impossible. They were brought back to the cave, and the Europeans without packs set out to clear footsteps in the newly fallen snow, and thus make possible the traverse of the great ice towers.

The following day, a good half of the loads were jettisoned, and thrown down the 5,000 feet precipice to the Twins Glacier. Thus relieved, the party could renew the struggle.

For once wayward Fortune smiled on them—the weather became fine. They gazed down, but could see no sign of any living beings either on the ice ridge or on the Zemu Glacier. It was not until two days later that they learned that all the ice ridge party were still alive.

Each of the two communication parties had had a great struggle in retreating. The exhausted porters continually fell, and avalanches poured down. Beigel and Aufschnaiter had suffered the worst. Between Camps Nine and Eight they were swept off their feet by small avalanches. Once the leader slipped when traversing slightly below the crest of a ridge; in another instant all must have been pulled off, and hurled down the precipices, but the party were saved by the presence of mind of the second man, who had time to leap into space on the reverse side of the ridge, and thus held his companions on the rope. This mishap resulted in the loss of both rucksacks, provisions and bivouac material, and a miserable night had to be spent on the ridge under a cornice without shelter of any kind. As a result Beigel was severely frostbitten in the feet.

At last with joy the upper party reached Camp Six. Communications had been severed from below. It took four days to plough down through snow many feet deep to the Base Camp. Everyone carried as great a load as possible. The sahibs broke the trail, sinking in below their knees. The porters followed, while last of the exhausted procession came Beigel, carried on a rough stretcher made from two tent poles, "silent and uttering no complaint." Even at the snout of the Zemu Glacier another weather catastrophe overtook the worn-out party. For three days it snowed and rained, and the snow covered bamboos and rhododendrons proved almost impassable. Poor Beigel, who had been carried, had perforce to walk. The mountainsides were alive with landslides; mud-shoots did their best to annihilate the party. "Dishevelled, dead-beat, our nerves worn out with the wild struggle against nature, with unkempt beards and covered with mud, we trod with heavy feet into the brilliantly lit dining room of the Lachen bungalow."

Thus ended one of the most gallant mountaineering enterprises ever carried out.

In one respect only is criticism justified. When they reached their highest camp at an altitude of 24,000 feet, they considered that they had overcome the worst difficulties. Such, however, is far from the case. These difficulties had scarcely begun. Altitude and its effects only begin to be serious over 24,000 feet, and being on the sheltered side of the mountain they had not yet begun to experience the terrible west wind which sweeps the upper part of the North Ridge with such merciless severity, and last, but not least, is the final pyramid, of which the climbing difficulties are certainly greater than those of the final pyramid of Everest. Colonel E. F. Norton, in an interesting letter in the *Himalayan Journal* analysing the respective difficulties of Kangchenjunga and Everest, lays stress on the time factor. He writes :—

" *Exclusive of false starts* it took the party just under a month from the foot of the ridge (17,060 feet) to Camp Ten at 23,290 feet. This includes the establishment of Camp Ten for six sahibs and four porters equipped ' for the fight for the eight thousanders.' (The meaning of this expression is not quite clear to me. 8,000 metres equals 26,600 odd feet, equals 1,500 feet below the summit, so I am not certain if they were equipped for the whole distance to the top.) This represented a climb of 6,230 feet.

"Compare Mount Everest ; in 1924 we estimated to establish a similar party (equipped to lay out one more camp and reach the top) at Camp Five (25,000 feet) in 15 days from the Base Camp (16,500 feet). This represented a climb of 8,500 feet.

"We failed; but that this was not an unreasonable estimate is proved by the fact that we established Camp Five in 1922 (including a four-day reconnaissance of the East Rongbuk Glacier—up and back again) with four sahibs in 19 days from first leaving the base camp, largely over an unknown route.

"Camp Five on Mount Everest was 4,000 feet from the top—an easy rock climb.

"Camp Ten on Kangchenjunga was 5,000 feet from the top, and judging from what Mr. Bauer says, the condition of the snow even at this height necessitated 'stamping a track.'

"Now the difficulties imposed by altitude only begin to be really serious from about 24,000 or 25,000 feet onwards, both as regards condition of the snow and rarity of the air.

"Next consider the time available on Kangchenjunga.

"Mr. Bauer's party started presumably in the tail of the monsoon (August 26), and got badly caught high up on the mountain by the first winter snowfall on October 3—after five and a half weeks. A party trying it in the spring can hardly kick off from the foot of the mountain until April 15 on account of the spring cold; the monsoon is due to arrive by May 21 (I am writing from memory)—again five and a half weeks.

"On Everest we reckoned on a season of from four to six weeks, i.e. from May 1 to the arrival of the monsoon on the north face of the mountain—any time between June 1 and 15. The penalty for being caught high on Everest in soft new snow is the danger of avalanches on only about 1,500 feet of descent from the North Col.

On Kangchenjunga there must be thousands of feet of such dangers—as Mr. Bauer found.

"Events may well prove me wrong: but on the face of it, Kangchenjunga appears to me a more formidable and more dangerous proposition than Mount Everest."

One cannot but concur with this admirable analysis. Time will always be the most important factor in any attempt on Kangchenjunga. Five and a half weeks is the maximum period during which weather and conditions suitable for climbing can be expected. It is significant also to notice that at their highest camp the Bavarians had begun to experience the west wind.

I mention these facts in no carping spirit, but merely to point out the difficulties to be expected. Given sufficient time, and weather of the right type, there is a remote probability that Kangchenjunga can be climbed by present day methods. But does a sufficiently long enough spell of good weather *ever* occur on the mountain? Can men acclimatise sufficiently to climb even moderately difficult rocks, and the upper rocks may be more than moderately difficult, between 27,000 and 28,000 feet?

There is no need to analyse further possible routes on Kangchenjunga. Every side has now been explored, photographed and mapped, and further reconnaissance is unnecessary. The mountain may require methods to overcome it which are at present not known to mountaineers, but even supposing medical science discovers means artificially to acclimatise the body so that as much work can be put out at 28,000 feet as at a much lower altitude, Kangchenjunga will still remain something more than a formidable antagonist.

CHAPTER III

PLANS AND PREPARATIONS

Only by comparison is it possible to obtain any idea of the scale of the world's greatest mountain range. Yet, even this method is unsatisfactory, for whether the mountaineer is toiling up Mont Blanc or Mount Everest, his feelings, apart from those imposed by altitude and the desire to achieve, are very similar; he is but a microcosm on the vast mountainside. Suffice to say that Mont Blanc is little more than half the height of Mount Everest, 29,002 feet; Kilimanjaro, 19,700 feet and Mount McKinley, 20,454 feet. The highest peaks of Africa and North America, would rank as minor peaks in the Sikkim Himalayas; and even Aconcagua, 23,000 feet, the monarch of the Andes, is no higher than the historic North Col on Everest.

Each group of the greater peaks has its own type of scenery, but none is finer than the magnificent massif that culminates at 28,156 feet above sea level in the summit of Kangchenjunga. The visitor to Darjeeling who climbs to the top of Observatory Hill sees it fifty miles away over range upon range of lower ridges, split with deep, gorge-like valleys, incredibly remote and icily aloof, lifting its glaciers like silver shields to the sky. There is no scale by which the observer can appreciate the size of what he sees. The apparently insignificant ridges over which his gaze passes are themselves as high as, or higher than, the Alps. The slit-like valleys and gorges are disclosed only by the mists, born of their steamy, tropical heat, that form towards noon and writhe slowly upwards in columns of massive cumuli. There is no standard of comparison, and experience alone can teach that the heights, depths, and distances are twice or three times as great as those in the Alps.

The eye can pass at a glance over these leagues of ridges and valleys between Darjeeling and Kangchenjunga, but the foot of man cannot take them at a stride. The problems of reaching the base of the greater peaks and of carrying sufficient food and equipment are second only to the problems of scaling the peaks themselves. It is largely due to these initial difficulties, and to the expense of organising and maintaining a large bandobast[1] of native porters that so few expeditions are undertaken in the high Himalayas. Yet, in an age when mountaineering in the Alps is said to have reached technical perfection, it is indeed remarkable that not one of the greater Himalayan peaks has been climbed.

Yet, if the summits of Everest and other giants over 25,000 feet remain untrodden, man has not been idle; he has climbed thousands of minor peaks and several expeditions that have been carried out in the High Himalayas have taught valuable lessons as regards the right personnel, the best kinds of food and equipment, and the easiest and most efficient methods of porterage. The three Everest expeditions and the 1929 Kangchenjunga expedition taught invaluable lessons. It is over the graves of former mistakes, and not on the wings of new ideas that

[1] Bandobast—a common Indian term meaning organisation, arrangement, party, etc.

the climber will at length tread the highest summits in the world.

Though it may sound " a glimpse of the obvious " there is only one way of learning Himalayan mountaineering, and that is to climb among the Himalayas. Useful asset though it is, a brilliant Alpine mountaineering record is no Open Sesame to a brilliant Himalayan record, the conditions are so different. In the selection of the personnel and equipment it was unfortunate that not one of the party that left Europe had experience of Himalayan expeditions. Schneider certainly had climbed in the Pamirs, but the conditions prevailing there are not the same as those of the Eastern Himalayas. Had it been possible, it would have been the wisest move to have invited at least one or two British or German mountaineers at the outset with past Himalayan experience. Apart from this vital omission, the party selected by Professor Dyhrenfurth was an exceptionally strong one. It possessed one important advantage over most other British parties that have visited the Himalayas—all its members had experience in winter mountaineering and ski-running, as well as summer mountaineering in the Alps. This was important because snow conditions approximating to Alpine winter conditions are frequently encountered in the Himalayas.

Climbing is mental as well as physical work. Mr. G. Winthrop Young devotes a whole chapter to the mental aspects of Alpine mountaineering in *Mountain Craft*. All that he wrote applies with even greater force to Himalayan mountaineering. The climbing party must be something more than a collection of expert mountaineers, it must be a team, and like a team of Test cricketers, one that pulls together in every department of the game ; and if it is a good team, it should also be a happy family. In no other pursuit is the best or the worst in a man brought out as it is in mountaineering. An old friend of civilisation may be a useless companion on a mountain. The 1929 Munich expedition had one great advantage over our own, they were all friends before they started from Europe. We were not, and the fact that everything went so smoothly must be set down to luck. There have, in fact, been other Himalayan expeditions the members of which were acquaintances, if not friends, which did not go so smoothly as our expedition.

In Professor Dyhrenfurth, the expedition possessed a leader of wide mountaineering experience, as well as an accomplished geologist. He has ascended more than seven hundred peaks in the Alps and Hohe Tatra. He is forty-four years of age, and comes of a hardy mountaineering stock, for his father, Dr. Oskar Dyhrenfurth climbed the Jungfrau at the age of sixty-nine,[1] and at the age of seventy-four, made a solitary climb on the Dachstein, in which he fell badly, but recovered. Professor Dyhrenfurth made his first climb at the age of nine, and at the age of thirteen, ascended the Rosengartenspitze, the well known peak in the western Dolomites. He was severely injured in 1921, when he fell twenty-one feet owing to a rope breaking when ascending the Drusenfluh. During the War he commanded a corps of mountain guides on the Italian frontier, and spent summer and winter at heights of over 10,000

[1] This is by no means an unusual age for mountaineers to make ascents. Many members of the Alpine Club have made greater ascents at considerably greater ages. The late Captain J. P. Farrar at the age of seventy-one climbed many first class peaks in the last year of his life. Mountaineering begets longevity and longevity mountaineering.

feet in redoubts among the Ortler mountains, and in dug-outs cut in the solid ice of glaciers. These experiences were of more use to him from a Himalayan point of view than any ordinary Alpine mountaineering.

Frau Dyhrenfurth is perhaps best known as an international lawn tennis player. She is one of the best players in mixed doubles in Switzerland. She has accompanied her husband on many expeditions, but few women have taken part in great climbs in the Himalayas, and by accompanying the expedition, she joined that select little band of Himalayan lady mountaineers, including Mrs. Bullock Workman, Mrs. Ruttledge and Frau Visser.

The second in command of the expedition was Monsieur Marcel Kurz, who besides being a climbing member, was our cartographer. He is the greatest living Continental authority on winter mountaineering, and his record of first winter ascents and difficult climbs is unique. His climbs included the first winter ascents of the Ober Gabelhorn and Taschhorn in the Zermatt district, the last two peaks in the Alps of Valais to be unclimbed in winter. He is an expert on snowcraft and avalanches, particularly from the point of view of ski-running. When climbing with Mr. H. E. L. Porter in the Southern Alps of New Zealand in 1927, he made a new route up Mount Tasman by the East Ridge, and also ascended Mount Cook, 12,349 feet, the highest peak in the New Zealand Alps, by a long and difficult route. He revised and brought up to date the famous Kurz guide-books on Mont Blanc and the Pennine Alps written by his father, and has also written *Alpinisme Hivernal* and a guide to the Alps of Valais. He has mapped Mount Olympus for the Greek Government, and published a monograph on the mountain from both historical and topographical aspects.

Herren Hoerlin and Schneider joined the expedition with as brilliant a record of great climbs as any young mountaineers in Europe. The number of great ascents made by them rivals that of the famous Swiss pair, Dr. W. Amstutz and Herr Schumacher. In 1929, they carried out a series of climbs on the range of Mont Blanc which included the first winter ascents of the Aiguille Noire de Pétéret and the Aiguille Blanche de Pétéret, as well as a ski traverse of Mont Blanc. They are an extraordinarily fast pair ; their time for their winter ascent of the Aiguille Blanche de Pétéret, one of the most dangerous climbs in the Alps, was actually faster than that for the summer ascent of the peak by Mr. Eustace Thomas and Josef Knubel, Mr. Winthrop Young's famous guide. They also ascended the Aiguille Verte and Les Droites in winter. Herr Schneider comes from Hall, in Tyrol, and is a geologist. In 1929 he took part in the Alai Pamir expedition led by Herr Rickmer Rickmers, in the course of which he climbed some fifteen peaks in the neighbourhood of 17,000 feet, eight 20,000 feet peaks and Mount Kaufmann (renamed Pic Lenin by the Soviet) the highest peak ascended in Central Asia. Herr Wieland, though not so experienced as his compatriots, is nevertheless one of the keenest of the younger German mountaineers.

Herr Hoerlin is a student of medicine. Though he only started to climb in 1922, he is recognised as one of the leading young German mountaineers, and is the president of the Akademischer Alpen Club, Berlin, the most exclusive mountaineering club in Northern Germany.

AT THE BASE CAMP

from left to right, DR. RITCHER ; WOOD JOHNSON ; PROFESSOR DYHRENFURTH ; DUVANEL ; FRAU DYHRENFURTH ; WIELAND ; HANNAH ; HOERLIN ; KURZ ; SCHNEIDER

Note the expedition boots

Dr. Richter was to act not only as surgeon, but as reporter to the German newspapers. He is a German army doctor, and though his experience of climbing was limited, he had had considerable experience of ski-ing, and was an excellent runner. He is a keen physiologist and hoped to obtain valuable data in connection with the effects of high altitudes on the bodily functions.

In order to ensure bringing back a first-rate film record of the expedition, Professor Dyhrenfurth engaged Monsieur C. Duvanel, who had previously made a number of aerial films for the Swiss Government, as well as instructional films of Alpine climbing and ski-ing. He is, like Kurz, a French-speaking Swiss, and comes from Lausanne.

The importance of having expert transport officers with a Himalayan expedition can hardly be over-estimated. It is one thing to climb a mountain but it is quite another thing to get to the foot of the mountain and having got there maintain an efficient line of communication. The expedition were fortunate in obtaining as chief transport officer Lieutenant-Colonel H. W. Tobin, D.S.O., O.B.E., the Darjeeling secretary of the Himalayan Club whose experience not only of Himalayan mountaineering generally but of local Darjeeling conditions made him an invaluable asset to the expedition. Upon him devolved responsibility for the enlistment of porters and the arrangement of the multifarious expedition details at Darjeeling, many of which though seemingly trivial in themselves are vital to the efficient working of a transport organisation.

In order to strengthen not only the transport organisation but the climbing party as well, Mr. G. W. Wood Johnson was invited to join the expedition. Like Colonel

Tobin he is well acquainted with local conditions. His enthusiasm for mountaineering may be gauged by the fact that he had come to India not only to learn tea-planting but to learn how to handle natives and speak Nepali in order to fit himself for a future Everest expedition. In these things he had prospered exceedingly under the able tuition of Mr. McKean his manager. Though he had then no previous Alpine experience he was a member of the Fell and Rock Climbing Club of the English Lake District and an expert rock climber. Alpine experience counts for little in the Himalayas without knowledge of travelling conditions, and an expedition undertaken by him in 1929 to peaks around Dzongri was to prove of more value to our expedition than any amount of Alpine experience.

Having chosen the personnel of a Himalayan expedition, the next thing to do is to equip it. Himalayan mountaineering falls naturally into two categories. There is the expedition that has for its object the conquest of peaks up to 23,000 feet high, and for this ordinary Alpine clothing and foot-gear are sufficient. Then there is the expedition that sets out to attempt the greater peaks of the Himalayas. This requires more specialised equipment, for owing to the effects of altitude and subsequent lowering of the vitality and bodily wastage, the winds that mercilessly sweep the upper ridges, and intense cold, it is essential to prevent frostbite.

There is only one way of efficiently clothing an expedition, and that is to study the lessons of the past, and to take heed of the lessons learnt, often at considerable cost, on expeditions such as Sir Martin Conway's in the Karakorams and the three Mount Everest expeditions. These lessons and the recommendations derived from them are all laid down and should be studied with the utmost care. Nor should the late Sir Ernest Shackleton and the clothing which he provided for his expeditions into the Antarctic be neglected, for he was one of the first to make a scientific study of *light* wind-and-cold-resisting clothing.

Professor Dyhrenfurth was fortunate in having the advice of Brigadier-General the Hon. C. G. Bruce, C.B., M.V.O., Lieutenant-Colonel E. L. Strutt, C.B.E., D.S.O., who accompanied the 1922 Everest expedition, and others. In the light of their experiences on Everest they were unhesitating in their recommendation that light clothing and light boots should be worn of a type similar to that advocated by Shackleton. On Everest, the best clothing was found to consist of woollen underclothes, Shetland wool sweaters, and outside a light jacket of wind-proof material. Boots were similar to those used in ordinary Alpine work, only lightly nailed and sufficiently roomy to take two or three pairs of stockings and socks. It is interesting to note that the porters who went highest, about 27,000 feet, did so in Army ammunition boots brought out from England and costing 15/6 a pair. Thus, in a properly equipped expedition, frostbite is usually due to the carelessness of the climber.

Bearing these things in mind, it was unfortunate that Professor Dyhrenfurth did not follow advice founded on many years experience, of equipping his expedition with light clothing and boots. He chose rather to adopt the diametrically opposed theory that one layer of heavy material is warmer than two or more layers of lighter material.

The following is a list of clothing that was supplied. A tricot coat weighing six pounds; breeches, three pounds, six ounces; sweater, two pounds, ten ounces; outer wind-jacket, three pounds. I can only describe the boots as portmanteaux. They weighed six and a half pounds a pair, and each was nailed with sixty clinker and tricouni nails. The soles were built up of layers of felt, rubber and leather, and the uppers, which came half-way to the knee, were felt-lined. Crampons supplied with these boots were proportionately heavy and weighed four pounds a pair. Allowing an additional two pounds for an ice-axe, and five pounds for underclothing, head-gear, socks, stockings and puttees, but not including gear and equipment such as is normally carried in a rucksack or rope, we were, therefore, expected to carry a total of thirty-two and a half pounds to the summit of Kangchenjunga. This, together with other equipment, etc., would in my case be *nearly a quarter of my own normal weight.* It goes without saying that this equipment proved totally unsatisfactory. The only occasion on which I wore the expedition boots was on the Ramthang Peak, and I shall not easily forget the effort of lifting them at an altitude of 23,000 feet. What would they and the clothing be like to the climber dependent on his last dregs of energy between 27,000 and 28,000 feet near the summit of Kangchenjunga?

It was with some inkling as to what was likely to be provided that caused me to purchase some equipment in England in addition to that with which Professor Dyhrenfurth was providing me. This consisted principally of Shetland woollies and Jaeger underclothing. Of the former, I had four sweaters weighing four ounces each purchased from W. Bill of Great Portland Street, London. I never found it necessary to wear more than three of these, and these three worn in conjunction with Jaeger combinations and a wind-proof jacket were definitely warmer than the tricot jacket, and the two pounds ten ounces single sweater. Unfortunately, the boots came as a complete surprise, and, like some of the other members of the expedition, I was forced to wear a pair of boots which I used to tramp from Darjeeling to the Base Camp, boots which would only take two pairs of stockings, and that at a squeeze, but which nevertheless proved perfectly satisfactory with a dozen or more tricouni nails knocked into each.

I know that in making such challenging statements I may arouse the wrath of my continental friends, who believe that weight and thickness alone spell warmth, but apart from my own former experiences in the Alps, during which I have made a close study of clothing and equipment, and apart from the experiences of former Himalayan and Polar expeditions, it cannot be doubted that several layers of light clothing are preferable to one layer of thick, heavy clothing, and that clothing one third of the weight of that which I have mentioned would be heavy enough, and warm enough for a man to reach without fear of frostbite the highest peaks in the world.

There is another thing that must be considered besides mere warmth—the ventilation of the body. Though the air temperature may be many degrees below freezing, the sun temperature is enormous at high altitudes. If the body is not sufficiently ventilated, perspiration cannot evaporate, and a sudden lowering of body temperature by wind, or the withdrawal of the sun may result in a severe chill. A single layer of thick material, while being wind-proof, is also ventilation proof. It is possible to have clothing which will both ventilate the body and protect it from the wind, and in this respect there is nothing better than several layers of Shetland wool.

The head and ears must be well protected, and here again one cannot do better than to wear two or three Shetland wool Balaclava helmets, while in the event of a severe wind, a leather flying helmet can be worn outside, although this again tends to retard ventilation.

Snow blindness must be guarded against. At high altitudes the ultra-violet rays of the sun are so intense that even on rocks it is possible to suffer snow blindness. No special protection, other than the ordinary bottle-green or dark yellow snow-glasses that can be purchased in Switzerland at one franc a pair, is necessary. Personally, I found Crookes' glass more restful, as it does not distort colour, and eliminates all glare by cutting out the ultra-violet rays. The sun also shines with such power that it strips the skin off the face like paper, a process which, incidentally, is assisted by the wind only too effectually. The best kind of protective face cream is that which both lubricates the skin and absorbs the ultra-violet rays, which are principally responsible for the painful stripping process.

Excellent gloves were provided. They were of the leather fingerless variety fleece-lined. Puttees have many opponents among mountaineers, but the Kashmiri puttees as recommended by General Bruce do not impede the circulation in the least degree and are wonderfully warm. Not only do they prevent the snow getting in, but they afford excellent protection against the inroads of leeches. Incidentally, while on this last subject, it is a useful tip to put tobacco leaves in the stockings. Although leeches enjoy one's blood, they object to having to chew tobacco first in order to get it.

Professor Dyhrenfurth did a wise thing when he decided to have separate tents for each European member of the expedition. Later on, I shall have occasion to remark on the psychological importance of this. Suffice to say that these tents made by Schuster of Munich were excellent, and stood up well to wind and rain. The only criticism that might be made is that there was not sufficient overlap in the flaps.

The best thing of all among the camping equipment was the synthetic rubber ground sheets. These were about one-third of an inch thick. Not only do they keep one dry, but they insulate one from the cold ground or snow, and are soft enough to eliminate the " inevitable stone."

Wise is the mountaineer who fusses over his sleeping bag as a cricketer fusses over his particular brand of bat. Individual taste should be satisfied, for the Himalayan mountaineer spends an appreciable portion of his life lying in his sleeping bag. Here again the lessons of the past are not to be ignored. It has been said of Everest sleeping bags that they were too narrow, and that at great altitudes, the climber had to wriggle, strain and pant in order to insinuate himself into his bag, an effort so great at 25,000 feet or more that he would lie for minutes exhausted by the effort. The warmest sleeping bag is not a tightly fitting one, but one in which there is plenty of room to change the position. Warmth also depends upon having sufficient air space round the body. Several years experimenting in Alpine conditions have convinced me that quilted eiderdown is superior to all other forms of material for a sleeping bag. Also that an outer covering of jaconet is advantageous. A plain sleeping bag, open only at one end is better than one slit down the side, for however well the side may be laced up, and the finicky business of lacing is, incidentally a labour, the slit is sure to coincide with the middle of the back during the night, and chilliness will result.

Unwilling to be standardised on this matter, I had a sleeping bag made by Mr. R. Burns, of 5 Lever Street, Manchester, to my own design. It was seven feet long, thirty-two inches wide at the head end, tapering to seventeen inches at the feet end, and weighing eight pounds, fourteen ounces. It consisted of two quilted eiderdown bags, one inside the other. The inner one was lined with Jaeger fleece, and the two bags were enclosed in an outer covering of jaconet. Both bags and the outer covering were fitted at the head end with a string-bag arrangement. The length was so ample that I was able to snuggle up right inside it with only my nose and mouth projecting through the drawn up opening.

The advantage of having two bags was a great one. It meant that in the lower tropical forests I could utilise the outer of the two eiderdown bags only, and sleep comfortably without being too hot. Higher up, the second bag could be utilised with its fleece lining, and on the snows both bags together with or without the outer covering. Thus, it was easily possible to regulate through a wide range of temperature the degree of warmth required.

It is interesting to note that when only one bag and the jaconet cover are utilised, the latter tends to condense the vapours of the body and wet the eiderdown, but with two bags this does not occur, owing to the air space between the bags. I slept for six weeks using both bags and the cover without the bag becoming damp. I slept well too ; in fact, during the whole expedition I do not remember shivering once during the night, and that fact, coupled with the excellent sleep I was able to enjoy, was of no small importance, and was undoubtedly responsible for my keeping fit during the expedition. I can unhesitatingly recommend these bags to other expeditions, and particularly those whose route takes them through a variety of climates.

The expedition bag was about the same weight, and was enclosed in a heavy canvas cover weighing five or six times more than the jaconet cover. It was narrow and slit down the side. The slit was done up with little wooden cross-pieces which had to be fitted through string loops, an awkward and irritating business, whilst the bag was so narrow, that more than once I heard my companions groaning as they strove to get into it.

The expedition took with it one large " Debrie " cine-camera with its manifold gadgets, including various telephoto lenses, three " Kinamo " cine-cameras, which take one hundred feet of film and can be loaded in a daylight charger, and no less than 60,000 feet of standard size film. In addition, practically everyone had his own camera, the majority of which were fitted for film packs. Of the latter we took an enormous quantity made by Messrs. Agfa, Ltd., each in an air-tight tin, and I am happy to add that they gave every possible satisfaction, and admirably stood the manifold changes of humidity and temperature they had to undergo between exposure and development. My own pet cameras were two thin pocket " Etui " cameras, one 6 × 9 centimetres, and the other 9 × 12 centimetres. Of the work done by them, I need only say that it was of the finest possible quality, and photographs taken by these little cameras appeared in newspapers all over the world. Both cameras were very light, and either could be slipped into the pocket. They were supplied by Sands, Hunter, Ltd. The disadvantage of cinematographic and photographic work on a large scale is the number of additional porters this entailed. I do not think that less than fifty porters were utilised in carrying our cinematographic and photographic apparatus and materials.

A large quantity of continental and English rope was taken, and regarding this all members of the expedition were agreed that the Alpine Club rope manufactured by Beale's was far the superior both in strength and general handiness.

There is no space here to mention the manifold items of equipment necessary for an expedition of this nature. I think a good deal of what we took might have come under the heading of luxuries rather than necessities, and had our subsequent transport difficulties been realised at the outset, it is safe to say that there would have been a drastic cutting down of individual and general equipment, and this without imperilling the party in any way. The seeker after information regarding Himalayan equipment should refer to the Alpine Club equipment report.

Turning to food, the importance of correct feeding can hardly be over-estimated. The mountaineer climbing at high altitudes should look after his stomach with as much care as most American millionaires are forced to look after theirs. Up to the Base Camp, normal eating and foods can be indulged in. Above that the health, and therefore the success of a Himalayan expedition, depends upon eating the right kind of food. Sugar is to the mountaineer climbing over 20,000 feet as petrol is to an internal combustion engine. Thanks to the generosity of many firms the expedition was able to leave Europe with enough food and chocolate to start a grocery store and confectioner's shop. Unfortunately, however, much of this food came under the heading of luxuries, and included such substances as caviare, paté de foie gras, tinned gherkins, Christmas puddings, tinned mushrooms and so forth. If in place of these, sugary foods had been taken, the subsequent ill health and upset stomachs which afflicted the expedition members at various times might have been avoided. As a substitute for bread, which is not to be obtained in most parts of the Himalayas, we took Swedish biscuits. These proved excellent, not only as a food, but as an aid to the digestion. The effect of high altitude is to make the stomach very acid, and food tends to ferment rather than be absorbed by the normal processes of digestion. Bismuth tablets are a spendid neutraliser of this uncomfortable condition. Owing to low pressure at high altitudes water boils at lower temperatures than at sea level. In order to facilitate boiling we took with us a patent high-pressure boiler. Though there was often some doubt as to whether or not it would blow up it was on the whole a great success.

No physiological subject during recent years has provided

a greater controversy than whether oxygen is useful or not at great altitudes. In spite of the fact that Colonel E. F. Norton and Mr. T. H. Somervell reached 28,000 feet on Everest without oxygen, there are those who still declare that oxygen is of value despite the weight of the cylinders containing it, and the apparatus to distribute it. Personally, I think a compromise will be reached so that the future climbers of Everest will carry one or two small oxygen cylinders as a reserve to boost their strength up for that last terrible few hundred feet. We compromised, but in a different way, and took with us oxygen cylinders, not for inhalation on the actual climb, but for use in tents, as it was thought that this "English air," as the natives called it, would serve as an excellent "bracer" to the day's work at a high altitude, and might be of use in resuscitating an exhausted man. It was certainly found to be useful in both these departments, but whether the expense of porterage and the apparatus was worth it is doubtful. I think, however, that for Everest or Kangchenjunga oxygen should be taken as a medicine, for its effect on an exhausted man is superior to that of alcohol.

Apart from oxygen, Dr. Richter took with him a special physiological apparatus in addition to the usual implements of his profession.

The foregoing is necessarily little more than an allusion to a few among many of the details that must be considered before an expedition can so much as set sail from Europe. It is intended only to give the reader some idea of the manifold things the leader of an expedition has to consider. No one could have worked harder than Professor and Frau Dyhrenfurth, and their work was inspired by the fact that in going to Kangchenjunga they were fulfilling a lifetime's ambition.

As regards the Press, it was arranged that I should act as Special Correspondent and Photographer to *The Times*. Messages were to be sent back by runners from the expedition and thence telegraphed to Europe through the *Statesman* newspaper in Calcutta, the Editor of which, Mr. Alfred Watson, was of great service to the expedition. So at last, on February 24, 1930, the first party consisting of Professor and Frau Dyhrenfurth, Dr. Richter, Duvanel and myself left Europe on the S.S. *Gange* of the Lloyd Triestino Navigation Company.

On our arrival at Bombay, we sent off six and a half tons of goods to Darjeeling. Our first task was to apply to His Highness the Maharajah of Nepal for permission to pass through his country. That that permission was granted was due partly to the kind offices of Mr. Howell, Foreign Secretary, and Colonel Dawkes, the British Envoy at Khatmandu, the capital of Nepal. It was considered also that an English speaking Gurkha N.C.O. would be most useful to us, and thanks to the kindness of Field-Marshal Sir William Birdwood, Bart., we were able to obtain the services of Naik Tikeram Thapa of the 2/8th Gurkha Rifles, who was specially selected by his Commanding Officer, Lieutenant-Colonel C. D. Noe.

These things being accomplished, we toured through India, visiting such show places as Delhi, Agra, and Benares. But the plains were hot and dusty, and we longed, all of us, to sense the keen air from the snows of Kangchenjunga and the High Himalayas.

CHAPTER IV

A FIRST GLIMPSE OF THE HIMALAYAS

In order to meet Wood Johnson and make some of the preliminary arrangements for the expedition, I left the first party at Agra, and travelled on alone to Siliguri. The "Darjeeling Mail" from Calcutta arrived there soon after dawn. The night in the train had been a stifling one, and intense heat had not improved a slight attack of dysentery contracted at Agra. Yet, it was impossible not to experience a thrill, for Siliguri lies at the foot of the Himalayas, and I craned my head out of the window to try and catch a glimpse of the great mountain range we had come so far to see. But nothing was visible save a few miles of the monotonous heat-soaked Plain of Bengal.

Alighting on the platform, I found my hand clasped by Wood Johnson. He said, "I knew it was you, because you are obviously a climber." I replied that at the moment I certainly did not feel like one, as my stomach appeared to be full of gnawing rats. "Oh! That's nothing," was the comforting reply, "everyone gets these little 'tummy' troubles out here."

It was during breakfast that I learned that I was expected to accompany Wood Johnson on the pillion of his motor-cycle to his tea plantation at Rangli Rangliot, 5,000 feet up, thirty miles from Siliguri and twenty from Darjeeling. Three years previously I had risen from a muddy ditch by the side of a remote road in Wales whither I had been hurled at a speed of forty-five miles per hour vowing that I would never again ride a motor-cycle. Now, this vow must perforce be broken.

I will not mention the make of the motor-cycle, as this might be considered derogatory by the makers. We had not proceeded a mile from Siliguri when a portion of the horn fell off. Many bullock carts were on the road, and vigorous blasting on the horn was required to move them. After a search, we retrieved the lost portion, and proceeded on our way.

The road from Siliguri is flat and straight, as straight as a Roman road, and with a fair metalled surface. On either hand is dense jungle ; tangled, knotted masses of trees and undergrowth, interspersed with tall, coarse elephant grass. Here are to be found elephant, leopard and tiger. Indeed, Wood Johnson told me that a man eater of the last species had recently caused considerable alarm in the district. The road we were on is a unique highway. It is the connecting link between India and Thibet, the great trade-way along which Thibetans pass to sell their goods in India, and the route followed by three Everest expeditions. After the sullen-eyed Bengalis of Calcutta and the plains, it was a relief to see the yellow-skinned, almond-eyed, alert little men from Thibet and Nepal, with their wide, cheery grins.

As we chugged and exploded through the silent forest, dim, unsubstantial shapes far overhead began to loom through the haze, the Himalayas. In no other mountain range that I have seen is the transition from plain to mountain so abrupt. One minute we were on the Plain of Bengal, as flat as a golfing green, the next the wooded jaws of the great Teesta Valley had enclosed us.

The Teesta Valley is one of the most superb valleys in the world. Though no snow peaks are visible from its lower portion, the traveller realises that he has entered the Himalayas. Above him the valley sides rise for thousands of feet at such a steep angle, it seems almost impossible that the dense tropical vegetation can cling to them; below, in a rocky bed of giant boulders carried down by the turbulence of the monsoon rains, thunder the melted snow waters of Kangchenjunga, and the glaciers of Northern Sikkim.

Where it debouches on to the Plain of Bengal, the valley floor is but a few feet above sea level. Luxuriously beautiful though the forests are at this low altitude, they serve but to breed one of the most malignant malarial mosquitos known to exist. It is said of Teesta Valley malaria that once it is fairly in the blood, the victim will never entirely rid himself of it. That this is a truism is shown by the poor physique of the Sikkim Lepchas, who inhabit the valley. This race of gentle mild-eyed people is being gradually, but ruthlessly exterminated by disease and malaria. Their plight is not helped by a strict conservatism regarding marriage, which decrees that they shall not marry Thibetans, their hereditary enemies. Thus the evils of inter-marriage are added to those of disease, evils that increase as the population decreases. It is only fresh and healthy blood that can save the Lepchas from extinction.

Soon after entering the valley, the road began to climb

in a series of hairpin bends. These Wood Johnson negotiated at a high speed, while relating to me how the previous year he had run off the road, fallen a considerable distance with the motor-cycle on top of him, and had to spend three months in hospital. Fortunately, it was on a straight section that the tyre elected to go suddenly flat. The valve was at fault, although had the tyre been punctured, it would have made little difference, as Wood Johnson possessed no repair outfit.

We were five miles from the nearest village where help could be obtained. First of all, we attempted to continue as before, but even at a slow speed the motor-cycle slewed unpleasantly about the road, and after I had received a bruise on the shin, I suggested to Wood Johnson that he should go on alone, repair the valve, and return. With no weight on the pillion this was possible, and a few minutes later he was out of sight.

To one who had but recently escaped from the cold, damp vapours of a London February, the heat seemed terrific. From all sides came a shrill symposium of innumerable insects, and the harsh clatter of frogs. It was my first experience of a tropical forest, and as I wished to see more of the Teesta Valley, I decided to continue walking along the road.

For the most part the hillside rises steeply and directly from the road, but at one part there was a comparatively level intervening stretch of forest. It was while passing this that I was suddenly startled by an unpleasantly malevolent snarl. Looking to the left I could clearly distinguish between the matted undergrowth the form of a large tiger, not more than five yards away. Apart from

Zoos and circuses, it was the first time that I had ever seen a tiger, and I must confess that Wood Johnson's story of the man eater recurred unpleasantly in my mind. My only weapon, a pocket knife, seemed a poor defence. It was a situation requiring tact. If I ran, the tiger might regard this as an indication of timidity, and follow me. If I stood still, he might assume me to be an attacker, and himself attack. The best compromise was to continue quietly walking down the road. Once I heard a rustle as though the brute was following me through the jungle, but after two hundred yards the flat jungle gave place to a buttress of crags abutting against the road. I could breathe more freely, for the tiger was scarcely likely to follow me along the open road. It was, of course, much to be regretted that I had not a rifle, for to have shot one's first tiger in such circumstances would have been unusual. The fact that farther along the road several natives passed me showed that in this district, at least, nothing is to be feared from tigers.

A mile or so farther on was a native hamlet, consisting of thatched, wooden houses resting on log piles. Here the road divided, one branch climbing the hill towards Darjeeling, the other continuing along the valley, after crossing a tributary of the main Teesta River by a well-made suspension bridge. By the bridge, I sat down to wait for Wood Johnson. At length, he arrived, and we continued once more on our journey.

I told him of my encounter with the tiger, and gathered that I should consider myself lucky seeing one so soon after arriving in India. Other men had been out for years, and had not seen a tiger. He, Wood Johnson, would have given a month's pay to have seen that tiger at the business end of a rifle. The tiger had already killed deer, and other animals. There was, of course, no question of it attacking human beings unless itself attacked. All this I gathered as I bumped painfully up and down on the pillion of Wood Johnson's motor-cycle.

Presently, we left the road in favour of a narrow lane that winds up the hillside to Rangli Rangliot, 4,500 feet above the Teesta Valley. In England, this lane would be much in demand by motor-cycling clubs as a test hill. People would line its one in three gradient and hairpin bends to cheer the intrepidity of the riders, but in this part of the world it is only one among many other hills of a similar character habitually traversed by the Austin Seven cars and motor-cycles of the tea planters. Wood Johnson said his record was twenty minutes for this particular ascent, but that out of consideration for my stomach he would not try to break it. Anyway, Fate willed otherwise. We had climbed but two or three hundred feet above the main road when the engine, after a few splutters and a sharp cough, stopped dead.

This time it was a twist-grip throttle control that had broken. A caravan of laden ponies under the charge of some natives was coming up the path. They wished to pass us, but this Wood Johnson would not allow. He said they would interfere with our future progress. First of all, we endeavoured by an ingenious arrangement of string to manipulate the throttle from the handle-bars, then Wood Johnson in the saddle, and myself and two natives shoving, the motor-cycle was pushed up the hill. After several attempts the engine suddenly elected to start with a gallant roar. I sprang on behind, Wood Johnson let in the clutch, and once more we shot up the hill. But we had not gone more than a few yards when the engine again spluttered and coughed to a standstill. The same laborious process was then repeated, after which we sat down exhausted amid a circle of interested natives.

The noon-day heat was appalling. Divesting ourselves of the majority of our clothes, and giving them to one of the natives with instructions to bring them up, we once more attacked the problem of our recalcitrant mount. First of all I thought of something ingenious, and then Wood Johnson thought of something even more ingenious. The result was always the same, a vulgar splutter and a sarcastic cough. An hour or two later we hurled the contraption to the side of the road, and sat down to consider the situation. We were very hot, Wood Johnson's hand was bleeding from contact with one of the sharp edges common to all motor-cycles, my stomach had not been improved. The motor-cycle tilted over by the side of the road at an inelegant angle, with its horn tied together by string and lurching drunkenly over one handle-bar, seemed to leer at us. There was nothing for it but to walk uphill. Luck was with us. We had not got half-way when we met some unladen ponies coming in the opposite direction, two of which we at once commandeered.

It was now possible for the first time since leaving Siliguri to appreciate the surroundings. As we climbed, the tropical heat of the Teesta Valley was gradually superseded by a temperature comparable to that of a warm English summer day. The jungle thinned, and abruptly we emerged from it on to open slopes covered in tea. A fresh evening breeze greeted us, seeming to whisper of high places and the snows. Thousands of feet below now was the Teesta Valley with its argent river thread. Northwards, rolling hills stretched like grass-grown slag-heaps towards the factories of the snows. These grass and forest-clad hills are but the foot-hills of the Himalayan wall, yet they are as great in scale as the main range of the Alps. In the Alps one may gaze down into a valley and see trim, neatly laid-out little villages and fields, roads, railways, and electric-power lines, but these give to the mountains an artificial taint, and even on the summit of Mont Blanc or the Matterhorn the mountaineer cannot escape entirely from civilisation. But amid these lower foot-hills of the Himalayas there are few signs of commercialism. True, man has hacked a way here, and scraped a clearing there, but generally speaking the country is the same as it always has been. Up there, in the evening stillness of the tea-gardens I experienced for the first time in my life that subtle feeling of joy and sorrow intermixed which comes to all who are born with the love for mountains. Joy for the vision and hope of the unknown, and sorrow in realising how many adventures there are to seek, and how pitifully short is the life in which to seek them.

Gielle Tea Estate, where Wood Johnson works, is one of the most beautifully situated among the Darjeeling district tea-gardens, and commands a view up the Teesta Valley towards the snows. A pleasant evening was spent there as the guest of Mr. McKean, Wood Johnson's manager, who had kindly given permission for the latter to accompany the expedition, although it meant single-handed work on the plantation for the next three months.

McKean had lived twenty years at Gielle, and it was largely due to his expert tuition in the handling of native labour that made Wood Johnson so invaluable to the expedition.

He presented me with a kukri as a memento of the occasion. The cutting powers of this heavy, curved knife in the hands of an expert Gurkha is amazing. It is said that with one blow a bullock's head can be severed from its body, whilst during the War it was a favourite amusement among men of Gurkha regiments to crawl across " No Man's Land " at night, lie " doggo " on the parapet of the enemy trench, and lop off the head of the unfortunate sentry or anyone else who happened to pass. But apart from its unique cutting powers, the kukri is useful in many other ways, and during the expedition I saw it employed in cutting up firewood, opening packing-cases, sharpening pencils, hewing down vegetation and other varied, if menial tasks.

That evening a number of tea-garden coolies came in with baskets of freshly plucked tea. Most of them were women, sturdy little Nepalis with gay coloured head-dresses, necklaces and earrings. In spite of a heavy day's work, for which they are paid but a few annas, they have always a smile at the end of it, and they stood outside the factory laughing and chattering like school children starting out for a treat. The gaiety of these hill people is indeed infectious, and one cannot but compare these lively little women of the hills to the morose Hindu women of the plains.

It was late when Wood Johnson and I left McKean's hospitable roof. Innumerable fireflies flitted round us as we passed through the silent plantation. Somewhere in the direction of the Himalayas lightning flickered restlessly. The profound quietude of the hills was broken only by the distant throbbing of a native band.

CHAPTER V

SUPERSTITIONS AND STORMS

Great mountain peaks usually excite superstitious awe in the minds of the simple peasantry who dwell in the valleys beneath them. Their height, their isolation from the everyday affairs of life and their grandeur impress men with a sense of their insignificance, persuading them against all judgment and reason that there are forces abroad beyond human ken.

During the Middle Ages the Alps were popularly reputed to be the abode of monstrous dragons ; the uneasy ghost of Pontius Pilate was believed to haunt the slopes of Mount Pilatus above Lucerne, and as late as the latter half of the last century, Edward Whymper wrote of the Matterhorn : " There seemed to be a cordon drawn around it, up to which one might go, but no farther. Within that invisible line gins and effreets were supposed to exist—the Wandering Jew and the spirits of the damned. The superstitious natives in the surrounding valleys (many of whom firmly believed it to be not only the highest mountain in the Alps, but in the world) spoke of a ruined city on its summit wherein spirits dwelt ; and if you laughed, they gravely shook their heads ; told you to look yourself to see the castles and the walls, and warned one against a rash approach, lest the infuriate demons from their impregnable heights might hurl down vengeance for one's derision."

With the advance of civilisation, however, most Alpine

superstitions became legendary. Sturdy guides haul tourists to the summit of the Matterhorn, the ghost of Pontius Pilate is enjoying a well-earned repose, and the dragons have fled before the hosts of Mr. Thomas Cook and the Polytechnic Institute.

Yet even in such an accessible mountain range as the Alps superstitions die hard, and the traveller who forsakes the tourist highways will still find ancient beliefs that have been handed down through countless generations. How much more, therefore, must superstitions be rife among the stupendous ranges of the Himalayas? The fact that their greatest peaks have defied the best efforts of skilled mountaineers, and that, of the sixty odd peaks over 25,000 feet, not one has been scaled, is in itself a justification of the belief that a cordon is drawn round the summits beyond which man may not enter, where dwell the gods in icy detachment from the world.

The most rationally minded of men cannot gaze from Darjeeling upon Kangchenjunga without experiencing something of the same emotions of the simpler-minded Sherpas and Lepchas who dwell in the valleys below. He will find himself wondering half in shame whether there is anything in the tales told him of the powerful god whose sacred throne rests upon its summits, the " Five Treasures of the Snow," and whether the snow-fields and glaciers suspended in mid-air above a misty ocean are indeed the abiding places of the Mi-go, the Abominable Snow Men. He will gaze on Siniolchum and reflect that if there is a God of Inaccessibility, his unapproachable halls and palaces must be fashioned beneath the icy flutings and sweeping scimitar-like ridges of that amazing peak.

It is easy to understand the superstitions of the natives who live round Kangchenjunga. Their fears and fancies are merely an outward expression of a primitive instinct that recognises in Kangchenjunga something beyond human understanding ; a world apart, akin both to Heaven and to Hell ; something to be revered, feared and worshipped.

At first sight it seems strange that men should flock so willingly to the banners of expeditions such as have attempted Everest and Kangchenjunga. The reason is not far to seek ; there is prestige and honour to be gained in daring the inaccessible and braving the wrath of the gods. The Sherpas may be the prey to superstitious fears, but they are men enough to be able to conquer them.

Mountain superstitions are much the same the world over ; it is, therefore, curious to find such a unique superstition as the Abominable Snow Men so firmly implanted in the native mind. Our porters, even the most educated among them, swore that they had seen them, and described them as being white-skinned and naked, but covered with thick hair. Whence did this belief originate ? Was there once a wild tribe that roamed the Himalayas—a tribe, perhaps, of white nomads from Southern Siberia, half ape and half man, to give to this superstition a foundation of fact ? During the last Everest expedition wild rumours were afloat that the expedition actually encountered these beings. Actually, however, no European has set eyes on a Snow Man. The nearest approach to fact was the experience of Mr. E. O. Shebbeare, who accompanied the 1929 Bavarian expedition to Kangchenjunga. He relates that when ascending to the Base Camp his porters begged him to come with them to see the footprints of a Snow Man in the snow. When, however, he arrived at the spot a fresh fall of snow had covered the ground.

Thunderstorms are common among the Himalayas. Most fine mornings see the cloudy galleons sweeping up from the steamy Plain of Bengal. Slowly they sail over the green foothills or float in lazy stateliness on the blue hazes of the deep valleys, their keels in shadow, their sails of massive cumuli bellying thousands of feet aloft in the sunlight. As they advance, they are augmented by the warm, moist air currents from the valleys. Magically they grow larger ; their girth and height increases every moment ; they are sifted by the upward breezes, broken and distorted into all manner of queer forms by vagrant winds ; momentarily dissipated by unexpected blasts. They become a mighty fleet and pass in splendid line ahead towards the huge wall of the Himalayas, where they assault in misty surges the snowy bastions of Kangchenjunga.

Towards mid-day the first thunder echoes in deep growls along the valleys. A smooth slaty pall of nimbus, underhung with coppery billows of cumuli, slides up the zenith. The thunder becomes louder ; its solemn booms are resolved into an angrier crackle. Spiteful lightning spears the whale-backed crests of the foothills and leaps among the clouds. A veil of rain is borne along by the thundercloud trailing hill and valley, blotting out the sunny hillsides, sweeping over the ridges.

Local thunderstorms occur almost every day among the foothills of the Himalayas ; they seldom attack the great peaks, and usually expend their wrath before the evening, their apparently indissoluble clouds melting into the night. But, occasionally, there are storms which are neither local nor confined to the foothills. I saw such a storm at Darjeeling.

The afternoon had been thunderous, and storm after storm had stalked over the hills, their hailstones bringing dismay to the tea planters whose leaves were ready for plucking. The sunset was wild as I climbed Observatory Hill. Long, tendrous clouds, bridging a gap between the dense curtains of cumuli, had been twisted by the wind until they appeared like bloodstained claws groping in the sky. The sky between was that ominous cat's eye green, a colour that mountaineers and seamen instinctively distrust. One doresque shaft of ruddy light striking through the turmoil of mists fell upon the Singalila ridge. Day was dying as I gained the summit of Observatory Hill, and sullen draperies had been drawn across the sunset. In the south lightning flicked a restless whip over Tiger Hill ; in the east, towers of cloud were occasionally revealed by fountains of lightning. Once again came thunder, long heavy vibrations shaking the earth ; lightning blue and vivid slashed the peaks of the Singalila ridge and Nepal.

On the summit of Observatory Hill there is a Thibetan temple, not a building, but a forest of prayer flags ringing a small space in which is set a primitive altar. Here, as though to propitiate the gods, and perhaps, in particular, the great God of Kangchenjunga, the lamas began to pray, a low mutter breaking forth into a wail of religious fervour, accompanied by the monotonous ringing of a hand-bell. I felt that indefinable sensation that every visitor to the East feels sooner or later—that time and space are limitless, that man is but the puppet of fate, a mere plaything of elemental forces beyond his comprehension or control.

Thibetan music is the epitome of that strange mountain land of the Himalayas. Its weird dirge-like monotone, its occasional passionate crescendo, suggests infinity, the presence of great mountains and limitless spaces, the fears and hardships of those foredoomed to dwell on bitter wind-swept plateaux and gaze for ever on the barren slopes and inhospitable solitudes of Central Asia.

The praying ceased ; between two rolls of thunder no sound disturbed the hilltop save the sigh of an awakened wind among the prayer flags and the distant clamour of Darjeeling.

The storm came up apace with glares of bluish lightning and staccato thunder that flung in waves of sound across the valleys or rolled and grumbled like immense engines on the ridges. Rain and hail swept the hill ; the lightning leapt in furious confused brilliance. Thunder, crashing and majestic, came hard on its heels. In a few minutes the storm was gone, its turbulence swallowed in the night. A small star gleamed tentatively, was extinguished by a cloud scud, and gleamed again more confidently. The subsiding groan of the wind among the prayer flags broke a heavy silence.

Other and more distant storms took up the tale. In the direction of Everest sudden floods of white light soundlessly illuminated the cloudy pavements of the sky, picking out in faultless detail the towers, minarets and cupolas of a cathedral of mist towering above the world. As though jealous of his supreme neighbour, the God of Kangchenjunga struck out with fierce blue swords and vicious darts of forked lightning. Somewhere over Bhutan and Thibet another cloud winked with bibulous persistence like some lesser mountain god delighting in this fiery combat of Himalayan giants.

No thunder was to be heard. From the depths of the Rangit Valley beneath, mist wraiths swayed upwards like jinns from the confines of a monstrous bottle. The moon was rising as I turned to go ; her calm radiance seemed to quell the stormy disputes between earth and sky. Beneath her contemptuous gaze the distant lightning became desultory and wan. The clouds were withdrawn from Kangchenjunga. Far up in the awakened stars something white gleamed steadfastly—the summit.

CHAPTER VI

OFF AT LAST

By the end of March all members of the expedition were assembled in Darjeeling. While in Delhi we had written letters to the Maharajah of Nepal, and to Colonel Dawkes, C.I.E., British Envoy at Khatmandu, requesting permission to attack Kangchenjunga from the Nepalese side. Owing, however, to political friction existing then between Nepal and Thibet, it seemed advisable not to worry the Nepalese authorities until matters had quieted down. The letter was left, therefore, with Mr. Howell, the Foreign Secretary, who had kindly undertaken to forward it at an appropriate date. The previous year, the Munich expedition had also applied for permission to enter Nepal, but though this permission had been eventually given, it had arrived far too late for them to avail themselves of it. Bearing these things in mind, we had no option but to plan an attempt on Kangchenjunga via Sikkim, and the eastern face of the mountain.

Apart from Colonel Tobin, who as previously mentioned, was appointed Transport Officer, Mr. J. S. Hannah, of the Bengal and Nagpur Railway, was invited to join the expedition. Hannah had had considerable experience of Indian travel, and had also climbed in the Alps. Most important of all he spoke Hindustani, and this, combined with the efficient way in which he handled transport and porters, was to make him an invaluable member of the expedition.

By whichever route we went, we hoped to leave Darjeeling early in April. The time during which an attempt can be made either before or after the monsoon is so short, that it was essential to be at the foot of the mountain, if possible, by the middle of April. This would allow some six weeks. But as General Bruce pointed out, the monsoon *might* come by the middle of May, and that this was possible was borne out by the experience of the tea planters and others living in the Darjeeling district. Assuming that the difficulties would be comparable to those encountered by the Munich expedition, four weeks was definitely too short a time in which to make the attempt. On the other hand, so far as could be seen from Darjeeling, the Kang La, the 16,373 feet pass we must traverse into Nepal was still so deeply snow-covered at the beginning of April that to have started earlier would have been impossible.

Attempting any great Himalayan peak must always mean a gamble with the weather. Had we decided in the beginning to tackle the eastern face of the mountain by the same route as the Munich expedition, we could have established our Base Camp early in April, and commenced to have attacked the mountain without delay. But Professor Dyhrenfurth had other objects in view besides attempting Kangchenjunga. North-east Nepal was practically unknown. No European had passed along the valleys to the west and south-west of Kangchenjunga since 1899, when Mr. Douglas Freshfield passed round Kangchenjunga. The upper branches of the Kangchenjunga Glacier were still unexplored. No one had seen the head of the Ramthang Glacier which falls from the western face of Kangchenjunga. There were valleys unknown, and peaks untrodden, and the district might confidently be expected to provide topographical and geological data of considerable interest.

Directly on arrival at Bombay we had dispatched the expedition's goods, weighing some 6½ tons, in a special truck by passenger train to Darjeeling. Though this cost £135, and should have taken no longer than four or five days in transit, over two weeks had elapsed, and still there was no sign of the truck. Imploring telegrams were sent to high officials, eliciting non-committal replies. The truck had been seen here, and seen there, but not one of the railways could tell us exactly where it was at the moment. Finally, as we were in despair, the goods arrived, but the expedition had been delayed two or three days, and every day was of vital importance.

A store-room was hired, and the 180 crates containing food and equipment unpacked under the supervision of Frau Dyhrenfurth. She was in her element, as clad in a neat apron, and armed with a pencil and notebook, she superintended operations, amid stacks of various foodstuffs, tins, rucksacks, boots, films, patent hot-water bottles, dangerous-looking magnesium flares, and a multitude of other things all heaped up amid a labyrinth of packing-cases and crates. There was one tragedy, a German firm had presented the expedition with a large quantity of honey. This had been packed in cardboard containers. Travel and heat had done their worst, and it had arrived a glutinous mass. It was not, however, entirely wasted, for it was much appreciated by the porters and countless children who gathered around the crate and licked the honey as it oozed through the cracks.

General Bruce had been emphatic on one thing in particular. "Don't forget to worm your porters," he had whispered into my ear at Victoria Station. Worms are a curse among the natives in India, and the strongest Himalayan porter may become anæmic and weak from them. Actually, Dr. Richter discovered but few porters who were suffering from this particular ailment. Possibly the Medical Officers of previous Everest expeditions taught them how to cure themselves with santonin and castor-oil. More prevalent among the porters was a species of scurvy, due most likely to under nourishment, that showed itself in the form of skin breakings, and boils. A number of porters were so badly affected by this that it was impossible to take them.

Owing to recent cases of smallpox locally, it was deemed advisable to vaccinate all porters. We anticipated some trouble here, and Frau Dyhrenfurth heroically offered herself as the first victim and example. But her public spirited offer was unnecessary. The porters took to vaccination with alacrity, and they roared with laughter at the lengthening of the faces of those being vaccinated as their arms were scratched.

Not warning Darjeeling of our coming had been a serious error, and meant much additional work for Colonel Tobin in enlisting every available porter. It was an exceedingly busy time for most members of the expedition and especially so for Colonel Tobin, who laboured with all his might to get the manifold preparations completed in time. About 400 porters were necessary if we were to attack Kangchenjunga from Nepal, and 400 good porters are not obtainable normally in Darjeeling. As had been proved previously on Everest and Kangchenjunga, the best types of Himalayan porters are Sherpas, Bhutias, and Thibetans. There is little to choose between these hardy races for carrying powers and endurance, but the Sherpa is the best mountaineer. Like the Bhutia, they dwell in the remote valleys of Northern Nepal, and have both Nepalese and Thibetan blood in them. They are used to withstanding cold and hardships on some of the most inhospitable portions of the world's surface, and are natural mountaineers. The men who did so well on Everest and Kangchenjunga were known as " Tigers," for their work in carrying loads at immense altitudes was tigerish in its strength and courage.

It may appear extraordinary that these men should so readily leave their homes and rickshaws in Darjeeling, where many of them make a comfortable living during the tourist season. Perhaps it is because of a born instinct for adventure, perhaps because of the prestige that is to be gained by being chosen to accompany an expedition to the greatest peaks of the world, and perhaps because they love the mountains with a primitive unreasoning devotion which finds expression in the belief that they are the abiding places of the gods. Whatever it is, and it would be interesting to get behind their minds in the matter, it is not entirely the prospect of monetary reward that impels these men to risk life and limb on Everest and Kangchenjunga.

There are many good men in Darjeeling, "rickshaw wallahs," most of them, but there are also many good men living in far-away hill villages, who, had they known, would have been only too willing to come too. As it was, during the fortnight we were at Darjeeling, a number of men came in from the hills anxious to join the expedition, including two from Nepal, who said that they had traversed the Kang La. So long as these men remain unspoilt in a world where commercial gain is becoming the only thing that matters, future expeditions, with mountaineering as their aim, will have no difficulty in finding the right men to help them on their enterprise.

Thus it was, that though the expedition was able to enlist a nucleus of keen, reliable men, it was forced also to enlist others who had no interest in its objects, " bazar wallahs" who were merely out to serve their own ends, and who had no intention of working or serving the expedition faithfully.

Four sirdars were engaged, Naspati, Gyaljen, Narsang and Lobsang. Of these, Lobsang was incomparably the best. Though only an ordinary " rickshaw wallah " of humble origin, and affecting none of the European clothes and manners of the other sirdars, and of little experience, having only recently been promoted from coolie to sirdar, he was a born commander of men. A Bhutia by birth, he was yet liked and respected by the Sherpas and Thibetans. His pock-marked, rugged countenance was the hardest I have ever seen in a native, and indicated a masterful personality. Perhaps it was this very personality that was responsible for adverse criticisms from some quarters, for Lobsang was of that rare native type which prefers being left to itself, to act largely on its own initiative. He was a genuine " tough " in the best sense of that word, and as Wood Johnson remarked, his work was equal to that of a sahib. Unfortunately, he was now too old to climb to the highest camps, but as commander of the general coolie

A TYPICAL SHERPA

organisation at the base, in the lower camps and on the march he would be invaluable.

Of the other sirdars, Naspati and Gyaljen were excellent men, especially in keeping pay-rolls, management of stores, and " office jobs," but for sheer drive and personality they were not to be compared to Lobsang.

Minor worries are to be avoided at all costs on a Himalayan expedition, and a good personal servant can do much to alleviate the trials and discomforts of life. General Bruce had given me a letter to his own personal servant, Lhakpa Chede, who accompanied him on the Everest Expedition. In this letter General Bruce flatteringly if inaccurately referred to me as his grandson. It is needless here to enlarge upon the admiration, affection and respect with which the Leader of two Mount Everest expeditions is regarded in Darjeeling. On many occasions natives stopped me in the streets of Darjeeling to ask whether the General Burra-sahib was leading the expedition. This charming fiction was of inestimable advantage to me personally, and I was soon known among our porters as the Nati-sahib (Grandson).

Lhakpa Chede had taken a post as a waiter, and was unable to come. Mr. Kydd, of St. Paul's School, suggested his own "rickshaw wallah," Nemu. It was a happy suggestion. Nemu had been " Sandy " Irvine's servant on Everest, and had ascended as high as Camp Five, a height of 25,000 feet. But that was six years ago, and Nemu was now thirty-six. For Europeans this should be the prime of life, but it must be remembered that these men are frequently old at thirty, whilst the majority of them die in the neighbourhood of fifty. Was Nemu therefore too old, was his strength, and power of resistance to cold, still equal to the task, did he really want to leave a comfortable and easy job in favour of the hardships and rigours of high mountaineering ? Nemu's keenness to come was in itself an answer to these questions.

I took an instant liking to the man. Clad as he was in a ragged and patched old coat, a dirty pair of aged corduroy breeches, frayed puttees, probably relics of the last Everest expedition, and a pair of apparently cast off boots, he looked at first glance a thorough old vagabond, but his face was broad and good-humoured, and his eyes were those of a hillman, possessing that subtle, far-away look of those accustomed to gaze great distances. Hazel brown, and set far apart, they were eyes indicative of honesty and trustworthiness. So I engaged Nemu, and had no cause ever to regret it.

There were many other seasoned veterans of Everest and Kangchenjunga who were anxious to come. "Satan" Chettan was secured by Schneider as his servant. Of all Himalayan porters he was the most experienced in mountaineering, for he had accompanied all three Everest expeditions, climbed with Dr. T. G. Longstaff and Mr. H. Ruttledge in Garhwal, and as the servant of Dr. Paul Bauer, the leader of the Bavarian expedition, performed miracles of endurance on Kangchenjunga the previous year. There was also Lewa, who put up a magnificent performance on the Bavarian expedition. Perhaps most important of all were the cooks, for on their efficiency much depended. The Bavarians had sung the praises of Ten cheddar, so we engaged him. He spoke a little English, and among his favourite expressions which we soon learnt by heart was " sometime coming." To him everything was always " sometime coming "—even death itself. There is a whole philosophy in " sometime coming."

Many of these porters produced tattered and dirty letters of recommendation from General Bruce and other members of the Everest expeditions, testifying to their courage and loyalty. One of the first questions was often whether the General Burra-sahib was coming. Happy indeed the man who can win the respect and affection of such men.

As nothing had been heard from Nepal, it was necessary to plan a provisional scheme to attempt Kangchenjunga via Sikkim and the Zemu Glacier. It was arranged that Wood Johnson and myself should leave Darjeeling about April 1, and proceed via Gangtok, the capital town of Sikkim, and Lachen, and blaze a trail up to the Zemu Glacier. It is possible to take ponies as far as Lachen, but above that, dense jungle would probably necessitate arduous trail making. It would also be the task of this advance party to find three camping sites between Lachen and the Base Camp, which we proposed to establish on Green Lake Plain on the north bank of the Zemu Glacier. With the way thus prepared, the main body of 150 porters and about 60 pack ponies would start from Darjeeling under the charge of Hannah, where they would be joined at Gangtok by the climbing party, who would travel in motor-cars from Darjeeling.

From Gangtok the main body would proceed on foot or ponies to Lachen, where a provision dump under the supervision of Colonel Tobin would be made.

The three temporary camps between Lachen and the Base Camp would be a day's march between, and would be used as stages in the relaying of loads from Lachen to the Base Camp. By this means we estimated to reach the Base Camp with 67 porters. Of these 25 would be sent back, leaving 42 porters to do the work of establishing the Base Camp, and the first two high camps on Kangchenjunga. By this method it would be the work of only eight or ten days to bring all the expedition's food and equipment from Lachen to the Base Camp.

Professor Dyhrenfurth was naturally loth to attack Kangchenjunga by the same route as that of the Bavarians the previous year so long as there was a possibility of climbing the mountain by any other route, but it was obvious that the ice ridge leading to the North Ridge was the only line that offered any possibility on the Sikkim side of the mountain.

It was at this stage, when all preparations had been completed, that the following charming letter was received from the Maharajah of Nepal :—

" Khatmandu,
" Nepal.
" 29*th March*, 1930.

" To Professor Dr. G. O. Dyhrenfurth,
" Darjeeling.

" Dear Sir,—I beg to acknowledge the receipt of your letter of the 16th March, 1930, giving information of the formation of an International Expedition to attempt an ascent of and make scientific observations on Kangchenjunga, and requesting permission for the expedition to enter Nepalese territory and approach the said mountain via Kang La, Chumbab La, Tseram, Mirgin La,

Khunza and Kangbachen, using the same route on return with the possibility of one party going over to Sikkim by way of Jonsong La.

"His Highness appreciates your remarks about the international character of the expedition which has for its object the cementation of international friendship and good-will among the countries concerned, coupled with the augmentation of human æsthetical and scientific knowledge, and desires me to inform you that he gladly accedes to your request. The Nepalese local authorities concerned are being ordered to permit the party the use of the routes mentioned in Nepalese territory.

"His Highness hopes that the expedition will be a great success in every way, and sends to you as the worthy leader of the expeditionary party the best wishes for that.

"I remain,

"Your obedient servant,

"(Signed) MARICHI MAN SINGH,

"Bada Kaji,

"Private Secretary to his Highness the Maharajah, Nepal."

Although a complete change of plans was necessary, no time was lost in rearranging matters. Had, however, we realised the difficulties confronting us, I do not think we should so willingly have abandoned the original scheme. The route to the Zemu Glacier is a relatively easy one compared to that to the Kangchenjunga Glacier and good paths along low valleys lead four-fifths of the way from Darjeeling. The road to the Kangchenjunga Glacier via the Kang La and Mirgin La passes is much more difficult.

Most important point of all—the winter was a late one, and snow lay low on the Kang La.

Mules could be employed only as far as Yoksam, five marches from Darjeeling. Thenceforward, we must rely entirely on porters, and as previously stated, 400 of these were necessary. We estimated that it would take us three weeks to reach the foot of the mountain, and once the base camp was established, communications had to be maintained, and fresh supplies for the porters obtained. Obviously, we must rely to a large extent on local help in Nepal. A telegram was sent to the Maharajah asking whether we could buy porters' food at Tseram or Khunza, two Nepalese villages we must pass through. We received a very courteous answer, informing us that everything possible would be done to help us, and that we could employ local porters and obtain local supplies. Thus was solved the greatest difficulty of all, for without local help, this route would have been absolutely impossible.

In order to avoid overcrowding at the camping sites, Colonel Tobin considered it necessary to split the expedition up into three parties. Wood Johnson and Hannah were to be transport officers of the first and second parties respectively, whilst Colonel Tobin was to bring up the rear with eighty mule-loads of provisions and equipment, which he would transport to Yoksam, where he would be met by 150 porters sent back from the first and second parties to carry his loads over the Kang La.[1] This arrangement was made assuming that local help in the shape of porters and

[1] This arrangement was known only to Professor Dyhrenfurth and Colonel Tobin and the fact that neither the transport officers, Wood Johnson and Hannah, of the first and second parties respectively, knew anything about it was largely responsible for subsequent transport difficulties.

food was to be obtained by the first and second parties on the Nepalese side of the Kang La.

It was an excellent scheme, but it was perhaps not sufficiently elastic in its allowance for failures. How were we to be certain that porters and supplies would be immediately forthcoming in Nepal. The Maharajah's commands would take some time to infiltrate from Khatmandu into a remote corner of North-east Nepal. Little time would be available for the Subadar appointed by him to look after our needs, and to collect porters' food and porters from the sparsely populated valleys. The weather was another important factor. Anything might happen on a pass as high as the Kang La. Even now, the beginning of April, almost daily storms were depositing snow at levels far below the summit of the pass, and boots were available for but a few of our porters, principally the "Tigers" intended for the work of establishing the high camps on Kangchenjunga. Was it wise to split up the party into three separate groups over such a difficult route? The discomforts of overcrowding in camping sites would have been well worth cohesion and unity. If I have dealt at length with this problem of transport, it is because it is a very real problem, and one on the solving of which the success of any Himalayan expedition depends.

The three Everest expeditions had a far easier task, for in spite of the length of their route from Darjeeling to Everest, they were able to take ponies and mules the whole distance. This meant employment of less than 100 porters, and these were all picked men. We had 400 porters, some very good, others very bad. In addition to attempting Kangchenjunga from the Kangchenjunga Glacier, it was proposed first of all to explore the southern face of the mountain above the Yalung Glacier, the face attempted by the ill-fated Crowley party, but like Mark Twain, our exploration got no farther than an examination through the powerful telescope at the Planters' Club at Darjeeling.

To appreciate the beauty and dignity of Kangchenjunga, the apparently smooth, sickle-like sweep of its ridges, the pale red of its granite precipices gleaming like a sun-caressed Devonian sea cliff through a blue Atlantic haze, it should be viewed with the naked eye. Seeing it thus it is impossible to grasp the scale of the mountain, and the mountaineer's analytical mind is peacefully submerged in a quiet ocean of meditation.

But seen through a telescope Kangchenjunga ceases to be an object of restful meditation. It is revealed in all its cruelty. The pale red precipices are resolved into fearful slices of unrelenting granite; the apparently smooth ridges resemble the blade of a knife seen through a microscope; broken and jagged, torn and hewn by wind and weather into edges, gaps and towers of fantastic and terrible beauty; what appear to the naked eye as straggling thin white threads are terrific ice-armoured couloirs, down which crash stones, and ice avalanches from disintegrating cliffs of rock and ice. Even looking through a telescope it was impossible not to gain some idea of Nature's forces that are ever at work slowly destroying the greatest peaks of the world.

But a minute's examination was needed to assure us that it was futile to seek a way from the Yalung Glacier. Though only the upper part of the route was visible, the long sloping icy shelf the mountaineer would have to ascend is exposed to avalanches of snow, ice and stones, while the ice-fall up which the party would have to go to reach the shelf, looked unassailable. The telescope effectively dispelled any nebulous schemes we may have cherished of attempting this side of the mountain.

At last the preparations were completed. On the night of April 5, the last load was packed and weighed by Frau Dyhrenfurth, assisted by many willing helpers. We had planned to reach the dak-bungalow at Chakung in one day by motoring to Singla Bazar, and from there riding to Chakung 4,000 feet higher. This was, however, a long march for the porters, so it was decided to send them off a day beforehand.

It is interesting to remember that there are days during every month when it is considered by the natives extremely unlucky to start on a journey. However, should a native find it absolutely essential to leave on one of these unlucky days, it is usual for him to send on his hat on a lucky day beforehand by a servant or friend. In this way the gods are deluded into thinking that he has actually started on a lucky day, and he may escape the consequences of his rash act.

It was important to have someone in Darjeeling who would look after our mails, and arrange for the sending of dispatches to Mr. Alfred Watson, Editor of the *Statesman*, of Calcutta, whence they would be forwarded to *The Times* in London. We were extremely fortunate in obtaining the services of Mr. W. J. Kydd, of St. Paul's School, Darjeeling. Mr. Kydd had been in the Secret Service during the War, and we felt we could not leave the work in more competent hands.

It was arranged that Herr Eberl, the German Vice-Consul at Calcutta, should accompany the expedition part of the way. Before leaving Calcutta he was able to arrange to have weather reports broadcasted for us by the courtesy of the Meteorological and Broadcasting Departments, and he brought with him a suitable receiving set complete with masts. He also loaned us some useful porters' tents, and presented to the expedition a number of gramophone records.

April 6 was a day of bustle and activity at Darjeeling. Each porter and his load was checked by Colonel Tobin. This was facilitated by the issue to each porter of a metal disc stamped with a number. The native population of Darjeeling was agog with excitement. Crowds lined the roads ; porters' wives were there to see their husbands off, some to give them a final cup of tea, others to wag an admonitory finger. The porters themselves swelled with conscious pride.

Kangchenjunga sympathised but little with these preparations for its discomfiture. It sulked behind sullen clouds, dispatching now and again sudden rainstorms, destined apparently for the express purpose of drenching and damping the ardour of the expedition.

That night before turning in Wood Johnson and I took a final stroll along the terrace of the Mount Everest Hotel. The weather boded ill. Lightning glared every few seconds through a rain-charged murk. Ghostlike swathes of mist eddied evilly from the valleys. From the direction of the Himalayas came long low growls of thunder.

CHAPTER VII

THROUGH TROPICAL SIKKIM

April 7 dawned mistily, but as the sun got up, the dense blanket of white, wet fog enwrapping Darjeeling quickly dissolved. Rifts were torn in the curtain disclosing Kangchenjunga, silvered, blue-shadowed, and remote. It was a morning full of a calm promise.

There were many friends and strangers to see us off, including an American lady, who seemed particularly anxious for our welfare, and asked us whether we did not expect to find it " turrible slippery " on Kangchenjunga.

Four Austin Seven motor cars had been engaged for the first stage of our journey to Singla. There we were to be met by ponies and continue on them to Chakung. From Darjeeling to Singla a rough track descends tortuously 6,000 feet, in a distance as the crow flies of about five miles. Frequently the gradient is as much as 1 : 3 or 1 : 4, and hairpin bends are such as to necessitate reversing, with the wheels but a few inches from the unprotected edge of precipitous drops.

" Baby " cars have done much to improve the social amenities of the Darjeeling district. A few years ago the tea planters, whose estates are scattered about the hill-sides, were forced to use ponies or mules for transport. As a result, their existence was frequently a lonely one, for many of the plantations are twenty or thirty miles from Darjeeling. Recently, however, one of the planters bought a " baby " car as an experiment. He found to his surprise and delight that it was capable of negotiating the narrow zig-zagging tracks, and terrific hills of the district. Now practically every tea planter owns one, and the social life of the district has been vastly improved thereby.

The climate of Darjeeling is temperate, and comparable

By courtesy of *The Times*

to that of England, the temperature seldom rising above 70°. That of Singla in the Rangit Valley is definitely tropical. At first we passed through woods and glades of oaks, firs, and beeches reminiscent of the hillsides of Shropshire. Then came more open slopes covered in dark green terraces of tea, and clumps of tall bamboos.

Kurz, Wood Johnson, and myself were in the first car of the little procession. We had not gone more than a mile or so from Darjeeling when we overtook a number of our porters scattered along the road, who had obviously only left Darjeeling that morning instead of the previous day. In reply to our query as to why they had not started, several of them said they were not feeling well. The cause of this was not far to seek. The advance pay intended for the upkeep of their wives and children in their absence had been spent in one last " beano " the previous night at Darjeeling. It was essential to get these men to Chakung the same day, and to Wood Johnson, as transport officer of our party, fell the unwelcome task of staying behind to see that they *did* get there.

As we descended, we were vouchsafed occasional glimpses of the snows. Below was the floor of the Rangit Valley, 2,000 feet above sea level, whilst forty-five miles away remote in heaven rose the summit of Kangchenjunga, 28,156 feet, a vertical height difference of over 26,000 feet !

Once we were stopped by a tea planter who cheerily wished us good luck, and insisted on taking a photograph. It became hotter and hotter. Several of us were wearing Terai hats, double wide-awakes with broad brims. These are worn mostly by tea planters, and afford excellent protection from the sun. The pith solar *topi* soon goes to pieces in the rains, but the Terai stands up to any amount of hard wear.

A peculiarity of tea is that given the right soil, and the requisite amount of rainfall, it seems to grow satisfactorily in any climate, varying from the temperate to the tropical. The highest Darjeeling tea garden is over 6,000 feet above sea level, and the lowest descends to the bottom of the Rangit Valley. We passed garden after garden, all picturesque and forming charming deep green foregrounds to the distant procession of woolly white clouds masking the distant wall of the Himalayas.

At Singla we were hospitably greeted by the planters of one of these lower plantations, and spent a pleasant hour sipping cool drinks in a shady bungalow.

Apparently on the principle that walking was good for us, only four ponies had been ordered, and we had to take turns in riding them. No doubt, the intention was a good one, but in the enervating heat of the Rangit Valley, such mortification of the flesh seemed both unpleasant and unnecessary.

At Singla Bazar a dismal tale awaited us. According to Narsang, one of our sirdars, a large number of coolies had not yet arrived, and they could not possibly get to Chakung that day. We would have to wait a day for them to catch up. There was much that was unintelligible, and little that was useful in his declarations, poured out as they were in weird and wonderful English learnt during service with a Gurkha regiment in France. And what had happened to the cook? Why was he not there waiting for us with lunch prepared? " The cook? He is gone on somewhere," and Narsang waved a hand with characteristic native vagueness.

In my rucksack was a large lump of dry gingerbread. This was broken up and handed round. Suddenly, Wood Johnson arrived. " Not get to Chakung? " Nonsense! Of course, the porters would, all of them. Within five minutes the peaceful serenity of Singla Bazar was replaced by a feverish activity. The lazier of the porters who had settled down for the day and the night at the village, found themselves, much to their surprise, on the road to Chakung. Our sheet anchor, Lobsang, was behind, bringing on the stragglers. The majority of the good porters, the Sherpas and Bhutias, had left the previous day, and were well *en route* to Chakung, it was only the Nepali "bazar wallahs" who were exhibiting such early slackness.

Singla Bazar is a picturesque little place. Its primitive thatched houses and shops rest in the shadow of spreading trees, but, like most native villages, the spaces between the houses were plentifully bestrewn with garbage. Therefore, there were smells, and there were flies. We were glad to leave it and jog leisurely along the valley.

Presently we came to a suspension bridge across the Ramman River, a tributary of the Rangit River. The former forms the frontier of Bengal and Sikkim, and there was a native frontier post at one end of the suspension bridge, with a corporal in charge. To him we showed the passes that had been given us in Darjeeling. Unfortunately, Dr. Richter and Eberl had left their passes in their rucksacks, which had been sent on ahead, whilst Wood Johnson, whom we had left at Singla Bazar, had forgotten his altogether. The former two had to wait until their rucksacks were returned, but Wood Johnson, we knew, would get across without a pass whether he was given permission or not. It transpired later that when the pass had been demanded of him, he had looked the corporal up and down until that unfortunate man had apologised for daring to insult the sahib by asking for the pass, and had humbly escorted Wood Johnson across the frontier.

The suspension bridge had tied to it numbers of little prayer flags, or perhaps more literally, prayer rags. All bridges in this part of the world are decorated thus in order to propitiate the river gods. It is usual, also, to throw a coin or two into the river when crossing a bridge to help, presumably, towards the upkeep of the river gods.

From the suspension bridge the path wound steeply uphill through dense jungle. The afternoon was close and boilingly hot, and a heavy slumberous silence was broken only by the whirring of insects. We turned a corner; a small spring of pure water was bubbling from a bank. By the side of the path in an orange garden a meal had been laid out on the grass, presided over by the grinning face of Tencheddar. Famished, we greeted it with a pæon of praise and thanksgiving, forgetting in the ecstasy of the moment to revile Tencheddar for his idiocy in having come this absurd distance before stopping to prepare a meal.

The orange garden is the property of the Maharajah of Sikkim. There are many such scattered about this fertile countryside, for orange-growing is the most important industry in Sikkim, and the revenue brought in from these scattered estates is surprisingly large.

With appeased appetites we lay back at last contentedly. Already we felt ourselves to be far from civilisation. Dotted about the hillside below were primitive little houses, above rude terraces of rice, irrigated by roughly cut channels along which flowed water from the mountain streams and springs. The day was drawing to a close, and between the blue cloud shadows moving across the broad bosomed hills, the forests were daffodil gold in the declining sun. Somehow I was reminded of an evening I once spent on Bowfell, in the English Lake District, one of those perfect evenings, still and peaceful, with soft colourful distances. Seated on a grey boulder I had watched just such a peaceful sunset and seen the hills imperceptibly annexed by the Kingdom of Night. But here everything was greater. In the Lake District, you may run down a hill into a valley and up another hill in an hour or so. In the foot-hills of the Himalayas, it is a day's hard work. The country over which we were looking was vaster than any of us had imagined. It produced in us almost a feeling of impotence. We were not ants, or flies, but mere microcosms toiling over the age-worn wrinkles of the earth.

Night was falling rapidly as we continued on our way. Now and again we passed porters. In the heat, they were making heavy weather of it, but a few days' marching would soon sweat out the fatty accumulations of soft living, and knit together muscles and sinew in preparation for the hard work ahead.

Presently the path rounded a shoulder and passed into the Ratho Valley, contouring along its southern side. The others were ahead, and I found myself alone. Night trod hard on the heels of day. Soon it was dark. Fireflies flitted out from the forest on either hand, like minute lamps in the hands of hurrying elves. Rain began to fall, each heavy drop drumming on the still leaves of the silent forest. The path divided, but my pony unhesitatingly took the left branch. A few minutes later I arrived at the dak-bungalow, just in time to escape a tropical deluge.

The dak-bungalows of Sikkim are theoretically run by the Government of that State, but actually it is the British

Government that is primarily responsible for their upkeep. Each bungalow is in charge of a native caretaker. All those at which we stayed were clean and comfortable. Their situation is admirable, and the sites of many of them were obviously chosen by someone with an eye for scenic beauty. The bungalow at Chakung stands on a wooded ridge separating the Ramman and Ratho Valleys close to the ruins of an ancient shrine, which was most likely formerly employed for the worship of some local deity.

The supper that evening was a merry one. Wood Johnson arrived in the middle of it, and later Eberl and Dr. Richter. Just as we were thinking of turning in, the corporal of the police put in a belated appearance. Recovering from his surprise at the suspension bridge, he had followed Wood Johnson with a tenacity worthy of the " Flying Squad." As he had no wish to get the man into trouble, Wood Johnson gave him a note to take to the Commissioner at Darjeeling. With this in his pocket, plus substantial *baksheesh*, the corporal returned to his post a happy man.

Heavy rain fell all night, and was succeeded by a dull grey morning and low sluggish mists. Already some of the Nepali porters had come to the conclusion that loafing in Darjeeling was preferable to work, and it was only with difficulty that we were able to get some of the more miserable specimens to start at all.

Our next stage was to Rinchenpung. From Chakung the route descended into the Ratho Valley, and crossing a stream climbed over a low ridge bounding the northern side of the valley. The path was bog-like in places, and the morning was as depressingly dismal and damp as an August day in the Highlands.

We had not gone far before we saw our first leech. Soon the path was swarming with them. Apparently they had their own telegraph system, and leeches all along the route had been warned of our coming. These pests are the most unpleasant feature of journeying through the tropical valleys of Sikkim. Ungorged they are about the thickness of a match, and a little shorter. Gorged, they attain the dimensions of a large slug. They are blind, and attack by scent alone, but their nasal acuteness more than compensates for their blindness. Stop for but a few moments, and they approach from all directions.

Their method of progress is peculiar and comical. Raising their heads in the air, they bend forward and attach themselves, apparently by the mouth, to the ground in front. The tail is then brought up against the head with the body arched between and the head makes another forward lunge. Had it not been annoying, it would have been amusing to see these eager little blood-suckers standing with their heads upright, like tiny serpents, waiting to affix themselves to their prey.

The powers of insinuation and penetration of a leech are great. They can insinuate themselves into an eyehole of a boot with the greatest of ease, whilst their drill-like head is capable of boring through at least one layer of a puttee. Personally, I found that the Kashmiri puttees given to me by General Bruce afforded excellent protection, and I was not once bitten on either foot. But the persevering little devils are not easily baulked of their prey. I was just beginning to congratulate myself on my immunity, when

I discovered two large ones firmly attached to my scalp! It is a mistake to pick a leech off once it has become attached to the skin, as its head will be left in the wound, and this may lead to blood poisoning, or at least a nasty festering sore. The usual way of forcing them to release their hold is by dipping a bag of salt in water, and letting the brine drip on to the leech, which soon drops off. Another excellent method is to apply a burning cigarette.

If, by virtue of boots and puttees, we were comparatively immune, it was a different matter for the porters and ponies. The majority of the porters preferred walking in their bare feet, and the leeches made the most of them. The ponies' legs streamed with blood, and it was necessary to keep a sharp look-out to see that the leeches did not crawl into their nostrils and ears. In the absence of human beings and beasts, how do leeches manage to exist?

From the ridge north of the Ratho Valley, we descended into the Rishi Valley. Both these valleys are side valleys of the main Rangit Valley, and are comparatively small and glen-like. A primitive little bridge of logs spans the Rishi River, and large boulders near by afforded a luncheon site free from leeches, for a leech hates a dry surface, and only lives in swampy ground, or comes out after rain.

It was a delightful spot, almost like a valley in South Devon. The water of the torrent was sweet and clear, and despite a formal protest on the part of Dr. Richter, we did not hesitate to drink it. It is only from these smaller streams that pass through villages that there is danger of typhoid or dysentery.

If there had been any doubts as to how Frau Dyhrenfurth would stand the strain of these marches through

Sikkim, they were soon set at rest, for the "Memsahib," as she was soon respectfully and affectionately known by all the members of the expedition, not only insisted on taking a man's share of the work, but was usually among the first to finish the day's march.

From the Rishi Valley, the path rose steeply to the ridge on which stands the Rinchenpung dak-bungalow. This is one of the prettiest bungalows in Sikkim, and from its well kept lawn and creeper-clad veranda, there is an enchanting view up the Rangit Valley towards the snows. Once again, the day ended in rainstorms of monsoonish intensity.

There were two other visitors at the bungalow. They told us that they were on a world tour, and had been "taking the Himalayas" as part of their Indian itinerary. The weather, they said, had been continuously bad, and they were now returning to Darjeeling without having had one satisfactory view of Kangchenjunga.

Wood Johnson and I preferred the fresh air of the veranda to the crowded little rooms of the bungalow. I woke at dawn next morning. The rain had ceased. From the still woodlands came the song of the coppersmith bird, a musical, yet monotonous note, like someone beating a sheet of copper with a metal hammer. As I raised myself in my sleeping bag, I saw between a gap in the nearer mists the crest of a great cloud high up in the sky aglow with the first pale light of day. But was it a cloud? It was too steadfast, too immovable. I rubbed the dimming sleepiness from my eyes. It was no cloud, but a snowy mountain. Even as I watched, the dawn came up fiercely, ruddily, a titanic conflagration sweeping the upper regions of the sky. The nearer mists dissolved; other peaks became visible, their summits glowing like the white tents of a besieging army reflecting the glare from some burning city.

I roused our tourist friends. Now, at last, they had seen the snows. I wonder whether they still remember that glimpse of them?

The morning was one of sparkle and freshness as we set out for Pemayangtse. Improving weather raised the spirits of the porters, and for once in their lives even the Nepalis seemed cheerful and willing.

I left well in advance of the party to try to take some photographs before the usual morning clouds concealed the peaks. I did not go unrewarded. For a little distance the path descended through woods, but in one place a landslip had swept out a clearance. Framed between the trees, and thirty miles away, I saw Kabru and Kangchenjunga. It was a view so overwhelming in its magnificence as would cause the most ardent photographer to despair of reproducing one tithe of its grandeur. The morning clouds gathering about the crests of intervening hills, or, rising from the valleys, served but to increase the visual impression of height and depth. How is a photographer to transfer such an impression to a film? Only by comparison can he hope to convey to the unsophisticated any suggestion of the real scale, and what method of comparison is there? The forests covering the lower hills are but a dark green cloak, over which the eye passes at a casual glance. The river in the valley beneath was a mere thread. The greatest works of man, his towns, his cathedrals, and his factories, would be lost in such a landscape. Place St. Paul's on the crest of one of the intervening hills; to the

KABRU AND KANGCHENJUNGA FROM RINCHENPUNG

eye it would appear as a mere dot ; on a photographic film it would be invisible. Only physically can one learn to appreciate the scale of the Himalayan foot-hills, and that by toiling over them.

Mentally, a man is lost in this country. Like an astronomer he can estimate distance only in figures. His brain is too small, too tied to the little houses, towns, villages, and hedgerows among which he is accustomed to live, to grasp the real magnitude of these immense landscapes.

As I came out of the forest on to the open hillside, the snows had all but vanished behind growing masses of cumuli. Only the summit of the nearest snow peak, Narsingh, was visible, and I had barely time to take a photograph before it, too, vanished.

The path passed along a ridge, decorated by a row of chortens (prayer shrines), at which it is customary to pray and give thanks to the gods, and then plunged in steep zig-zags down a precipitous hillside.

At the junction of the Kalet and Rangit Valleys we found ourselves once more in tropical heat. The Rangit Valley here becomes gorge-like, yet so fertile is the soil, trees and other vegetation somehow manage to eke out a precarious existence on ledges and crannies of precipitous cliffs and crags.

Some women from a neighbouring hamlet were washing clothes in the river. Their method was to dip the clothes in the water, then, holding them up, beat them violently with a piece of flat wood. This must be the method employed by my local laundry when washing my dress shirts.

Thanks to the efficiency of Mr. Kydd, we were overtaken here by a runner, and spent a pleasant half-hour in the shade reading letters from home, and the latest murder sensations and French railway accidents in newspapers.

Some members of the party had seen a large snake, the markings of which they described to Wood Johnson. He said it was probably a king cobra. If so, they were lucky not to be attacked, for the king cobra is one of the few snakes that attack human beings without provocation. It is said that it can overtake a running man.

We lunched near a small hamlet, at which Duvanel and his ciné camera created considerable excitement, and afterwards trudged up to Pemayangtse. It was scorchingly hot, but the gradually increasing coolness as we gained height was well worth the effort.

The dak-bungalow at Pemayangtse is admirably situated on a grassy sparsely wooded ridge, and commands superb views to the north and south. We had barely arrived when we were greeted by an imposing little procession of Lamas from the neighbouring monastery. They were barefooted, and clad in long gowns of a dingy red colour, on top of which was the " patched robe," the emblem of poverty. From the girdle encircling their waist were suspended various sacred instruments and relics, such as pencil holders, knives, and purses. Their heads were close cropped like black flue brushes, but the tropical sun seemed to have little effect on them. Most of them were young, with somewhat vacuous faces, dull, unintelligent eyes, and loose lipped smiles. There was, however, one old monk of dignified carriage, who was most likely the Proctor of the monastery, for his face bore the stamp of character and intelligence. Standing before the bungalow, they commenced a low, monotonous intoning, possibly praying for

THE HEAD LAMA OF PEMAYANGTSE MONASTERY CHATS WITH WOOD JOHNSON

our souls, while the old man came forward and burst forth into a torrent of Nepali and Thibetan. After considerable difficulty, we were at last able to get his meaning. Yes, they were glad to greet us, but we had only come in the nick of time. Had we a Doctor Sahib? Then would he cure them of this terrible thing that was afflicting the monastery? "What was the terrible thing?" we enquired. His answer was simple and expressive, "Worms!" And as for himself, for his sins, he was possessed of a terrible ear-ache.

A little later, a number of Holy Men might have been seen imbibing large quantities of castor oil and santonin with every appearance of gusto and enjoyment, whilst the old monk lay on the ground in order to have oil poured into his bad ear. Gratitude in the form of eggs and skinny chickens arrived later, and it was arranged that they should give us a devil dance the following morning.

Devil dances are a religious observation. They are usually given in honour or propitiation of some deity. In this particular instance, the deity was the God of Kangchenjunga.

That evening we made merry with the gramophone. This was always a never ending source of amusement to the porters. Scarcely had the first record been put on, when the doorway of the dining room was filled with dirty faces grinning appreciatively. The classical masters were little appreciated, but Messrs. Layton and Johnstone, and the bass voiced vocalist in "Give Yourself a Pat on the Back," never failed to produce roars of merriment.

Before turning in, we sat on the veranda, arguing as to whether something white far up among the stars, lit by the rising moon, was a mountain top or a cloud. Most argued cloud, but when hours later I woke in the middle of the night, and looked out, the " cloud " was still there, watched over by trembling stars.

We rose early next morning, and passed up the roughly paved road leading to the monastery. The approach to the monastery was lined with high poles decorated with prayer flags, consisting of long, multi-coloured strips, inscribed with prayers, nailed longitudinally to the poles. These prayer flags are common all over Thibet, Sikkim, and Nepal, and are supposed to have been originated by Asoka, the Constantine of Buddhism, who ordered pillars to be erected, inscribed with prayers and extracts from Buddhistic laws. Planted in the ground more than twenty centuries ago (B.C. 253–251) there are six set up by him in India still standing. Sometimes prayer flags display the dragon-headed horse, one of the great mythical animals of China.

The Pemayangtse Monastery stands on a wooded ridge about 7,000 feet above sea level. So fierce are the storms that sweep across the Himalayas, that its wooden roof was once carried away. It is now secured by iron wires to the ground. It is a tall building of stone and wood, gaudily painted in red and yellow, the two holy colours of Thibet.

The Lamas were waiting to receive us grouped round the Head Lama, a charming old gentleman who greeted us with a warm smile of welcome. While not engaged in conversing with Wood Johnson, our transport officer, who spoke Nepali, he was ceaselessly engaged in telling his rosary of yellow beads, keeping up a low, monotonous mumble at the same time, which is appropriately called "purring like a cat."

General Bruce relates that on one occasion when visiting the Pemayangtse Monastery he was for some reason put under a spell by the Head Lama. The spell took the form of a severe stomach-ache which General Bruce was told would last until mid-day. It did, in spite of efforts made to cure it, but punctually at mid-day it disappeared as "miraculously" as it came.

Telling beads is one convenient method of praying, but perhaps the best of all methods, as it gets through the greatest number of prayers in the shortest possible time, is the prayer wheel. This consists of a copper or brass cylinder, which is made to revolve on a wooden handle. Inside the cylinder is a roll of paper or parchment on which are written as many prayers as can be squeezed in. As every revolution is equivalent to reciting all the prayers inside, it is possible, by assiduously revolving this apparatus, to get through some millions of prayers a day.

The Head Lama told us that he would be pleased to offer up a prayer to the God of Kangchenjunga for the safety of the expedition, and also volunteered the information that the weather would remain fine. This was an excellent idea, as we knew it would put great heart into our porters. If he possessed such powers over General Bruce's internal economy, the ordering of meteorological conditions should present little difficulty.

Before the monastery was a large grass-covered quadrangle, enclosed by pavilions and outhouses on three sides, whilst a flight of steps leading up to the imposing and fantastically painted portico of the monastery, overhung with tapestries, formed the fourth. Arranged in a line before the monastery was the band. The instruments consisted of two long metal-chased and ornamented horns, from twelve to fifteen feet in length, smaller horns, flutes, drums, and cymbals. Some of the bandsmen wore cowls, which gave to them a curiously Ku Klux Klannish appearance, and others a curved, cockatoo-like crest to their hats.

Shortly after our arrival, the band crashed forth into what was presumably a welcome. My first impression was of a hideous medley of sound, which, judged by European standards, was completely tuneless and unintelligible. Yet, as my ears became accustomed to the din, I became aware of a perceptible rhythm. The music began to take shape and form in my mind. Gradually, I felt myself borne away, as it were, mentally, from the Twentieth Century, conveyed on the wings of this strange music into the very heart of this mystic mountain land, where time and space are limitless, and man is re-incarnated through eternity. The bass note of the great horns, surely the deepest note of any known musical instrument, seemed to boom of the might of the gods, the thunder of their avalanches, the roar of their torrents, the solemn roll of the thunderstorms that beat about the buttresses of their mid-aerial thrones.

The music dropped into a dirge-like monotone, then rose suddenly into a passionate crescendo. Two hideously masked figures appeared in the portico of the monastery. Leaping down the steps they dashed into the quadrangle, spinning round and round with wide-spread arms and swirling silken robes.

The band had previously taken up a position in the

THE BAND OF THE PEMAYANGTSE MONASTERY

pavilion. Seated in front was the Head Lama amid a horde of acolytes. In one hand he held a bell which he occasionally rang vigorously as a signal for changes of music, or to call in more devil dancers.

The duty of these first two devils was apparently only to announce the more important devil participants in the dance. Suddenly the band, which had stopped for a rest, blared forth again, and four figures slowly descended the steps, and commenced to dance.

They wore long silken robes, beautifully embroidered, and on their heads the most fantastic masks we had ever seen. Intended primarily to represent animals, fowls, yaks, eagles, goats, horses, and sheep, they were yet ghastly mockeries of nature—the phantasmagoria of a madman's imagination. At first the music was dirge-like, and the dancers' movements correspondingly slow. It quickened gradually. Other dancers joined in. Lines, circles, and squares were formed as in folk dancing. Movements became more rapid, arms were flung wide with gestures of abandon, legs kicked high in time with the banging of the drums, and the boom of the great horns. They pirouetted round and round with incredible speed, their heavy garments flying upwards and outwards like human catherine wheels. The music mounted to a terrific pitch of frenzy. Suddenly, above the din, came the sharp ringing of the Head Lama's bell. The music dropped, the dancers retired after a final twirl and obeisance, and sprang quickly up the steps into the monastery.

Duvanel was naturally anxious to secure " shots " of the dancing, but at first it was plain that his machinations were regarded as savouring of black magic. However, directly he commenced to turn the handle of his camera the Lamas appeared considerably relieved. Obviously this complicated machine was nothing but a new and improved form of prayer wheel.

Lastly, there appeared several monsters of ferocious aspect, accompanied by two small boys dressed to represent demons. Possibly, they were intended to represent the devils which worry beasts in the form of insect pests and leeches, for armed with long yak-hair whisks, they proceeded to goad the monsters into fury until they reared, stamped, and charged about the quadrangle, whilst once again the band obliged with a crashing crescendo of sound.

As though in answer to this demonstration in its honour, the cloudy draperies of morning were drawn aside, disclosing Kangchenjunga. One silver banner of cloud trailed from its crest. The attendant fairies of the great God were " baking their bread."

From Pemayangtse to Tingling was an easy march, but a hot one. Once again, we descended into and across the upper Rangit Valley. On the descent we passed a well-built, modern looking temple. It was here that the Dalai Lama stayed during a tour of Sikkim. As, in view of his extreme holiness, it was thought necessary to erect a temple at every place at which he spent a night such a tour must be something of a drain on the purses of the local taxpayers. Several members stopped to bathe in the Rangit River. The current of these mountain torrents is dangerously strong, and Dr. Richter was nearly carried away. Had he been so, he would certainly have been drowned.

We forgathered for lunch in a cool, shady spot by a

DEVIL-DANCERS OF PEMAYANGTSE MONASTERY

small brook, afterwards dozing and resting during the heat of the day. But cool, shady spots in Sikkim are only too liable to harbour leeches, and it was not long before Schneider had a large one affixed to his bare arm.

At Tingling we camped for the first time. It was a charming site for a camp. Close at hand was the little village of Tingling, which stands on one of the few flat bits in Sikkim, and we pitched our tents at the edge of a wheatfield.

Prior to the expedition, Professor Dyhrenfurth had had tents made for each member. Actually, they were two-men tents, so that there was plenty of room for one man. The dweller in civilisation may argue that for each man to have his own tent is unnecessary and unsociable. Travellers and explorers, however, know the psychological value of privacy. During the months of monotony and hardship of a Polar expedition—and the same thing applies in a lesser degree to Himalayan expeditions—the best friends may become sick of the sight of each other, and little habits of speech and manner that count for nothing in civilisation may jar intolerably. Only by being able to escape for a while is a man able to tolerate things which normally he would not give a care to.

Nemu, my servant, was an expert in the art of camping. He was usually among the first to arrive at the end of a day's march, and had an unerring eye as to the best place to pitch a tent. This, combined with a never failing capacity for looking after his master's interests, made him an invaluable servant. He was an old soldier, and had the North-west Frontier Medal, and like most old soldiers, he was an adept in the gentle art of scrounging. Not that I ever missed so much as a cigarette, but in the event of my breaking or losing anything, it was sure to be replaced in some mysterious way. Both on the march and on the mountains Nemu proved a tower of strength, and I can see now his broad good-natured face, with its philosophical eyes, and occasional broad grin, that flashed out always when least expected.

At Tingling an unpleasant incident occurred. One of the coolies ran amok with a *kukri*, and before anyone could stop him, had run another porter—one of our best men—through the chest. The wound was a serious one below the heart, and had it not been for the skilful treatment of Dr. Richter, the injured man would probably have lost his life.

His assailant was brought along to the Mess Tent, under the charge of Tikeram Thapa, to be interrogated by Wood Johnson. While doing so, he managed to pick up a large stone, and made as though to try and brain me as I was standing back to him outside the Mess Tent, but was fortunately promptly collared by Tikeram. The man was obviously demented, and we were forced to tie him up, hand him over to the Head Man of Tingling, and send a runner to the police at Gangtok.

Apart from this unpleasant incident, Tingling will always remain in my mind as one of our most charming camping sites. There is no view of the snows from it, but perhaps that is as well, for the gentle verdure-clad hills around are reminiscent of Glen Affric, and any intrusion on such a scene by the more restless forms of nature would tend to detract from the peaceful beauty of the landscape.

Late that evening, several of us went to the Head Man's

house to see after our injured porter who had been lodged there. Climbing a rickety, wooden ladder, we entered a low-roofed room, like the upper story of a Swiss cowherd's châlet. In the middle was an open stone fireplace, in which crackled a log fire, the flames of which lit the wrinkled face of the Head Man and his friends, as they squatted round. The atmosphere was close and heavy, even the pungent smoke not altogether successfully combating the odour of bodies unwashed since birth. The injured man had been wrapped in rugs, and placed on a bed of straw. He appeared comfortable. We ordered hot milk to be given to him at intervals throughout the night. Such is the toughness of these people, that despite the severe injury, and the obvious risk of subsequent infection and blood poisoning, we heard later that he was on his feet again in less than a fortnight.

It was good to be in a tent again beneath the stars, and I lay long in my sleeping bag that night looking between the flaps at the sentinel trees on a neighbouring ridge dimly outlined against the sky.

From Tingling to Yoksam was a longer march than that of the previous day, although the horizontal distance was no greater. A sharp ascent brought us to the crest of a wooded ridge north of Tingling. As we breasted the last rise, we were surprised to be met by a sudden blare from a band. The monks of the neighbouring Kachöperi Monastery had come to greet us, and had erected two little shelters of gay chintz-like material, for all the world like little beach bathing tents, in which fruit and tea were pressed upon us. The latter appeared to be made from aromatic herbs, and was rich, thick, and buttery. The day was very hot, and we were thirsty; I, for one, drank several cups of the sickly stuff, and for the remainder of the day wished I had not. The monastery band, complete with long poles to which were fastened various prayer flags and pennants, lined along the path outside the tent and did honour to us in a crashing crescendo of sound.

From the ridge we glimpsed the summits of Kangchenjunga and Kabru. A silver lock of cloud was trailing from Kangchenjunga. Standing there in the still morning, perspiring gently under a fierce sun, it was difficult to realise that had we been up there we might have been fighting for our lives in death dealing cold and a *tourmente* of wind-flung snow.

From the ridge we had to descend once more into the Rangit Valley. The valley here begins to narrow, and bold crags jut out through a tangle of vegetation on its steepening sides.

The trudge up to Yoksam was a hot one but we were fanned by a fresh southerly breeze. As we progressed, we were puzzled to hear a series of pistol-like reports, and an intermittent crackling, like rifle fire. Turning a corner, we saw that the jungle was ablaze. Dull red flames were leaping high into the air, amid a pall of black smoke. Hastened by the breeze, the fire was sweeping with great velocity along the hillside. One moment some majestic tree would stand defiantly in its path, the next it would disappear in a smother of flame and smoke, reappearing as a gaunt, blackened corpse. Owing to the clearings made by the natives of Yoksam, the scope of the fire was limited, but its fierceness and the speed with which it swept the hillside reminded me of boyhood tales of prairies and pampas.

THE FIRST CAMP : AT TINGLING

Like Tingling, Yoksam is situated on a shelf clothed in pasture land, rice and wheat-fields. We pitched our camp on the terraces of a rice-field. Soon after we arrived we received word that the second party, under the charge of Hannah and Wieland, was two marches behind and that the convoy of mules under Colonel Tobin had left Darjeeling.

Yoksam is the last village. Thenceforward our way must lie through wilder country, and along rougher tracks towards Dzongri and the Kang La. Soon we would be at grips with things. Already the veneer of civilisation had lost its polish, despite the restraining and elevating influence of the "Memsahib." Table manners were already at a discount. Beards were growing steadily, and it was a matter of speculation as to who would win the race for length and bushiness. At present the honours were fairly evenly distributed between Professor Dyhrenfurth, Dr. Richter, and Duvanel. My own particular effort promised to develop into what I believe is technically known as a "King Beaver," or a beard bright red in colour.

The following morning, April 12, saw us strolling across the open pastures of Yoksam, or between fields of ripening grain. Then the path degenerated into a narrow, rough track and the forest enclosed us once again.

The paths in this part of the world are a fair indication of the character of those who make them. The native, of course, lives only in the present; the future holds no interest for him. Therefore, he goes about everything in the easiest possible way, the thought that by a little extra trouble he might save himself work in the future never occurring to him. It would not have been difficult to have made the path north of Yoksam contour the eastern side of the Rangit Valley. It would never have occurred to a Swiss Verschönerungs Verein to have done otherwise. But generations of native yak-herds and travellers over the Kang La have thought fit always to follow the line of least resistance, irrespective of time and future convenience. Thus, the path was continually climbing up, or dropping down to avoid the direct traverse of a steep piece of hillside. It was an extremely irritating path to the ordered and practical mind of a European.

But passing through this magnificent primæval forest cloaking the Upper Rangit Valley one can forgive the path its vagaries. None of us had ever seen an Amazonian forest, but it can scarcely be finer than the forests that line the trench-like valleys of the Himalayas. Yet, to one who finds pleasure in tramping the windy moors, fells, and bens of the North Country, there is something indescribably depressing about such a forest. The dense walls of vegetation on either side of the narrow straggling track and the interlacing canopy of vegetation far above the head shut out the health-giving sunlight and breezes. An awed silence seems somehow to hold in its arms a breathless suspense. There exists undefined menace, suggested perhaps by the dank odours of rotting vegetation. I experienced a feeling of being imprisoned in a vault, and longed to escape into more open places, to breathe air untainted by the miasmal odours of decay. Even the creepers that writhe about the trunks of the trees, or hang snakelike from the branches, appear ready to grip the traveller, and drag him to some horrible death in the gloomy recesses of the forest. There is little of good, and much of evil about such a place, and as Wood Johnson said, its impenetrable depths might hide anything, even the dreaded Snow Men.

To the botanist, however, there is much of interest and beauty in the flora of these forests. Quoting from Sir Joseph Hooker : " The vegetation consisted of oak, maple, birch, laurel, rhododendron, white Daphne, Jessamine, Arum, Begonias, Cyrtandaceæ, pepper, fig, Menispermum, wild cinnamon, Scitamineæ, several epiphytic orchids, vines, and ferns in great abundance."

As the path progressed it became worse. Here and there it was built up of bamboos and logs against the sides of precipitous crags. Mr. Freshfield found it " a great trial of temper." So, too, did we, or perhaps I should say, the porters. For loads such as ski and tent poles are a considerable nuisance in such a place.

Professor Dyhrenfurth was anxious to make a double march, and reach Dzongri in two days instead of three from Yoksam. But these three stages had not been arranged without reason, and Wood Johnson, who had traversed this same route the previous year, pointed out the inadvisability of a double march under such difficult conditions for transport. We accordingly camped in the usual camping place at the end of the first day's march, where there is a flat shelf and the forest is not too dense to allow of tents being pitched. This camping place harboured an unpleasant form of tick, a crablike insect about the size of a little finger nail, the bite of which was both painful and poisonous.

The scene at night was a curious one. Every flat place on the hillside above the camp was occupied by the porters. Their fires twinkled through the gloom like the fires of goblins. Like us, they were depressed by the forests, but their depression found adequate expression in the simple belief that devils and other unpleasant characters dwelt therein. That is, perhaps, the chief difference between the workings of the native mind and the European mind. Scenery may depress or exhilarate the European mind in exactly the same way as it does the native mind, but the European mind is educated sufficiently to be able to analyse consciously, or subconsciously, the reason for its reactions. The European tells himself that his feeling of depression is due to the gloom, the smell, or the appearance of what he sees, but the native mind is too clogged with superstition to be able to reason out its reactions. It must look for a simpler and more direct explanation, and such an explanation usually takes the form of belief in devils, gods, or other figments of the imagination. These he is able to propitiate and thus set his fears at rest. Thus, where the European is able to conquer his feelings by the exercise of will power, and so remain mentally superior to his environment, the native is able to arrive at exactly the same result by completely different means. Thus, that evening it was thought necessary to propitiate the devils of the jungle, but this having been accomplished, our porters settled down for the night perfectly happily, with no fears that anything untowards was likely to occur.

Mists hung low in the great ravine up which we were passing as we set off the following morning. The path became gradually worse and worse. In some places it was blocked by fallen tree trunks. Sometimes it was necessary to jump from one boulder to another across turbulent torrents. For a considerable distance the path vanished

THE RANGIT VALLEY

altogether beneath the débris of a landslip of considerable size. Here shattered tree trunks were piled in an inextricable confusion, and dense undergrowth that had sprung up between made progress fatiguing and difficult.

The way had to be cleared with *kukris*, and it was interesting to watch how quickly and neatly these were wielded by expert hands. Many who are reading this will have seen the batting of Frank Woolley, the great Kent cricketer. Seemingly little force is put into the stroke, yet the ball is at the boundary before the spectators have realised what has happened. The secret is hitting the ball exactly in the driving centre of the bat, combined with perfect timing of the stroke. The same methods apply to cutting with a *kukri*, and it was interesting to watch the dexterity with which heavy branches were lopped cleanly off, and a way cleared through the undergrowth.

It was during this march that I began to feel ill. The forest had repaid my dislike for it by presenting me with a severe chill. Of course, it was my own fault—a chill always is the fault of its victim in the tropics. I did not have to cast back far in my mind to remember how the previous evening I had neglected to change damp clothes until I had been actually shivering. The tropics allow no latitude for foolishness, and to look after one's physical well-being with scrupulous care is the first essential of Himalayan travelling.

We crossed the eastern branch of the Rangit River, where it divides south of Dzongri. It was a wild spot. Mountain and cloud seemed to roof us in ; the air was damp and chill. Far above we could just discern streaks of snow projecting like white fangs through the lowering mists. The glacier-born river roared sullenly over its rocky bed ; cold spray beat upwards from its grey waters. Even more than in the forest did we feel enclosed and shut in. As Eberl said, it might have been the end of the world.

Into the forest again, and up the hillside, where the feet sank into leaves rotting into leaf mould, or crushed into blackened débris, and decayed branches. A storm was threatening as we camped on a slope under dismal trees. No doubt my recollections are prejudiced, for my voice had completely disappeared, and I crawled into my sleeping bag ill and feverish, but this camping site remains in my memory as the most depressing one at which it had been my ill fortune to spend a night. Fortunately, Dr. Richter gave me some excellent medicine and throat spray which considerably relieved me, but sleep was impossible. The weather broke that night in a thunderstorm accompanied by torrential rain. Though lying ill in a sleeping bag, with the rain from a leaky patch in the tent oozing through, there was an element of magnificence in listening to this warring of the elements on the very edge of the Himalayas. The blue glares of lightning were answered by majestic crashes of thunder that seemed to be precipitated from hill to hill and peak to peak in volleys and waves of sound like music in the nave of some immense cathedral. The very echoes were indicative of vastness. In a flat country the thunder seems to dominate, but in the Himalayas, it is but the mouth-organ of the giants.

The storm died of its own fury, and morning dawned clear and cold. The forests above were dusted with new-fallen snow which extended down to as low as 8,000 feet. Such weather boded ill for the crossing of the Kang La.

My lungs had been touched by the chill, and breathing was painful and difficult when walking uphill. Had it not been for the encouragement of Wood Johnson, who stayed with me during this trying time, I do not think I could have struggled up the 5,000 feet to Dzongri.

As we ascended, oaks and chestnuts gradually gave place to firs. The dense tropical tree roof under which we had been marching for the past two days thinned. Shafts of sunlight illuminated a ground covered no longer in the rotting débris of tropical vegetation, but in fir cones and needles. The fresher and purer air from the snows brought with it a fragrance of sun-warmed resin. Beneath the firs were clumps of giant rhododendrons already budding, and as we got higher, these thickened, and the path twisted tortuously between their snaky, mangrove-like stems. The sun melted the snow on the fir branches above, sending it down in little showers of water drops, that filled the forest with patterings and murmurings.

Wood Johnson and I rested in a hillside glade, but before we had sat down for more than a minute we saw dozens of malignant leeches making for us with a stern resolution. At this height, above 8,000 feet, we had expected to be rid of the pests, but they seemed to thrive in spite of the cold. Actually, they were the last we saw until returning to Darjeeling.

The snow-drifts became more frequent. At length the path was completely snow covered, in places to a depth of two or three feet. Only a small portion of this snow had fallen in the night, and what we were encountering was obviously the lees of winter snow. To find such deep snow below 10,000 feet was disquieting, and doubts as to getting barefooted porters over the Kang La returned with redoubled force.

The rhododendron belt seemed interminable, but at length we emerged from it on to an open hillside clad only in dwarf rhododendrons, which are but two or three feet high, as compared to giant rhododendrons which attain a height of fifteen to twenty feet. The scene was more Alpine than Himalayan in character. The gentle snowy summits of the Singalila Ridge to the west put me in mind of the summits around Kitzbuhel in Tyrol. Normally, at this time of the year these slopes should have been mostly grass covered, but now, so large was the amount of snow on them, they suggested ski-ing rather than walking.

The trudge, or perhaps it would be more correct to say stagger in my case, up to Dzongri remains in my mind as the most severe physical effort I have ever been called upon to do. As we breasted the last slope, on the summit of which flutter a few forlorn prayer flags, we were met by a biting wind from the north, bringing with it a hurrying swarm of snow-flakes.

The sky was greying as we walked over the bleak upland pastures on which stand the huts of Dzongri. The few remaining blue pools of sky were engulfed in the advancing tide of a blizzard. Wood Johnson went on ahead to look after the porters. On arriving at the camp he at once ordered a Thermos flask full of hot tea to be sent back. Narsang also carried my rucksack. Thus, I was able to reach Dzongri without having to be carried.

The two primitive stone huts of Dzongri which afford shelter to the yak-herds later in the summer, stand on a rolling upland, the crest of which separates the Praig Chu

BETWEEN TINGLING AND YOKSAM

and Rathong Valleys. Though Dzongri would appear to be a prey to every wind that blows, it is the obvious climbing centre for this part of the Kangchenjunga Range, and its comparative easiness of access from Darjeeling demands that a proper shelter hut, run on the same lines as a Swiss Alpine Club hut, should be built. There are a number of fine peaks, for the ascent of which Dzongri would make an excellent starting point : Kabru, 24,002 feet, Little Kabru, 22,000 feet, Simvu, 22,360 feet, Pandim, 22,010 feet, and the rugged range to the south of it. All these peaks would appear to be possible to a strong mountaineering party.

Dzongri itself stands at 13,200 feet, and immediately to the north of it is 15,480 feet Kabur, the culminating point of the Dzongri Ridge. The great gneissic boulders that are strewn about the slopes hereabouts form an interesting geological problem. How came they to be there ? Sir Joseph Hooker's theory that ice once covered the whole spur, and in moving downwards transported these boulders from the upper crags to other parts of the spur is most likely the correct explanation. At all events, it is curious to find these grassy, rolling downs littered with boulders lying in the midst of savage snow and rock peaks.

That evening the threatened blizzard broke. Once again I lay sleepless listening to the fury of the elements. Two days before we had slept in the moist, enervating heat of a tropical forest, now the snow slashed our tents, and the mercury of the thermometer shrank into its bulb.

CHAPTER VIII

THE KANG LA

A calm morning succeeded an angry night. Winter had ousted spring and snow lay over six inches deep. The sky was a clear washed blue, and far to the south blue hazes indicated the heat stricken Plain of Bengal. The crests of Pandim, and the peaks to the south of it were fringed with a faint iridescence as the rising sun shone through their delicate eaves, cornices and flutings of snow and ice. We had little time or inclination to admire the beauties of the scene, for the blizzard had done something more than transform the hillsides, it had turned the hearts of the Nepali porters into water. They refused to go on. Wrapping their blankets round them they cowered in the snow, weak, miserable specimens of humanity.[1]

Cajolery and argument were useless. It was necessary to separate the good men from the bad. Even though it meant delay in bringing some of the loads over the Kang La, it was better that we should get rid of these poor creatures now, rather than find ourselves at their mercy in a less favourable position. Wood Johnson, accordingly, ordered those men who wished to go back to stand to one side. They were indeed a sorry looking crew. The Sherpas and Bhutias eyed them contemptuously. The deserters numbered fifty, and the abandonment of their loads was a

[1] Considering that they were clad only in cotton clothing and were unequipped with boots they are scarcely to be blamed for refusing to traverse the snow covered Kang La.

serious matter. It meant that they would have to be brought over the Kang La by relays of porters. Such a *modus operandum* had little to recommend in it in view of the uncertain weather, late winter and low snow-line. Having sent back the shirkers, and issued snow goggles to our faithful porters, we were at length able to start, not forgetting to leave a reliable man in charge of the dumped loads.

For some distance the path contoured along the south-west slopes of Kabru, then dropped in a series of steep zig-zags into the Rathong Valley. In places it was deeply snowed under, and trail making was tiring work for those in front. It was here that we began to appreciate the sure-footedness of the Sherpas and Bhutias. Though many of them wore rope soled Thibetan boots without any nails, whilst others had no boots at all, they descended with that easy gait characteristic of hill men.

Somehow the Rathong Valley reminded me of the upper reaches of Glen Nevis. There was the same luxuriant vegetation, sky line of crags and firs, and clear torrents hurrying down the hillsides, or hanging in thin, gauzelike water veils from beetling cliffs.

Much to our relief we saw that the lower part of the valley leading up towards the Kang La contained but little snow. The Kang La itself, and the peaks north and south of it were buried in clouds suggestive of another blizzard. Snowflakes were falling as we mounted rhododendron-clad slopes into the Kang La valley, but presently the bleak sky was tempered by a fugitive sun, and the clouds rolled back.

We pitched camp on a bed of dwarf rhododendrons.

Apart from these, the valley was distinctly Alpine in character, and the stern rock walls on either hand dark stained by oozing water, turf-crowned slopes above and below, interspersed with occasional slopes of scree and drifts of snow provided scenery of a type typical to the Alpine gneissic ranges.

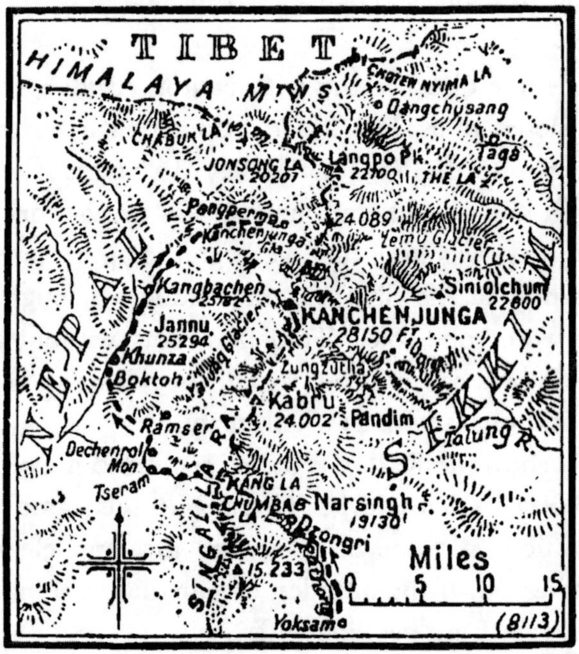

By courtesy of *The Times*

Thanks to Dr. Richter's treatment, plus a tough constitution, my chill was already better, and I was able to take my place at mess that evening. Seated on packing cases, we ate our supper in the open, warmed by the sun's last gleams. Up to date Tencheddar's cooking had met with approval, although not always unqualified approval. We were getting used to the varieties of food and cooking he expected us to stomach. It is indeed strange what men can get accustomed to in the wilds. Even the assistant cook's confirmed habit of pulling his shirt out of his trousers, and wiping the plates with it met with no more than a conventional grunt of disapproval. Our servants waited upon us, and it was a point of honour with each one of them to see that his own particular sahib got more than anyone else. As time went on, we would endeavour to vary the monotony. At this Schneider displayed most aptitude, and his favourite concoction consisting of toasted cheese, salad dressing, Worcester sauce and gherkins remains an unholy memory.

One unfortunate result of splitting up the expedition into three parties was the absence of alcohol in our own party, and it was not until we had crossed the Kang La that we discovered that Tencheddar had accidentally packed some bottles of rum in mistake for Worcester sauce. It was the only mistake he ever made that ended happily.

As soon as the sun disappeared it became very cold, and a bitter wind got up, hustling down the valley from the snows. It was necessary to let the world know something of our doings, and I sat up late that night hammering on a portable typewriter, until numb fingers no longer functioned and an overwhelming desire for sleep, after two bad nights, submerged journalistic considerations.

The porters had now been marching for ten days without a rest, and an off day was certainly theirs by right, but the unsettled weather, and the possibility of another snowstorm decided Professor Dyhrenfurth to push on over the Kang La without delay, and not only this, but to try to cross it in one day from our present camp. In view of the quantity of snow on the pass, one day certainly meant a very long and tiring march, for our camp was not more than 13,000 feet, and the Kang La is 16,373 feet. In addition, none of the sahibs or porters were acclimatised yet to altitude, and 16,000 feet to an unacclimatised body is more of a strain than 20,000 feet to an acclimatised body. Porters, also, were carrying a load of sixty to eighty pounds each. Taking all these considerations into account, it was doubtful whether such a long march was advisable.

To our delight and relief, the following morning dawned brilliantly. The wind had dropped, and a benevolent sun warmed the chill air of the upland valley. Our porters were if anything more susceptible bodily and mentally to weather conditions than we, and on this occasion they started off in great heart.

For a short distance above the camping site the valley floor is almost level, and covered in loose stones. We mounted over an ancient and steep terminal moraine. Thenceforward, the way lay entirely over snow.

The direct heat of the sun, and the reflected glare of it from the snow were terrific. Unfortunately, protective glacier face cream was not available, and all we had were some tubes of ordinary cold cream. These proved almost completely useless and despite liberal applications, we could feel our skin becoming dried up, scorched and burnt. As we gained height, there were backward and enchanting views. The great foot-hills that had enclosed us during our march through the tropical forests to the snows seemed now mere rucks and folds in the earth's surface. The deep valleys along which we had laboured had sunk out of sight ; belts and bands of translucent blue haze, from which white cumuli clouds born of steamy earthen heat were beginning to nose their way upwards like white whales, alone told of them. It was as though we were gazing out upon some ocean from a viewpoint of few miles inland, the nearer peaks forming the broken edges of the coastal cliffs overlooking the long rollers of the foot-hills.

Hoerlin and Schneider with their usual indefatigable energy left early with the intention of climbing the Kang Peak, 18,280 feet. This rises south of the Kang La, and if Mr. Graham's description is correct would appear to have been climbed by him. Their ascent would act as an excellent spur to the porters.

On the Sikkim side of the Kang La there is a small uncrevassed glacier which is joined by another glacier from the north. This northern glacier, which boasts a considerable ice fall, leads up to the foot of a symmetrical snow peak, the delicately pointed summit and sharp ridges of which invite exploration and conquest. Southwards, were a number of rock peaks and ridges, one of which bears a striking similarity to the well-known Dent du Géant and Rochefort Ridge, on the range of Mont Blanc.

As we plodded through the soft snow we experienced for the first time that Himalayan malady known as glacier lassitude. In our case, this lassitude, the mental and physical weariness induced by climbing the long snow slopes, was due probably to the fact that in six days we had ascended no less than 13,000 feet. But glacier lassitude is due to something more than mere lack of acclimatisation ; sun and glare have much to do with it, as does also a curious lifelessness in the air. In the snowy trough we were ascending the air seemed dead and incapable of vitalising lungs and body. It lacked oxygen, and was as depressing to breathe as flat soda-water is to drink. In Himalayan glacier hollows evaporation in the tropical sun is so rapid that maybe the air is deprived by absorption of some of its oxygen. Only in snow and glacier hollows does lassitude attack the mountaineer, and by climbing a ridge he may rid himself of its baneful effects in a few minutes. It is also interesting to note that lassitude only makes itself felt on windless days, and that wind always restores energy to the apparently fatigued body.

We halted for lunch on a level place some 500 feet below the crest of the pass. Directly above rose the steep slopes of the Kang Peak, and on them were the minute figures of Hoerlin and Schneider. How slowly they seemed to move. In the soft snow they were finding the going very laborious. They were making for one of the ribs falling from the summit ridge, and by the time we had finished lunch they had gained it. Thenceforward, the way looked less exacting physically, though more difficult from a climbing standpoint. The porters watched interestedly, forgetting their own tiredness.

The last slopes of the Kang La remain in my memory as entailing something more than a weary trudge. I was, of course, still weak from fever, and every upward step meant an expenditure of will power as well as physical energy. At long last the slope eased off, and stepping on to an outcrop of rocks, I gazed down into Nepal. Little was to be seen save battalions of fleecy clouds struggling up the snow-filled and desolate valley leading to Tseram.

From a scenic standpoint the Kang La is not an attractive pass. Like some of the passes across the Alps, such as the Brenner, the Simplon and St. Gotthard, it is fatiguing

AN OLD GENTLEMAN FROM THIBET

without being particularly interesting. Perhaps its greatest charm is the sense of isolation and remoteness from the world of men inspired by it. It is suggestive of some Arctic landscape, frigid and hostile to flesh and blood. Looking down the way we had come, I could see the men strung out in a long line of slowly moving dots. It was difficult to realise that these dots on the vast counterpane of snow were indeed men, and each man, in addition to the load he was carrying, carried another load of care and trouble, joy and sorrow.

Did I really soliloquise thus? I doubt it. It is only now, seated in a comfortable chair, and breathing the air of Primrose Hill approximately 200 feet above sea level that I can think of what I ought to have thought of on the Kang La, and forgetting for a moment the grumble of traffic, and a distant yet audible inferno of pneumatic drills, conjure up in my mind's eye that string of little men toiling up the weary snow-slopes.

After a short steep slope on the Nepal side of the pass, the snow filled valley curved gently downwards. After the labour of the ascent it was an easy matter descending through soft deep snow. It was an interesting fact that however much altitude may effect a man climbing in the Himalayas, he can, given easy ground, descend almost at an Alpine pace. Some remarkable instances of this occurred on Everest where slopes that had taken hours to ascend were descended in a few minutes.

The "Memsahib" was as usual well to the front of the party, and we congratulated her on being the first European woman to cross the Kang La. After a short distance, the valley floor dropped in a steep boulder strewn pitch.

Below this was another level section, and there, among stones and patches of snow we pitched camp.

Two or three of us arrived with jarring headaches. It was the first and last time on the whole expedition that I was affected thus, and it is tolerably certain that the headaches, which seemed to strike through the head from the back of the neck to the eyes, were induced by intense sun glare plus an altitude to which our bodies were not yet acclimatised. We found aspirin tablets the best remedy and under their influence the headaches disappeared in a few minutes.

The northern side of the valley on which we were camping, had been almost denuded of snow by the sun, but the unbroken snow covering the valley floor on the opposite slopes seemed to offer possibilities of ski-running. Actually, ski would have made the traverse of the Kang La much easier, but it seemed hardly fair to use them in view of the laden coolies, and it was necessary, too, for the Europeans to stamp out a track through the soft snow. Descending, however, we had no such scruples, and Dr. Richter set an example by running down the upper slopes on ski, which in lieu of bindings, he had tied on with odd bits of string.

Scraggy dwarf rhododendrons were growing on the slopes above the camp, and soon a dozen or more little fires were smoking on the ledges and crannies, as the coolies cooked their evening meal. The day had been a hard one, an exceptionally hard one, even for our toughest Bhutias and Sherpas. The Alpine porter seldom carries more than a load of forty of fifty pounds, and this as a rule only along paths up to huts ; on mountain ascents he carries considerably less. Our men had carried sixty to eighty pounds each over a pass higher than the summit of Mont Blanc. They had, of course, been used to carrying heavy loads from early childhood, but even so their work that day had been simply magnificent.

An hour or two after we had arrived Schneider and Hoerlin rejoined us. Their attempt on the Kang Peak had been crowned with success, albeit the ascent had been scarcely enjoyable in view of the bad snow conditions. The view had been marred by mist, but once they caught a glimpse of Jannu, 25,294 feet, which had impressed them as being a magnificent mountain.

We had camped at about 4 p.m., but as the evening drew on stragglers were still coming in, some of them very tired. Of Wood Johnson, who was bringing up the rear, there was no sign. As it was likely that he was experiencing difficulty in getting the last of these stragglers over the pass, I set off alone from the camp to meet him.

Night was falling swiftly as I plugged uphill. The evening was a calm one, and there was not even the faintest whisper of wind. For some distance I could hear the murmur of the camp beneath, and smell faintly the odour of burning rhododendrons, but soon nothing was to be heard. The gaunt, craggy sides of the mountains enclosed me. The murmurous trickles released by the sun had been clenched by frost to their channels. The silence of the high mountains at eventide was unbroken. I felt very lonely. Had it not been for the track stretching before me, a mere thread drawn across the snowy waste, I might have felt myself the sole inhabitant of a frigid planet. There was indeed an element of unearthliness about the scene. In the High Alps a man may find himself temporarily removed from civilisation, but always at the back of his mind is the thought that he has but to turn downhill, and in a few hours at the most he will regain civilisation. But in the High Himalayas such sub-conscious knowledge does not exist, and the wanderer experiences the genuine meaning of solitude. Above me the sun glowed redly, cruelly, on the peaks, but round me the snows were livid, deathlike, and the black rocks jutted through like unburnt coals amid the white ashes of the world.

So I trudged on, conscious only of the pounding of my heart, and the crunch of the crusted snow beneath my nailed boots. Far above, on the last slopes of the pass, some black figures appeared, moving slowly and jerkily, like marionettes operated by tired hands. They approached, a sorry little procession of exhausted men. Wood Johnson was with them to cheer them on. He, too, was very tired. He said it had been necessary to *drive* them over the pass. They were so tired, he said, that they had sat down and asked to be left there to die in the snow. He had himself been forced to carry loads up the last slope to the pass. Both physically and mentally he was worn out with the strain. If we others had known difficulties of this sort were likely to arise, we would, of course, have remained behind to help, but we had not known, although in view of the trying day it had been even for unladen Europeans we might have guessed.

Three or four of the porters could hardly stagger, but we supported them as well as we could, cheering them on and telling them that they had but a short distance to go. Several loads had been abandoned on the pass, but there was one grey-haired old man, who looked the oldest of our porters, who, although in bare feet and as exhausted as any, steadfastly refused to abandon his load. To him it was a point of honour to get it to camp at any cost. I wish I could remember his name. So we continued down the snow slopes towards the camp, a little army of exhausted men.

All the peaks were livid now, and the reflected glare of the sunken sun illuminated the snow-fields in a weird opalesque afterglow.

Leaving the others, I hurried on to the camp, and rousing it, returned with men carrying lanterns. It was quite dark by the time we had got back to the tired porters. Willing hands relieved them of their loads or supported their faltering steps. It was bitterly cold as we stumbled down the last ice-glazed rocks to the camp.

The poor old man's bare feet were frost-bitten, happily not seriously, and he and the remaining stragglers were completely exhausted. It was only due to Wood Johnson that the casualties were not more serious. Thus ended the march over the Kang La.

The weather maintained its promise, and the next day dawned fine. Eberl decided he would take advantage of it, and return to Darjeeling and Calcutta. His leave of absence was not long enough to permit of him coming to the Base Camp, and he could not afford to take the risk of being held up by bad weather returning over the Kang La. We parted from him with regret.

The sun glare of the previous day had done its work only too efficiently, and I awoke conscious that my face was a temporary ruin. Edward Whymper in "Scrambles among the Alps" gives a harrowing description of the effects of sunburn.

"They have been scorched on rocks and roasted on

glaciers. Their cheeks—first puffed, then cracked—have exuded a turpentine-like matter, which has coursed down their faces, and has dried in patches like the resin on the trunks of pines. They have removed it, and at the same time have pulled off large flakes of their skin. They have gone from bad to worse—their case has become hopeless—knives and scissors have been called into play ; tenderly and daintily, they have endeavoured to reduce their cheeks to one uniform hue. It is not to be done. But they have gone on, fascinated, and at last have brought their unhappy countenances to a state of helpless and complete ruin. Their lips are cracked ; their cheeks are swollen ; their eyes are blood-shot ; their noses are peeled and indescribable."

Wood Johnson had not unnaturally suffered most, for he had been far longer exposed to the sun, and in his anxiety for the porters had neglected to look after his face. The non-mountaineering reader may think I am making a lot of this affliction, but those who gently brown, either artificially or naturally on the sands of Margate or the Lido, have little conception of the truly dreadful state that the Himalayan sun reduces the countenance to. Anyone who has ever experienced the agony of eating and smiling, or the sleepless nights it may cause will have good cause to remember it. As a Doctor once remarked to me : " Take a man straight from England, and sit him for a few hours without clothes on in the middle of a snow-field in the sun, and he would most probably die." I believe he would.

The previous evening I had eyed the snow-fields around with that sort of longing that every ski-runner knows. Now

I determined to try my luck on ski. We had brought with us ski for every European member of the party. Made by Schuster of Munich, they were a compromise in length and weight between ultra short or summer ski as used in the High Alps, and standard length winter ski. The wood was hickory, and the bindings detachable clip-on ones, of a breed not familiar to me, a compromise between Huitfeldt and Alpina.

Unfortunately, however, these bindings had already left in one of the porter loads by the time I was ready to start, and like Dr. Richter I had recourse to string, and odd lengths of yak-hide thongs. The porters watched my preparations with intense interest. I think they thought that the ski constituted part of some flying machine by the aid of which the sahibs would alight on the summit of Kangchenjunga. In the narrow forest paths, their porterage had been an irritating and difficult business, but the porter carrying them had treated them with the utmost care and respect. Had he known that they were not part of a flying machine he might possibly have been tempted to throw them away.

Dirty faces grinned expectantly as I fastened them on. Willing hands helped to tie the cat's cradle-like bindings of odd bits of string. At length I was off, shooting down the slopes into the middle of the snow-filled valley. The snow was board hard, with a delightful loose crystalline surface into which ski could be edged. It was very similar to early morning spring snow in the Alps, but in the Alps a two or three inches deep surface of crystals is only experienced after a snowfall ; normally, the surface is conducive to skidding, and the traverse of steep slopes is tiring. But on this Himalayan snow which gains its crystalline surface from the heat of the mid-day sun, any swing is possible, from the Telemark to the stem Christiania.

The running was of its kind the most perfect that I have ever experienced. Would that it had been longer. As I glided down the valley I was scarcely conscious of movement ; only the procession of mountains on either hand, the gentle slush of the snow beneath my ski, and the breeze meeting my face suggested it. I felt Einsteinian. It was I who was stationary, and the world that was slipping away beneath me.

The valley floor dropped in another pitch ; it was necessary to make downhill swings. I became more conscious of movement, and movement swift, fierce, exhilarating. Some porters were marching down the side of the snow. I swooped past them in tremendous style, leaving them gaping in wonder. My triumphant progress was short lived. Suddenly both ski came off together. The world ceased to slip, it revolved with great velocity and in revolving dealt my nose a shrewd blow. I arose, my neck was full of snow, and my mouth full of hard words. From above was borne down faintly a roar of laughter ; the prestige of the flying machine had vanished for ever.

We descended from winter into spring. A softer air lubricated our tortured countenances. There were patches of grass and dwarf rhododendrons, whereon we flung ourselves down for a few moments of delightful repose. We turned a corner. Below was the emerald green Alp above Tseram, where Mr. Freshfield pitched his camp thirty years previously. Behind were the snow-clad peaks of the Kang La. Over the ridge to the north we could see some glittering summits in the neighbourhood of Jannu, forming the culminating points of acute ice ridges, defended beneath by ribbed curtains of blue ice. They looked, and probably are, unassailable.

The vegetation became more luxuriant as we descended. Small flowers peeped shyly out between the boulders of an ancient moraine. Everything was green and glad in the sunlight. A rough path led us gently downwards to Freshfield's camping site.

Since Yoksam our camping sites had been poor ones. It was pleasant, therefore, to find a level pasture of dry, springy turf on which to pitch our tents. Around were woods of firs and giant rhododendrons. The air was permeated with sweet scents. Near at hand the voice of a crystal clear stream babbled a friendly welcome. Majestic snow-clad peaks stood watch and ward over this little Eden.

At one end of the pasture a new hut, constructed of rough-hewn timbers, intended for yaks and their herds, had been built, but of the yaks and herdmen, or more important, the Nepalese Subadar, whom we had hoped to find waiting for us with coolie food, there was no sign. Doubtless, our coming had not been observed, and it was possible that the Subadar might be waiting for us in the hamlet of Tseram, which was some twenty minutes' walk farther on. But it was not so much the beauty of our surroundings to which we first turned our attention, as to the great wall of snow-covered peaks to the north of Tseram and the Yalung Valley, peaks very similar in steepness and general appearance to those hemming in the Gastern Valley, near Kandersteg in the Bernese Oberland. Did the way via the Mirgin La to Khunza lie over this wall? We knew that we must cross the Mirgin La, but the map and Mr. Freshfield's description had not led us to expect anything so formidable in appearance. Already, the Kang La had forced us to realise how great was the task that we had embarked upon in attacking the Nepalese side of Kangchenjunga.

Coolie food was running short, and it was imperative to find the Subadar without delay. Accordingly, that afternoon, Wood Johnson and I set off for Tseram.

A rough path oozing with snow-drifts led down the mountainside, through a tangle of giant rhododendrons into the Yalung Valley. Less than a year previously, the young American, Farmer, had passed this way with his porters *en route* to the Yalung Glacier, whence he made his attempt on Kangchenjunga which ended so tragically. We had received a telegram asking us to make every possible enquiry and search for him, and in particular to visit the Decherol Monastery, which, according to the map, was situated some distance up the Yalung Valley, below the terminal moraine of the Yalung Glacier.

A quarter of an hour's walk brought us down to a muddy torrent, flowing from the Yalung Glacier, which we crossed by a small bridge. During the flood season, Himalayan torrents must be immense. The width of the torrent bed, and the jumbled confusion of great boulders carried down by the flood waters bear witness to what the Yalung River is capable of, but now it was no bigger than an Alpine torrent from a glacier of moderate size.[1]

As we ascended the north bank of the stream, a head rose cautiously over a large boulder. We shouted a greeting, but it abruptly disappeared, and its owner, a boy, bolted

[1] See Appendix: "Glaciology: Snow Conditions and Avalanches."

precipitately as though all the devils of the district were at his heels. There came a furious clamour of dogs, and a few instants later we approached a rude hut, long and wide-eaved, with the boards of its roof weighted down with stones. A wizen-faced old man wearing high Thibetan boots and a dirty black robe girdled at the waist came forth to greet us. Behind him was his wife, twisting her fingers in shyness and embarrassment, while eyeing us half fearfully with narrow, dark, restless eyes, under a tattered fringe of hair. Close at hand, two savage Thibetan sheep dogs strained at the cords with which they were fastened to stakes in the ground.

The old man was the yakherd of this remote valley, and if being dirty constituted good yakherdmanship, he was certainly efficient at his job. There was no question of any high-water mark round his neck, for no tide had ever penetrated as far. Yaks were obviously his great enthusiasm in life. He smelt of them too. His wife was, if anything, dirtier and more odorous.

From them we learned that the Nepali Subadar had been staying at Tseram waiting for our arrival for some time, but not hearing anything of us, he had gone down the valley the previous day. This was most unfortunate ; we must find him and obtain coolie food at all costs. The best man for the job was our Gurkha, Tikeram Thapa, and we arranged with the old man for the loan of his son as a guide. Meanwhile, should our coolie food run out entirely, there were always the yaks. We were told that their owner, who lived in the lowlands, had kindly sent up a message to say that if necessary we could slaughter one. If possible, however, we wished to avoid feeding our coolies on meat, as they are vegetarians, and meat has a deleterious effect on them.

We asked the yakherd for information regarding Farmer. He was not able to tell us much. Farmer and his porters had not passed through Tseram itself, being unwilling to attract attention owing to the fact that they had crossed the Nepalese frontier without permission. They had avoided Tseram by traversing the rhododendron-clad hill-side above that hamlet. As for the Decherol Monastery, that had been a ruin for thirty years or more. This was all he could tell us, but we decided if we had time, we would go some distance up the valley and attempt to discover traces of Farmer.

The evening was chilly, and we adjourned into the yakherd's hut. One end of it was reserved for yaks, the other end for the yakherd and his family. A mass of dirty straw, alive with fleas, was the family couch. At one corner were piled some sacks of grain, rough cooking utensils, and wooden drinking cups. The rough and uneven floor was paved with stones and dried mud. A fire of rhododendron wood was burning on a primitive stone hearth, but as there was no chimney the smoke had to find its way out through chinks in the roof, a process more efficient in theory than in practice.

The old man and his wife, and two or three of our porters, who had come down from the camp, squatted round the fire, and a greasy looking concoction of some buttery substance was brewed, but fortunately, we were spared having to drink it. It was a scene simple and primitive, that will live in my memory. The last gleams of sunset filtered through the cracks ; there was a glimpse of forest and mountain. Is happiness to be measured in terms of modern invention? Was not this old man in his old hut, through the chinks of which he could watch the sunset and the stars, with his simple philosophy and his yaks, happier than many dwellers in a city?

In the last light we walked back to camp. A profound quietude enwrapped mountain and valleys. Below, the lazy smoke from the yakherd's hut lifted gently upwards, mingling imperceptibly with the night. For the yakherd and his family it was just the end of another day, the passing of another spoke in the wheel of life.

That evening after dinner we sent for Tikeram, and acquainted him with the urgency of the situation. He was keen and willing to start at once. "I am here to help," he said, and set off at once on his journey through the night, guided by the yakherd's son with a lantern.

Whether or not we were forced to remain at Tseram until food arrived, it was essential to rest the porters. It is not too much to say that we had arrived a dilapidated party in health and morale. Several of the porters had bruised or cut feet, and one or two, including the plucky old man who had refused to abandon his load, minor frost-bites. Worst of all, a number of them were suffering from snow blindness. There was no real excuse for this, for they had been issued with snow glasses, but the native is both careless and improvident. Snow blindness is, as I know from personal experience, extremely painful. Its first effect is by straining the optic nerve to put the vision out of focus. A profuse discharge follows, and the eyes ache abominably. It is impossible to open them in the light without severe pain, as the light seems to strike them almost like a blow. Fortunately, ordinary snow blindness is as brief in its effects as it is painful, and two or three days' rest and treatment are usually sufficient to effect a complete recovery. Our porters, however, did not know this. They thought they were dying, or about to become completely blind, and it was a pitiable sight to see them cowering beneath their blankets, pathetic bundles of humanity, outside Dr. Richter's tent.

News came that Hannah and Wieland were in difficulties. Their porters, not unnaturally, had refused to traverse the Kang La without boots. The next day, therefore, we called for volunteers to return over the Kang La to carry boots to their help. Thirty-seven of our best men immediately responded, and were sent off under the charge of Lobsang.

The situation was certainly not promising. Every day was of vital importance, and here we were relegated to Tseram for an indefinite period.

That morning, Kurz left early to map the lower portion of the Yalung Glacier and Valley. He returned later, confirming the statement of the yakherd that the Decherol Monastery was indeed a complete ruin.

Had it not been for our anxiety over the transport, and the painful state of our faces which made eating a misery, and sleeping difficult, we might have enjoyed our four days enforced rest at Tseram. To while away the time we rigged tape between two upright poles, made a quoit from rope, and played deck tennis. Even at such a moderate elevation as 10,000 feet, we found this somewhat strenuous, but exercise had the excellent effect of quickening acclimatisation.

That evening Wieland arrived, and acquainted us with

the situation on the other side of the Kang La. It was not a good one, but we knew that we could rely upon Hannah and Lobsang to get their men across. For the rest, everything depended on the weather. Actually some of Hannah's men had already arrived, carrying light loads, having marched direct from Dzongri.

On April 20, Wood Johnson and I, with Nemu who had accompanied Farmer to show us the way, visited the Yalung Valley to search for traces of Farmer. From Tseram a rough track traverses the north side of the valley. It was evidently the former route to the monastery, for we passed a number of rude walls and shrines covered in inscriptions.

Like most large Himalayan glaciers, the Yalung Glacier terminates in a great moraine some 1,000 feet high. Above this, the glacier is moraine covered for so great a distance that Lobsang, who was with Farmer, told us that they had had to march for three days before they trod ice.

It was while resting after lunch on the slopes of the valley near the terminal moraine of the glacier, that two curious incidents occurred. The first was an earthquake shock, the same shock, I believe, that was experienced in Turkestan and which we afterwards saw mentioned in the newspapers.

The second incident was an amusing one. As we sat smoking, we saw something moving in the valley beneath, half hidden by a huge boulder. Whatever it was, it seemed too large for any animal likely to be met with thereabouts. Nemu, however, had no doubts upon the matter, and fell on his belly with a frightened whisper of " Bad Manshi, Sahib ! Bad Manshi ! " (Bad Men, Sir ! Bad Men !)

This was interesting ; were we at last to meet one of the redoubtable Snow Men in person? Lying flat and motionless behind the rocks we peered intently down into the valley. For perhaps ten minutes we gazed, and we were beginning to wonder whether what we had seen had been a mere figment of imagination, when suddenly with majestic tread out walked—an enormous yak. Needless to say, we burst into a roar of laughter at poor Nemu, who had been trembling with terror, but his superstitions were not to be so easily over-ruled. He declared that like other of our porters he had on several occasions actually seen the "Bad Manshi," and described them as being huge men, white skinned and naked, but covered with thick hair.

Native temperament is childlike in many respects. Given work to do, or some object in life to fulfil, our porters were happy, but after having been left to their own devices for two or three days, they were only too liable to get into mischief, or work up some imaginary grievance. Among our porters were one or two men who, had they lived in England, would make admirable paid labour agitators or "tub thumpers" in Hyde Park. As it was they did their best to stir up strife among the rest of the porters, and to a small extent they succeeded in deluding the more credulous.

That evening, we were eating our supper in the Mess Tent, when there came an excited babble of voices. We took no notice of them until we had finished our meal, then Wood Johnson went outside. As usual, the trouble had originated with a few of our more unreliable porters. The Sherpas and Bhutias stood eyeing the scene passively, if curiously. A few minutes later, thanks to Wood Johnson, the agitators were slinking away amid the laughter and jeers of the remainder of the porters. The trouble had

SOME OF OUR "TIGERS"

arisen simply owing to Narsang forgetting to issue a ration of sugar. To get behind the native mind would indeed be to get behind the mind of a child.

Late that evening, Tikeram Thapa arrived with the welcome news that he had found the Nepali Subadar, and that the latter was coming up to Tseram the next day, bringing a few local porters with loads of coolie food. Tikeram told us that he had marched over twenty miles down the valley in the night, guided by the yakherd's son, although he had fallen and damaged a knee. It was a capital bit of work.

The same evening we made the discovery of the bottle of rum which as previously mentioned had been accidentally substituted by Tencheddar for a bottle of Worcester sauce. Despite the transport thorns besetting our way, we went to bed happy that night.

The following day we decided to shift the camp to Tseram, and carry as many loads as possible up the mountainside above in preparation for the start to Khunza. Diplomatically, we had made friends with the yakherd by presenting him with a number of empty tins which he had obviously coveted, and as a result he was willing to guide us to Khunza by a route over the Mirgin La that was well known to him. In such a remote part of the world an empty condensed milk or bully beef tin obviously possesses a very definite value.

The hillside above Tseram scarcely belies its apparent steepness. It is steep, but nowhere dangerously so. We returned to find the Subadar had arrived. He proved to be a thin-faced, sad, somewhat anæmic-looking man, with a long, straggling, and ill-nourished moustache. He was clothed in baggy white breeches and a black jacket. The only indication of any rank was the Nepalese coat of arms in gold above his turban. He seemed a cultured and educated man. We told him of our labour agitators, and he proceeded to tell them exactly what he thought of them. Making a number of comments on their ancestry, their personal appearance, and their chances of future salvation which, if he was to be believed, were nil, he ended up by telling them that the Maharajah of Nepal, whose country they were now in, had given orders that every assistance should be given to the expedition, and that he, the Maharajah's representative, was there to see it done. If, he concluded, it was not done, there was always the time-honoured custom of chopping off a few heads. There were no more labour troubles.

CHAPTER IX

IN UNKNOWN NEPAL

We broke camp on April 22. After the enforced inaction of the past few days, it was a relief to be again on the march. It was a brilliant morning, and fragrant odours of sun-warmed firs and flowers permeated the still air as we trudged up the hillside. We emerged from the forest on to open slopes of grass and boulders. There we were greeted by Kabru, and for the first time found ourselves gazing at its eastern face. Thus early in the morning it was in deep blue shadow, but the reflected light from the snow-fields of the peaks opposite across the Yalung Valley revealed the clean-cut edges of its hanging glaciers, and lit with a greenish sheen its icy steeps and snowy mouldings.

If Kabru turns a serene and benevolent countenance towards Darjeeling, it has, like a two-headed giant, another face, and this face which overlooks the Yalung Glacier is savage and cruel. Even as I watched there came a distant roar, the snowy lips of the giant writhed back, and an avalanche was spat out from between its teeth. A mere puff of white dust it seemed at that distance, and only the thunderous roll of its falling told of the tens of thousands of tons of grinding ice blocks crashing down thousands of feet to the Yalung Glacier. As though ashamed at the meaningless ferocity of its twin brother, a cloud was detached from the warm, sunny face of the mountain, and was wafted gently over the ridge. Dispassionately, it slid along the precipices, growing larger as it did so, and finally wrapped the mountain in a soft, grey shroud.

It was not long before we came to the snow. It was still frozen hard, and I determined to hurry on to try and obtain a glimpse, and if possible, a photograph of Everest. The mountainside which appears from Tseram a smooth,

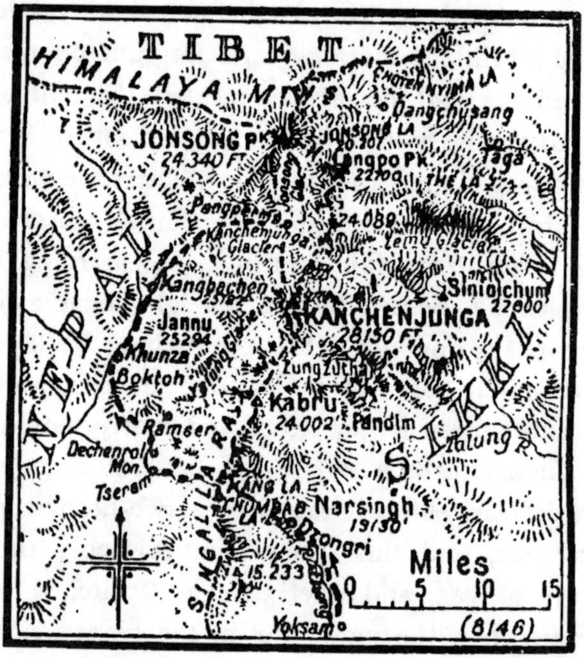

By courtesy of *The Times*

unbroken face topped by small, rocky summits, is in reality broken up into subsidiary ridges and valleys, and rounding a shoulder, I found myself in one of these snow-filled valleys leading upwards to the first of a series of snowy cols we must cross.[1]

As I mounted the snow slopes, I saw over a low ridge to

[1] This first col is actually the highest point traversed between Tseram and Khunza and is 15,361 feet high.

the left a solitary peak rising above a sea of woolly clouds. In shape its summit was a symmetrical sugar loaf like the Zermatt Weisshorn, and to the north and south its ridges swept down in graceful parabolas to perfectly proportioned shoulders. It was Makalu, Everest's 27,790 feet high neighbour. When Everest has been climbed, Makalu may defy many generations of future mountaineers, for it is one of the most terrific peaks in the world. By the time I had reached the col, it had disappeared behind clouds welling up from the warm depths of the Arun Valley. Of Everest there was nothing to be seen.

From the col I looked across a desolate snow-clad hillside, broken into rounded shoulders and stony hollows. Here and there the snow had melted, disclosing grass and straggling patches of dwarf rhododendrons. On one of these I had my lunch. The day was sunny, and the grey rocks warm to the touch. I was alone. Some may not appreciate the charm of solitude, but the true mountaineer, even if temperamentally of a gregarious nature, realises the value of occasionally parting from his companions in order to contemplate mountains as they should be contemplated, alone. On an expedition escape from one's fellows is seldom possible, not that one often desires it, but there are times when an inexplicable and fierce desire demands temporary release from the bonds of sociability.

I sat down, ate my lunch, and afterwards inhaled a contemplative cigarette, lolling among the dwarf rhododendrons, with my back fitting comfortably into a hollow of a rock. For a while I was merely a body clogged with an excellent lunch, gazing with peaceful digestion and bovine appreciation at the landscape. But presently and unexpectedly the dull pudding of my mind was stirred by the spoon of inspiration. I seemed to become a part of the hillside on which I was resting. I felt very old, and yet eternally young. The hills had been my companions through æons of time. I had seen them created, raised, and fashioned by the forces of the earth. I had seen vegetation clothe them, and snow cloak them, ruin overtake their more fanciful and extravagant constructions. I felt that I had always lived with the hills, and on the hills, and that the hills had treated me kindly. How else could a man be born with the love for hills? There is eternity both ways.

Men came over the col, one after another, a string of them. The silence was broken by the clatter of voices. I did not resent their presence, for I had had my hour alone on the mountain.

The snow was soft and fatiguing to march through. For some distance the path to the Mirgin La contours the mountainside. It was a long, hard day for the porters, especially for those who had had to carry loads all the way from camp. Once I came across Nemu. From somewhere he had acquired a pair of truly remarkable breeches. As there were no fifty shilling outfitters at Tseram, I was at a loss to imagine how he had got them, and Nemu himself never enlightened me on the subject. I say that they were remarkable breeches, because they did not look as if they were intended to be breeches at all. They were made of some curious balloon-like cloth, that hung down in loose folds like a collapsed parachute, and as Nemu walked, the breeches gave forth an important sort of swishing noise.

I think he experienced some mental strain in wearing them at first, for sahibs and coolies would gape at them, laugh, or make uncomplimentary remarks, but nevertheless he wore them in, as it were, until they became as much part of the expedition as Duvanel's beard, or Wieland's sun-skinned nose.

But Nemu was by no means alone as regards eccentricity of costume. One porter boasted an officer's khaki tunic, another a bandsman's jacket, then there was a villainous looking fellow with what might have been once an old Etonian tie, and two or three who sported engineers' overalls. Everest equipment was still greatly prized, and one man possessed a pair of Everest puttees, ragged and worn, sacred relics of which he was very proud. Like ladies, they allowed their imagination to run riot in the matter of head-gear. My own impression as to the constructive principles underlying the latest shapes in ladies' hats is that you take a perfectly ordinary hat, such as a Homburg, and then proceed to knock, kick, crush, and cut it in a fit of berserk fury. After such treatment, it is styled the latest mode or shape. This is precisely the treatment meted out by our porters to their own headgear. Any fashionable Paris hat designer, desirous of obtaining new ideas, can hardly do better than go on an expedition into the Himalayas, taking with him Sherpa and Bhutia porters.

We reached the Mirgin La, 14,853 feet, under a greying sky. Hailstones were falling, and from the east came an occasional thunder growl. Below, the snow slopes fell away into a desolate valley, ribbed with ancient moraines, like the embankments of a railroad fallen into disrepair. A few tattered prayer flags fluttered on the summit of the pass.

Viewed thus under a leaden sky, with light and shadow merged into one universal monotone, black-jawed crags jutting from livid featureless snow slopes, and a chill wind sighing through the gap, it was a depressing scene.

No depressing thoughts occurred to the porters as they breasted the pass, and they grinned broadly at the prospect of descent. Among them were several women, who had been with Wieland's party. In weight-carrying powers they were the equal of a man, and their powers of endurance were prodigious. These women did much to keep up the spirits of the porters, and relieved the tedium of the march with many verbal leg pulls and jokes which, according to Wood Johnson, it was fortunate the " Memsahib " did not understand. Now, one of these women, with a load on her back, sat herself down in the snow, and commenced a glissade down the steep snow slopes. For a few yards all went well, and she slid slowly and with dignity, then suddenly a hard icy patch of snow supervened. She uttered a shrill scream as her speed suddenly increased. The next moment she spun round, something happened, and her skirt was blown up over her head. Her load went one way, and she another, both rolling over and over to the bottom of the slope. A roar of laughter followed her from the assembled porters.

It was an easy matter descending these upper slopes, but tedious work lower down. There we encountered for the first time a type of soft snow that is fortunately seldom met with in the Alps, but which is, however, all too common in the Himalayas. It is not that it is simply soft, but the direct heat of the sun appears to have the effect of shrinking the snow beneath the surface, so that holes are formed into which the climber may sink up to the waist. For a few steps the surface crust may bear, and then, all at once, it collapses.

Walking under these conditions is extremely tiring and irritating, especially for laden porters, who sink in at almost every step. The Nepali Subadar, who was in front, was making very heavy weather of it. I came across him energetically digging in the snow with his hands to retrieve one of his shoes that had been left in a hole. Snow passes were evidently not to his liking, and the wan smile with which he greeted me was in sad contrast to his magnificent bearing on the previous day. I offered him a chocolate biscuit as solace for his woes, but he was unable to eat it owing to his religious principles, which forbade the eating of food handled by anyone outside his own particular caste. Nevertheless, he eyed it wistfully. It must have been about this time that he got severe frostbite, which resulted in his nearly losing a foot.

Perhaps, it would be as well to explain here that there are three stages of frostbite. The first is merely a temporary numbness, a loss of circulation which may be restored by rubbing or warmth. In the second stage frostbite manifests itself in blisters and swellings charged with fluid. And lastly there is the worst stage of all, in which the whole area affected, usually the extremities, becomes gangrenous. In this case, amputation may be necessary. The Subadar most likely came from one of the warm valleys or plains in Southern Nepal, and was not able to resist the cold as were our porters, with their more active circulation and thicker blood. Perhaps he had not even realised that he was being frostbitten when one foot lost sensation.

As we stood in the snow, Dr. Richter and Kurz shot by on ski. Their progress was to be envied. At the same time, someone had to make a track for the porters. To have to walk oneself at the expense of considerable effort, and to be passed by someone else travelling with but little effort rouses the worst passions. It is like trudging along one of those incredibly dull by-pass roads on the outskirts of London, and being passed by fat, opulent men in luxurious motor vehicles. Of course, if you are one of the fat, opulent ones, your viewpoint is different.

Dense, black clouds were massing as we struggled down the valley. Spiteful stilettos of lightning stabbed the peaks, and thunder crackled like a giant shelling walnuts. Once I descended into a hole up to my chest between two boulders. One foot jammed, and I was unable to extricate it for a quarter of an hour. I mention this purely as a point worthy of note among solitary climbers. I have seen a man so trapped that it took half an hour or more of hard work, plus considerable ingenuity, to get his feet out from between two boulders. Death by starvation thus would not be pleasant.

We pitched camp on a miserable spot on the north side of the valley. Had it not been for the porters, we should have continued the descent, and camped below the tree line, but the day had been a heavy one for them, and it was necessary to camp at the first available place.

From our camp we looked across the Kangbachen Valley, in which, out of sight, lay Khunza, to a range of peaks rising to 21,000 feet. They were for the most part massive mountains, with indeterminate ridges, between which flowed steep and broken glaciers. Owing to a lack of definite ridges, and the consequent difficulty of finding a continuous route to their summits, they looked decidedly awkward of access.

The day ended wretchedly in a heavy snowstorm, whilst a miserable supper turned out by Tencheddar did little to alleviate the general gloom.

The clouds snowed themselves out during the night, and morning dawned clear and cold. With memories of Signor Sella's wonderful photograph of Jannu in Mr. Freshfield's book in our minds, we set off up to the ridge running south-east from the Sinon La, the last pass we must cross to reach Khunza. We found, however, that the ridge above the camp was only a subsidiary ridge of the main ridge. Some decided to go on, but Schneider and I favoured descent to the " flesh-pots " of Khunza.

A good path led up to the Sinon La, but we found that on the north side of the pass formed the head of a long and steep couloir filled with hard snow, which must be descended some distance. It was a place where a slip might well end fatally, and we stamped secure steps for the porters. A number of other snow-filled couloirs had to be traversed, after which we found ourselves in rhododendrons. Somehow, I was irresistibly reminded of the descent to Chamonix from the Grands Mulets. Not that there was much in common between the Chamonix and Kangbachen Valleys, except a certain trench-like monotony. The Kangbachen Valley is far wilder than the Chamonix Valley, and on either side rise peaks to an altitude of 20,000 feet or more.

We strolled down sunny slopes to the crest of an indeterminate ridge from which we looked down to Khunza, a little cluster of brown dolls' houses thousands of feet beneath, and far up the valley we must go towards the Kangchenjunga Glacier. But this view, fine though it was, had not the dramatic quality of the view up the Yamatari Valley to the east. Curving round the corner were the moraines of the glacier, which has its sources in the southernmost recesses of Jannu, and above rose a range of rock and ice peaks of terrific aspect.

One of the curses of being a mountaineer, is that an analytical mind, trained as it is in seeking routes and estimating their relative difficulty, tends to detract from æsthetic enjoyment. In other words, the humble tourist, unversed in the art of mountaineering, is sometimes more able to appreciate the beauty and magnificence of a scene than is the mountaineer with his mind clogged with technicalities. But here was a scene so magnificent as to submerge the sharp, ugly rocks of analysis and technical considerations beneath the smooth rollers of pure contemplation. The thought of how these peaks might be climbed did not intrude. I did not see couloir or ridge, did not endeavour to win a theoretical way to a summit. Even Mark Twain would have put aside his telescope and been content to gaze with unfettered eyes up that sylvan valley with its background of stupendous ice peaks.

As I lay on the flat summit of a moss-clad boulder, something of my boyhood's simple adoration of the hills returned to me, that half wild yearning for an unattainable "something." It is a yearning that becomes dulled by time and experience. But such is the magical influence of the hills that sometimes they are able to recall it at unexpected moments, and this was one of them. However much a man

AN UNEXPLORED VALLEY : THE YAMATARI VALLEY

may delude himself into thinking the contrary, he becomes as expert in his mental appreciation for the hills as he does in his physical appreciation for them. The unsophisticated moments of youth are to be prized and cherished.

We lunched and lounged in the sun, then plunged down through the rhododendrons by a steep zig-zagging path. Soon we were among the firs, strolling by the side of the torrent from the Yamatari Glacier. The path entered on to an open grassy glade, a smooth sward as flat as a cricket ground. What a cricket ground it would make too ! With the dark fir woods as a natural boundary, and snowy mountain tops as pavilions—surely more conducive to century-making than the dingy villas and gasometers of the Oval, or the sulphurous vapours of Bramall Lane.

We had found our way to this delightful spot easily enough, for the path had ended there, but we could not find any way out and down to Khunza for some time. Yet who would wish to escape from such a fairy glade ? However, presently we crossed a little bridge over a stream, and found ourselves on a good track. At a turn of the path we could gaze down to the village, a trim little place, with neatly laid-out fields. It was strange to think that no European had passed through here for thirty years. It might have been a village in Switzerland or Tyrol.

Porters passed us. They were tired after two days hard marching, but they were cheerful at descending from the snows once more.

As we ran down the last part of the path, we were puzzled to see various little water-wheels revolving in the streams. They seemed to have no practical use. Then it dawned upon us that they were prayer wheels. The inhabitants of Khunza are lazy but ingenious. Unwilling to expend time and energy in revolving prayer wheels by hand, they utilise the abundant water power of the vicinity, and had rigged up a number of water-wheels, on which are carved many prayers. Every time a wheel revolves, so many prayers are "said" for the village. Literally millions must go out every twenty-four hours, and if these prayers mean anything, the gods that dwell on the mountains round Khunza must look very favourably on its inhabitants.

Our camp was pitched on a flat field at the southern end of the village. The inhabitants eyed us with curiosity; small children stood round, sucking their thumbs in round-eyed wonder at these strange reincarnations of something or other that had come down from the mountains.

The Subadar had arrived early that morning ; he had not camped with us, but lower down in the woods. We did not then know that he was frostbitten, and it was not until later that a gangrenous sore developed. Narsang was there too, having preceded us to arrange about food. Actually, he had done nothing, and the reason was plain to see ; the hospitality of Khunza had proved too much for him. With magnificent optimism he declared that though no food had come up from lower down the valley, we could have as much food as we wanted, and unlimited coolies from Khunza. That no food had come up was a serious matter. We had hardly one day's coolie food left, and whether enough would be forthcoming from Khunza with which to carry on to the Base Camp was doubtful. The fact that there was no food or coolies available, as kindly promised us by the Maharajah of Nepal, was partly due to the slackness of the Subadar who had been sent up to arrange for it. He was aware of our intended route, and all he had done was to collect some food in the lower valleys several marches away. It was exasperating to be confronted with such difficulties when within easy reach of our goal, and Wood Johnson told the Subadar that if coolies and food were not forthcoming, we should have no option but to report him to the Maharajah. This threat had an immediate effect on the Subadar, and he at once informed the Head Man of Khunza of our requirements. We had no wish to deplete the village of food, but the Subadar said there was plenty to spare, and that to take it would mean no hardship to the villagers. We were, of course, prepared to pay a good price for it. The Head Man was, therefore, given a day in which to collect the food.

That evening several of us decided to call upon the Head Man, the principal reason being that Wood Johnson had promised us a drink of an intoxicating liquor known as marwa. The Head Man's house was a large building constructed on the châlet principle. Built of sturdy timbers, with a wide-eaved roof weighted down with large stones, it looked fully capable of withstanding any storm. On entering, we found that half the inhabitants of the village were present. In the middle of the floor a large log fire was burning, and round this we squatted, cross-legged on rugs. Presently, a mixture of water and fermented hempseeds was brewed in a large cauldron, presided over by a withered old hag, whose wrinkled face and claw-like hands, illuminated by the ruddy glow of the fire, were positively witch-like. The atmosphere was heavy and close, and a strong reek of smoke from burning rhododendron branches fought a losing battle against a stronger reek of unwashed bodies.

Presently, the concoction was brewed, and was ladled out into cylindrical wooden metal-bound pots. These had a lid, in the centre of which was a metal cone, with a round hole through the top. Through this hole was thrust a bamboo stick, up which the liquor had to be sucked. I cannot pretend to describe the taste of this drink, it is enough to say that it is by no means unpleasant and, taken in sufficient quantities, is decidedly intoxicating.

Heavy rain was roaring on the roof by the time we had finished, but we splashed back along the village " High Street " to camp happily enough singing the latest music-hall airs.

Theoretically, the following day, April 24, was a rest day, but not for Wood Johnson. His was the disagreeable task of getting blood out of a stone, or in other words, food out of the Head Man. That individual, lulled doubtless into a sense of security by the patronage of his house by the sahibs the previous evening, had done nothing. Probably, this was due not so much to wilful neglect, as to native inability to appreciate the value of time. What mattered a week, or two weeks, or even a month to the sahibs? What was their hurry? Why were they so anxious to undergo hardships on the mountains when every day was bringing the summer nearer? Such was his philosophy—the same sort of philosophy in these regions that decrees that when you are invited to a wedding you find it usually more convenient to turn up two or three months after the ceremony.

We repaired to the Head Man's house to find him peacefully tilling his garden. The Subadar was furious. He saw his reputation being destroyed, his authority set at nought, possibly even his head removed on his return to Khatmandu. After a volley of invectives, he grasped the cowering Head Man, seized some rope lying handy, and proceeded to lash him up to a post. " Produce the food, or have your head cut off"—that appeared to be the gist of the conversation for the next few minutes. Of course we interceded. We had no wish for our way through Nepal to be littered with the heads of Head Men. Nevertheless, the situation was not without its humour. Imagine a portly and worshipful mayor of some British provincial town tied to a post in his own back garden, and told to supply a party of complete strangers with food, or have his head cut off in the event of not doing so. So the Head Man was released from his bonds. The thunder clouds disappeared from the brow of the Subadar, and Khunza slumbered peacefully in the sunlight once more.

That afternoon we visited the Khunza Monastery. This is situated outside the village on the west bank of the Kangchen River. A rickety suspension bridge, the safety factor of which it would be scarcely wise to enquire into, spans the river. Entering a stone gateway, on which were carved the usual prayers, we passed through a forest of dilapidated prayer flags.

Khunza Monastery is a branch of the famous Khampa Dzong Monastery in Thibet. Normally, the Buddhistic religion imposes celibacy upon the Lamas, but so lax have conditions become at Khunza that from the Head Lama downwards, they intermarry with the villagers. There were also chortens. These are stone monuments erected in honour of some former Lama saint. On the summit there is usually a crescent moon, sun, or lotus, whilst sacred relics, such as the ashes of Lamas, are placed in a niche.

A Thibetan monastery is more in the nature of a village than a single group of buildings. For instance, about 8,000 monks reside at the De-pung (Rice-heap) Monastery near Lhasa. Compared to the great Thibetan monasteries, Khunza Monastery is, of course, small. Its wooden buildings are primitive, and display none of the grandeur of the great Thibetan monasteries. Passing along a narrow street, bounded by primitive two-storied houses, where circulated many varied and powerful odours, we were ushered through a doorway and up a flight of wooden steps, deeply furrowed with the passage of countless feet, into the monastery temple. As our eyes became accustomed to the gloom, we found ourselves to be in a barn-like room with uneven wooden floor. At one end gleamed little Aladdin-like oil lamps on altars, lighting the enigmatical face of a carved Buddha and effigies of former lamastic saints. The decorations were of the usual garish mixture of red and yellow, the beams across the roof and the pillars supporting it red and the tapestries and friezes yellow. Dozens of little lockers filled with sacred books lined the walls. Presently, the stairs creaked beneath a heavy tread, and the Chief Lama, a very fat man with a dough-like face and crafty smile, entered the temple.

On this occasion the hospitality consisted of some conventional devil dancing by a number of Lamas, but this was only the preliminary to a religious ceremony the purport of which was difficult to understand. Possibly it was intended as a blessing upon our expedition, but this

KHUNZA

was doubtful in view of our unpopular demands in the matter of food and coolies.

The ceremony consisted of numerous incantations by the Head Lama, accompanied by the monastery band, and repeated by the Lamas, varied by an occasional vigorous ringing of a small bell by the Head Lama. Sometimes the band would stop, and only the low mutter and wailing of the praying Lamas would be audible, like the rise and fall of wind in the rocks of a mountain top. Put such a scene on the stage of a London music hall and it would scarcely induce anything but boredom, but here, many marches from the nearest outpost of civilisation, it produced a strange impression upon us. The crowding cares of the Twentieth Century seemed to fade away. We were back in a mediæval land caring nothing for progress, a land fiercely jealous of its ancient rights, its conservatism looking askance upon modernity and the outer world. Perhaps it is happier so.

At the conclusion of the ceremony everyone was handed small quantities of rice and seeds which were cast into the middle of the floor. Among other things, the Head Lama showed us a knotted raw-hide whip, stained with blood, with which the Lamas are accustomed to keep order among the villagers, for they have the powers of life and death over the inhabitants of the district.

Much of the power wielded by the Lamas over the destinies of Thibet, Nepal, and Sikkim is due to their preying on the superstitious beliefs of the people. While on the expedition there was related to us a story concerning a certain high dignitary. The dignitary who owned a large and scattered estate decided to visit an outlying portion of it. There were, however, strong reasons why he should not do so. It appeared that a considerable portion of the revenue accruing from the estate had been pocketed by the Lamas of a neighbouring monastery. Therefore, he was told that there was a large and thoroughly malevolent devil who had taken possession of this portion of the estate, and that should its shadow fall upon him he would die an agonising and lingering death. Naturally the dignitary was loth to come to such an unpleasant end, and decided to postpone his visit. It was then that some ingenious person suggested that if he carried an umbrella the devil would be unable to cast its shadow over him. This idea was seized upon gladly, and the estate was visited under the devil-proof shelter of an enormous umbrella. It is to be hoped that the embezzling Lamas were brought to book.

We had with us our portable gramophone, and suggested that the Head Lama might care to hear some white man's tinned music. Thus it came about that for the first time in its history the religious gloom of the monastery was broken by Messrs. Layton and Johnstone and "Sunny Side Up." The Lamas gazed open mouthed for none of them had ever seen or heard a gramophone before, while the Head Lama forgetting his dignity squatted on the floor and gazed with great curiosity up the horn, seemingly under the impression that Messrs. Layton and Johnstone were the reincarnated voices of two holy English Lamas.

Before we departed our host insisted on our drinking large quantities of marwa. It was a more intoxicating brand than the Head Man's and the suspension bridge seemed to sway unpleasantly to more than one member of the expedition.

It was necessary to establish a provision depot at Khunza, and we decided to leave Tikeram Thapa in charge, for he had displayed considerable aptitude in the making up and paying of accounts. Meanwhile, the Subadar would go down the valley, and arrange for food to be sent up on the backs of local coolies. Such was the procrastination of the Head Man that the porters' food did not arrive until late that night. Fortunately, its quantity exceeded our expectations, and we finally turned in happy in the knowledge that with eight maunds[1] we had sufficient food to feed our porters for at least a week, and could carry on without further delay to the Base Camp.

The majority of the party were away early the next morning *en route* to Kangbachen. It was a perfect morning ; a myriad water jewels gleamed on the pastures of Khunza ; the peaks rose serenely into a stainless blue sky, little puffs of mist eddying enquiringly from their shadowed hollows and meeting with annihilation from a brilliant sun. Wood Johnson remained behind to supervise the transport, and see that all the coolies were evacuated from the village. This last was important, because our men had not unnaturally made the most of their rest at Khunza. If the Sherpa or Bhutia has any vices, the only one I know is predilection to strong liquor at any and every opportunity. But this is not so much a vice as another indication of their childlike disposition, for, like a child, they will eat and drink more than is good for them, without a thought as to the consequences. Unfortunately, they are

[1] One maund=eighty lbs.

liable to become quarrelsome when intoxicated, and at such times, like an Irishman at a race meeting, they pick up the nearest weapon and proceed to run happily amok. Luckily, we had no serious damage done in this way, save for the porter stabbed at Tingling, and Dr. Richter was spared having to stay up all night, as did Mr. Somervell in the last Mount Everest expedition, sewing up scalp wounds.

The march promised to be a long one, but Wood Johnson had the brilliant idea that he and I would ride on yaks. Accordingly, the Head Man was summoned, and told to parade the local yaks.

A yak was produced for Wood Johnson. Never have I seen a more inoffensive looking beast, and with its long hair and mild brown eyes, it might have been a child's toy. Personally, I felt a little doubtful about it, and remarked to Wood Johnson that yak-riding was not numbered among my accomplishments. I also suggested that it would be unpleasant to be thrown over the edge of a mountain path. Wood Johnson's reply was contemptuous. He said : " Walk if you like, *I* am going to ride. No tea planter has ever been known to have been thrown by a yak." Suiting his actions to his words, he vaulted with Wild West abandon on to the back of the yak. Watching him do it, I felt that there was nothing that he did not know about yaks, and that he had ridden them since infancy.

For a few moments the yak stood peacefully. It turned its head and looked at Wood Johnson in a gentle, enquiring, pleading sort of way. Wood Johnson sat nonchalantly, but then with the idea of getting the yak to move, he hit it. The yak *did* move. From a gentle, doormat-like creature it became suddenly possessed of seven devils. It commenced to tear rapidly round and round in circles, and in the middle of one of these circles its back arched bow-like, and Wood Johnson sailed through the air, alighting heavily on his back. He got up. The yak had stopped, it was nibbling a bit of grass, its mild brown eyes contemplating Wood Johnson with a sort of gentle, pitying, reproachful look. In the background stood the Head Man, his face a mask of Eastern passivity.

A few minutes later I was walking along the path, having declined the yak that had been thrust upon me, leaving Wood Johnson swearing that he would ride a yak that day, or perish in the attempt.

It was a delightful walk. The path lay through pine woods and glades yellow with primulas. Pine tops vignetted glimpses of cathedral-like peaks. It was a morning overflowing with jollity and good humour. The little brooks hastening down the hillside towards the river gurgled and chuckled with merriment. Below in its rocky bed the river laughed more ponderously. The Pipes of Pan played softly in the treetops.

The path was so good for the first few miles that I was always half expecting to come across a Beer Garden full of fat men in shorts noisily drinking beer. Certainly, in Switzerland such a sylvan valley would have been so defiled every kilometre or so. There would have been red paint on the trees to guide the tourist from Beer Garden to Beer Garden. There would have been benches for them to rest upon ; the pine woods would have been cut down and laid bare in order that a view should be obtained from these seats, though this would have been unnecessary, for you could have bought picture postcards of the mountains, the coloured ones costing five centimes more than the plain. But here was a Switzerland unspoilt, Alpine beauty on a loftier, nobler scale, its paths traversed only by yaks and their herds.

Presently the path descended into the torrent bed, which is here nearly a quarter of a mile wide. Great boulders, some of them as large as cottages, are piled in it, their rounded smoothness telling of terrific floods that have carried them down like pebbles, rolling them over and over. Once the path passed through a considerable stretch of forest that had been blasted by fire, indicating that long spells of dry weather sometimes occur in these parts.

Some four miles from Khunza the stream was bridged. It would have shortened the day's march to have crossed it, and continued up the western side of the river, but not unnaturally we followed the route marked in Professor Garwood's map. Judging from the stony banks of the torrent, the floor of the valley was composed of an ancient moraine, in which the present stream is busily engaged in carving out a larger and larger channel. We were given an unpleasant example of the speed at which this old moraine is being eroded when crossing a steep slope of loose stones more than one hundred feet high above the river, for boulders, large and small, were constantly falling down this slope, while some blocks of rock, weighing many tons, seemed ready to come down at any moment. It was not a place to linger in.

The path got worse and worse as we ascended, in places it was so overgrown with giant rhododendrons that it had to be cleared with *kukris*. Once we passed an enormous boulder fifty feet high at least, under which there was a cave with a fire blackened roof, and a small patch of cultivated ground outside which suggested that it was possibly inhabited by a hermit, for there was no grazing ground handy for yaks.

Finally, the path emerged from the forest, and we found ourselves confronted by the snout of the Jannu Glacier, which pushes a huge dyke of ice and moraine almost across the valley. Should this glacier advance and dam the streams from the Kangchenjunga Glacier and those of North-eastern Nepal, the consequences might be disastrous for villages lower down the valley.

The glacier snout is fully 1,000 feet high, and it was weary work clambering up its high moraine. Curiously enough, we were all feeling the effects of altitude, though the altitude was less than 15,000 feet. Mr. Freshfield remarked the same feeling of tiredness and listlessness between 14,000 and 17,000 feet. Is it because at this altitude the body undergoes a definite physical change? Acclimatisation would appear not to be gradual, but taking place in stages, though these stages are not necessarily at the same heights for everyone. There should now be enough evidence for physicists to be able to draw some conclusions. Personally, I was in addition still suffering from the effects of my chill, and I could scarcely drag my unwilling body up the wearying slopes of loose stones.

The afternoon mists had long since gathered, and cold, clammy vapours swirled over the drab stone covered hills of the glacier. It might have been difficult in the mist to have found the way over the moraine mounds, but for

Tencheddar who had gone on ahead and built cairns every few yards. At length we reached the other side. The mists lifted, and we gazed down to the flat valley floor where stood the huddled châlets of Kangbachen. Seen thus beneath the mists, this barren and treeless valley, unrelieved by a single shaft of sunlight, appeared inexpressibly dreary. It was a scene that recalled to mind a similar evening in the Pass of Glencoe, when a low roof of mist divorced the world from its good wife the sun, and seemed to oppress me with a sense of gloom, foreboding, and death, so that I hurried through the grim defile, unwilling to linger on a spot rendered ghastly by its association with a fiendish crime.

But as I slithered down the moraine, a light pierced the gloom. A tiny window of blue sky was disclosed, and in it was thrust a summit, red hot from the furnace of the setting sun. It was Jannu, 10,000 feet above me. Even as I watched, the glow faded from it. For a few seconds, before the mists closed in again, it gleamed down palely white, like some nun, disdainful of the world, yet peering curiously upon it from some high window of an unapproachable convent.

There came a sound of yak-bells, a sound, at once homely and calling up memories of Switzerland. Gloom was replaced by cheerfulness. A small boy was driving the yaks back to Kangbachen from the neighbouring pastures. He was crooning a song to himself as he did so, a monotonous little tune of infinite repetitions. At Kangbachen, one day is but a repetition of the last, and music is but an echo of life itself. When he saw me the tune froze on his lips. I did not blame him, for what he saw was a villainous looking fellow, with a stubbly red beard, an old slouch hat, and an aged pair of plus fours. He might have been forgiven for thinking me an apparition, a Mi-go, or some other unpleasant and undesirable character. Having, however, after a critical scrutiny, assured himself that I was in reality, perfectly harmless, he jumped on to a yak, which splashed through the torrent leaving me wondering whether the latter would have suffered Wood Johnson.

I followed, and arriving at the camping site found our servants had mostly got in before us, and my own tent already pitched. I was surprised to see Nemu washing something in the stream. On inspection, it proved to be a dishcloth with which he was wont to clean my plate, knife, and fork. As this dishcloth had already reached saturation point as regards grease and dirt, I wondered by what process of reasoning Nemu had decided to wash it at this particular hour and place, even though he had always a capacity for doing the unexpected. As one of the porters carrying some of my luggage had not arrived, and did not arrive until the next morning, it is possible that the washing of the dishcloth may have been simply to propitiate my probable wrath. The workings of the native mind are curious.

A number of the porters did not get into camp that night. This was largely due to the carousals at Khunza, and their inevitable aftermath of headaches. However, they were quite happy bivouacking out in the woods around fires. Wood Johnson arrived proud and happy, having with characteristic bull-dog determination succeeded in mastering the yak and actually ridden it for the first few miles.

We awoke next morning, April 26, to see Jannu, and its attendant peaks, in all their magnificence. From this side there is no possibility of climbing Jannu, and nothing I have seen is more hopelessly unassailable than the terrific sweep of its northern precipices. The peaks to the south of the Jannu Glacier and to the west of Jannu, though considerably lower, look equally hopeless. They are but acute wedges of rock, the ribs and ridges of which are plastered in ice that has been fashioned by time and weather into mere blades and biscuits. These peaks possess no main ridges, they are upflung indeterminate wedges of extraordinary steepness and complexity, and their ribs and ridges usually end in complete cut-offs, consisting of rock precipices, or hanging glaciers. Looking at such peaks, one is forcibly reminded of the geological newness of the Himalayas as compared to the Alps and other mountain ranges. They have not weathered sufficiently to present the mountaineer with feasible routes. They are still elemental and savage masses spat out by fire and eruption. Time has had little softening influence on them. Restless looking, inhospitable peaks they are, grand to look upon but evil to climb.

Kangbachen is situated at the junction of the Kangchenjunga and Thangchen rivers. The last named flows down a valley, which was formerly traversed by traders between Thibet and Nepal, but owing to political friction between these two countries, it would appear to have fallen into disuse. During what must have been more profitable days, Kangbachen must have flourished, and its inhabitants were most likely of good physique, but with the closing of this trade route, it was cut off from the world. Among so small a population, the evils of intermarriage soon manifested themselves, and at the present time a number of its

NEPALI DWARFS AT KANGBACHEN: THE EVIL EFFECTS OF INTER-MARRIAGE—NOTE THE BABY ON THE WOMAN'S BACK

inhabitants are crétins, not quite the ghastly type as depicted and described in Whymper's *Scrambles Among the Alps*, but nevertheless stunted, dwarf-like and seemingly possessed of but little intelligence. Several of them collected round our camp, and eyed it with curiosity. Two, a man and his wife, were but three feet high, and the woman carried on her back a baby almost as large as herself, which seems to show that physical development is arrested at an early age, judging from this couple, at the age of five or six. By no means all the inhabitants were thus stunted, and several of the children appeared quite normal and healthy.

It was desirable, if possible, to replenish our larder. Wild sheep were known to be in the vicinity, and as local knowledge might be helpful, we engaged an old gentleman, who styled himself the village Shikari.

Before breaking camp, I went a short way up the valley for some photographs. I had not walked more than two hundred yards from the village when, on turning a corner, I found myself face to face with a wild sheep. He was a fine specimen, with a splendid head, and had I taken with me a rifle, I could have shot him easily, as he stood staring at me without moving for more than a minute. But soon fear overcame his astonishment and curiosity. With a tremendous and agile leap he was away up the hillside, and in a few seconds was lost to sight among the grey boulders.

It was impossible to leave Kangbachen early that morning, owing to many of the bivouacking porters not having arrived. The march from Khunza to Kangbachen had been a hard one for them, and it was necessary to give them an off-day, or at least a very short and easy march. At Wood Johnson's suggestion, therefore, it was agreed that they should have no more than three hours marching. This does not sound much, but with full loads of sixty to eighty pounds carried at a height of 15,000 feet, it was enough for tired men. The porters, having been told of this through Lobsang, were perfectly willing to go on.

Passing through the evil-smelling, refuse strewn main street of Kangbachen, we found ourselves on an excellent path running along the western side of the valley. As yet, we had had no glimpse of Kangchenjunga, but some of its snow-clad neighbours were now visible far ahead up the valley. The snow-fields of one peak in particular aroused our ski-ing enthusiasm. The path, in keeping with the usual evil habit of paths in this part of the world, presently petered out into a stony waste formed by the terminal moraine of the Kangchenjunga Glacier. In order to save time we had engaged several locals from Kangbachen who knew every inch of the way to the upper pastures by the side of the glacier where they are accustomed to graze their yak herds. Among these was the local milkman, or Dhudwallah, of Kangbachen whom we had engaged to bring up fresh milk to the Base Camp at regular intervals. This old man, who was to prove distinctly useful to us later on, was a picturesque figure. With his lined, seamed and weather-beaten face, he might have been any age, but his bright eye, and the speed with which he walked up the hillside on broken ground betokened the born hillman. He was *exceptionally* dirty, and exuded a strong odour of yaks and other things, and more than one of us had qualms in entrusting the milk to his care. Also, he expectorated, a vice not common among natives, and expectorated with an accuracy of range which I have seldom seen surpassed. This accuracy we hoped would save the milk.

As in the valley lower down, denudation had worn a deep rift in the old valley floor, but here the slopes of loose, insecure boulders were much larger—in places over a hundred feet high—and the danger of traversing beneath them was proportionately greater. Above these slopes, the mountainside at one place appeared dangerously unstable, owing to an outward dipping strata of rock. Rock falls were obviously not uncommon, and one of many tens of thousands of tons had only recently taken place. For more than a hundred yards we scrambled as quickly as possible over masses of scarred boulders. It was a relief to leave the vicinity, for though the risk of crossing such a place is small, it exists, nevertheless. In view of the communications that must be maintained and constant passage of porters up and down between the Base Camp and Kangbachen, it would perhaps have been better to have gone a longer if more fatiguing way round.

Wood Johnson and I were last, and with such an easy march in prospect, we sat ourselves down on every convenient grassy patch, and lounged in the sun.

In its lower portion, the Kangchenjunga Glacier is so moraine covered that the inexperienced might be forgiven for thinking that there was no glacier there at all. This stony camouflage has, indeed, often led travellers, and even surveyors, into the mistake of thinking that Himalayan Glaciers are much shorter than they actually are. These moraines tell a tale of destruction, and their size alone is eloquent of nature's forces that are ever engaged in pulling down the proud peaks of the Himalayas.

As we ascended the valley, the scenery became wilder and the ridges on either side rose in height. Farther up the valley we caught a glimpse of the Wedge Peak, with its amazing rock and ice precipices. Heavy clouds began to gather, the sun was obscured, the temperature dropped, and a bitter wind charged with snowflakes smote down from the snows.

The porters, believing that the march was to be a short one, had taken things easily, and Wood Johnson and I hurried anxiously on. But there was no sign of the others having stopped to camp. The weather worsened, it began to snow heavily. Evening was drawing on apace as we reached a little group of huts marked in the map as Ramthang, 15,431 feet. There camp had been made. The actual marching time for unladen Europeans had been about five hours.

The day ended with a heavy blizzard. Less than half the porters arrived, the remainder spending the night in the blizzard, many of them without shelter.

The snow lay over six inches deep next morning. Above the huts of Ramthang, the way lay over flat, stony pastures. With the new snow covering the ground, plus the hot sun piercing the dissolving mists, our faces were threatened once again with disaster. In a desperate attempt to save mine from further destruction, I donned a white cotton veil. I found little to recommend in it. It tended to produce a feeling of breathlessness, whilst it was apt to strain the eyes, thereby producing a headache. The latter disadvantage was, however, overcome by cutting holes for the goggles.

Presently, the mountainside became so steep that it

KANGCHENJUNGA FROM THE BASE CAMP

forced us down to the Kangchenjunga Glacier. Himalayan glaciers have usually a convenient trough between the ice and the mountainside. Were it not for this trough, the ascent of most of them would be very tiring as they are usually very bumpy. To give some idea of the moraine covered portion of the Kangchenjunga Glacier, I can only say that it resembles a road-mender's paradise, or a London thoroughfare that has been erupted by pneumatic drills.

It was curious how badly we were going at this moderate altitude. Kurz and I had our lunch together, and we both agreed that though we were only about equal in height to the summit of Mont Blanc, we were feeling the altitude more than we had ever done on that mountain. Possibly, it was because glacier lassitude is at its maximum in a glacier trough. Members of the Everest expeditions remarked the same thing in the trough of the East Rongbuk Glacier.

After lunch we toiled on again. The trough was lost in a maze of moraine mounds, and we toiled over miniature summits, and along stony valleys. Once more, with the coming of afternoon, the sky had clouded. It grew leaden, and a strong, biting wind hinted at another blizzard as we ground up a stony slope. Above was a flat shelf of coarse grass. Here we decided to make the Base Camp.

Wind and snow harassed us as we pitched our tents on the leeward side of a little knoll. It was a dreary welcome. All the porters got in that evening but they exhibited little enthusiasm at so doing, they were too tired. We crept into our sleeping bags with a flurry of snow beating on the tents. As I lay in mine, I thought over the events of the past three weeks. We had met and overcome certain transport difficulties, but these were by no means at an end. Difficulties of the route, and lack of time, had meant working the porters very hard indeed. On the last Everest Expedition they had been given one rest day in every four or five working days, whenever possible or circumstances justified it. Our porters had been marched for the first eleven days without a rest day, including a double march over the Kang La, a march which must have stressed the physique of the fittest of them. The march from Khunza had also been a tiring one, whilst the march from Kangbachen to Ramthang is better forgotten. Would even our best men, the "Tigers," on whom so much depended stand up to the strains and hardships of Kangchenjunga?

CHAPTER X

THE BASE CAMP

The temperature dropped to zero Fahrenheit in the night, and the morning of May 27 dawned cold and clear. As I pulled aside the frozen tent flaps discomfort was forgotten. It was a morning of silver and blue, silver where the rising sun sparkled on the crystals of newly formed snow, blue in the shadows. Opposite the Base Camp, rising in one clean sweep of 8,000 feet above the Kangchenjunga Glacier, was the Wedge Peak. It is appropriately named. Other mountains may be termed fanged, or sugar loafed, but the Wedge Peak seen from the north is nothing more or less than a gigantic elemental wedge. It is a brutal mountain, possessing neither the structural massiveness of Kangchenjunga, nor the fairy-like ethereal remoteness of Siniolchum. The last named mountain has been called the " Embodiment of Inaccessibility," yet who would think of Siniolchum in terms of accessibility or inaccessibility ? it is too beautiful to be defiled by man. The Wedge Peak is different, its very aggressiveness challenges the mountaineer to pit himself against it, yet what mountaineer would accept that challenge ? Even as I watched, it flung an icy gauntlet to the glacier, and the still morning air trembled to the dull boom of an avalanche. Look at it through glasses, if you will, and seek a way up the sliced granite precipices, but when your gaze has passed up these, it will halt aghast upon the ice slopes above. Even imagination will boggle at the thought of having to climb them, at cutting and cutting for hour after hour, and getting—nowhere. Even imagination slips and is cast headlong down the precipices. Turn to the skyline.

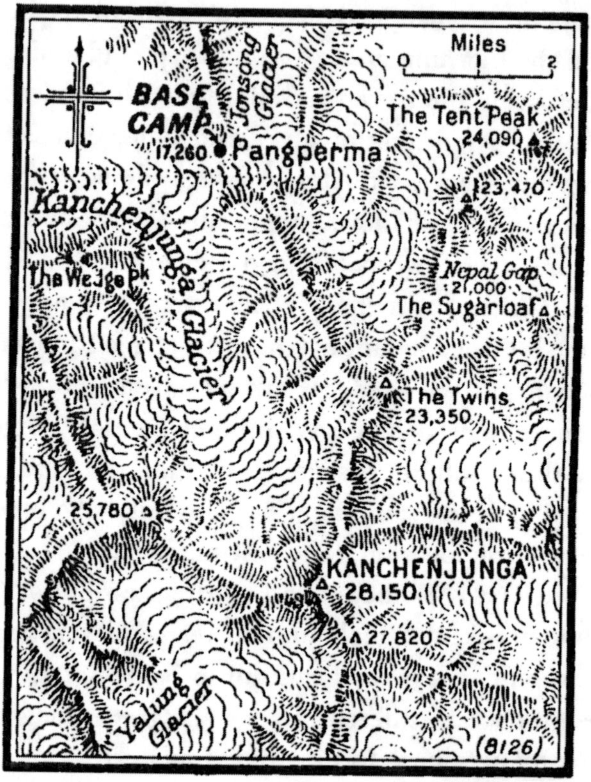

By courtesy of *The Times*

There ice, not ordinary ice, sharp-edged and unbroken, but ice hacked and tortured by the winds, clings to the ridges ; thin flakes of ice through which the sun gleams with a cold fire ; pinnacles of fairy-like delicacy, elegant busts, daring minarets, extravagant mushrooms, a strange goblinesque procession, drunken and tottering, frozen in a downward march.

I tore eye and mind away. Eastwards rose the Twins : peaks more staid and comfortable, not merely elemental and savage, but displaying that dignity and grandeur of the nobly proportioned and adequately buttressed. Framed in this magnificent gateway is Kangchenjunga. It is farther away, but distance enhances rather than detracts from its intrinsic grandeur, so great is its scale. It is built up of icy terraces one above the other. Rock cliffs separate each terrace. Glaciers rest on the terraces, their lower edges forming ice walls anything up to 1,000 feet in height—tiers of fortifications guarding the precipices from assault.

If the difficulties of the Wedge Peak are blatantly obvious, those of Kangchenjunga are less obvious. At first sight, the difficulties of Kangchenjunga on this side fail to impress. Glancing at the apparent angle of the mountain, with its sloping snow-covered terraces, one tended to exclaim involuntarily " It will go ! " But, gradually, as first general impressions were superseded by a closer analysis, optimism was ruthlessly uprooted ; the easy became difficult, the difficult impossible, and the impossible appalling.

The face of the mountain is nearly 10,000 feet in height. Compare this to some of the greatest Alpine mountainsides. The southern side of Mont Blanc rises 11,000 feet from the Val Veni, yet compared to Kangchenjunga, this cannot strictly be called a genuine mountain face, for the lower part of it is grass and forest covered, whilst it is broken up into a series of ribs and ridges radiating from the summit of Mont Blanc. The west face of Kangchenjunga is a mountain wall of almost equal height, rising not from a green valley, but from a glacier, and cloaked in snow and ice. To compare Kangchenjunga with the Alps is like comparing a pygmy with a giant. But it is the only possible form of comparison, and the only one which the reader unacquainted with Himalayan conditions will be able to appreciate. It is a better comparison than to state that it is equal to so many Snowdons piled one on top of another, a comparison which only vaguely suggests height. Height and scale can only be thought of in terms of a more direct comparison.

The view we were looking at was similar to that seen by Mr. Freshfield. His camp, however, was a little farther up the glacier, on the corner he calls Pangperma, where the Jonsong Glacier unites with the Kangchenjunga Glacier. One thing was very clearly impressed upon us at the start, and that was that if such an expert mountaineer as Mr. Freshfield considered that Kangchenjunga offered the greatest chance of attack on this side, it must indeed be a formidable mountain.

There is probably no great peak in the Himalayas on which so much snow is precipitated every year. Strictly speaking, it is not on the main watershed of the Himalayas which separates the arid plateaux of Thibet from the northern states of India, it juts out like a rugged peninsula from the main mountain coast. The Everest group is on the main coastal watershed, and by reason of the intervention between it and the plains of India of many inferior ridges, receives the south-west monsoon after much of its fury has been spent. Such hills as there are separating

THE WEDGE PEAK FROM THE BASE CAMP

Kangchenjunga from the plains are not high enough to break the monsoon, and the mountain, and its satellite peaks, receives almost the full force of it. It would be interesting to know what the annual precipitation is on Kangchenjunga as compared to Mont Blanc. It is possible that the amount of snow that falls on the upper part of the mountain is two or three times greater than that of the Alpine giant. Only evaporation prevents the glaciers of Kangchenjunga from extending far down into the lower valleys.[1]

Mr. Freshfield's analysis of the possibilities of this side of Kangchenjunga was a shrewd one. He considered that the greatest difficulties would be experienced on the lower part of the mountain. Once the upper terrace immediately under the highest summit had been gained, he considered that the final climb would be practicable. "The mountaineer," he writes, "should search to the left between the saddle which connects Kangchenjunga and the Twins." Unfortunately, this saddle is hidden by the shoulder of the Twins, and he did not see it. Had he done so, his report could not have been anything but a pessimistic one, and we, in all probability, would not have planned an attack on this side of the mountain. As it was, we hoped to find a way on to the North Ridge which connects the highest summit to the Twins.

Though Mr. Freshfield considered that the Kangchenjunga Glacier was the most likely line of attack, he was seriously under-estimating the difficulty of the mountain when he wrote that "the peak is hardly likely to be gained with less than two nights spent on its actual face." We

[1] See Appendix: "Glaciology: Snow Conditions, and Avalanches."

estimated that a minimum of six camps would be required. It is necessary to add, however, that when Mr. Freshfield made his journey, little was known about the effects of great altitude upon climbers, or the difficulties of snow, ice, and weather above 23,000 feet. On Everest six camps were established above the Base Camp, and Everest is, technically speaking, an easy mountain. Kangchenjunga is in everything but actual height an infinitely more difficult mountain than Everest.

The Base Camp was separated some five miles from the foot of the western face. At this distance it is difficult to form a just estimate of mountain difficulties and dangers. Also, we were not far enough away to escape the illusive effects of foreshortening, or near enough to be able to see whether or not a route might be found even up the glacier, that was not likely to be swept by avalanches from the huge hanging glaciers of Kangchenjunga and the Twins. Mr. Freshfield found himself in a similar predicament when examining Kangchenjunga, and although of the opinion that the most practicable route existed on this side, wisely committed himself to no definite statement. While admitting that "the whole face of the mountain might be imagined to have been constructed by the Demon of Kangchenjunga for the express purpose of defence against human assault, so skilfully is each comparatively weak spot raked by ice and rock batteries," he was yet not prepared to say Kangchenjunga was not possible. "Perseverance and good judgment may meet their reward."

Our plan, then, boiled down to this, we must reach the North Ridge, if possible, at the lowest point—the col between Kangchenjunga and the Twins. We must climb this ridge, and make our last camp somewhere on the upper of three glacier-covered terraces, about 1,500 feet, beneath the summit under the final rock pyramid.

There was one alternative, to gain the first or lowest terrace, and from it climb directly up the mountain face, past the second to the upper terrace. If the first terrace could be gained, the upper difficulties did not appear to be insuperable. It was by no means certain, however, what sort of climbing would be found on the rocks and ice between the three terraces. Also, in the event of a heavy snowfall, retreat would be impossible, owing to the danger of snow avalanches, for the obvious route between the terraces formed a natural funnel down which they might be expected to sweep. But the chief difficulty would be in gaining the lower terrace. So far as we could see from the Base Camp, the ice wall forming the lower edge of this ran without a break across the mountainside. Only on the extreme right did there seem any possibility of getting up to it, but even if this was accomplished, the mountaineer would be exposed for over a mile to the risk of ice avalanches while traversing to the left towards the second terrace.

Kurz had previously suggested this route, but one glance at the mountain was enough, it was hopelessly and desperately dangerous. Owing to the interposing shoulder of the Twins, we could not tell whether or not the lower ice wall petered out to the left, but the general lie and form of the mountainside suggested that it swept right round to beneath the col between Kangchenjunga and the Twins. A prolonged examination revealed the disturbing truth that there was no chance of successfully attacking any portion of the mountainside visible from the Base Camp, and that any direct assault on the face from the head of the main Kangchenjunga Glacier was foredoomed to failure. The only hope was that held out by Mr. Freshfield, that rocky shelves might lead easily upwards from the Eastern Tributary of the Kangchenjunga Glacier to the col between Kangchenjunga and the Twins. The fate of the expedition would be decided by what lay round the shoulder of the Twins.

It was a fascinating, yet depressing view. It was fascinating to let eye and mind wander over that huge mountain wall, to pass up the granite precipices, and over the defending bastions of gleaming ice, resting finally on the summit where the streamers of wind-blown snow were being torn off by the westerly wind. But it was depressing to think that where the eye might wander so easily, the body could not follow.

The weather had relapsed into a capricious vein. The morning was a beautiful one, and under the warm sun the snow vanished as one looked at it. But towards midday dank, snow-charged clouds began to gather. A cold and hostile wind was signalled, and came rushing up the valley ; snow began to whip across, frothing the ground.

A base camp must be something more than a starting point, it must be the G.H.Q., the hospital, and provision dump of an expedition, and not least, the peaceful haven at which tired and worn-out climbers can recuperate their strength. In fact, the psychological importance of a good base camp to a Himalayan climbing party is great both to Europeans and porters.

KANGCHENJUNGA, SHOWING PROPOSED ROUTE, FROM THE BASE CAMP

The thick, peaty turf lent itself admirably to the building of huts for the porters. Duvanel, Wood Johnson, and myself were the leading surveyors, architects, and builders. A piece of ground was levelled, and the construction of a building that was to serve both as a cookhouse and porters' quarters was commenced.

The methods adopted by Wood Johnson and myself were primitive. Having prised out stones, we piled them on top of each other, filling up the intervening spaces with clods of earth. Duvanel, however, was not so easily pleased. He displayed a praiseworthy and unexpected aptitude for the work. With that meticulous accuracy and attention to detail that are such admirable qualities in the Swiss, he proceeded to build a wall that will stand through all time. Not for him clods of earth piled higgledy piggledy, but stones that fitted into one another ; and corners that *were* corners, and not tottering masses of stones and turf.

At length the task was completed. With a large sheet of canvas stretched from wall to wall as a roof, and with a low front, it presented such a curious pavilion-like appearance that it inspired me to nail to it a notice that read, " M.C.C. Members Only." Then we stood back with a sigh of satisfaction to admire the result of our labours. But the next moment a puff of wind came up the valley, and the whole front of the pavilion, which had been constructed by Wood Johnson and myself, collapsed, leaving Duvanel's wall alone standing. Perhaps our type of architecture was too Gothic in its conception ; Duvanel's was Norman, and so his wall stood. Generations hence, when the descendants of Sir Henry Lunn and Mr. George Lunn run fortnightly tours to the Pangperma Palace Hotel and Kangchenjunga, people on their way to the Helicopterdrome for the ascent of Kangchenjunga will pause and gaze in astonishment on Duvanel's Wall. Honeymoon couples will sit under it in the moonlight, and hoarse-voiced local guides will bellow opinions and lies as to its origin and antiquity.

A day or two after we had dug ourselves in, a large pole was carried up from below Kangbachen and various prayer flags were affixed to it, not only as a propitiation to the gods in the future, but in expiation for our crimes in the past. Most important of these latter was the releasing of sundry devils by the rash removal of stones during our building operations. It appeared that the sole function of stones is to act as a shelter for devils, and by moving stones we had evicted any number of them. As a result they were highly indignant with us, and unless propitiated might wreak dire vengeance upon us.

A special medicinal tent was allotted to Dr. Richter, the atmosphere of which soon became impregnated with the unpleasant and insidious odours associated with the profession of medicine. During the march Richter had trained one of the porters in elementary first-aid. This man had been presented with a Red Cross armlet, the psychological effect of which, combined with Richter's teaching, had produced such an excellent effect, that he had become quite expert in the art of applying iodine and bandaging.

Soon after we arrived at the Base Camp we were submitted to the usual tests of breath-holding, pulse rate, lung pressure and capacity, etc. Though the height was but 16,500 feet, I found that I was still unacclimatised, and could only hold my breath for twenty-five seconds. It is interesting to note that three weeks later, at a height of 20,000 feet, I was able to manage thirty-five seconds.

Acclimatisation is, of course, one of the most important factors in high Himalayan climbing. In the short season available for attempting peaks such as Kangchenjunga and Everest, it is very desirable that the climber should become acclimatised as quickly as possible. Whether a climber climbs better after he has become quickly acclimatised or slowly acclimatised is doubtful. Experience on Everest would seem to show that the likeliest man to reach the summit is not the man who acclimatises quickly early on in the expedition, but the man who acclimatises so slowly that he is at his best towards the end of the expedition. The experience of Mr. Odell on the last Everest Expedition affords an interesting example of a man who acclimatised so slowly that he was not at his best until nearly the end of the expedition, at which stage he was fitter than those who acclimatised earlier.

Against slow acclimatisation on Everest and Kangchenjunga must always be set the all important factor of time. We could not reasonably expect more than a month of good weather in which to attempt Kangchenjunga, and even this short period might well be curtailed by the early breaking of the monsoon.

It was with this in mind that Dr. Richter had devised two methods which he hoped would aid the climbers in acclimatising quickly. The first was by withdrawing 200 cubic centimetres of blood from each climber. The object of this was to lessen the blood pressure, in order to counteract to some extent the low pressure of the atmosphere.

Mountain sickness (lack of acclimatisation) is due not only to lack of sufficient oxygen in the air, but to the low pressure of the atmosphere as compared to that to which the body is accustomed normally. This low pressure reacts unfavourably on the blood and nervous centres, producing headaches, general lassitude, and in some cases, nausea.

These ill effects are automatically countered by the body, which increases the number of hæmoglobins in the red corpuscles of the blood. So far as it is known, it is only by increasing the number of these hæmoglobins that the body is able to adapt itself to the low pressure and lack of oxygen at high altitudes. It was difficult, therefore, to see what practical use withdrawal of blood could be. For one thing, taking such a large quantity of blood away must inevitably result in a temporary weakening of the body, and therefore the climber's powers. Also, it is well known that the body quickly remakes and replaces any blood that has been lost. At all events, I refused to part with my blood, and so, too, did the rest of the party with the exception of Professor Dyhrenfurth and Duvanel. The first, no doubt, through a sense of duty towards the scientific objects of the expedition, and the latter because he seemed to like it. The remaining members withstood the doctor's vampirish entreaties for their blood.

There was more to be said for the second experiment. The state of an acclimatised body at a high altitude closely resembles the effect of anæmia at a normal altitude. Anæmia is a poverty of blood due to the lack of red corpuscles and hæmoglobins, but it has been found that ordinary liver eaten by the patient has the effect of increasing these, and thereby the quantity of blood. The mountaineer at a high altitude suffers not so much from poverty of blood, but from a lack of the essential hæmoglobins. It was hoped that eating a concentrated liver preparation would have the effect of increasing these hæmoglobins, and hastening acclimatisation. High altitude also induces wastage of the body, so that anything which would strengthen the blood is advantageous. Therefore, each climber was presented with a bottle filled with tablets of concentrated liver, three of which had to be taken three times a day. I regret to say that being somewhat absent-minded by nature, I took mine for only two days, after which I usually forgot to take them at all. Sometimes, however, I would find the bottle in my pocket, or at the bottom of my rucksack, and I would then swallow a large number of tablets at once in an endeavour to make up for what I had forgotten. Such irregularities are to be deplored, and it is to be feared that the liver tablets were not so beneficial as they might have been had I taken them more regularly. Schneider was, however, meticulous as to taking them, and I used to see him rolling his ration meditatively round his tongue, instead of swallowing them as per instructions, after meals.

In the evening we would gather in the mess tent, where, muffled up to the ears in sweaters, we would eat our dinner and endeavour to preserve some semblance of cheerfulness while wind and snow beat without. In order to delude ourselves into thinking that we were really enjoying life a porter would be told off every evening to work the gramophone, which he would keep in full blast for the duration of the meal. Once or twice the temperature was so low that it froze up the vitals of the gramophone, which after slowing down into a dismal dirge, would finally stop altogether with a protesting groan.

It was necessary to remain at the Base Camp some days in order to rest the porters, and prepare the plan of campaign. As yet, owing to the non-arrival of the second and third parties, we were still without much necessary equipment, and what news there was as to the state of the transport was not altogether satisfactory. In fact it seemed probable that the delay to Colonel Tobin's bandobast on the Kang La, which had been caused by bad weather and lack of porters, owing to desertions from our party and our consequent inability to send back sufficient help, might result in a serious shortage of food. It was, therefore, decided to slaughter a yak which had been sent up from Kangbachen. I felt sorry for this yak, for it was a depressed looking beast, and its sad brown eyes seemed always to follow us about piteously, as though aware of its impending fate. Wood Johnson was its executioner, and the fell deed was done with Professor Dyhrenfurth's rifle. Although Wood Johnson tried on several occasions to get near to wild sheep it must be confessed that this was the only useful rifle shooting accomplished, unless the assassination of a tame pigeon at Khunza is included.

On April 29, we decided to explore two peaks, both of about 20,000 feet, to the north of the Base Camp. It was arranged that Wieland should tackle one, and Wood Johnson and myself the other. The weather was good when Wood Johnson and I set off up the stony moraine slopes above the Base Camp. From the crest we had an excellent view of our objective, a cone-like peak with a sharp summit of snow, which formed the culminating point of a long rock ridge set at a comparatively easy angle.

We halted for some minutes in the sun to enjoy the glorious panorama of Kangchenjunga and its neighbouring peaks and glaciers. From the Tent Peak to the Wedge Peak nothing was hidden, save only the two upper tributaries of the Kangchenjunga Glacier, and in particular, the bay of the Eastern Tributary Glacier and the slopes to the North Ridge, on the feasibility of which so much depended. The upper ridges were smoking with blown snow, telling of a fierce westerly wind. One silvery banner from the crest of Kangchenjunga streamed far out against the blue sky. Since we had arrived at the Base Camp we had not seen the mountain unassailed by wind. Was it always so, we wondered. The chances of climbing the North Ridge in the face of such a relentless opponent would be nil.

Himalayan peaks are cruel. The Alps are the " Playground of Europe," the Himalayas the Playground of the gods. The Alps provide physical and æsthetical enjoyment, the Himalayas, the fiercer joys of achievement. In the Alps, when you have climbed a mountain, you want to climb it by other routes, to explore every ridge, tramp every glacier, to make a friend of it. You get to know its moods, learn to appreciate its weather vagaries. There is nothing friendly about a Himalayan peak. You feel that it is coldly hostile, that it resents intrusion. It allows no latitude, it seizes upon the slightest mistake. It will kill you if it can. And so if you climb it, you climb it only to conquer it for the sake of achievement. To do so you may have to mortify the flesh, steeling yourself to overcome bodily and mental weariness. When you have reached its summit, you have finished with it. There is no desire to renew acquaintances, or make a friend of Himalayan peaks, they resent familiarity. And always they will kill you—if they can.

How is it that the mountaineer should gain such an impression? Is it merely the height, the scale, the distance from civilisation, the weather, the clearness of the atmosphere, the unknown? Theoretically, I suppose, a combination of all these things. Actually, you cannot help feeling that these peaks are imbued with a fanatical hatred towards the intruder. They are as conservative in their attitude towards modernity and progress as the humans who dwell in the valleys beneath them.

We continued on our way, passing under the snout of a small glacier that descends from the north-west slopes of the Cone Peak, as we subsequently called it. This glacier is very broken, yet there were a few crevasses in it. The ice, which is curiously stratified, was hummocked and pinnacled, for its surface had been raised and broken by internal pressure. There were few actual crevasses, and many of the ice pinnacles were markedly bent. In the Alps such bending would be impossible without a fracture, and one is led to the conclusion that Himalayan ice is more plastic than Alpine ice. This plasticity is doubtless due to an enormous range of temperature.[1]

Toiling up a slope of scree, we found ourselves on the crest of an easy rounded ridge of loose stones, leading upwards towards the summit. We began to experience wind,

[1] See Appendix: "Glaciology: Snow Conditions and Avalanches."

and worse still, the weather began to cloud up for the usual afternoon snowstorm.

Wood Johnson and our two servants, Ondi and Nemu, whom we had taken with us, were going slowly, but my own progress was funereal. Though we were but 18,000 feet or so above sea level, I was feeling the height severely. Every step was an effort, and every flat stone suggested a rest.

Snowflakes began to whip across, stinging our cheeks with their icy particles. Grey mist rags writhed over the ridge. We donned our spare clothing and gloves, and with heads bowed to the blast, struggled on.

The hog-backed ridge narrowed to a nearly horizontal ice ridge, abutting against the summit cone of rock and ice, which rose steeply for perhaps 200 feet. With crampons it would have been an easy matter to have walked along the crest, or on one side of this ice ridge, but without them we had to cut steps. The ridge was not possible on the side sheltered from the wind, and the crest bore the brunt of its fury. We were forced, therefore, to cut along the exposed side, which consisted of steep unbroken ice slopes falling to the glacier beneath.

We tied on the rope, and leaving the porters in a sheltered place under some boulders, advanced to the attack. There was nothing to break the cruel force of the wind. But if it was cruel, it possessed one good attribute, it completely banished my lassitude. I felt fit for anything, fit enough to cut steps for hours in the ice.

I cut steps as quickly as possible, until the whole length of rope between us was out. It was Wood Johnson's first experience of ice-work, but he is an excellent rock climber and his sure-footedness precluded a slip. The wind was no longer blowing steadily, it was coming in gusts of increasing strength that threatened to blow us from our steps. Our clothes were becoming sheeted in ice, and our fingers were rapidly losing sensation. Retreat was inevitable. With axe picks driven well in at every step, we slowly descended the ice to the friendly rocks. According to an aneroid, we had reached a height of 20,000 feet, about 150 feet from the summit.

Our servants were glad to see us back, for sheltered from the wind as they were, it had nevertheless been a chilly wait for them. After slow movement on the ice, it was a relief to feel the blood circulating again in tingling finger-tips. We rattled down the easy ridge. It had been an interesting experience. If this wind at 20,000 feet had been sufficiently strong and cold to turn us back, what would such a wind be like on the summit ridge of Kangchenjunga?

We arrived back in camp to find that Hannah and his porters had come up that day. Wieland had been more successful than us. His peak had proved a lower and easier one, and he had reached the top without difficulty, and descended before the storm broke. As this peak was to the west of ours, he had been able to look into the Eastern Tributary of the Kangchenjunga Glacier, but his report of what he had seen was not encouraging. There were no easy rock shelves leading to the North Ridge. A cirque of sheer cliffs and hanging glaciers walled in the head of the glacier, apparently barring approach to the North Ridge.

With the arrival of Hannah and much of the vital equipment necessary for establishing the high camps, Professor Dyhrenfurth decided to start on the morrow, June 1. He hoped to establish camps One and Two. The route to the North Ridge would have to wait until a closer inspection would enable us to estimate its difficulties and dangers.

The weather would have to improve a lot. At present, it was still wintry. Only with its aid would Kangchenjunga be climbed.

That evening, Wood Johnson harangued the porters. He said, " You have had a hard time, you will have a much harder time, and you will be faced with privations and dangers. Let any man who wants go back to Darjeeling." None did. They replied with burst after burst of cheers.

CHAPTER XI

THE FIRST ATTEMPT: THE GREAT ICE WALL

We left the next morning, May 1, in good weather. The party consisted of Professor Dyhrenfurth, Kurz, Wieland, Duvanel, Wood Johnson, and myself. Hoerlin, Schneider and Dr. Richter were to follow in a few days ; the first two were not fit, and had been bothered by stomach trouble, whilst Richter was suffering from a strained heart. Hannah also was to follow in a day or so, and remain in charge of Camp One.

Whether or not the rest at the Base Camp had been as beneficial to the health of the party as had been hoped was doubtful. It is a curious fact that during the whole expedition we never felt really fit at the Base Camp. Probably, it was not so much the altitude as the damp and boggy ground on which it had been pitched, and the relentless winds and snowstorms that chilled us every afternoon. At all events, we were glad to leave it, and get to grips with our opponent.

In order to get on to the middle of the glacier, we had to thread our way between and over moraine mounds ; the route had, however, been facilitated by the erection of cairns the previous day by Schneider and Kurz, who had visited the glacier for mapping purposes.

For a considerable distance the gradient of the Kangchenjunga Glacier is a gentle one, and in five miles it does not rise more than 1,500 feet. The day before, Wood Johnson and I had noted a snowy corridor running up the middle of the glacier, which seemed to offer an easy routes and this we gained after negotiating the maze of moraines.

As we marched on up the glacier, the mountain wall, began gradually to shut us in on either hand. We were passing through the portals of an immense gateway into another world. Kangchenjunga gained in magnificence as we approached the foot of its northern face. From the Base Camp the edges of its hanging glaciers had looked but a few feet high, but now we began to appreciate their real scale—huge walls of ice hundreds of feet in height. Once there came the sound of an avalanche from the icy recesses of the great mountain ; its deep growl echoing menacingly from peak to peak seemed to threaten us for our invasion of these solitudes.

The corridor, at first wide, became a narrow trough through ice hummocks. The sun poured down upon us a fierce heat in which the snow became more abominable every hour. Once again we experienced the energy sapping effects of glacier lassitude.

Progress was slow, but there was no need for hurry, save at one place, where we were forced by the roughness of the glacier under the cliffs of the Twins. Here, the glacier was liable to be swept occasionally by ice avalanches discharged from a hanging glacier and we hurried across a level stretch which was strewn with fallen ice blocks.

The way became rougher. Presently, there came into view an unknown mountain to the west, about 23,000 feet high, situated between the Wedge Peak and the North-west Ridge of Kangchenjunga, on the watershed of the western tributary of the Kangchenjunga Glacier and the Ramthang Glacier. Between it and the Wedge Peak a steep glacier flows downwards to join the main ice stream of the Kangchenjunga Glacier. It is a serene and stately mountain, with icy ridges converging to a summit of

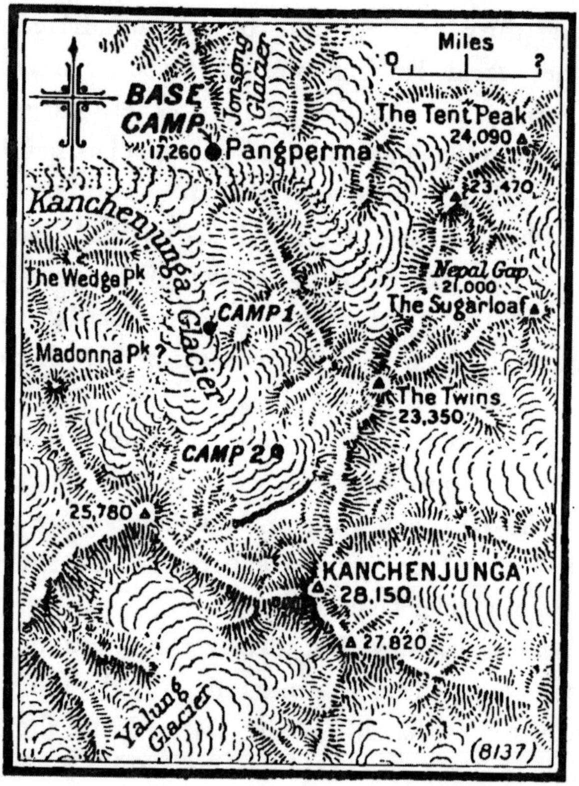

By courtesy of *The Times*

purest snow. So impressed were we by its beauty, that we named it the Madonna Peak. This name was, however, subsequently changed by Professor Dyhrenfurth to Ramthang Peak.

The Indian Survey authorities have wisely decided to

adhere to native nomenclature in the Himalayas. They are justified in doing so by the fate that has overtaken the peaks of the American and Canadian Rockies, where anyone with any pretensions to fame, and sometimes none at all save to be the first to tread a summit, has dubbed his name (or it has been dubbed by admirers) to inoffensive mountain tops. Only in very exceptional cases is there any justification for this. Among these may be mentioned the case of a member of the Alpine Club, who, hearing that a peak had been named after him, considered it his duty to make the first ascent.[1]

We were anxious to see round the corner of the Twins, and up the Eastern Tributary Glacier to the North Ridge, but soon we saw that the glacier dropped so steeply above its junction with the main ice stream of the Kangchenjunga Glacier that no view would be obtained until we had mounted some distance up it.

The first object was to find a suitable place for Camp One. It was necessary to camp out of range of ice avalanches from the Twins and Kangchenjunga. The most level site for a camp was under the cliffs of the Twins, but as this was by no means safe, we were forced to pitch camp some way out on the glacier itself. Here the glacier was very rough, and there were several crevasses near the camp artfully concealed by snow. Professor Dyhrenfurth fell into one of them up to the waist. It was a deep one, and he was unroped. Had all the snow-bridge given way, the odds are he would have been killed.

A few yards from the camp we discovered another deep crevasse running in the direction of the camp itself.

[1] Mr. L. S. Amery.

Determined probing, however, failed to reveal any crevasse actually under the camp, so that there seemed reasonable hope that we and our tents would not disappear into the bowels of the glacier in the middle of the night.

We were a happy party in camp that evening. Happier than we had ever been at the Base Camp. The feeling of lassitude so often experienced at the Base Camp had disappeared ; we felt fitter and stronger. Most important of all, we were sheltered by the Ramthang and Wedge Peaks from the abominable afternoon winds. Only an occasional puff stirred along the snowy surface of the glacier. Higher it was different. Far above, the icy bastions of Kangchenjunga jutting defiantly out into space thousands of feet above our heads like the prows of some ghostly mid-aerial fleet, were being lashed by tortuous columns of snow spray. Thin shreds and sinuous tendrils of blown snow writhed from the crest of the North Ridge. Sometimes they would rise steadily, like smoke from a factory chimney on a calm day, the next moment they would be captured by the vortex of a local whirlwind, and drawn upwards convulsively, to vanish into the deepening purple of the evening sky.

For once the weather was kind to us. The evening snowstorm was a mild, desultory affair, lacking its usual venom. The sun gleamed through the gently falling snow, illuminating its crystals, until they gleamed like showers of diamonds distributed by the prodigal hands of the mountain fairies. At sunset, the clouds rolled back, leaving only light grey skirts of mist that clung to the knees of the peaks. The peaks took to themselves the splendours of evening, and the snow around us gleamed opalescently with their reflected glories. We stood outside our tents entranced, and mindless of the cold. Blue deepened to purple, purple to ink-pot. Stars glittered frostily ; the low mists dissolved into the night. It was very silent, yet not quite silent. From somewhere came a sound, more felt than heard, like the distant surge of Atlantic breakers heard from far inland—the wind.

There was no mess tent, and we ate our dinner lying in our sleeping bags. A candle placed on my tin-box served to illuminate my own abode. At regular intervals the honest face of Nemu, with its habitual slightly worried expression, thrust itself between the flaps, and two horny hands would press upon me such delicacies as the cook thought fit to inflict upon us. These included portions of the yak Wood Johnson had shot, but I found them only suitable to sharpen a knife on for the next course.

I awoke next morning to see the sun stealing across the glacier, pushing before it the cold shadow of the Twins. With a short march in prospect, nothing was to be gained by starting until we were thoroughly warmed up. During the expedition, we did not once have occasion to leave a high camp before the sun had risen. To have done so on many occasions would have been to have courted frost-bite, and it was doubtful whether the porters could have been induced to start until the life-giving rays of the sun had cheered them.

Professor Dyhrenfurth had brought with him a small horn, of a pattern not unlike those used on foreign railways as a signal for the train to start. With this horn he was wont to arouse the camp in the morning. In theory, the three blasts which he used to blow on it were the signal for climbers and porters to tear themselves from their sleeping bags. In practice, Wood Johnson and I would, if it happened to wake us, turn over with a sleepy curse and enjoy another forty winks. Finally, Wood Johnson managed to steal it, but shortly afterwards another one was produced. However admirable the intention, there is something abhorrent in being awoken thus on a mountainside in the morning. A more human method is for the leader himself to go round to the tents shouting into each one, " Get up, you lazy louts," or some such appropriate remark.

Leaving Camp One, we set out up the glacier, and soon reached the foot of the Eastern Tributary Glacier, which rises steeply from the main Kangchenjunga Glacier for some distance. Under the cliffs of Kangchenjunga it is considerably broken, and pours over a low rock cliff, down which the unstable ice topples hourly with thunderous roars. Under the cliffs of the Twins it was less broken, and extensively moraine covered, and we mounted it without difficulty.

Wieland and I were leading. Anxious to see the head of the glacier, and solve the problem that had been exercising our minds, we climbed as fast as possible. The going was simple, nothing worse than an occasional step to chop out. The slope eased off, and we stepped on to a level terrace of snow.

Leaning on our ice-axes, we regained our breath, gazing upwards at the same time. What we saw was doubly disappointing. Before us, the glacier rose in unbroken snow slopes set at a moderate angle, yet steep enough to obscure all but the crest of the ridge connecting Kangchenjunga to the Twins—the ridge we must gain. But what *was* visible was very unpromising. Here were no easy rock shelves and snow slopes, but sheer ice-armoured precipices. Only the face directly beneath the highest summit of Kangchenjunga seemed to offer any hope. If the lower terrace could be reached, it might be possible to establish a camp there, traverse to the left, and climb a slope of 1,500 to 2,000 feet to the crest of the North Ridge. The slopes leading upwards from the end of the terrace did not seem so excessively steep as those dropping directly from the North Ridge to the glacier. Yet, we were looking up and foreshortening had to be taken into account. At all events, one could say offhand, the climbing would be decidedly difficult.

But how to reach the terrace ? Did the ice wall defend its whole length ? If so, what was the alternative ? We were in a horseshoe of mountains. From Kangchenjunga on the east to the Twins on the west, the precipices swept round without a break. The sole alternative to attacking the North Ridge via the terrace was to retreat. Discussions and opinions were unnecessary. Optimism's flower was already withered as we trudged up the snow slopes.

The glacier here forms a trough into which the sun was beating with piercing intensity. To have gone up its centre would have meant lassitude in its most disagreeable form. On those concave snow slopes we would be like flies in the middle of a burning glass. Accordingly, we traversed the northern slopes of the trough. Even on these the heat was bad enough, but it was relieved now and again by puffs of cold wind. We came to crevasses, only occasional ones, but cunningly concealed in places, with only a slight ripple or depression in the snow to indicate their presence, and once or twice, not even that. The snow was soft, and stamping a trail was hard work. We took turns at it ; a quarter of an hour at a time was enough.

Already we were beginning to learn something of the secret that makes for good uphill walking at high altitudes ; it is rhythm. Heart and lungs must keep in time with the movements of the legs. Each upward step must synchronise with the breathing. It does not matter how many breaths are taken to each step, as long as always the same number are taken. Once let this synchronisation fail, and it is necessary to stop and puff. The secret of maintaining it is a pace not varying by a fraction of a second in the interval of time elapsing between each step. To begin with, it is necessary to concentrate on the maintaining of this rhythm, but soon it becomes automatic. This is one reason why ground calling for a variety of pace is much more tiring to negotiate at a high altitude than ground on which the same pace can be kept up continuously. Above 20,000 feet it is much easier to ascend a snow slope in good condition than the easiest rocks, provided, of course, steps do not have to be kicked or cut.

As we rose, we were able to gaze up the Western Tributary Glacier. Like the Eastern Tributary Glacier, it falls in a steep ice-fall in its lower portion, but above the ice-fall unbroken snow-fields rise gently to a low col separating the Ramthang Peak from the Kangbachen summit of Kangchenjunga. The Ramthang Peak itself rises gracefully, but seen from this direction the Wedge Peak loses something of its grandeur.

Our pace was painfully slow, for quite apart from rhythm, or the lack of it, we were by no means acclimatised. Like the lower slope, the one we were on eased off on to an almost level terrace. Above the terrace the glacier rose again, but this time it was broken into an ice-fall which appeared to extend its whole width. We decided to camp on the terrace, for there seemed little chance of getting through the ice-fall the same day, and the porters, like us, were making heavy weather of it in the soft snow under the broiling sun.

Now at last we could see the whole of the face separating the North Ridge from the Eastern Tributary Glacier. Our hearts—I know that mine did—sank, as we gazed at it. There was no question of climbing it. The only possibility, if "possibility" it can be called, was directly over the ice wall, under the face of Kangchenjunga. This runs as a clean-cut barrier 600–800 feet high for some three miles across the face of the mountain, but under the North Ridge it is broken up into a series of ice waves and subsidiary walls. At one place a steep shelf sloped upwards from left to right, but above it towered a huge mass of unstable pinnacles that were liable to fall at any moment and sweep the shelf from end to end with their débris. Indeed débris lying on the shelf and below it showed that such falls were a frequent occurrence. Even had the shelf offered an easy climb, the steep ice of its lower and most dangerous portion would necessitate a staircase being cut. The sole remaining "possibility" was directly over the ice wall, where it was most broken, but I must confess that until it was pointed out to me as such I had not given it a second thought.

It was a pleasant spot for a camp. The sun lingered long upon us. The only drawback to it was the fact that there were one or two concealed crevasses in the vicinity, but we gave the porters strict orders not to go more than a yard or two from the tents.

Afternoon merged into evening, and the sun fought its daily battle with grey snow clouds. The cook was preparing the evening meal, and tempting odours were being wafted across the snow as, anxious to obtain some photographs, I strolled down the track for a short distance. Far beneath, the last half-dozen porters under the charge of Wood Johnson were toiling up the snow slopes. How small they looked, how painfully slow their progress. They halted ; I heard a faint shout. Doubtless they were glad to be within sight of camp. Now they were moving again. I heard another shout, and then another ; not so much a shout, as a curious high-pitched cry. This immediately struck me as strange. Men going uphill at nearly 20,000 feet do not waste their hard-won breath in shouting. There came a whole series of these cries. They seemed to come from a distance of a mile or so away, in the direction of the cliffs of the Twins. But between me and these cliffs the snow stretched unbroken, with no sign of any living thing on them. And still these strangely insistent, almost eerie, cries came.

Wieland joined me, and we both listened. An eagle perhaps ? Wood Johnson approached, and calling down we asked him if he heard them too. " Perhaps it is a Mi-go," he said, half jokingly, and then asked if Ondi, his servant, had arrived. I went back to the camp. Yes, Ondi had arrived, said the others. But where was he now ? There was no sign of him. At that the truth began to dawn upon us and Wieland and I hurried across the snow in the direction of the cries. Soon we came across a single track, coming from the camp ; there were no returning footmarks. We followed it cautiously. After a few yards the track ended in a small hole, not more than two feet across. Approaching it, we gazed down between the jaws of a crevasse. From the depths came a moan and a faint despairing cry.

We hastened back to camp. While Wieland returned with ropes and porters, I strapped on crampons in order to be ready to go down, if necessary. By the time I returned, a rope had been lowered. Fortunately, Ondi still retained sufficient presence of mind and strength to tie himself to it. With half a dozen sturdy porters hauling on the rope, he was soon dragged out. We quickly ascertained that he had no bones broken, but he had been badly bruised, his back and hands were skinned and bleeding, and he was half frozen and suffering severely from shock. He had fallen fully thirty feet before wedging between the walls of the crevasse, and had been down there for fully two hours. His extremities were white and numb, but we managed to prevent frostbite by massaging them. So severely was he suffering from shock, that, in the absence of Dr. Richter, I took upon myself the responsibility of giving him a double dose of belladonna. Whether or not this was the right treatment I do not know ; at all events, it sent him to sleep in a few minutes, and when he woke up next morning, he was much better and no longer suffering from the physical effects of shock.

It must have been a terrible experience for him, and many men less tough would most likely have succumbed. The next day he was sent down to the Base Camp, but after two days there he insisted on returning. Such was the spirit of the man. But the accident had a lasting effect on him. Prior to it he had been an excellent servant in every way, after it he became morose and sullen, dirty and careless in his work. It was only towards the end of the expedition that he began to recover something of his old spirit. I hope that by now he has completely recovered from his terrible experience.

Night fell, accompanied by the usual snow flurry, but the weather next morning was perfect. Unfortunately, Kurz, who had been afflicted with earache and general altitude debility which had rendered him unable to sleep, decided to return to the Base Camp. This he did for a large part of the way on ski. Professor Dyhrenfurth, also, was not feeling well enough to continue. This left only Wieland, Wood Johnson, and myself.

As Professor Dyhrenfurth was anxious to attack the ice wall, it was necessary to establish a camp at the head of the glacier. It was, therefore, arranged that a day should be spent in working out a route through the ice-fall to the upper plateau of the glacier. With this end in view we set off in two parties, Wood Johnson and myself on the leading rope, with Wieland and a porter carrying a ciné camera on the second.

Traversing first of all towards the cliffs of Kangchenjunga, we turned up a snowy corridor. The difficulties and complexities of the ice-fall proved far greater than they had appeared from a distance. First came a short, steep wall of ice. This ice, like all ice we subsequently encountered on Kangchenjunga, was of a rubber-like toughness, and many blows of the ice-axe were needed to fashion a step. The work served to remind us once again that we were by

THE RESCUE OF ONDI

no means acclimatised to even this moderate altitude, 19,500 feet, and I felt my icemanship lacking in vim as Wieland, with a wicked grin, proceeded to post himself on a snowy hump and film my efforts.

Above this pitch we found ourselves on the lower lip of a huge crevasse, which appeared to traverse the whole width of the ice-fall. It was a formidable moat, several yards wide and not bridged by a single tongue of snow. Even supposing we got across it, it was by no means the only difficulty, for there were wider crevasses beyond equally formidable. As there was no possibility of crossing it on the left, I told Wood Johnson to anchor himself, whilst I explored as far as the rope would allow me to the right. The ice lip I was on writhed upwards sneeringly. There seemed little object in going on, but I gingerly ascended to its delicate crest. It was a happy move; for but a short distance farther did the ice-fall continue towards Kangchenjunga, before becoming lost in smooth snow-slopes offering no difficulty whatever, which led easily up to the plateau above.

We retraced our steps, and passing along the foot of the ice-fall, gained these snow slopes. There was certainly no difficulty in circumventing the ice-fall by this route, and a gentle walk took us quickly uphill. It was, however, not quite certain whether these slopes were entirely free from danger. Though we were separated by nearly half a mile of level snow-field from the foot of Kangchenjunga, the huge masses of hanging glaciers suspended on the great face of the mountain told of forces held in check which if released must result in avalanches of cataclysmic dimensions which might well sweep the whole breadth of the snow-field. Indeed, one solitary block of ice lying near at hand and projecting through the newly fallen snow seemed to make this unpleasant possibility very real.

The reader may think that I am making much of the problematical, but one of the first lessons the Himalayan mountaineer learns is that exceptional forms of danger are more likely to encompass his disaster than ordinary forms of danger. In the Alps accidents usually occur through ordinary causes and neglect of ordinary rules. There is a certain mediocrity in Alpine dangers; the mountaineer knows that in one place he may be in danger from falling ice or stones, and in another he is not. In a word, the Alps are a well regulated mountain range. They have passed through so many geological epochs that they have acquired a certain staidness of demeanour. The Himalayas are different, they are not entirely divorced from their catastrophic epoch. Their scale is so vast, their weather conditions so different that they are still capable of producing the exceptional. Thus, I think it may truly be said that until the mountaineer has learnt to appreciate the huge scale of things and the catastrophic size of ice avalanches his chances of annihilation are infinitely greater than on the most difficult Alpine climbs.

Tacking up the snow slopes, we reached the little plateau above the ice-fall. Having satisfied ourselves that it was the obvious site for a camp we continued on up towards the ice wall. We had not gone far before we came across more artfully concealed crevasses. Wood Johnson went through into one, but I had him so tightly on a rope that I was able to jerk him outwards and backwards almost at the same instant. The snow was soft and fatiguing, and we decided that it would be best to return and save our strength for the morrow.

We descended quickly, and in less than an hour were back in camp. We had done what we had set out to do—to discover a camping site as high up the glacier as possible. We had also ascertained that there was no possible way to the North Ridge save over the ice wall and the lower terrace.

That night I was awakened several times by the sound of great ice avalanches. Heard thus, through the darkness, there was something indescribably menacing in their deep growls. It was terrifying to be disturbed from sleep in this way ; one felt pitifully small and helpless amid these vast and wrathful mountains. The porters felt something of the same, but in a different way. In the avalanche they heard the voices of the gods, in the moan of the night wind the jeering of the Snow Men. Once I heard a mutter from their tent, a low intonation rising and falling—they were praying.

The morning of May 4 was warm, sunny, and windless. Professor Dyhrenfurth was not well, he was suffering from severe high altitude throat, and could only speak in a whisper. These throats are induced by the dryness of the air, and the necessity for breathing through the mouth. The throat becomes painful and congested. At its best it is a nasty infliction, and reduces climbing efficiency considerably ; at its worst, it may be really serious. On Everest, Mr. Somervell's throat became so congested that he could scarcely breathe, and had he not been able to cough away the obstructing matter he might have been suffocated.

Professor Dyhrenfurth decided to return to the Base

Camp. Before leaving he gave us his instructions. As the route over the ice wall was the only way to the North Ridge offering any hope, we were to make every effort to overcome it. We were to establish a camp on the terrace, and attack the slopes above it leading to the North Ridge. Once on the latter, there were two routes worthy of consideration to the upper terrace immediately beneath the final rock pyramid. The first lay directly up the ridge. Immediately below the terrace, however, which at its junction with the ridge formed an extensive scree shelf, the ridge rose in an abrupt step which looked far from easy. The other route left the ridge below the step in favour of steep, crevasse riven slopes on the east face overlooking the Zemu Glacier. By crossing these, the upper and easy portion of the great rib attempted by the Munich party would be reached, and this followed to the terrace above the step. This route possessed the advantage of being on the leeward side of the mountain, and not exposed to the terrible west wind that constantly harries the North Ridge. On the other hand, the possibility of avalanches was not to be disregarded on this traverse, and the loose snow blowing over and off the North Ridge might well form wind slabs[1] of the most dangerous nature. If this was so, it would be best to keep to the crest of the ridge, but the great step below the upper terrace suggested something more than ordinary rock climbing difficulties, and by "ordinary," I mean the difficulties that a mountaineer may be expected to tackle with some degree of confidence at a height of 26,000 feet.

[1] The most treacherous form of avalanche : often found in the Alps during the winter months. The whole slope of wind-compacted snow comes away in a solid slab, which breaks up into a cataract of hard snow blocks.

THE RAMTHANG AND WEDGE PEAKS FROM ABOVE CAMP TWO

The reader must forgive me if the pictures I paint in his mind are done so with a brush steeped in the blues of pessimism, but the more we examined that huge mountain face, the more difficult and dangerous did it appear. Retreat in the face of such obvious difficulties and dangers would have been dishonourable neither to ourselves nor to mountaineering. After all, mountaineering is not to be classed with one of the modern crazes for sensationalism and record breaking at the possible cost of life and limb. It is an exact science, a perfect blending of the physical and the spiritual. It is not, and should not become, a desperate enterprise. There is no sport worthy of the name that has not its own peculiar risks, but no one has any business to walk deliberately into danger, and if risks are to be taken, they should be taken only by those who are fully alive to them.

Following our tracks of the previous day, we were soon up on the plateau. Leaving the majority of our porters to make camp there, and taking with us our personal servants only, we started off to the foot of the ice wall, accompanied by Duvanel with his little cohort of porters carrying various cinematographic apparatus and gadgets.

The snow had not improved since the previous day, and we sank in almost knee deep as we ploughed up the slopes. We kept as far as possible to the left, for the danger of ice avalanches sweeping the slopes to the right was obvious, and the ice blocks of former avalanches were strewn about them. Higher up, we were forced by some crevasses to the right for a short distance, but were soon able to traverse back to the left again.

As we approached the ice wall its magnificence

increased. It towered over our heads, cold and green, in tier on tier of ice, laced and friezed with snow. Immediately beneath it was an almost level terrace of snow about a hundred yards in breadth intersected longitudinally by a large crevasse. As far as we could see there was only one bridge over the crevasse, and that did not appear particularly solid. Driving two spare ice-axes into the snow, one on either side of the crevasse, we fixed a rope between them, which would serve as a safety hand-rail in the event of the bridge collapsing.

Beneath the lowest point of the wall was a clean-cut mass of ice some fifty feet high, under the shelter of which we sat down for a few minutes. It seemed a safe place in the event of anything falling from above. This lower mass could hardly count as a part of the main wall, and we were able to circumvent it on the right, and mount to its crest up an easy snow slope. It was at this point that the real work began.

Immediately above us rose an overhang of ice some eighty feet high. Above this was an icy shelf sloping upwards to the left and outwards to the edge of the overhang at an angle of at least fifty degrees. Above this shelf rose another sheer wall of ice. The shelf was the only break; we must gain it, and traverse it to the left to an easier slope that bore up to the foot of another ice pitch about one third of the distance up the ice wall.

The slope to the right afforded convenient access to the shelf. At first sight it appeared to be a snow slope, but actually it consisted of an ice slope evilly overlaid with a foot or more of floury snow. This snow had to be shovelled away, and firm steps cut in the ice substratum. It was an easy enough place and a snow avalanche was not to be feared, but it took time.

The ice was, as usual, tough and glue-like, and an altitude of 21,000 feet discountenanced severe exertion. Wieland and I took turns at the cutting, whilst Wood Johnson and the porters enlarged the steps to the dimensions of Wapping Old Stairs. We drove three pitons in, and fixed ropes thereto to assist the loaded porters in the future. These pitons were of a special type advocated by that great German mountaineer, Herr Welzenbach. They are barbed like an arrow, and we drove them into the ice with a broad-headed metal mallet. This type of piton has fastened to its head an iron ring. In addition to pitons, we carried a number of clip-on oval rings. These we could attach to the permanent ring on the piton, and afterwards fix a rope through them without the bother, and possibly the danger, of having to unrope. The procedure was for the leader to advance, drive the piton into the ice, clip on to its ring one of the detachable oval rings, and clip the rope through the oval ring. Thus, he could be securely held on the rope at every stage of the step cutting. The detachable oval rings were not, of course, used to thread the rope as a permanent hand-rail. In this case, the rope was threaded through the piton ring, and then tied.

By the time we reached the shelf it was beginning to snow. The hours had passed like magic, and the afternoon was well advanced. Thus far, the work had been easy, it now became very different. First of all, it was necessary to cut out a secure "jumping off" place in the ice at the end of the shelf from which the party could be securely held if need be. Duvanel took this task in hand, and soon fashioned a platform sufficiently broad on which to stand his ciné camera tripod.

It was while commencing to cut steps along the shelf that Wood Johnson's voice came up from below informing me that a hundred feet or so higher a large semi-detached flake of ice weighing a hundred tons or so was leaning unpleasantly over the route. I had already noticed this, and I am afraid, therefore, that I did not take Wood Johnson's information in the spirit in which it was meant, and after growling something about keeping up the morale of the leader and sundry damaging remarks anent the ice flake, which might justifiably have retaliated by falling upon me, I addressed myself once more to the task of step-cutting.

We were in a curious frame of mind. We knew that the place was dangerous. Had it been in the Alps, we should have gone back, but as the route was the only possible chink in the armour of Kangchenjunga the attack was persisted in, and the risks tacitly accepted. It was an understandable, yet false attitude of mind, but it is one that has warped the judgment of Himalayan parties in the past and will continue to exert its evil influence on other parties in the future. Suffice to say, that there will be many and terrible disasters before the greater Himalayan peaks are conquered, and before Himalayan mountaineering attains to any standard of sobriety.

Step-cutting on the shelf was weary work. First of all, the snow had to be cleared away, and beneath that a sort of flaky coating of ice before a step could be cut into the honest ice beneath. As in walking up-hill at high altitudes, so with cutting—rhythm. As each upward step in walking must be attuned to the breathing, so must each swing of the ice-axe. It has often been said that Mallory had some trick of climbing at a high altitude. I wonder if this was a scientific cultivation of rhythm. Mallory was one of the most graceful climbers that ever lived, and grace is the child of rhythm. It may be that the rhythmical grace with which he was wont to climb on the most difficult rocks of Great Britain or the Alps proved of inestimable value to him on Mount Everest.

A spell of twenty minutes' cutting was sufficient. I returned, and Wieland took my place. Twenty minutes' cutting, a few hard-won steps; it was not much. It was now snowing hard, but fortunately there was no wind, and it was reasonably warm.

Through the murk the great ice wall loomed coldly hostile. I have experienced fear many times on many mountains, but never quite the same dull, hopeless sort of fear inspired by this terrible wall of ice. I have often had occasion to remark how like men mountains are; some are friendly and others unfriendly. Kangchenjunga is something more than unfriendly, it is imbued with a blind unreasoning hatred towards the mountaineer. Sir Leslie Stephen once wrote: "But we should hardly estimate the greatness of men or mountains by the length of their butcher's bill." Kangchenjunga has every claim to majesty, and though the mere slaughter of those who attempt to reach its summit can scarcely add to it, the deaths that have occurred, and will occur, testify to the greatness of the mountain, and its supreme contempt for its wooers. The beautiful is often dangerous. Strip Kangchenjunga of its icy robes, and it would become weak and defenceless, a mere rocky skeleton. In its dangers lie its beauties, and no right thinking mountaineer would have it otherwise.

As we turned to descend, the mists thinned for a few moments. As though signalled by the rise of a curtain, a great ice avalanche blasted forth on to the snowy stage. Dimly, to the left, we could see clouds of wind-blown snow belch out from the mountainside, and the echoes boomed and crashed from precipice to precipice like the thunderous applause of some huge audience.

We returned to camp. Bad news awaited us. Owing to lack of local porters and our being unable to send back enough men to help him, Colonel Tobin was experiencing great difficulty in getting the transport to the Base Camp. We had sent back as many porters from Khunza as possible, but these were unreliable men. Not only had they refused to help Colonel Tobin, but they had looted a dump of stores at Dzongri, and stolen many articles of value. Colonel Tobin wrote that as far as Yoksam everything had gone well. There he had engaged local porters to bring his loads on to Dzongri, but these had refused to traverse the Kang La. He had experienced bad weather, and his assistant sirdar, Phuri, had died of exposure on the Kang La, whilst his chief sirdar, Naspati, had proved physically unequal to the task, and had returned ill to Darjeeling. Lobsang, whom we had sent back from Tseram, was now working with relays of men to get the loads over the Kang La. Colonel Tobin had laboured heroically against great odds, and as a result was physically worn out, and had lain ill for some days at Tseram. Also he had fallen and hurt his arm. He did not feel equal to the task of coming on to the Base Camp and had decided to return to Darjeeling as soon as adequate arrangements had been made to send on the remainder of the expedition's stores and equipment.

No one could have worked more for the expedition than Colonel Tobin, but the task that had been set him was an impossible one, and he was in no way responsible for transport delays. With only a few porters at his disposal, he could not be expected to get his transport to the Base Camp. Worst of all, Wood Johnson and I were unaware of the arrangements that had been made between him and Professor Dyhrenfurth regarding the sending back of porters, otherwise such a situation could hardly have arisen as Wood Johnson would have arranged to send back local porters from Khunza. Thus, a serious situation had arisen.

Something had to be done, and done quickly. Already sahibs' food was running short ; there was only about a week's supply left, and we were lacking many vital necessities, to say nothing of those little luxuries which help to alleviate the rigours of high altitude climbing. At sea-level yak meat should be an excellent diet for those gifted with a cast-iron digestion, but at a high altitude it is totally unsuitable and difficult to digest. At the Base Camp, even Schneider had expressed a dislike for it, and had turned with obvious relief to Welsh rarebit, salad dressing, and Worcester sauce. We were still without many items of equipment ; the wireless set had not arrived, and it was sad to think that every evening weather reports for our especial benefit were being broadcast from Calcutta.

There was nothing for it but for Wood Johnson and Hannah to leave Kangchenjunga, collect local porters at

Khunza with the assistance of the Nepali Subadar, and return over the Mirgin La to the help of Colonel Tobin at Tseram. It was extremely hard luck for them to have to leave Kangchenjunga when at grips with it, but it was some consolation for them to know that the work they would be doing would be of the utmost value to the expedition. Hannah had already come up to Camp One, and had moved it to a site a little farther up the glacier where it was less exposed to ice avalanches from the Twins. He had returned to the Base Camp directly he had received news of the transport difficulties. We had got back to camp too late from work on the ice wall for Wood Johnson to do likewise, nor could he be expected to do so after such a heavy day. Some time later, when he returned, after successfully helping to solve the transport problem, he told me that though it had seemed hard to have to abandon climbing he had somehow felt that what had transpired was all for the best. And perhaps that is so, for had he remained with the climbing party, he might have lost his life.

We slept fitfully that night, awakened at frequent intervals by the thunder of ice avalanches. During the nineteen days that we were on Kangchenjunga ice avalanches seemed to fall more frequently at night than in the daytime. At first sight, this may appear strange. The coldest period of the twenty-four hours should serve to knit together the unstable masses of ice. Actually, this tendency for avalanches to fall during the coldest hours is probably due to expansion owing to water freezing in cracks in the ice and forcing the masses asunder. Another avalanche period is in the early morning. In cases where freezing water has wedged the ice apart without forcing a fall, the frozen water tends to bind the ice together. Thus, a mass on the edge of a hanging glacier may not be forced to part from its parent glacier until it is well past the point of unstable equilibrium, owing to the ice mortar that is binding it to its parent glacier. It may be just a matter of a few pounds that prevents it from falling. When the sun penetrates the crack the restraining influence of the ice mortar may be removed, and the mass of ice, with nothing left to support it, topples to destruction.

A striking illustration of this thesis occurred on Mont Blanc. We were ascending by the classic Brenva route, and halted on the Col du Trident to watch the red glow of the dawn sun creeping down Mont Blanc. We were debating as to the advisability of following a French party who were making a short cut to the crest of the Brenva Ridge, or of going the longer and safer way round via the Col Moore, when the rising sun touched a mass of hanging glacier above this route. Almost at the same instant that it did so a great avalanche was let loose, which swept the route between us and the French party. The slight warmth of the sun had been just sufficient to tear the unstable mass of ice from its parent glacier. After that we went the longer way round.

The next day, May 5, dawned gloriously. It was with great regret that we parted from Wood Johnson. Only Wieland, Duvanel, and I were now left to continue with the work of making a route up the ice wall. Carrying with us several hundreds of feet of rope, and two or three dozen pitons, we returned to the attack.

The previous day we had cut steps to a point about half way along the shelf. The work was useful in one respect for we were becoming acclimatised, and were climbing every day with increasing vigour.

We went to work on the shelf with a will, the leader cutting fair sized steps, the second man enlarging them, and lastly the porters, who seemed positively to enjoy the work, hacking out platforms large enough for an elephant to stand on. An hour or two's strenuous work and the traverse to the shelf was completed. From a snowy ridge at its end we could gaze back with satisfaction at the long line of steps, and a comforting hempen hand-rail of fixed rope. The most formidable ice slope loses much of its terrors when so decorated.

The snowy ridge we were on led upwards for one hundred feet without difficulty. It was a gift from the gods of the ice wall, and we accepted it gratefully. Our gratitude was a trifle ill-timed. We should have realised that the gods, like the morbid inventor of a cross-word puzzle, had only invented this easy bit for a joke. The joy departed from our hearts as we stood on an almost level ledge of snow. Above the ledge, the ice wall rose in what a mountaineer, despairing of a suitable descriptive term, might call a "vertical overhang." It was certainly vertical for twenty-five feet, and, about fifteen feet up, the ice bulged out forming a genuine overhang. To left and right the ledge thinned out into precipices of ice. Only from the point where we were standing was there the remotest possibility of climbing the wall. Twenty-five feet above our heads it "eased off" to an angle of about 70 degree. This "eased off" portion extended through a vertical height of about two hundred and fifty feet ; crowning this slope and leering down upon us, rose a final and vertical barrier of ice fifty feet high.

As we stood, gazing silently, I tried to recall to my mind climbing of a similar nature in the Alps. I was unable to do so. In fact, it is probably safe to say that ice work of this nature had never been tackled in the Alps. Why should it be when it can always be avoided? The most continuously exacting ice climbing on record is that done by the Munich expedition on Kangchenjunga, but some of our porters, who had been with that expedition, assured us that though the work had been much longer, there had been nothing to equal this ice wall for *continuous* difficulty.

It is a well-known optical illusion that a slope looked at from below appears considerably less steep than looked at from above. The ice wall before us was a notable exception; it looked steep and it *was* steep.

A few mouthfuls of food, a drink of hot tea from a Thermos flask, and we set to work. At one place, a shallow splayed out chimney ran up the ice wall. It was too shallow to be of any use for body-wedging purposes, but we preferred it to the more exposed walls of ice on either side. Higher up, however, it became overhanging, and an upward and outward traverse to the right would be necessary. We debated whether crampons would be of any assistance, but decided that they would destroy the steps and would generally be more dangerous than useful, especially in view of the possibility of the leader falling off and spiking any unfortunates who happened to be beneath.

It was on Mont Blanc that I had undergone the exquisite torment of having a man stand on my shoulders in crampons. Even tricouni nails are bad enough, and I can sympathise with Wieland, and his request for me to be as quick as possible, as I stood on his shoulders. Reaching upwards, I hammered a piton into the ice, and clipped the rope into the oval ring. Supported by the rope running through the ring, I cut steps from the bottom of the wall. The easiest method of doing so was to place the feet in the steps already made, and leaning outwards and backwards on the rope, cut the next step above. Having reached the level of the piton, a fresh piton was driven in above, and the rope clipped into another oval ring. The lower piton could then be removed.

It was hard work ; two or three steps at a time was as much as a man could manage. Leaning back on the rope did not improve matters, for it compressed the upper part of the body and made breathing difficult. The ice was white and flaky on the surface, but underneath of a blue-black transparency, like the cold depths of the ocean. It was difficult to swing the axe effectively, and we had to peck at the ice like an aged chicken seeking grubs in a farmyard. At the altitude, every stroke represented a definite piece of work, and every step a stage in a day's hard labour.

To the mountaineer who revels in the art and craft of icemanship, there is no music finer to his ears than the ringing thump with which an ice-axe meets the yielding ice, and the swish and tinkle of the dislodged chips beneath him. But æsthetical and poetical sentiments were not for us. We wearied of the dull thud, thud, as the pick struck the ice. The musical ring of pitons driven well home found no answering ring in our hearts. We felt no excitement, no enthusiasm, no hope, no fear. We became mere dull automatons, as dull and as automatic as the driver of a racing car towards the end of an attempt on a non-stop distance record. Such is difficult ice work at 21,000 feet.

THE GREAT ICE WALL

The day was drawing to a dull close, and the usual snowstorm was pouring vials of snow powder on the world, as we stood together at the foot of the pitch, eyeing the scene of our labours. We had done eighteen feet, no more, but the steps were good ones. We would finish the lower wall on the morrow, and the day after that get up to the foot of the last wall. Yet one more day should see us up the final wall. Five days for five hundred feet of ascent ! Was it worth it ? Even with fixed ropes could laden porters ever be got up to the terrace above ?

We returned to camp tired and dispirited, there to meet Schneider who had come up that day from the Base Camp, and a Schneider brimful of energy and enthusiasm. To me his presence was doubly welcome, for, as the most experienced member of the party, I had felt myself to be saddled with more responsibility than I cared for. The difficulties and dangers were too obvious to be ignored. The porters realised the former, but did they understand the latter ?

The next morning, May 6, found us once more at the foot of the ice wall. Wieland and I were tired mentally and physically, and it was a relief to us to see the business-like way with which Schneider went to work. He is a splendid iceman, cutting steps with a methodical neatness and quickness equal to that of a first-class Alpine guide. He uses a short ice-axe with such a long and heavy pick that only a man with his strength of wrist and forearm could wield it effectively.

Even with three men on the job, it was a day's work to climb the last few feet of vertical or overhanging ice.

From the top of the shallow chimney it was necessary to traverse across a slightly overhanging bulge to the right.

Here the ice was of a slightly more flaky nature than lower down, and it was not altogether pleasant leaning outwards, trusting that the piton would remain firm, and not pull away from the ice. Duvanel had come up with us, and took a number of " shots " of our struggles on the ice. Surely no film camera has ever been used in quite such a situation. We might have got farther that day, but we were hampered by a heavy snowstorm that set in soon after mid-day. So thickly did the snow fall that within an hour or so it was six to eight inches deep.

By the time we turned to descend, so much snow had fallen that our upward steps and fixed ropes had been obliterated completely. The steps along the shelf were difficult to find. Duvanel and his porters carrying the cinema apparatus were the first to descend. They were about half-way across when Duvanel slipped, and slid quickly downwards towards the eighty feet overhang beneath. Apparently, he had not reached the hand-rail when he slipped. It seemed that the three porters with him must be pulled off too, but the porter next to him, I think it was Sonam, an old Everest " Tiger," had such a tight rope that he was able to hold him and stop him before he had slid more than ten feet. It was a splendid bit of work—none of us could have done it better—and shows to what a state of mountaineering efficiency these porters have been brought by their experiences with former expeditions. But the slip had the effect of unnerving the remainder of the porters on the traverse, and one of them promptly followed Duvanel's example. This man had no ice-axe, but fortunately he was held from the platform at the end of the traverse, and was drawn up on the rope wriggling like a fish by two lusty porters.

Roping on to Nemu, I followed the first party. The new snow made the traverse treacherous. Unfortunately, the fixed rope did not extend the whole distance across, but only stretched across the steeper portion. For several yards the passage had to be made without its aid. The newly fallen snow made the going distinctly tricky; not in all cases did the steps made by the descending porters correspond with the ice steps below, and one of them collapsed beneath me. I was well supported by my ice-axe pick, and driving it in, was able to arrest the slip before it was properly started. But never shall I forget Nemu's agonised " Oh, sahib, sahib ! " It was a relief to get hold of the fixed rope, and walk across the remainder of the shelf.

The snowstorm was an unusually heavy one, and looked as though it might continue all night. But as we ploughed down the snow slopes towards the camp, the snow stopped falling, and the clouds, relieved of their burden, began to dissolve. Below, grey mists swirled and eddied in the glacier valley ; and above, the peaks stood forth in the radiance of a perfect evening. It was one of those transformation scenes that mean so much to the mountaineer. For hours we had wrestled with the ice wall, wrestled in gloom and snowstorm, and now, like love in a world of hate, the sun shone through to cheer our downward march.

The mists beneath became less turbulent and ceased their eddyings and swirlings, lying in the valley like November vapours over a sodden meadow. The last cloudy rags were being thrown into the purple dustbin of the evening sky as we reached camp.

As I stood outside my tent after supper, watching the unity of earth and sky in the bonds of night, the harsh labours of the day were forgotten. Strange imaginings possessed me. In the profound quietude I heard the whisper of small voices ; the liquid notes of some strange harmony stole across the glacier, seeming to rise from the very snow I was standing on, then—a shattering, bellowing roar from Kangchenjunga ; snow whirling upwards and outwards ; a grinding thunder of echoes rolling and crashing from peak to peak, booming, murmuring, dying into an affrighted silence. But the voices and the music I heard no more.

The party had been further strengthened by the arrival of Hoerlin, and Wieland and I felt that we could justifiably leave him and Schneider to continue with the attack on the ice wall. Since leaving the Base Camp, we had worked solidly for six days, and a rest was necessary if we were not to crock. Such ice work at high altitudes as we had been doing is not of a type that can be kept up indefinitely, and coming thus early in the expedition, we were both feeling the strain of it.

Hoerlin and Schneider put forth a great effort, and climbed the slope to the foot of the final wall. During the day we watched them, mere specks crawling upwards with the slowness of an hour hand. While they were at work, a large avalanche broke away from the left-hand extremity of the wall, and swept the lower part of the sloping terrace which we had decided was too dangerous to be climbed.

They returned with the news that there were two possibilities of getting over the final wall. One was directly up it, and the other by engineering a way up a crack, which separated the lower portion of the ice wall from the ice of the terrace. It would be necessary to keep as far to the right as possible, in order to avoid getting beneath some unstable-looking ice pinnacles on the terrace. On the other hand, they regarded with disfavour the crack, which seemed to suggest that the portion of the ice wall outlined by it to the right was breaking away from its parent glacier. They considered that the work would be completed on the morrow, and the terrace reached, and proposed to take up all the porters with loads, to establish Camp Three on the terrace. If the upper wall turned out to be harder than was anticipated, the loads would be dumped as high as possible. They had roped up all the upper part of the route, but it remained to be seen whether the porters could go safely up and down. Even if they could, keeping up the communications would be a much harder task than on Everest, where porters were able to go up and down unaccompanied between camps. Here every convoy must be under the charge of a European.

But would it be possible to maintain such communications at all ? As we had seen two days previously, a slight fall of snow had altered the complexion of things completely. A heavy fall would undoubtedly isolate Camp Three. And what of the other camps above that ? At least six were anticipated between the Base Camp and the summit, and this number might well be increased by the difficulties of the climbing and the altitude to eight. With the beanstalk severed just above the root, it would both cease to climb and die.

Apart from snowstorms, something worse than an awkward situation might be created by the collapse of any part of the ice wall involving the route. Even supposing no immediate deaths resulted, it might be difficult, or even impossible, to descend.

One primary fact had not been realised, and that was that Kangchenjunga is something more than an Alpine peak on a large scale. Not one of the party could deny that the route was liable to be swept by ice avalanches, but it was not realised exactly to what an extent risks were being taken. A party in the Alps sometimes deliberately incurs a risk of being overwhelmed by an ice avalanche when passing beneath a hanging glacier, or under an unstable ice pinnacle in an ice face, but such a risk is seldom incurred for longer than a few minutes. We had been exposed to these risks for four consecutive days, and were to be exposed to the same risk for yet another day. And this was not all ; the risk would last as long as we were on the mountain. Communications between camps must be maintained, and porters go to and fro. Thus, the ice wall and the slopes beneath would have to be traversed not once, but many times, and the probability of accident was greatly increased thereby. As I have pointed out, Himalayan porters appreciate difficulty, but not danger. They place implicit confidence in their sahibs, whom they are prepared to follow anywhere. This confidence should not be abused.

That day, and late into the night, I sat in my tent writing up a sadly overdue diary, and also a dispatch to *The Times*, which last was sent down the same day to the Base Camp. In the former I wrote :

" Our camp is pitched on the only safe place in the cirque, for the hanging glaciers that cling precariously to the hollows of precipices frequently let loose enormous ice avalanches that sweep the snow slopes beneath with cataracts of ice blocks. Yet were one of these catastrophic ice avalanches—the collapse of a hanging glacier—such as are common among the Himalayas, to take place, we would be brushed like a speck of dust from the earth. Even as I write there comes at almost regular intervals, the boom and roar of ice avalanches from Kangchenjunga. It is almost as though the mountain was pulsating to the fierce beats of her restless heart. Unhurriedly masses of ice are riven by the downward motion of the ice-fields from the edges of the red rock cliffs. They totter forward, masses as great as the Houses of Parliament, breaking up into disintegrating ice masonry, which strikes the precipices beneath with an appalling crash, and pours down in an irresistible torrent of ice, concealed by billowing clouds of snow dust flung before it."

My dispatch to *The Times* concluded with these words : "As I write, avalanche after avalanche is roaring off Kangchenjunga, each one seeming to proclaim defiance and warning."

CHAPTER XII

THE AVALANCHE

I lay long in my tent that evening writing, and it was nearly midnight before I blew out the candle, and composed myself to sleep. But sleep would not come. I was quite comfortable, my digestive organs were in good order, and acclimatisation had reduced my pulse-rate to nearly normal. The night was curiously warm, in fact, the warmest night we had had since we arrived at the Base Camp. Now and again came the long-drawn-out thunder of avalanches.

Perhaps it was the atmosphere, or maybe some trick of the imagination, but the sound of the avalanches seemed dull and muffled. It was as though Kangchenjunga was choking with suppressed wrath. My body was ready for sleep, but my mind was not. It was troubled and restless, groping in a catacomb of doubt and fear. I have known fear before on a mountain, but that was fear of a different nature, sharp and sudden in the face of an immediate danger, but I have never known what it was to lie awake before a climb, tortured by the devils of misgiving.

Some people may call this a premonition, but I do not think it can be so defined. Premonition of danger is, after all, an anticipation of danger, where, theoretically, danger ought not to exist. That danger existed in this case cannot be denied. The mind had brooded over it consciously and subconsciously to the detriment of the nerves, and these had become temporarily unstrung. That is a more logical explanation than the acceptance of the premonition theory, which is more dependent upon a belief in psychical phenomena.

When, at last, I fell asleep, I was troubled with terrible dreams. These dreams were not dreams of personal danger, but of danger to the porters. They were always getting into an impossible position, and would turn to me appealingly for help. But I was unable to help. Afterwards, Wood Johnson told me he used frequently to dream this too. Possibly it was due to an innate sense of responsibility. Others on Himalayan expeditions have probably experienced the same sort of dreams. It was a bad night.

I crawled out of my tent the next morning, dull, heavy, and unrefreshed. I looked at the ice wall, and the weary track leading up through the snow to it, with loathing. Neither mentally nor physically did I feel fit to start.

The morning was ominously warm and a steamy heat beat down through sluggish mists. The sun was obscured, but for the first time on the mountain we were able to sit outside and keep reasonably warm without its rays on us.

It was decided that the scheme arranged the previous day should be adhered to. All except the cook and myself were to leave and try to establish Camp Three on the terrace.

Schneider with his usual boundless energy was the first to leave. He was accompanied by his servant, " Satan " Chettan, who was carrying a considerable load.

There was no porter in the expedition of a finer physique than " Satan," and I remember watching him swing on his load with effortless ease, and start off in the wake of his master, his legs propelling him uphill in shambling powerful strides, the gait of a born hillman and mountaineer.

Duvanel and three porters carrying cinematograph apparatus came next, as the former wished to obtain "shots" of the last party, which consisted of Hoerlin, Wieland, and eight porters carrying heavy loads. For a while I sat on a packing case, watching them as they slowly plodded up the slopes of soft snow, then I adjourned to my tent in order to write some letters.

Perhaps half an hour later I was startled by a tremendous roar. Two thoughts flashed through my mind. Firstly, that only an exceptionally large ice avalanche falling close at hand could make such a din, and secondly, with a sudden clutch of horror at my heart, that the noise came, not from the usual direction of Kangchenjunga's face, but from the ice wall!

I dashed outside. What I saw is indelibly engraved on my memory.

An enormous portion of the ice wall had collapsed. Huge masses of ice as high as cathedrals, were still toppling to destruction; billowing clouds of snow spray were rushing upwards and outwards in the van of a huge avalanche. On the slope below was the party, mere black dots, strung out in a straggling line. They were not moving. For an instant, during which I suppose my brain must have been stunned, the scene was stamped on my mind like a still photograph, or perhaps a more apt comparison would be a ciné film that has jammed for a fraction of a second. Then everything jerked on again. I remember feeling no surprise, it was almost like a fantastic solution to something that had been puzzling me.

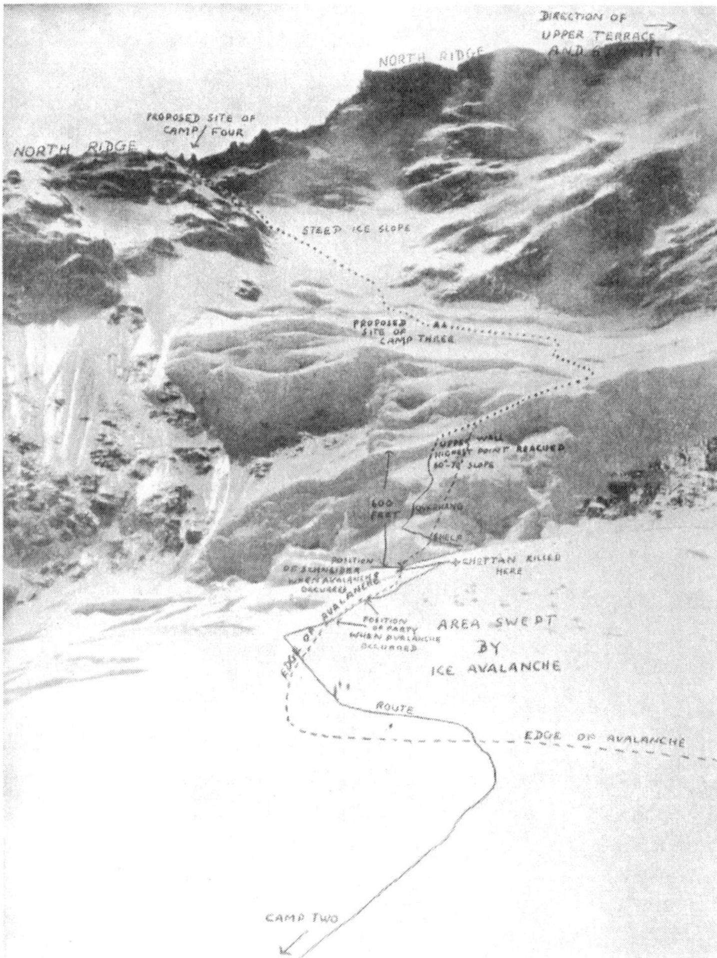

THE ROUTE UP THE GREAT ICE WALL

Now the dots were moving, moving to the left ; they were running, but how slowly, how uselessly before the reeling clouds of death that had already far outflanked them. The next moment the avalanche had swept down upon them ; they were engulfed and blotted out like insects beneath a tidal wave.

In the tent I had been conscious of noise, but now I was no longer aware of it. The clouds of snow swept nearer. At first they had seemed to move slowly, but now they were shooting forwards with incredible velocity. Vicious tongues of ice licked out under them. Here and there solitary blocks broke free from the pall ; behind them I caught a glimpse of a confused jumble of ice blocks, grinding together like the boulders in a stream bed caught up by the flood waters of a cloudburst.

The thought of personal danger had not occurred to me at first, but now, suddenly, came the realisation that the avalanche might sweep the camp away. I glanced round for the cook—he was standing outside the cooking tent—and yelled to him to run for it.

I had stood and watched the avalanche like one rooted to the spot in a nightmare. Running was nightmarish too. The feet sank deeply into the snow ; at the height (20,000 feet) every step was an effort. We floundered along for perhaps twenty yards, then heart and lungs gave out, and neither of us could continue. We looked round ; the avalanche was stopping two hundred yards away. Though I had not been conscious of any noise after the initial roar, I was paradoxically conscious of it ceasing.

The avalanche stopped, only the clouds of snow, driven by the wind displaced by the falling masses, writhed far into the air. There was no sign of my companions. I turned to the cook : " They are all killed, but we must do what we can." We retraced our steps to the camp, seized ice-axes, and set out for the scene of the disaster. We tried to move quickly, but it was impossible at the altitude, it was better to go slowly and steadily, and how slow this was.

The clouds of snow began to settle, the veil thinned. It was a terrible moment. I expected to see no sign of the party. Then, to my immense relief, I saw dimly a figure away to the left, and then some more figures. We toiled upwards, skirting the edge of the avalanche ; it was sharply defined, and the ice blocks were piled several feet high. Beyond it the snow was untouched, save where it had been scored by solitary blocks flung forwards from the main mass of ice.

Two hundred yards from the camp the track vanished beneath the débris of the avalanche. We reached a little group of porters. They were standing stupidly, without moving or speaking, on the edge of the débris, all save one, who was probing energetically with an ice-axe between the ice blocks. It was Nemu. I asked him what he was doing, whether there was a man buried there, and he replied, " Load, sahib, I look for load." In order to run and escape from the avalanche he had dropped his load, and this was seriously worrying him. Who were alive and who were dead did not concern him, he had dropped his load, the load entrusted to him by the sahibs.

I counted the party, two were missing. Hoerlin, Wieland, and Duvanel I could see above me. The missing ones were Schneider and Chettan. Two hundred feet higher I saw Wieland approaching something sticking out between the ice blocks. It was Chettan's hand. By the time I had climbed up he had been dug out. He was dead, having been carried down at least three hundred feet, and crushed in the torrent of ice blocks. His head was severely injured, but as a forlorn hope we administered artificial respiration for over an hour. In the middle of it Schneider reappeared. He had had a marvellous escape. He had actually been under the ice wall when it came down. He said : "I heard a crack ; then down it came, huge masses of ice from hundreds of feet above. I thought I was dead, but I ran to the left, and the avalanche missed me by five metres." Chettan had been too far behind Schneider to save himself.

The remainder of the party had amazing luck. They had been on the track where it ran farthest to the left. Had they been ten minutes earlier or later, nothing could have saved them. Even so, they had had to run for their lives, and the track was swept almost from end to end. Duvanel told me that when he saw it coming, the thought of being able to escape never even occurred to him. But, like the others, he had run to the left, as it seemed better to be killed *doing something* than waiting for apparently certain death. So narrow had been the escape of the main body of the porters that some of them had actually been bruised by blocks of ice on the edge of the avalanche. The escape of the party can only be called a miracle of the mountains.

The portion of the wall that had fallen had been that outlined by the crack noted by Hoerlin and Schneider the previous day. In falling it swept the route on the ice wall diagonally, completely obliterating the lower part of the route that Wieland and I had made, destroying the snow bridge over the crevasse, and the ice hump under which we had sat. In fact, the topography of the route we had made at the expense of so much labour had been altered completely. The area of snow slopes covered by the débris must have been nearly a mile square, and the avalanche can scarcely have weighed less than a million tons.

We returned to camp, two of the porters taking turns at carrying Chettan. According to those who had been highest, another crack had opened up above the ice wall, and there was a strong possibility of another avalanche, possibly greater even than the first, which might conceivably sweep away the camp. It was advisable to retire to Camp One with all speed. But before doing so we buried Chettan.

It was a simple, yet impressive ceremony. A hole was dug in the snow, and the body, dressed as it was in climbing clothes, laid within with folded arms. A handful of rice was roasted by the porters, and this was scattered over the body to the accompaniment of muttered prayers. We stood round with bared heads. Then someone gave an order, and snow was quickly shovelled into the grave. As this was done the mists dispersed, and the sun shone through for a few instants. Almost one could see the brave soul winging its way over the mountains. We drove in an ice-axe to mark the spot, and silently turned away. We had lost not a porter, but a valued friend. We left him buried amid one of the grandest mountain cirques in the world.

So died a genuine lover of the mountains, a real adventurer at heart, and one whom members of several Himalayan expeditions will mourn.

By courtesy of H. Ruttledge

CHETTAN

We descended to Camp One in a wet and soaking snowstorm, that later developed into a blizzard. Word was sent down to the Base Camp of the disaster, requesting that Professor Dyhrenfurth and Kurz should come up and discuss matters.

Wind was howling, and snow lashing the tents, as we ate supper and crept miserably into our sleeping bags.

CHAPTER XIII

THE SECOND ATTEMPT: THE NORTH-WEST RIDGE

On May 10, the day after the accident, Professor Dyhrenfurth, Kurz and Dr. Richter arrived from the Base Camp, and a conference was held on the situation. " Conference " is perhaps a little misleading. It is a word conjuring up a picture of frock-coated gentlemen seated round a long mahogany table, the highly polished surface of which reflects waistcoats ornamented with gold watch-chains, and earnest countenances on which responsibility and a heavy lunch sit heavily. In the present instance I must ask the reader to imagine the sombre interior of the large porters' tent, the thick canvas of which reduces the light within to a faint depressing green, whilst a pungent reek of smoke struggles with a faint, yet perceptible odour of unwashed bodies that have lain there during the previous night. In the middle a heterogeneous collection of packing cases do duty as a table. Seated on other packing cases are a number of unsavoury looking ragamuffins with unkempt hair, frowsy beards, cracked sun-scorched countenances, and eyes bleared by the snow glare.

The first suggestion made by those who had remained at the Base Camp was that the attack on the ice wall should be renewed, but this was very properly rejected by all those who had shared in the attack. The sole remaining alternative was to attempt the North-west Ridge which rises from the western tributary of the Kangchenjunga Glacier. This ridge ends in a snow and ice terrace beneath the Kangbachen summit, 25,782 feet, of Kangchenjunga. Even supposing the terrace to be reached, however, the most we could hope for was to ascend the Kangbachen summit, as there was no possibility of traversing to the highest summit, as both distance and difficulty were too great. Personally, I must confess to a longing to flee from the mountain altogether, and be able to lie in a sleeping bag at nights and sleep undisturbed by the fear of annihilation from ice avalanches. I suggested, therefore, that we should retire, cross the Jonsong La, and attempt the Jonsong Peak, 24,344 feet high. This idea met with no support, and it was decided to attempt the North-west Ridge. Should we fail, as it seemed certain we must do, judging from appearances, at all events we could ascend the Western Tributary Glacier, explore its head, and possibly climb the Ramthang Peak.

In order to do this, it was decided to move Camp One across the glacier to the foot of the rocky spur separating the Western Tributary Glacier from the glacier falling between the Wedge Peak and the Ramthang Peak. This new site would have the advantage of being considerably safer than the present one, for it was by no means certain that we were safe in the event of an exceptionally large ice avalanche falling from Kangchenjunga or the Twins. This uncertainty was emphasised the same afternoon in a startling fashion.

We were aroused from an after-lunch siesta by the thunder clap of a great avalanche. We issued from our tents in alarm. Thousands of feet above us on the face of

Kangchenjunga masses of hanging glacier were collapsing. Sweeping the precipices with appalling violence, the avalanche crashed down to the glacier, and roared straight across at us.

Huge clouds of snow were raised by the wind blast from the surface of the glacier, and came rushing down upon the camp. They concealed the falling ice, and it was hard to tell whether the camp was safe or not. My own inclination was to run for it, and I was about to bolt precipitately when I saw Duvanel calmly turning the handle of his ciné camera with that sang-froid peculiar to his calling, the tradition of which demands that the handle of a ciné camera shall be turned in the face of charging elephants, and at shipwrecks, fires, explosions, earthquakes and other catastrophes. Fired by his example, I pulled my own folding camera from my pocket, and took a hurried snap. As will be seen from the accompanying illustration the avalanche resembled the white clouds of some new and deadly form of gas attack. The God of Kangchenjunga is evidently well up in the technique of modern warfare. The roar of the avalanche subsided. We knew that we were safe from ice débris, but the clouds of snow continued to pour down the glacier towards the camp with extraordinary velocity. The next moment a wind blast struck the camp, and a blizzard of snow sent us scuttling into shelter.

The blizzard lasted some minutes, and when it had cleared the upper part of the glacier was seen to be covered in nearly an inch of wind-blown snow. The actual ice débris of the avalanche had stopped well short of the camp, but it had swept quite half a mile down the glacier. This was not

THE ICE AVALANCHE THAT FELL TOWARDS CAMP ONE

the only avalanche; other lesser ones fell, but none of such terrifying dimensions. It was obvious, however, that it was a mere question of volume and momentum whether or not the camp was to be swept away by a future avalanche. If it was a rest day for tired bodies, it was scarcely so for nerve-racked minds.

It was a simple matter moving camp the next day, and the new site on the other side of the glacier was safer than any we had yet discovered. We had not been able to bring down all our equipment from Camp Two, so some porters under the charge of Kurz went up to fetch it. Schneider and Duvanel, meanwhile, descended to the Base Camp, the former in order to make a new track up the glacier to our new Camp, the latter to develop some ciné film. I was left in charge of the evacuation of the old camp, and took the opportunity of donning a pair of ski, and making short runs on the glacier. The snow was excellent and similar to late Spring Alpine snow.

The new Camp One was pitched in a fine situation. There was a delightful view northwards up the moraine-stacked Jonsong Glacier winding sinuously up towards the little notch of the Jonsong La. The background was dominated by the rocky mass of the Jonsong Peak. Farther to the east, rose a ridge of icy peaks running northwards from Kangchenjunga and the Twins, from which the Tent Peak, 24,089 feet, rose head and shoulders above everything else. It is as aptly named as the Wedge Peak, for its horizontal summit ridge with its small points at either end resembles a tent, the ridge of which sags between its supporting poles.

Some useful stores arrived from the Base Camp that day,

among them being synthetic rubber ground sheets for the tents. Though light and spongy, and weighing but a pound or so each, the difference they made to our comfort was amazing, and we were able to sleep then and afterwards far more warmly and comfortably than we would have done otherwise, insulated as we were from the snow. There is no question that they are far superior to any ground sheet, and form an item of equipment that no future Himalayan expedition can afford to leave out, for they induce the sleep which is so essential if climbers are to keep fit.

Relieved by the thought that we were tolerably safe from avalanches, we slept well that night. It would have been wise to have started early the next morning while the snow was still hard from the overnight frost, but we did not get away until the sun had thawed its crust sufficiently to let it break beneath our weight. The obvious route up the Western Tributary Glacier was a trough between the glacier and the rock ridge forming its northern containing wall. The trough was snow-filled for most of its distance, except for one section where a scree slope interposed. These troughs, which form such a convenient line of least resistance up the glaciers of this district are perhaps the only thing vouchsafed by Kangchenjunga which seems to have been intended for the benefit of the long suffering mountaineer.

Wieland and I, with some porters, were the first to set off. Hoerlin, Kurz, and some more porters were to follow, but at the last moment Kurz, who was again not feeling well, decided to return to the Base Camp.

The snow in the trough was in the worst possible

condition. We floundered waist deep into holes between concealed snow covered boulders, and wallowed in hollows where the snow was soft and watery. An hour passed ; we had made but little progress. I suggested to Wieland that we should leave the trough in favour of the ice-fall of the glacier. In making this suggestion I was actuated by the fact that at one place the trough seemed likely to be swept by falling stones from the cliffs above. Hoerlin, however, was of a different mind ; he would stick to the trough. As things transpired, he was right ; the danger was more apparent than real.

Ascending the ice-fall was fatiguing work on account of the soft snow. Snow-shoes eased the porters' labours to some extent, but there were not enough pairs to go round. Considering how broken was the ice, it was remarkable how few crevasses there were, but these few were dangerous ones, subtly concealed. We toiled up and down over hummocks, or threaded our way between pinnacles. The devil of doubt began to gnaw at our hearts ; would we be able to get through the ice-fall ? The sun beat down upon us mercilessly, and glacier lassitude sapped the strength of sahib and porter alike. At last we saw a sort of corridor leading from the ice-fall into the upper part of the trough. We could see that the trough was perfectly safe, but had it been dangerous, we should still have preferred it to the sweltering gullies and hollows of the ice-fall, for glacier lassitude tends to undermine the judgment and warp the conscience of the mountaineer.

A crevasse barred the way. We stepped gingerly on to a fragile snow bridge. Icicles were dislodged and went tinkling down into the green depths with a noise like the banging together of small chandeliers. The corridor stretched ahead ; its smooth, snow floor looked innocuous, but Wieland suddenly disappeared up to his waist in a concealed crevasse : it was merely one of Kangchenjunga's little jokes.

At the top of the trough, where it debouches on to the glacier, above the worst of the ice-fall, there is a short section liable to be swept by ice avalanches from a hanging glacier forming the edge of a snow plateau on the Ramthang Peak. While still within the danger area we were startled by a sudden crash, but all that came down were a few boulders and blocks of ice.

The porters were by now very tired, and they begged us to camp as soon as possible. We promised to do so as soon as we were out of range of ice avalanches. The sun was declining, and evening mists gathering around us as we reached the smooth slopes above the ice-fall, where stretched Hoerlin's straggling track, man's first score on these snow-fields. Here we decided to camp, while Wieland went on with ski to bring down Hoerlin, who had camped some distance further up the glacier.

The evening was strangely still save for an undercurrent of sound, as though the goblins and witches who haunt the cliffs of Kangchenjunga above were murmuring at our coming. As usual, it was the wind. An upward glance disclosed the snow eddying and swirling from the polished ice cliffs defending the snowy terraces. The sun set calmly. Barely had its last rays faded when they were replaced by silver moon sheen behind the North Ridge of Kangchenjunga. The snow blown off the ridge by the wind was illumined from behind, and Kangchenjunga took to itself a glowing aureole of light. Imperceptibly the upper snowslopes were resolved from the darkness ; ghost-like, unreal, they shimmered far above the world. Mindless of the cold, we stood outside our tents entranced by the glorious spectacle. At long last the laggardly moon peered over the ridge in a shy, self deprecating sort of way. It seemed to wither and shrivel as it mounted into the frosty sky and its radiance, at first soft and wan, became a hard, cold electric blue. Details stood forth as clearly as in daylight. Only the shadows were black, and in these lurked the darkness of a pit.

The cold gripped us. We crawled into our tents, and with numbed fingers laced-to the flaps. As Sir Leslie Stephen wrote : " Bodily fatigue and an appreciation of natural scenery are simply incompatible." He might have added cold and discomfort.

The sun reached us early the next morning, and we were off betimes. Our first business was to move camp farther up the glacier to a site that would form a convenient upper base for operations against the North-west Ridge. As we marched up the glacier we were able to examine the latter. First impressions are not always accurate and it is never easy to assess the difficulties of a mountainside or ridge at their true worth. As that great mountaineer, Captain J. P. Farrar used to remark : " You can never tell what rocks are like until you have rubbed your nose against them." Yet, even bearing these things in mind, no ridge I have ever examined affected me with the same feeling of utter and complete hopelessness as that of the North-west Ridge of Kangchenjunga. Picture a ridge rising 4,000 feet. Thin, trim and whittle down its edges until they are as keen as a Gurkha's *kukri* ; then hack deep gaps into these edges and perch rocky towers hundreds of feet high on them. Armour every smooth bit with ice, and mask every ledge with snow, and you will perhaps obtain a faint glimmering of an idea of the North-west Ridge of Kangchenjunga. The ridge attempted by the Munich party is formidable, but it cannot compare to the North-west Ridge. Ice pinnacles alone had to be surmounted on the former ; spiky rock pinnacles bar the way on the latter, and between these are some of those extraordinary ice ridges peculiar to the Himalayas. In appearance and sensationalism they are comparable to those on the Wedge Peak. There are the same tottering masses, the same biscuit-like flakes through which the sun gleams, the same extravagant forms, hacked and torn by the wind, lurching and tottering at the behest of gravity, and the same ice flutings to emphasise by their graceful lines the appalling steepness of the slopes they decorate. If we had been forced to attack the ridge from its base, I think we would have relinquished any idea of attempting it at the outset, for the lowest rock towers are hopeless from a climbing point of view. It looked possible, however, to gain the crest of the ridge above these initial pinnacles, by a steep snow-filled couloir about 600 feet high, leading upwards from the glacier to one of the gaps in the crest of the ridge.

Camp was pitched on the glacier, and leaving the porters to make it comfortable we set off to climb the couloir. The lower half was simple; then the angle steepened. It was not difficult, but care had to be taken that the footsteps kicked in the floury snow that masked rock slabs and ice did

THE NORTH-WEST RIDGE OF KANGCHENJUNGA

not collapse. The last hundred feet were very steep. The angle must have exceeded 60 degrees, but we were comforted by the thought that we could fix a rope to facilitate descent. A small cornice leaned over the summit. The leader, Hoerlin, hacked and flogged it down, and squirmed through and over to the gap, Wieland and I following one by one. The ascent had taken only forty-five minutes, indicating that we had become well acclimatised to altitude.

My first impression was probably somewhat similar to that experienced by a house-breaker, not a burglar, but one of those phlegmatic gentlemen who stand on the dizzy edges of aged and tottering walls knocking bricks off into space with a pick-axe. But surely no house-breaker has ever stood on top of such an unstable wall as we found ourselves on. A modern £25 down and balance in rent villa could scarcely be more "jerrybuilt" than the place on which we stood. On either side of us the rocks were piled in loose masses needing but a touch to send them crashing down on either side of the ridge below us. On the opposite side of the ridge to that which we had ascended loose yellowish precipices dropped to the head of the Ramthang Glacier. From our gap it appeared possible to descend to the glacier down another steep gully, scarred with falling débris. Such a descent would, however, involve unavoidable dangers. And far above this scene of perpetual decay rose the great ice slopes and ice walls of Kangchenjunga.

Is there any hope of ascending Kangchenjunga from the Ramthang Glacier? The answer must be, no, unless the climber is prepared to take his life, *and* the lives of his porters, in his hand. Like the face above the Kangchenjunga Glacier, that above the Ramthang Glacier is defended by enormous walls of ice running across the mountainside. At one point only is there any hope of climbing the *lowest* of these ice walls, and this point is also liable to be swept at any moment by ice avalanches from another and tottering ice wall above. Kangchenjunga was not built for the mountaineer.

Leaving rucksacks and spare rope, we commenced to climb along the unstable ridge. Almost immediately, we were forced off the crest to avoid a decrepit rocky tower. A traverse had to be made on the southern side of the ridge over steep, loose rocks, here and there treacherously covered in snow. It was a place not so much difficult as dangerous. There was not a reliable rock round which a rope could be placed to secure the party, and had a slip occurred, it would in all probability have been attended by the worst results.

From the traverse, an upward ascent brought us into the mouth of a loose gully, the head of which consisted of slippery slabs disagreeably covered by a few inches of unstable scree.

It is curious how on any climb the mental equilibrium of the mountaineer is liable to be upset by bad rock. Difficulty is one thing, danger another. The nerve-stressed mountaineer needing a safety valve for his feelings frequently finds an outlet for them in forceful language. I make no excuses, therefore, for certain improper remarks when clambering up these rocks. I cannot remember what Hoerlin and Wieland said, I had not yet learned the English translation of the German epithets that they held

UNKNOWN PEAK SEEN FROM NORTH-WEST RIDGE

in reserve for such occasions, but once, Hoerlin turned and remarked to me in perfect English, "These rocks are * * * !" sentiments which, happily, I was able to return with interest.

The principal advantage of taking photographs on a mountain is that the mountaineer is thus enabled to stop at frequent intervals and recover his breath. That is why most elderly mountaineers carry cameras. Taking a photograph is a much more convincing excuse for a halt than a boot-lace or braces that need adjusting. All those liable to be touched in the wind should take a camera. With what the reader will no doubt consider admirable foresight, I had brought up my camera with me, and not left it at the gap. I was not blown, but the ridge beyond the top of the little gully appeared so uninviting that I decided to stop there and photograph Hoerlin and Wieland doing it.

Seated in a sheltered place, with the sun glancing warmly down upon me, I was able to appreciate the situation to the full. For a short distance the ridge appeared possible, and although extremely loose, not excessively difficult. But beyond the next tower it was very different. It rose abruptly in a huge pinnacle, quite three hundred feet high, and above this pinnacle, connecting it to the next pinnacle, was the first of those appalling ice ridges. As I sat there I tried to think of an Alpine ridge comparable to it, but I could think of none. The Péteret, the Brenva, the East Ridge of the Jungfrau, none would fit.

How were porters to be got up? Even supposing ropes were to be fixed the whole way up the smooth slabs of the first great pinnacle, they would not be able to climb with anything but a light load ; also we had lost so much rope in the avalanche that we certainly had not enough to spare for even this first pinnacle. There was, however, no necessity for experiencing renewed pessimism. What we were now seeing simply confirmed the opinion that some of us had formed when gazing from the glacier below.

Hoerlin and Wieland were moving slowly and carefully, but even so they could not avoid dislodging many rocks which thundered down the precipices of the Ramthang Glacier. They turned a corner, and disappeared from view, but presently I saw them on the top of another minor pinnacle. There they remained, and I conjectured that they could not advance farther.

The usual mists gathered, but without threatening anything beyond desultory snow flurries. Occasionally, they rolled aside to disclose a beautiful snow mountain, unknown and unnamed in a south-westerly direction, apparently on the ridge separating the Yalung and Ramthang glaciers. This peak was in shape something like the Ober Gabelhorn, and possessed the same sweeping lines as the graceful Zermatt peak. Jannu should have been visible beyond, but mists obscured it. Almost immediately beneath us was the camp we had just established. We seemed to be looking almost vertically down upon it so steep were the precipices below. It seemed that a jump would have landed us on our tents. Above the camp, the Western Tributary Glacier swept up serenely to the col separating the Ramthang Peak from the first rock towers of the ridge we were on. The Ramthang Peak itself was playing hide-and-seek in a fitful mist but what was visible of it reminded me forcibly of the Mönch seen from the Jungfrau Glacier. There were the same graceful lines and flowing yet defiant massiveness.

It was late when we returned to camp, where we found Professor Dyhrenfurth, Schneider and Duvanel, who had come up that day from Camp One. I fear none of us were particularly optimistic over the day's work, and it was refreshing to find that Professor Dyhrenfurth did not agree with an opinion that the ridge was hopelessly inaccessible and considered that we should continue with the attack towards the terrace above.

For once, the afternoon clouds, instead of thickening for a snowstorm, dissolved. The evening was a calm and beautiful one, sky and world were unsullied by a single speck of cloud, a profound silence brooded over the sanctuaries of the snows, and only an occasional streamer of wind-blown snow sallied into space from the upper reaches of Kangchenjunga. Slowly night's floods filled the valleys, and the peaks became steeped in gaudy hues, like waxen deities covering their countenances with rouge and lipstick. Imperceptibly, the aerial pageantry died, but its riot of colourings was superseded by an afterglow which released the peaks from night's bonds for a few instants revealing them as cold statues of purest alabaster against a sky of deepest indigo. It was of such a day's end that Mr. G. Winthrop Young once wrote :

When in the hour of mountain peace,
The tumult and the passion cease,
As the red sunfloods sink,
And the pale lords of sovereign height,
Watch the cold armies of the night
Mustering their first assault.

Who would suspect evil to lurk in such a sunset? Yet, somehow, its superlative colourings put me in mind of a sunset I had once watched from a tiny ledge 12,000 feet up on the south face of Mont Maudit. *That* had been a sunset preceeding a heavy snowstorm in which retreat had been no easy matter.

I awoke some hours later to hear the pattering of snow on my tent. In the quietude it sounded like the light tread of fairy feet. Presently, I became aware of a faint undercurrent of sound like the far off throb of a train down some pastoral valley. The train approached, its distant murmurings rising gradually to a booming crescendo of sound. A gust of wind struck the tent, hurling the snowflakes against it with rude fierce spatterings. The gust passed, but soon came another and stronger gust. In a few minutes the blizzard burst, furiously sweeping upon our encampment. I snuggled more closely into my sleeping bag, for strong though the tent fabric was, it was not entirely proof against this bitter onslaught at a height of 20,000 feet. We had thought to be sheltered by the Northwest Ridge, but it afforded no protection, for the wind seemed to pour over it like a cataract, and descend almost vertically upon the camp.

The gusts grew stronger, they wailed and shrilled, rising to a roaring sort of boom like an express train racing through a tunnel. I could feel the tent floor rise as though malicious wind devils were undermining it with the object of my abode flying upwards into space. The wind dug viciously at the sides, or strove with strong fingers to tear apart the flaps, and burst the tent asunder. I prayed that Nemu had driven the pegs firmly and deeply into the snow, and then I recollected that the guy ropes were pitifully thin, no thicker than a sashline. There seemed every possibility of the tent carrying away ; if it did, there would be little fun in being overtaken by such a disaster clad only in underclothes, so I struggled out of my sleeping bag, pulled on my climbing clothes, and packed my rucksack with some necessaries.

The storm had now reached a pitch of intensity I had never before experienced when camping, and the night was filled with thunderous volleyings. Sometimes the wind would sink to a mysterious calm, during which it was possible to hear the storm snarling and worrying on the North-west Ridge as a preliminary before gathering its forces for a fresh charge on the camp. It was during one of these temporary lulls that I heard a sort of wailing outside, a wailing more human than storm-like. Peering through the flaps, I could just perceive a figure crawling through the snow. It approached my tent. In the light of my electric torch I saw the white, frightened face of Nagpa, the cook.[1] " Sahib ! Sahib ! " he cried, " Tent go ! Tent go ! " Opening the flaps wider, I glanced out, the porters' tent was intact ; the cook had merely lost his head. I was unwilling to have him for a bedfellow, and told him to go back. The cook, however, was completely demoralised, and shielding his face from the blast, he crawled down the line of tents with his constant wailing of " Sahib ! Sahib ! Tent go ! Tent go ! " Eventually, he found sanctuary with Wieland and Schneider, but as they explained later, they took him in not for love or charity, but simply as additional ballast for their own tent ! It

[1] Tencheddar had been left at the Base Camp.

was the solitary untoward incident of the storm. Well and truly had our tents been pitched.

An hour or two later the wind began to subside, and ere dawn it withdrew with some last mutters and snarls, leaving a clean sky picked out with stars against which the windy banners of Kangchenjunga softly lit by moonlight streamed in ghostly rivalry to the starry constellations.

We awoke to a warm sun glancing benevolently over the Twins. The North-west Ridge was plastered with new snow, and our steps in the couloir had been obliterated. As there was a possibility of avalanches occurring, we decided not to renew the attempt that day, and devoted the morning to building a wall of snow blocks on the windward side of the camp. Hoerlin was not feeling well ; somehow he had contracted a severe chill. Duvanel was also by no means fit, and only his devotion to his cinematographic duties had torn him away from the Base Camp.

At the head of the glacier on the ridge separating the Ramthang Peak from the North-west Ridge of Kangchenjunga is a small point about 20,800 feet high. This Wieland climbed by himself, using ski most of the way, and returned reporting that he had had a splendid view of the Ramthang Glacier and the North-west Ridge. It was decided, therefore, that the whole party should ascend to this point the following day, and carefully examine the latter to see whether it was worth while persisting in the attempt to climb it.

The following morning, May 15, dawned fine. Unfortunately, Hoerlin was so ill that there was no option but for him to return to the Base Camp. This was a serious loss to the climbing party ; at the same time, the prospect of getting any distance up the North-west Ridge was so utterly hopeless that it did not really matter.

After the experiences of the past fortnight, it was with something more than relief that we set out to climb something that could be climbed. It has been said that on Everest the climbing party were so heartily "fed up" with the mountain, its weather, and the effects of altitude that their sole wish was to get the job over and done with, no matter who did it. Our attitude towards Kangchenjunga was the same. I do not think there was one of us who was not sick to death of work on the mountain. At exactly what height mountaineering ceases to be pleasurable is not easily defined, the matter is rather one of individual temperament, but I do not think there is one mountaineer who has climbed on Everest or Kangchenjunga who can honestly say that he enjoyed the work. Achievement may be good for the soul, but it is not necessarily enjoyable. It was a relief to turn away from our exacting opponent for a day and *enjoy* ourselves.

The 20,800 feet point is easily reached along the ridge connecting it to the Ramthang Peak, but from sheer exuberance we chose to ascend by a little rock face rising from the glacier. We raced each other up by various routes, and subsided puffing and blowing on the summit. What a summit it is—one of the most extraordinary that I have ever stood upon. From the Western Tributary Glacier it appears a mere knob, an insignificant excrescence, but had we stood on the Ramthang Glacier we should have seen an "impossible" peak. Seldom have I gazed down such abysmal precipices as those falling to the Ramthang Glacier. They were as long as the south-eastern face of the Finsteraahorn, and as steep as the Dolomite wall of the Winklerthurm. The seamed and wrinkled surface of the Ramthang Glacier was spread out beneath us like a relief map, and we gazed down upon it like pilots from the nose of a bombing aeroplane. The upper portion of the Ramthang Glacier rises very steeply in an almost continous ice-fall. From the col we had reached in the North-west Ridge we had been separated by but a few hundred feet from it, but the drop from Point 20,800 must be at least 4,000 feet, and as this point is separated from the col by only about a mile, the inclination of the glacier is a steep one.

At its extreme head the Ramthang Glacier forms a snowy plain beneath the west face of the Kangbachen summit of Kangchenjunga. This face resembles closely the north face above the Kangchenjunga Glacier. There are the same impregnable ice walls stretching across it from which ice avalanches fall at least as big as those that fall from the north face. At the southern end of the face, where it abuts against the main West Ridge of Kangchenjunga, which separates the head of the Ramthang Glacier from the Yalung Glacier, there appeared to be a remote possibility of ascending between the ice walls and gaining the West Ridge. But, like the route we had already tried to the North Ridge, the possibility of success was more than counterbalanced by the possibility of annihilation, for the whole of the route was liable to be swept at any moment by ice avalanches. Even if the West Ridge was gained, what then? At the best it could only lead to the Kangbachen summit. To traverse the ridge between the

THE SUMMIT OF POINT, 20,800 FEET

Kangbachen summit and the highest summit, over the third highest summit, would be beyond the powers of any party. Therefore, it can be said without hesitation that Kangchenjunga is definitely unassailable from the Ramthang Glacier.

But if this side of Kangchenjunga is disappointing as regards its climbing potentialities it is hardly so otherwise. Great tiers of ice, gleaming steeps, and terrific red granite precipices combine to form a mountain face of a magnificence and grandeur worthy of the high summits it defends.

We had looked upon the last portion of Kangchenjunga to be properly seen by man, and what we had seen but confirmed out opinion that there are no group of mountain tops defended so impregnably as the " Five Treasures of the Snows." We tore our eyes away from those terrible ice walls and glanced for relief along the winding trench down which flows the Ramthang Glacier, and up over the sea of peaks to the west. Woolly clouds were rising from the valleys and draping themselves about the shoulders of the peaks. Once the cloudy waves rolled back ; in a distant trough a great peak rose in noble solitude above the world. Someone said, " Everest." Then the mists closed in, and we saw it no more.

We turned to the North-west Ridge. Our view of it was an end-on one, but if it was impossible to gauge its length, its height and difficulty were apparent. Below us on the glacier was the camp, a mere smudge on the immaculate expanse of snow. The terrace we must gain was 4,000 feet higher. The North-west Ridge was the connecting link. I have already described its knife-like edges of ice and its rocky towers. Seen thus, end on, they were jumbled one against the other, and one gained but little idea of the real length of the ridge. Perhaps it was this that deceived Professor Dyhrenfurth into deciding to continue with the attack. To those used only to Alpine scale, it is easy to be misled by the length of these Himalayan ridges. But if the length was not apparent, the difficulties were, and one could not but wonder how porters were to be got up, and camps established along that tremendous crest. There was no answer to this question. Even supposing the upper ice wall, against which the ridge abutted, to be climbed, and the terrace gained, what next? There was no possibility whatever of reaching any of Kangchenjunga's summits. The terrace did not extend right across the mountain to the North Ridge, there was a cut-off of impassable precipices. At the best, we could only hope to reach the Kangbachen summit, and that was separated from the terrace by 1,500 feet at least of formidable granite precipices. The most we could do was to climb as high as possible, perhaps even as high as the Bavarians, but what was the practical use of that? I fear my companions thought me a pessimist, but what else could one be taking everything into consideration? Anyway, the decision was made. We were to go on. This settled, we sat and lazed two or three hours away in the warm sun, happy hours, but trammelled by the thought of the morrow. The evening mists saw us jogging down the glacier to the camp.

The party that left the next morning consisted of Professor Dyhrenfurth, Schneider, Wieland and myself, with two porters, Lewa and Nima, the last named not to be confused with Nemu, my servant, both experienced

Everest men. The couloir was in bad condition, and steps had to be kicked or cut through an upper layer of powdery snow a foot deep. The porters were not happy; neither of them had experienced similar climbing before. Lewa stuck gamely to the task, but Nima was constantly slipping from his steps. I was next to him on the rope, and had several times to hold him. The ridge itself was also in a worse condition than it was during our reconnaissance.

We climbed on two ropes, Schneider, Wieland, and Lewa on the first, and Professor Dyhrenfurth, Nima, and myself on the second. The duty of the second party was to drive in pitons and fix ropes to the rocks. Nima caused us some anxious moments. It made one shudder to see the way he climbed on the loose rocks, hauling himself up on his hands without testing loose holds. So poor a show did he put up that we decided to leave him on a broad and safe part of the ridge, a decision that relieved him as much as it did us. Lewa was, however, an excellent rock climber, and followed Schneider and Wieland without difficulty to the top of the pinnacle, which had been the farthest point reached during the reconnaissance.

From the top of the pinnacle a vertical and holdless slice of granite drops to a gap. The climber must descend the granite slice on the rope, and alight on a sharp edge of snow. A piton was driven into a crack on the pinnacle, and a double rope fixed to it. Schneider and Wieland then descended hand over hand down the fixed rope, while being held at the same time from above on another rope by the remainder of the party. It was the sort of place fiction writers would make much of. Their descriptions would bristle with "unfathomable abysses," "like a fly on a wall," "beetling precipices," and so forth. The mountaineering guide-book writer would, however, describe it simply as "a twenty feet absail"[1] and as a grudging compliment to the place add "sensational." In this case, however, the fiction writer would convey a better picture to the mind of even the most sophisticated reader than the guide-book writer. To add to the sensationalism might be added the fact that the cracked and disintegrating pinnacle on which we stood exhibited a distinct tremor if rudely handled. I distinctly remember thinking, a trifle morosely, what a grand finale it would make to the expedition if the thing collapsed, and toppled into the "unfathomable abyss" with its human load.

As Wieland swung over the edge, the dirty and battered topi he was accustomed to affect looked strangely incongruous in these surroundings of rock, snow and ice, and, as he bumped and rasped down the rough granite, I half hoped that it would be knocked from his head and go spinning down the precipices, arriving at the camp below a pulped and shapeless mass. No such diversion occurred, and soon he had joined Schneider in the gap on the snow ridge.

Professor Dyhrenfurth and I remained on the pinnacle for an hour or two. We were privileged in witnessing one of the finest feats of climbing we had ever seen. Immediately above the gap rose a semi-detached mass of rock; beyond was another small gap, above which rose the great pinnacle in three hundred feet of slabs set at an angle not far removed from the vertical. Ice in the interstices of these slabs had forced them apart in many places and dangerously

[1] A German term for double roping.

unstable flakes rested against the face. Every ledge was loaded with snow or ice. On an Alpine climb of exceptional severity the ascent of this pinnacle would be a formidable proposition ; at 21,000 feet it bordered on the impossible.

Wieland ensconced himself on top of the semi-detached mass, and Schneider descended, without much difficulty, into the secondary gap, and began the ascent of the slabs. Methodically he worked his way upwards. The exertion of hard rock climbing at such an altitude was obviously severe, and after each upward heave he was forced to halt and rest. At length he reached a small stance, a tiny triangular recess, where Wieland joined him. Above this rose a slanting crack formed by the edge of a projecting flake the upper part of which bulged out unpleasantly. It was not a place to linger over, and Schneider did not linger. A foot scrape on the wall, a hand wedged in the crack, a quick upward caterpillar-like movement with nought but tiny hand holds to prevent a backward topple, and the hardest part had been accomplished. In the silence, unbroken save by an occasional whisper of wind, I could hear the sibilant sucking in of breath by sorely stressed lungs. A few feet more of difficult, but not such exacting climbing brought him to a sloping shelf. Wieland followed, and although burdened by both ice-axes and a rucksack, he came up without relying on the rope.

So far, so good. For a few feet the work was easier ; then the slopes steepened once more. In places they were dangerously ice glazed, and their sloping icy shelves were masked by snow. Ice-axes were called into play to clear holds. Now and again loose flakes of rock were dislodged.

Hurtling madly down the cliffs towards the Ramthang Glacier, they loosed other rocks until a perfect torrent of crags set the echoes thundering from the cliffs of Kangchenjunga.

Two hours work, two hundred feet of ascent, such was the climbing on the great pinnacle. Professor Dyhrenfurth and I watched the struggle with intense interest. It was, probably, the finest piece of rock climbing ever done at such an altitude. We forgot for the moment that the real problem was not the ascent of the ridge by the Europeans but the establishing of camps and the getting up of porters over this gaunt, inhospitable backbone of rock and ice.

The weather restored pessimism, grey mists came flying up from the west, a chill wind sobbed over the ridge, driving before it small moths of snow. Schneider and Wieland were out of sight now. Occasionally we could hear their voices, whilst an occasional stone crashed out news of their advance. We rose, stretched our cramped limbs, tied on Lewa, and started to descend.

We had collected Nima but were still above the col when we were startled by an enormous roar. Millions of tons of ice had broken away from the ice wall and were thundering down to the Ramthang Glacier. Instantly, the whole upper basin of the glacier was filled with a writhing hurricane of snow. Whirling up at us, it enveloped us in a blizzard, that whitened and sheeted our clothes in snow. The sky was darkened ; the whole district seemed to be filled with the wind-blown snow dislodged by this monstrous avalanche.

Such an avalanche, had it occurred in the Alps would command widespread attention, newspapers would refer

GRIM WORK ON THE NORTH-WEST RIDGE: SCHNEIDER AND WIELAND ON THE GREAT PINNACLE

to it as a " Cataclysm of Nature," and questions would be asked in the Swiss Parliament about it. But on Kangchenjunga, such avalanches are not the exception, but the rule—almost an everyday occurrence in their season.

Kangchenjunga is by no means the only Himalayan peak to discharge avalanches of such magnitude, but it is probably safe to say that there is no other Himalayan peak that discharges them with such frequency. This is due, of course, to its great snowfall, the quick downward movement of its glaciers.[1] A good instance of the size of a Himalayan avalanche is that which occurred during the late A. F. Mummery's attempt on Nanga Parbat. The party had bivouacked on a rock rib which projected some five hundred feet from the mountainside, but when they returned to their bivouac site after an unsuccessful attempt on the mountain, they found that their gear had been swept away by an ice avalanche. The avalanche had fallen diagonally and taken the five hundred feet rib in its stride ! The size and destructive power of Himalayan avalanches is the first thing that should be studied when climbing in the Himalayas. A purely Alpine-trained mountaineer finds it difficult to appreciate the scale on which such avalanches occur. Mummery paid the penalty of not realising this when he made his final and disastrous attempt on Nanga Parbat. No trace of him and his two Gurkha followers was ever discovered. We narrowly missed paying the same penalty too, and had we been wiped out during our attempt to reach the North Ridge of Kangchenjunga, we should have received our just deserts.

[1] See Appendix : " Glaciology : Snow Conditions and Avalanches."

It must be remembered that Himalayan ice avalanches *habitually* sweep the whole breadth of glaciers. To illustrate this I can but add that were the peaks in the vicinity of the well-known Concordia Hut in the Bernese Oberland enlarged to Himalayan scale, the mountaineer staying at the hut would not be safe from ice avalanches falling from the peaks on the opposite side of the Aletsch Glacier.

It was a relief to leave the rotten rocks, and to stand once more in the col ; and it was pleasant to escape from the cutting wind, and seizing the fixed rope that hung down the steep upper part of the couloir step blithely down the capacious ladder of holds towards the camp.

We glissaded down the lower part of the couloir, and for the first time that day Nima's worried expression gave place to a broad grin of delight. The porters are children at heart, and they have all the enthusiasm for a glissade down snow that a child has for a toboggan. For the benefit of the uninitiated I should explain that there are two methods of glissading. One is to stand upright, and the other is to sit down. The former is best employed on hard snow, the latter on soft snow. A certain degree of expertness is necessary for the stand-up glissade. Many commence in elegant style. With ever increasing speed, they slide down the slope. Presently, as the speed becomes faster and faster, they become flustered. From stability, they are reduced to instability ; their elegance, their dignified deportment is lost, their balance is upset, they struggle wildly to regain it, then the snow comes up and hits them on the nose. They go head over heels, their ice-axes are snatched from their hands, their hats torn from their heads, their rucksacks wind themselves round their necks, endeavouring to strangle them, snow is forced down their collars, up their sleeves, and into their pockets and trousers. Over and over they go in a series of somersaults, to subside finally at the bottom where they rise to their feet vowing it was good fun. On this account, the inexpert and less venturesome prefer to glissade sitting.

There is one other variety of glissade worthy of mention, and that is glissading on a rope. This is one degree worse than ski-ing on a rope. What usually happens is this : the leader, without troubling to enquire whether the second man is ready, shoots off with great velocity, despite the agonised cries of the latter. In a moment or two, the rope tightens on the second man who has barely had time to start, snatching him forward on to his head, and squeezing the breath out of him. The jerk arrests the leader, who hurls an uncomplimentary remark over his shoulder at the unfortunate second man, who meanwhile slides, or somersaults pell mell past the leader. Then, before the leader has time to continue, he is in his turn dragged in the wake of the second man. And so it goes on, a vicious cycle, until they have reached the bottom, where they sit side by side in the snow roundly abusing one another.

We reached camp in desultory snow squalls. Mists concealed the North-west Ridge, but now and again they blew aside and we scanned the rocks a little anxiously for signs of Schneider and Wieland. It was not until evening that we saw them descending, mere dots silhouetted against the jagged skyline. Dusk was falling when they returned. They reported immense difficulties, difficulties both of rocks and ice. Short of roping the great tower up from top to bottom, there was no possibility of getting the porters up it, and even with ropes, it would most likely prove impossible for laden men. The prospect of further advance beyond the tower was doubtful in the extreme. The whole crest of the first knife-like ice ridge would have to be hacked away before a passage could be won. At the end of this ridge, there was another tower, not so high as the first, but more difficult, in fact, probably impassable. Its summit was capped by a boss of ice which flowed down its sides like icing on a cake. There was no avoiding this tower, for the precipices on either side were sheer and offered no hope of a traverse. Above this tower, other ice ridges rose, a whole series of them, up to the terrace. Nowhere, said Schneider, was there a place on which a camp might be pitched. There were not even any ice pinnacles of a type suitable for bivouac caves. And the weather? What would be the position of a party caught high up on this great ridge in bad weather or high winds? The storm on the glacier three nights previously had been bad enough, but what would it have been like on the ridge? Retreat would be impossible. It would probably mean two weeks hard work to reach the terrace, even supposing camps could be established, and porters brought up, and by then the monsoon would most likely have broken. Each of these facts taken separately was sufficiently weighty to militate against any attempt; accumulatively, they were overwhelming.

There was no alternative but to abandon the project, and the following day Wieland and I accomplished the dreary task of collecting and bringing down the fixed ropes. Kangchenjunga had beaten us, beaten us not by bad weather, so much as by sheer difficulty. We had examined every portion of the faces above the Kangchenjunga and Ramthang glaciers. Nowhere was there a chink in the armour of the giant ; nowhere was there a route at which the mountaineer might look and say, " Well, it *might* go." Others sceptical as to the truth of these assertions may follow in our footsteps, but they too will return disappointed, and like us they will lie awake at nights and tremble, even as the ground trembles, at the roar of the great ice avalanches that seek their destruction, and like us, their hope and optimism will be ruthlessly crushed beneath the icy heel of Kangchenjunga.

CHAPTER XIV

THE RAMTHANG PEAK ON SKI AND FOOT

I have already had occasion to mention the beautiful snow and ice summit rising from the head of the Western Tributary of the Kangchenjunga Glacier. This peak, which is about 23,000 feet high, had inspired the appellation of Madonna Peak, for its sweeping robes of snow and ice suggest an unapproachable virginity, but Professor Dyhrenfurth had, in the interests of topography, subsequently rechristened it Ramthang Peak in deference to the Ramthang Glacier which is fed by its southern snow-slopes.

On May 18, the day after our decisive and final defeat on the North-west ridge of Kangchenjunga, we decided to push camp as far as possible up the mountain and so bring the summit within reasonable reach. With this end in view, it was agreed that Schneider and I should start before the main body of the expedition, and explore the route, with a view to ascertaining whether it was possible to establish a camp on a snowy shoulder at the foot of the eastern ridge of the peak which we hoped to follow to the top.

I was the first to leave, and soon after the sun had struck the camp strapped on ski and started alone up the glacier, which in its upper portion is practically devoid of crevasses and perfectly safe for a solitary ski runner.

The morning was a lovely one ; scarcely a zephyr of wind disturbed the delicate ice crystals formed by a sharp overnight's frost on the surface of the glacier ; a host of hoary peaks lifted silvered heads into a sky of gentian blue. Slowly the sun flooded over the snow-fields, his slanting rays revealing the most delicate folds and unsuspected wrinkles and undulations on the time-worn countenances of the peaks. I almost felt myself to be the invader of some moonscape, fantastic, unreal and beautiful.

A load of care had been lifted from my mind by the abandonment of the attempt on the North-west ridge. Now at last we were to attempt something that offered some prospect of success. Even my ski seemed to hiss joyfully beneath me, like a carefree ostler grooming a horse, and my ski-sticks drove into the crusted snow with a light triumphant plop at every forward lunge.

Impelled by sheer exuberance I climbed quickly, too quickly, for soon my lungs began to labour reminding me that I was not on the slopes of Mürren but 20,000 feet up in the Himalayas. Gladness departed ; what was mere flesh and blood that it should stride about the mountains in this way ?

I halted, and puffed myself into a more sedate frame of mind. Like walking uphill at great altitudes, so with ski-ing, rhythm. And, once cultivated, an easy rhythm. Despite the heavy hickory boards, I found myslf climbing more steadily, and making height more quickly, than if I had been on foot. Unconsciously, I began to keep my upward lunges in time with the slow beats of an old and sentimental music-hall ditty. I had not heard it, or sung it, for years, yet now, high up on the Ramthang Peak, it jogged through my brain in harmonious time with the forward movements of my ski.

Leaving Point 20,800 feet on my left, I climbed up and round in a wide arc, and began to ascend to the snowy shoulder. The slope I was traversing gradually steepened, and presently, on glancing down, I saw that an ice cliff two or three hundred feet high was below me. For fifty yards, where the snow was resting but a few inches deep on hard ice, a ski jump down the ice cliff was the penalty of slipping, and I advanced cautiously, stamping my ski well in at every step.

The slope eased off, and I found myself on the shoulder. From beneath it had looked almost flat and a good site for a camp ; actually, it was by no means flat and was, moreover, exposed to the full force of the wind. At all events, there was little object in advancing camp thus far, when only half an hour's extra work would be entailed on the morrow if we pitched it as high as possible up the glacier.

Above the shoulder rose an ice slope nearly 1,000 feet high, and forming a cut-off in the eastern ridge of the peak. The ice was too steep for crampons to be effectively used, whilst an evil glitter from its polished blue-black surface suggested a long and hard bout of step cutting.

Schneider joined me. Together we lazed in the sun. The view was an extensive one. The whole of Kangchenjunga's northern precipices were outspread before us. Our gaze swept along their granite façets, with their tiers of icy escarpments that stretched across the face of the mountain like the galleries of some colossal stadium. Now and again avalanches boomed through the still morning air telling of an ever restless and malignant activity.

South-westwards rose Jannu, 25,294 feet high. It would be difficult to conceive a more inaccessible looking mountain.

THE ROUTE TO THE RAMTHANG PEAK

Like many Himalayan peaks it is wedge-like in formation, with two summits set at either end of an almost horizontal ridge. Once gain this ridge and the ascent of either summit should be feasible. But how to gain the ridge? On the side facing us the precipices lifted in one smooth, terrible façade of granite ; on the other side, to judge by photographs, are equally fearsome cliffs. Can either summit be reached directly? The answer is, No. Both ends of the wedge end in hopeless precipices. Such is the problem presented to the mountaineer by Jannu, a rival of the famous Mustagh Tower in the Karakorams, and one of the most appalling rock peaks in the world.

Northwards, was the Jonsong Glacier, its irregular moraine strewn surface looking as though it had been riven by the picks and drills of a million mad navvies. Far up it stretched the ugly moraines, and it was only at its head that the forces of ruin and decay relinquished their grip, and gentle snow slopes stretched upwards to the snowy notch of the Jonsong La. West of the Jonsong La, the Jonsong Peak, 24,344 feet, rises grandly, its massive summit forming the culminating point of the ranges of North-eastern Nepal and North-western Sikkim. On this side, the south-eastern face, it throws down great cliffs friezed like Kangchenjunga with hanging glaciers. Dr. Kellas had, we knew, attempted it from the north-west. Given sufficient time before the arrival of the monsoon, that would be also our line of attack.

Then the range of peaks directly to the north of the Base Camp attracted our attention : fine precipitous rock peaks standing out from torrential glaciers. One of them, with a horizontal roof-like ridge rising to an acute spire at one end, bore a curious resemblance to a church.

At first we were observant and critical, but as we reclined in the snow, warmed by the sun, mind and muscles relaxed, and the peace of the high places laid soothing hands upon us. Through half closed eyelids I gazed at a world unsubstantial and dreamlike. Once again I seemed to hear music, but this time music solemn and slow, a majestic symphony from the massed orchestras of the hills. Its slow pulsating waves bore me away into space—the music was drowned in a sudden roll of drums. I tried to escape from the insistant din. I could not. It closed in on me, surrounded me. There was a thundering crash. I awoke. My opened eyes were dazzled by the snow glare, but the thunder still smote on my ears—a great avalanche was roaring off Kangchenjunga.

There is no peace to be found on these mountains. Solitude, yes, but peace, no. Every hour the mountaineer is reminded of the destructive forces that are ever at work ceaselessly endeavouring to reduce the grandeurs and beauties of the mountains to the uninspiring uniformity of the plains. To discover the peace that dwells upon hilltops you need go no farther than our Homeland hills. On them, among their rocks and heather, you will be given something that not even the lords of the Himalayas are able to give.

We unclipped our sealskins, thrust them into our rucksacks, and strapping on ski set off down towards the little worm-like caravan of porters who were toiling up the glacier far beneath.

I had barely started when Schneider was half way down to the glacier. He is a splendid ski runner, combining the dash of the first-class racer with the shrewd judgment of the mountaineer. To him, as with me, ski are something more than wooden boards, and ski-ing something more than a winter sport.

We had reached a height of between 21,000 and 22,000 feet, and I found ski-ing downhill at this height more tiring than ski-ing downhill at Alpine levels. One good point about mountaineering on foot at high altitudes is that it is no more fatiguing to *descend* moderately easy ground than it is in the Alps. The same does not apply to ski-ing. Balancing at low levels is automatic, but at 20,000 feet a conscious effort is required, whilst a swing is distinctly hard work. After a few swings the knees tend to become weak, and balancing more difficult. For a moderate class runner like myself, really to enjoy a long descent, it is best to stop and rest now and then.

The snow was of a delightful quality, hard, but with a loose crystalline surface into which the ski edged well. On such a surface the jerked Christiania was a simple matter. So much for the technique and the drawbacks of ski-ing at high altitudes ; how can I describe the delights ? The swift rush with body tensed and crouched, the song of the wind, the slow procession of the mountains, the fierce exhilaration of pure speed, and far below a little line of laden porters ascending the glacier, halted in amazement at these strange pranks, rushing upwards towards me. As Mr. Arnold Lunn once remarked, " Ski-ing is the finest form of locomotion known to man."

Camp was pitched on the gently sloping glacier under Point 20,800 feet. Unfortunately, Professor Dyhrenfurth, Wieland and Duvanel were not fit, and it looked as if

Schneider and I alone would be able to make the attempt on the morrow. Duvanel was worst; he had worked very hard on the taking of his film, and had not spared himself. The unfitness of the party was due, partly, to the wrong kind of food, and partly to nerve strain. Owing to transport delays, we had been forced to exist for ten days on food scarcely suited to the peculiar requirements of high altitudes. Now, thanks to Colonel Tobin, Wood Johnson and Hannah, the transport had been reorganised and food cases were arriving every day at the Base Camp. But the harm had been done, stomachs had rebelled, and constitutions had been undermined. Yet, compared to nervous strain, food is of secondary importance. We had escaped annihilation on Kangchenjunga only by a miracle, and during the eighteen days we had been on the mountain we had never felt safe from ice avalanches. At the back of our minds there had been always the feeling that we were only there on sufferance, and did Kangchenjunga choose, it could kill us. However philosophical a man may be, and as regards danger he *does* become philosophical at high altitudes, such mental strain tells on the physique. The period spent on Kangchenjunga was the most nerve racking that I have ever experienced. Wieland and I had been up the whole time, and we were both tired, mentally as well as physically. We were sick of the unvarying glare of snow, and longed to feast and rest our eyes once more on green grass. Schneider alone was brimful of energy, for he is of a type impervious to "nerves," besides being a man of extraordinary physique.

I spent the remainder of the afternoon seated on the snow ridge above the camp between Point 20,800 feet and the first rock towers of the North-west ridge. Among other dainties that had come up from the Base Camp, were some boxes of fruit jellies, and I lay contentedly in the snow eating them for hours, with the appreciative mechanical regularity of a small boy possessed of a generous, if misguided uncle.

Mists gathered ere evening, their light luminescent filaments serving to enhance the beauty of the peaks. Once again I thought I saw Everest, like a blue jewel resting on cotton-wool clouds.

Towards sundown a chill wind rose, and I was glad to retire to the camp. We had thought it to be protected from the wind, but that capricious element poured over the ridge above and descended on us in a bitterly cold douche. There were fifty degrees of frost as we vainly endeavoured to boil some hot tea over a Meta cooker, and so quickly did the heat radiate from the aluminium cooking pan, that it was impossible to get more than a lukewarm brew.

Among other good things that had arrived were some tins of cranberries. These mixed with condensed milk formed a delicious dish, and Duvanel, who had undertaken the onerous task of cooking, distributed them to us.

We were glad to get into our sleeping bags and warm numbed hands. The wind increased in force during the night, and once I awoke to hear the driven snow lashing my tent like raw-hide whips.

At dawn the wind had not dropped, and the cold was still severe, but, nevertheless, Professor Dyhrenfurth gallantly blew the conventional three blasts on his horn. But for once he blew without effect ; there was no competition among my companions to " show a leg." A few minutes later I heard him passing down the line of tents endeavouring to rouse their occupants to a sense of duty. Eventually he stood before mine. " Herr Smythe, it is time we started." No answer. Louder : " Herr Smythe, it is time we started." I emitted a lusty snore. A few minutes later the camp was slumbering peacefully again. It was not until eight, by which time the wind had abated and the sun was warm, that we were tempted outside.

By 9 a.m. Schneider and I were away. The wind had dropped completely, and the morning was as perfect as that of the previous day. Following our former tracks, we were soon on the shoulder. There we took off our ski, and made preparations for the final climb.

More as an experiment than anything else I had brought with me the pair of expedition boots that had been supplied to me. These weighed no less than eight and a half pounds the pair, and each boot bristled with over sixty nails. So far during the expedition I had not been able to pluck up enough courage to put them on, except when camping, and I had worn ordinary light Swiss-made climbing boots, which had kept my feet perfectly warm. The expedition boots were designed to guard against frostbite, and their uppers, which came half-way to the knees, were lined thickly with felt, whilst their soles were constructed of layers of rubber, felt and leather. As regards weight, the same remarks might be applied to the climbing suits supplied to the expedition. These again were excellent for use in camp, but were too clumsy and heavy for difficult climbing on a mountain. My own favourite garb consisted of Jaeger combinations and shirts plus several light Shetland sweaters weighing about two or three ounces each, with a wind-proof jacket on top, a pair of strong tricot breeches, one pair of socks, and one pair of stockings, and as additional protection to the legs, a pair of light and warm Kashmiri puttees that I had got from General Bruce. Two or three light Balaclava helmets on the head afforded ample protection to the ears and neck, whilst in the event of a particularly strong, cold wind, a leather flying helmet could be added. Fleece-lined leather fingerless gloves, are superior to all others.

In addition to the portmanteau-like expedition boots, it was necessary to wear crampons. These weighed about four pounds the pair. Thus, I was carrying a load of twelve and a half pounds on my feet, nearly an additional stone of weight, and I felt something like a cross between a leaden-footed diver, and one rooted to the spot in a nightmare after a heavy dinner. Thus attired, I began to lift my two foot portmanteaux up the snow slopes, with a slow, tread-mill-like action, trying to keep up with Schneider who was wearing ordinary light climbing boots. I felt fortunate in being with Schneider, for he exults in hard work on a mountain, and would, I hoped, make all the steps. If he did, it might be just possible for me to raise myself, plus boots and crampons, to the top of the mountain.

The slope soon steepened, and step cutting became necessary. Schneider went at it with a will, swinging his heavy ice-axe with that graceful yet vigorous style of the born ice-man. The ice was blue-black, polished and hard. Step after step was hewn out. The slope seemed interminable, and it needed a glance backwards down the long ladder of steps to assure us that we had made progress.

Professor Dyhrenfurth, Wieland and Lewa arrived on the shoulder, and sunned themselves, while waiting for the work to be finished. Cutting went steadily on ; the thud, thud, thud of the ice-axe becoming gradually monotonous to the ears. I occupied myself with enlarging the holds.

Suddenly came a mighty roar. We looked round. Huge masses were falling from the edge of the upper terrace of Kangchenjunga. Sweeping downwards with fearful force, a million tons or more of ice poured on to the Eastern Tributary Glacier. Sweeping forwards with lightning speed, the avalanche seemed to leap across the glacier, obliterating our former route between upper and lower Camp Two, and so far as we could see the site of lower Camp Two. The clouds of snow raised by the wind shot cannon-like across the mile-wide glacier and beat furiously against the precipices of the Twins. It was a tremendous avalanche, the largest we had ever seen. It confirmed, if confirmation was needed, the fact that nowhere within a mile or so of Kangchenjunga's north face is the mountaineer safe.

As quickly as possible I got my camera out of my pocket, and bracing myself firmly in my ice steps, took two hurried snaps. The illustration on the opposite page is one of them. It shows the head of the avalanche about to sweep the route between upper and lower Camp Two. The roar subsided, but it was long before the clouds of wind-blown snow began to settle. We turned again without a word to our task.

About half-way up the slope we decided to try our luck by traversing to the left to where snow appeared to overlay the ice. Our speculation was justified, and to our delight we found ourselves on hard snow in which only a couple of

THE GREAT ICE AVALANCHE SEEN FROM THE RAMTHANG PEAK

good kicks were necessary to make a step. Without further difficulty, we gained a subsidiary ridge falling from the main east ridge of the mountain. The snow here was wind-blown, hard and icy, and without crampons another hour's cutting at least would have been required. As it was, we walked, our faithful spikes biting well home. The angle, at first steep, gradually eased off. We found ourselves on the main ridge. It was almost horizontal at its junction with the subsidiary ridge, and we sat down for a welcome rest. My legs felt as if they had been afflicted with varicose veins since birth, and I anathematised the foolish spirit of experimental inquiry that had led me to don the expedition boots.

If Schneider is included in a party, that party does not get much rest. Now, he was fairly bubbling with suppressed energy and enthusiasm, and unable to wait, untied the rope, and set off along the ridge, which appeared quite easy for a considerable distance. A minute or two later he disappeared over a snowy hump, and I was left to myself. I did not feel like going on, my calves ached abominably, but I supposed it had to be done, and so heaving myself to my feet, I set off on the wearying task of dragging the expedition boots up the final five hundred feet of ridge to the top.

With a superhuman effort I gained the crest of the hump, wondering vaguely whether it would be practical to take my foot luggage off, and proceed in stockinged feet. Schneider was halted some distance along the ridge, and he called to me urgently. Beyond him the ridge was obviously much more difficult, narrowing to a mere blade of ice, of a type so characteristic of the Himalayas. I gathered that without me he did not like to go on alone.

With an inward, if not outward groan, I galvanised the expedition boots into activity, and together we toiled along the ridge.

There certainly appeared to be one or two distinctly formidable pieces in the ridge. Immediately above Schneider it was split by a curious crevasse, and above the crevasse was a nasty, unstable looking ice flake. Roping on to Schneider, I paid him out while he carefully bestrode the crevasse, and cut steps up and along one side of the flake. After a short upward traverse, he cut up directly to the top of the flake, and commenced to hew its crest away with a cheerful abandon. The flake became thicker, and the work easier. Soon he reached a broader portion of the ridge, and there, comfortably seated in the snow, bade me cheerily to come on. I did so, cautiously propelling the expedition boots upwards from step to step.

To the non-mountaineering public, there are only three kinds of mountaineering difficulties. There is the vertical, or overhanging precipice, the dizzy ledge, and the knife-like ridge. All these figure conspicuously in novels purporting to present the thrills of mountaineering. In actual practice, however, they are seldom met with. The Matterhorn, for instance, can be climbed, and not one of them will be encountered, and it is necessary to go to special districts such as the Aiguilles of Mont Blanc, or the Dolomites to find plumb vertical, or overhanging precipices, and genuine dizzy ledges. The knife-like ice ridge scarcely exists at all in the Alps, and the only examples I can recollect are the ice ridges on the Brenva face of Mont Blanc, and in particular the classic ice ridge of the Col de la Brenva, along which Mr. A. E. W. Mason's heroes and villains crawled in *Running Water*. But even the Brenva ice ridges, airy though they are, cannot compare to the ice ridges adorning Himalayan peaks. It was with something of satisfaction, therefore, that I found myself on a ridge, the knife-like merits of which not even the most earnest seeker after the sensational could carp at.

On my left the slopes dropped with tremendous steepness towards the Western Tributary Glacier ; on my right, I looked down the most extraordinary precipice I know of. Not extraordinary so much from the point of view of steepness—the Alps can produce a nearly vertical face of 4,000 feet in height—but in its appearance. Great uncouth lumps of ice clung to it, bulging outwards like the primitive sculptures of Mr. Epstein on the " Underground " building at St. James' Park. Leering, gargoyle-like heads suspended from thick, goitrous-like necks of ice peered over into the abyss ; great boiler plates and sheets of black ice coated the smooth granite slabs ; icy stalks, marrows, and pumpkins, grew from every wrinkle, niche and cranny.

How ice could cling to rocks at such an angle passes the comprehension. Such formations are not seen in the Alps. Only once before have I seen anything to approach this precipice, and this was strangely enough on Ben Nevis during an Easter climbing holiday. In that case, however, the ice was due to freezing moisture-charged winds from the Atlantic beating against the sunless northern cliffs of the Ben. In the present instance, it was more likely temperature fluctuation that enabled the ice to stick glue-like to the all but vertical precipice.

Needless to say, I did not think of all these things at the time ; my attention was concentrated on getting over the narrow bit as quickly as possible to the broader and more comfortable ridge on which Schneider was sitting. The ice was obviously tough, but the crest tended to curl slightly, but unpleasantly outwards over the right-hand precipice. This tendency was perhaps slightly exaggerated in my mind by Schneider's reference to " gefährlichkeiten " and earnest exhortations to me to hurry. In a minute or two it was no longer essential to emulate the stealth of a cat-burglar, and treading more boldly, I rejoined Schneider.

For a short distance the ridge was easier, then once more it narrowed. This time it was not so much a knife-edge as a leaf. The ice was curiously stratified, each stratum indicating a previous snowfall which had gone to help build up the leaf, but the latter was so thin and under-nourished that it needed but a blow to knock a hole through it several feet below its tapering crest. There was no going along that crest, the sole way of negotiating it was to traverse below it on the Kangchenjunga side. It was steep work ; hand-holds were as desirable as foot-holds. The expedition boots did not like it at all, and struggled clumsily to maintain a grip in the steps cut by Schneider. Given one good kick with them, the leaf would most likely have collapsed.

The length of the leaf was quite short, not more than twenty-five feet. It thickened gradually, and presently Schneider was able to cut directly up. He put his head over the top like an evil disposed small boy peeping cautiously over the wall of an orchard. Satisfied that the leaf was thick enough to support him, he hauled himself on to its crest, and advanced a few steps until it widened out considerably, and there was no longer any doubt as to its stability. There he halted, and shouted back that it was the last difficulty. I followed. Half way along I found myself opposite an awesome hole, a yard in diameter, through which I was able to put my head and shoulders, and gaze down the other side of the ridge. My sensations were no doubt similar to those of one who gazes out for the first time from the attic window of a New York "skyscraper." One glance was sufficient, and I popped my head back again. The downward view from *my* side of the ridge was sufficiently nerve harrowing. Presently, with a tremendous effort, I hauled the expedition boots on to the crest, and a few instants later flopped down thankfully beside Schneider.

The difficulties had been conquered ; snow slopes alone separated us from the summit. We grinned at each other, but my own grin was a trifle wan. Three hundred feet of soft snow slopes to do in the expedition boots at nearly 23,000 feet ! The ascent had taken longer than we had anticipated ; time was getting on, it was well after mid-day, and the afternoon mists were forming, and getting denser every instant. Leaving all our spare kit in our rucksacks, including, I regret to say, my camera, we set off on the last push to the top.

Dense mist concealed the way, and in its enveloping folds the snow slopes seemed to stretch never-endingly upwards. Fortunately, it was remarkably warm and windless.

On the way up the snow had been bad, but its vileness had been compensated for to some extent by the interest and excitement of the climbing. Now, with interest and excitement evaporated, and with nothing else to think about save getting to the top, we realised how vile it was, and what a purgatory we were undergoing. At every step Schneider sunk in well above the boots, but he persisted in leading, and his indomitable energy seemed in no whit abated. I plodded after him, cramp numbing my calves, my knees weak and trembling from the strain of raising the expedition boots.

It was not all plain sailing. At one point a half choked crevasse rifted the slope, and its steep upper lip necessitated a few steps being cut. Above that the slope eased off.

We trudged resolutely, if slowly, upwards. The mist thinned. The sun glared down upon our labours; its suffocating heat scarcely served to lighten them, rather did it seem to sap all energy, so that despite well acclimatised bodies, every step became a gasping toil. We topped the slope, and found ourselves on an easy snow ridge sloping gently upwards. The summit became dimly visible. Schneider leapt forward; soon he was fifty yards ahead, plugging with the tireless regularity of a machine through the soft snow. The fitful mists closed in upon us as we trod that last remote ridge-pole of the world.

We stood together on the summit. The mists lifted for a few seconds; once more sunlight and shadow chased about us. Below steamy clouds eddied and boiled from deep glacier cauldrons. A bitter breath of wind sallied out of the west, causing us to knock gloved hands together, and shuffle chilled feet. The world was not visible; we felt ourselves to be far removed from it. A picture flashed through my mind of civilisation, its hateful clamour, its sweatful heat. Up here, all was peace. When we had gone, the wind would fill our footsteps with snow, and remodel once more the serene crest of the snow ridge we

THE SUMMIT RIDGE OF THE RAMTHANG PEAK

had trampled under foot. All would be the same, and continue the same. When we die, may our spirits linger on the high places to which we have dedicated our youth.

We turned, and strode downhill. An immense vitalising relief coursed through my tired body. I was no longer lifting the expedition boots, I was simply swinging them forwards, and allowing them to drop. How mercilessly long the ascent had seemed, how mercifully short and easy the descent.

In a few minutes we were sitting in the snow by our rucksacks. For a while we lazed, but time was drawing on, and the descent had perforce to be continued. The flake and the knife-edge were soon traversed. Jumping the crevasse, we threw off the rope, and fairly raced along the ridge. At the end of it we found Professor Dyhrenfurth and Lewa. Though far from well, the Professor had pluckily climbed until he could go no farther. Wieland had ascended to the shoulder, and then turned back. A welcome drink from the Professor's flask, and we were off once more.

Facing inwards, and with picks driven well home, we carefully descended the long line of steps. Half way down, where the snow gave place to ice, and the route traversed across the slope, we found a convenient streak of snow. Stamping our crampons well in, we pelted down to the shoulder.

During the latter part, at least, our haste had been induced not so much by the desire to get down as by the knowledge that a large tin of fruit had been left on the shoulder. We had been the prey to grim forebodings that they might no longer be there, but these proved to be without foundation, and soon parched mouths and throats were being lubricated by delicious Californian peaches and their accompanying juice.

We did not loiter, for the afternoon wind was increasing in strength every minute, and stinging particles of snow from a greying sky were whipping across the shoulder. With stiff fumbling fingers I pulled off crampons and expedition boots. The latter, with their armoury of nails, seemed to leer at me. I thrust them out of sight into my rucksack, registering at the same time a solemn vow never again to burden myself with them on a mountain. I strapped on ski, swung my heavy load on to my back, and turned downhill for home.

Schneider had decided to descend direct to the Base Camp, and he suggested that I should leave my load at Camp Two for the porters to bring down the following day. This was a first rate idea, for like him, I hungered for the comfort and luxury of the Base Camp. With no boots to change, Schneider was off first. Taking everything straight, he shot skilfully down the snow slopes, and was soon a mere insect on the vast counterpane of the glacier. I followed. For a while, all went well, but then, instead of being sensible, and kick turning at the end of every traverse, I essayed a downhill Christiania swing. Instantly, the expedition boots retaliated ; the heavy rucksack swung me off my balance, and I pitched headfirst down the slope, where my nose, already raw and peeled, clove through the crusted snow like the prow of a ship. For a while I lay too winded even to curse, but then the humour of the situation suddenly dawned on me, and the breath I had regained was lost in an uncontrollable fit of laughter.

Kick turn by kick turn, I descended to Camp Two.

A circle of grinning faces greeted me as I entered the porters' tent, and hurled the expedition boots to the ground. Somewhere in the gloom a Primus stove was roaring ; a dirty hand pressed a large cup of steaming hot tea upon me. The porters were genuinely pleased that we had got to the top, as pleased as small boys would be at the success of their schoolmaster in an International rugger match. What splendid fellows they are ! Their devotion to duty, their uncomplaining fortitude, and unvarying cheerfulness on Kangchenjunga can never be forgotten. The ground is well prepared for the corps of native Himalayan guides that General Bruce and the Himalayan Club are anxious to form.

The light was poor when Schneider and I started off for Camp One. The basin of the Western Tributary Glacier we were leaving seemed sombre and sad, the ice walls of Kangchenjunga shone greenly, malignantly in the fading light, and the jagged rock towers of the North-west ridge stabbed the livid mists like grim watchful sentinels. How long will it be before man again visits this lonely corner of the World ?

We ski-ed in long smooth sweeps down the gentle breast of the glacier. Gradually, the angle steepened, the keen air tightened in nostrils, whooped past Balaclava-covered ears. Swish ! A swing one way, a long sideways skid on the hard frozen surface, snow crystals raised in a scintillating shower. Swish ! A swing the other way. The ski whipped round like live things. Walking up through the soft snow we had been exposed for perhaps half an hour to the risk of ice avalanches from the ice cliffs below the shoulder of the Ramthang Peak. Ski-ing down, we swept across this dangerous area in a few seconds.

Schneider soon disappeared ahead; he had as usual, taken everything straight. My ski-ing is, however, not of the type that allows me to take steep slopes straight without disaster, or at least frequent and unpleasant crashes, and I entered the corridor alone. In it I was forced to tack to either side of Schneider's straight track several times. It was during one of these tacks that I went into a crevasse. In the dull light the slight concavity in the snow-crust concealing it was not visible. I was running moderately fast when the snow beneath me collapsed. There was no time in which to do anything, no fraction of a second in which to make a desperate spring forwards, my legs dropped into nothingness, my body, owing to its forward impetus was flung violently against the opposite lip of the crevasse. There I lay, half in and half out of the crevasse utterly and completely winded. My legs were numbed with the shock, and my back felt as though it were broken, as well as every other bone in my body. I certainly ought to have broken both ski and legs, yet, by some miracle, both were intact. It was a nasty moment that drop into space; I remember vividly the noise of dislodged fragments of snow and ice as they fell with a sort of shush, shush, shush, into the bowels of the crevasse. Minutes later I was able to make an effort and haul my legs and ski out on to *terra firma*, where for some time I lay, still partially winded and feeling not a little sick. As I lay I remembered the wise words of an American friend of mine who fell into a crevasse the first time he had been escorted on to a glacier. He said : " Never again ! I guess it's *terra firma* for me in future, less terror and more firmer."

Taking off my ski, I walked down the remainder of the

corridor, following the porters' tracks. Dr. Richter was at Camp One. He had some hot tea ready for me and, what was even better, rum. Both served to steady shaken nerves.

The way between the Base Camp and Camp One had been well prepared by Schneider and Duvanel ; it was not only a good route for foot slogging, but first rate for ski-ing, and soon we had left Camp One far behind.

The angle at which the main ice stream of the Kang-chenjunga Glacier rises is deceptive. From the Base Camp the glacier looks practically flat, but actually it slopes downwards at a much steeper angle than at first appears, and we skimmed gaily down it for quite three miles with scarcely a stop.

Dusk was falling as we reached the maze of moraines separating the snowy middle of the glacier from the grassy terraces of Pangperma and the Base Camp. Seated on a boulder, we gazed back towards the scene of the labours, bitternesses, hopes and fears of the past nineteen days. The evening was a still one ; the glacier rivulets were already hushed and awed in the grip of frost ; only the occasional slither and splash of a dislodged stone falling into a glacier pool broke a profound quietude. Through a window, where the mists were melting into the first stars, stood Kangchenjunga, its precipices aflame in the setting sun. Before us curved the great glacier down which we had come, like a ghostly road stretching to the foot of some Goblin fortress. All day long the avalanche juggernauts had roared down upon it ; now they rested cold and silent in the garages of the hills, and "Policeman Day" retired wearily from his long beat.

We turned to go, leaving our ski and sticks on the stones.

Two figures came scrambling over the moraines to meet us, Nemu and Nima with a thermos of hot tea for each of us. It was a kindly thought, something to remember when other and more grandiose events have passed into oblivion.

I had expected to feel very tired. On the Ramthang Peak it had seemed an impossibility to get down to the Base Camp that day, but seven thousand feet of descent had stimulated muscle and will jaded by altitude, and I found myself trudging over the moraine feeling little more tired than at the end of an Alpine day.

Tropical night fell like the lowering of a curtain. As we stumbled over the last stones more figures emerged from the gloom and we clasped hands with our companions.

Though defeat on Kangchenjunga had been our lot, it was a cheery crowd that gathered in the mess tent that evening. What a joy to be able to sit and eat dinner with one's fellows once more, instead of " pigging " it cramped up in one's own tiny tent. Even Tencheddar's " Soup sometime coming," as we sat and waited hungrily for dinner, could not damp the general cheerfulness.

Transport difficulties had been solved, and Wood Johnson and Hannah were back from their arduous tasks, which they had accomplished so successfully. Wieland and Duvanel had come down that day ; the latter was far from well. Only Professor Dyhrenfurth and Dr. Richter remained in the upper camps, and they with the remainder of the porters and equipment would be down next day.

Kangchenjunga had beaten us, and claimed a brave soul in so doing. That the toll was not greater was not due to any skill on our part, it was a Divine Providence.

CHAPTER XV

THE JONSONG LA

On May 20 the remaining camps on Kangchenjunga were evacuated, and all members of the expedition and porters assembled at the Base Camp. Rest and reorganisation were the first essentials. The general health and condition of the party was by no means what it should be ; several members were still suffering from the relaxing effects of altitude throats and Hoerlin was weak from his chill. Our greatest anxiety was Duvanel, who was seriously ill with a chill on the lungs and severe altitude throat. It was a question whether or not he should be sent down straight away to the lower valleys, if not Darjeeling, but he was determined to carry on, if possible. Frau Dyhrenfurth had stood her trying time at the Base Camp wonderfully well. She had organised the dispatch of stores and equipment to the other camps most efficiently and her untiring efforts, and especially her unvarying cheerfulness, had been real assets to the expedition.

In order to attack the Jonsong Peak, 24,344 feet, which was now our main objective, we had to cross the Jonsong La, 20,200 feet. Though, technically speaking, an easy pass, the crossing of it was by no means an easy undertaking for two reasons, firstly, weather, and secondly, porterage. Every day was bringing the monsoon nearer, and on such a high pass heavy snowstorms and deep snow must be expected. Apart from the monsoon, purely local storms might well prove embarrassing. The question of porterage was, however, the most serious one. We had dismissed the majority of our porters, retaining eighty of the best, and two hundred and fifty loads had to be trans-

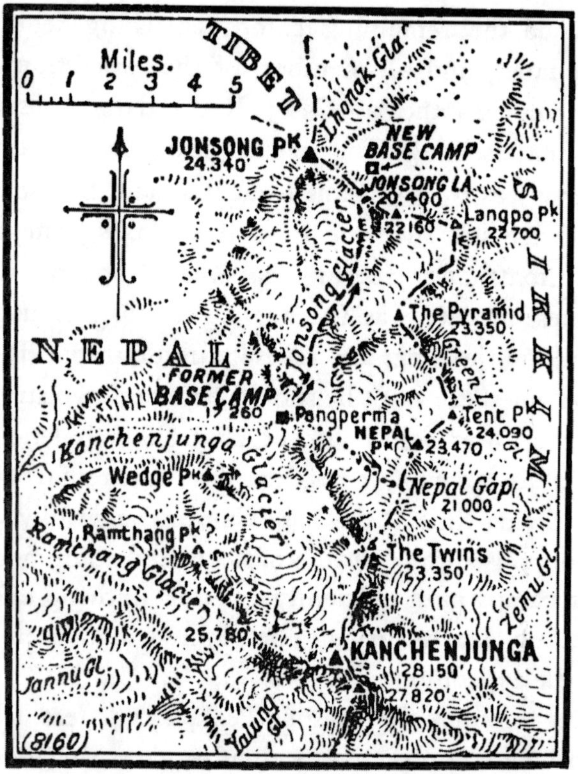

By courtesy of *The Times*

ported. A new Nepali Subadar had come up in place of the former one, whose feet had been severely frost bitten, and he promised to enlist for the expedition all the local porters available, but we knew that we could not rely upon obtaining more than twenty or thirty at the most. There was another factor, dissatisfaction among the porters, and this, it must be admitted, was not entirely without reason. During the expedition the porters had been worked very hard, harder, it is probably safe to say, than they had ever been worked before on any other expedition. On Everest, it was customary to give them one rest day in every four or five working days. These rest days naturally depended on circumstances, but they had been set aside whenever possible. Our porters had marched without a rest from Darjeeling to Tseram, eleven days' marching, with full loads of sixty to eighty pounds per man, which had included a total of something like 35,000 feet of uphill work, and marches in tropical heat. Since Tseram, owing to the breakdown of the transport arrangements and difficulty in obtaining sufficient local food, they had frequently been on short rations, or had to eat food to which they were not accustomed.

Furthermore, a quantity of clothes had been lost or stolen *en route*, and a number of Sherpas actually had worked on Kangchenjunga for several days before their full complement of high climbing clothes had turned up. Another grievance, confined to the Bhutias, was that clothes had been issued only to the Sherpas on the mountain, and the Bhutias, who had been told off for the donkey work of bringing up loads to the Base Camp, had not had the extra clothes that had been promised them. Naturally, we had no option but to clothe the high climbing Sherpas in preference to the Bhutias, but the latter's grievances were nevertheless easily understandable. An ugly situation that threatened to resolve itself into a strike and general desertion of the Bhutias was once more saved by the tactfulness of Wood Johnson, and the Bhutias agreed to cross the Jonsong La on the condition that the clothes promised them should be recompensed for by a cash equivalent on our return to Darjeeling.

As regards transport, Wood Johnson told me that when he and Hannah had gone back, Hannah had arrived at Khunza first, and took what coolies he could find over the Mirgin La to Tseram. Subsequently, Wood Johnson, who had followed him to Khunza, went through that place with a fine comb, and got women, boys, and men from villages below, in fact every available coolie in the district, and sent them to Tseram. As a result of these efforts, ninety-eight loads were got from the Kang La and Tseram to the Base Camp; the remaining loads were mostly looted. Incidentally, sixty-eight Darjeeling men and twenty-three Khunza men were sent back from the Base Camp the day after we arrived there, but as they did not reach Colonel Tobin, they must all have deserted. Fortunately, while at Khunza, Wood Johnson made arrangements to send up coolie rations, meat, eggs, and vegetables to the Base Camp. The situation had been got well in hand by May 11, when Colonel Tobin left Tseram for Darjeeling, after having sent on all loads to Khunza.

Wood Johnson now suggested that in view of the limited number of coolies available, only a small and light party should cross the Jonsong La and attempt the Jonsong Peak; the remainder of the expedition should return to Darjeeling, turning aside to attempt Kabru, 24,002 feet. The snow would have melted from the Mirgin La and the Kang La, and even during the monsoon there should be no difficulty in crossing these passes, as they were not high enough to be snowed under, while there would be little risk of the transport breaking down. The only other alternative was to get the loads over the Jonsong La by relays of porters. Such a scheme was all very well in theory, but there were grave objections to it in practice. In the event of a severe snowstorm, it was bound to break down, and we might find ourselves in the unpleasant position of having one half of the transport on one side of the pass and the other half on the other, with all intervening communication cut off. Bad weather might well result in a wholesale desertion of the porters, or at least the underclad Bhutias. In spite of these objections it was decided that this scheme should be proceeded with. That it succeeded was due entirely to luck, the greatest piece of luck the expedition was blessed with.

Owing to the expiration of his leave, Hannah had to return to Darjeeling, but before doing so he climbed with Wieland the 20,000 foot peak on which Wood Johnson and I had been beaten by bad weather. We parted from him with real regret. His work on behalf of the transport had been invaluable. In fact it is only fair to say that without him, Colonel Tobin, and Wood Johnson to do the spade work, the expedition would not have reached the Base Camp.

Now that the main object of the expedition had been frustrated, Professor Dyhrenfurth wisely decided to make all use of the large party under his command, and by splitting it up, explore as much new country as possible. With this end in view Schneider and Wieland were told off to explore the 21,000 feet high col known as the Nepal Gap, which forms the lowest point on the ridge separating the head of the Zemu Glacier from the Kangchenjunga Glacier. Dr. Kellas had attempted to reach it from the Zemu Glacier no less than four times. In 1907 he made two attempts ; on the first he reached 18,000 feet and was forced to retreat by a thick mist, and on the second 19,000 feet, at which height impassable crevasses again enforced retreat. His third attempt in September, 1909, was defeated by a heavy snowstorm 1,000 feet below the col, whilst on his fourth and last attempt in May, 1910, he almost reached the col, but did not climb the small rock wall just beneath the summit.

I should have liked to have accompanied Schneider and Wieland, but the claims of journalism and photography relegated me to the Base Camp. It was arranged that the Nepal Gap party should leave on May 23, and the main party for the Jonsong La the following day. Dr. Richter and Duvanel, who was now recovering from his chill, were to remain at the Base Camp until it had been cleared of all loads. Meanwhile, an urgent message had been sent to Tikeram Thapa at Khunza, telling him to collect and bring up as many local porters as possible.

The few days rest at the Base Camp had been most welcome. It had been good to feel the soft turf beneath the feet again, and to rest eyes strained from the glare of glaciers and snow-fields. The weather was now very warm, an ominous warmth, which seemed to herald the monsoon. Unfortunately, the wireless set had arrived completely shattered, and we were unable to obtain news as to when the monsoon might be expected. It was small consolation to know that every evening messages were being broadcast for our especial benefit from Calcutta. Among the loads

ON THE WAY TO THE JONSONG LA

that had arrived intact was the dark room photographic tent, a sinister looking affair, like the lair of a fortune-teller, in which we developed a number of negatives and cinematograph films. For the interest of photographers I need only remark that so brilliant was the light at 20,000 feet that an exposure of $\frac{1}{50}$ of a second at an aperture of f.22 was sufficient, save during the early morning or late afternoon.

Given good weather, no one can fail to get over the Jonsong La. Whether the passage is to be a fatiguing one, or a relatively easy one depends largely on finding the best way through the labyrinth of moraines covering the Jonsong Glacier. Mr. Freshfield found it a troublous business descending on this, the Nepal side, and camped twice between the pass and Pangperma. He was, however, much hampered by snow covering the glacier. In former times the pass was frequently used by salt traders between Khunza and Lachen, and we were astonished to learn that the Dhudwallah, who had been engaged in bringing milk up to us regularly from Kangbachen, was fully conversant with the route. We engaged him, therefore, as our guide.

In order to find a good camping place for our first camp, Hoerlin and Wood Johnson went up the Jonsong Glacier the day before the party left. They returned after having found a grassy shelf on the west bank where tents might be pitched.

The morning of May 24 was a beautiful one, and Wood Johnson and I strolled up the grassy moraines feeling at peace with the world. On the way we passed Nemu, who was laden with a miscellaneous assortment of my luggage, including my aluminium washing basin which jerked up and down with a mournful clang at every step. For some distance we followed a well defined path which seemed to show that the Jonsong La was frequently crossed in the past, or that yaks were brought up to graze on the stony pastures of Pangperma. Possibly, it was the latter speculation that caused me to halt and sniff, and remark that there was a strong smell of yaks. Wood Johnson, however, seemed to take this as a personal reflection.

Between the moraines and the mountainside were a number of old snow-drifts, composed probably of avalanche débris. These had been resolved by the hot sun and dry atmosphere into groups of beautiful little snow pinnacles a foot or two high. These are known in the Andes of South America as *nieves penitentes*, owing to their resemblance to a penitent congregation. The most common explanation as to how they are formed is that winter and spring snowstorms form snow-drifts, which are blown into ridges. As the snow of these ridges is not of the same consistency throughout, the less dense snow tends to melt and evaporate, leaving the denser masses, which are subsequently sculptured into pinnacles by sun and evaporation. As with ice pinnacles on Himalayan glaciers, the origin of *nieves penitentes* is also influenced by temperature fluctuation. I have only once seen anything to approach them in the Alps, and that was in the exceptionally hot summer of 1928, when the snow on the surface of the glaciers became so rough and spiky in the broiling sun, that one could only assume it to be in the first stage of being formed into *nieves penitentes*.

In the corner of Pangperma where the Jonsong and Kangchenjunga glaciers unite, we sat down and rested awhile. Are there grander or nobler peaks than those surrounding the head of the Kangchenjunga Glacier? A snowstorm was raging on Kangchenjunga, and dark slate-coloured clouds sailing up from the south were adding their quota to the snow-fields and glaciers. A few clouds detached themselves from the main masses, and sailed inquisitively up the glacier, strewing snow-flakes in their wake, before being disrupted and annihilated by the dry Thibetan winds from the Jonsong La. Other and heavier clouds pouring over the ridges from the south advanced to the attack. The Wedge Peak received their first furious assault, and became impenetrably shrouded in the murk of a snowstorm. The storm clouds advanced in a solid phalanx, but the north wind counter-attacked vigorously. A writhing mêlée took place above the glacier basins. The storm clouds were held, but now and again they sallied desperately forward, bombarding us with hasty flurries of snow. Impotent against the north wind, they retreated sullenly; the latter pressed its advantage irresistibly and, sweeping through their once proud ranks, forced them back in a confused and hopeless rout. A searchlight of sun pierced the gloom. Like the flood-lit summit of a lofty spire, the Wedge Peak stood forth from the blue veils of snow. Once through the shifting murk concealing Kangchenjunga came the deep growl of an ice avalanche. The great mountain was bidding us begone.

We gazed up the glacier towards the Nepal Gap, arguing as to which was the most probable route taken by Schneider and Wieland. Was it a trick of the imagination, or did we see two minute dots descending the broken glacier from the ridge north-west of the Gap? Some porters were passing, and Wood Johnson directed their keen eyes to the place. Yes, they saw the dots too. Schneider and Wieland were evidently busy at their task of finding a way over the Gap.

Continuing on our way, we passed the corner of Pangperma and looked up the stony reaches of the Jonsong Glacier. There are many peaks hereabouts that would yield to determined assault, and some look decidedly easy. Dr. Kellas must have realised this when he crossed the Jonsong La from the Lhonak Valley to climb the Langpo Peak, 22,800 feet, at the head of the glacier.

The passage of many porters had trodden out a good path along the moraine. Turning the corner at Pangperma seemed to bring us into a different country and a different climate. Everything pointed to a much drier climate, the very ground was more dusty than at the Base Camp, whilst the defeat of the storm clouds suggested that the strong, dry winds of Thibet protect the Jonsong Glacier to a large extent from many of the snowstorms that attack Kangchenjunga. Were a number of meteorological stations to be installed between Kangchenjunga and the Jonsong La, they would most likely exhibit striking differences of precipitation and humidity.

Camp had been pitched on a charming spot—a small grassy shelf above the moraine of the glacier. The shelf ended in a spur on which a number of flat stones, obviously arranged by the hand of man, suggested a former encampment, possibly Mr. Freshfield's. Ranged along the shelf was a drift of *nieves penitentes*. They occupied most of the width of the shelf, and there was but little room in which to pitch our tents. Had we known how this icy

THE JONSONG PEAK FROM CAMP ONE, JONSONG GLACIER

congregation was to protect us, we should scarcely have resented their usurping so much space. Opposite the camp rose a fine snow peak of about 22,000 feet, which appeared climbable. On this side, it lets fall a steep glacier to the Jonsong Glacier. Were it in the Alps, this glacier would by reason of its steepness be much crevassed, yet here, so plastic is the ice, and so capable is it of accommodating itself to the irregularities and steepness of the ground down which it flows without breaking or cracking, that, though hummocked and lumpy, there was scarcely a crevasse to be seen in it.

Half a mile farther on up the glacier, another steep high glacier flowed down to join the main ice stream of the Jonsong Glacier, the pinnacles of which made a fitting foreground to the great southerly walls of the Jonsong Peak. From our position the mountain appeared to full advantage. South-westwards from the summit, smooth unbroken snow-fields descend for some distance, but like Kangchenjunga, they come to an end above precipices thousands of feet high, and like Kangchenjunga these snow-fields, which are hundreds of feet thick, are constantly breaking away at their edges in huge ice avalanches, which set the echoes grumbling round the great cirque of peaks, whence the Jonsong Glacier draws its strength.

That afternoon the sky was covered with gossamer-like clouds, floating above the mountain tops. Wood Johnson eyed them suspiciously, and gave it as his opinion that they preceded the monsoon. He added a grain of comfort, however, by declaring that we need have no immediate fears, and that we might confidently expect another week of fine weather. We could well believe in the imminence of the monsoon, for these clouds were strongly reminiscent of those which forecast a bout of *föhn* in the Alps.

The majority of the porters were sent back the same day. Professor Dyhrenfurth's scheme was that they should leave the Base Camp early the following morning bringing up more loads, and continue with us up the glacier. Lobsang had been given instructions that this was to be done. The porters, however, not unnaturally, regarded such a procedure as being in the nature of a double march, and though they left the Base Camp early enough, they took good care not to arrive until it was too late to start another march up the glacier. This gave us no option but to postpone our advance for another day.

This attempt to double march the porters had an unfortunate effect on their morale. When at length they arrived, they gave it out as their intention to strike. Collecting in a sullen group, they declared they would not continue farther. Once more Wood Johnson was forced into the onerous position, in which he should never have been placed and over which he had no control, of having to placate our disgruntled labour. The porters were quite reasonable. They regarded the attempt to double march them as being the forerunner of other double marches and continual hard work without rests. Their experiences on the march out from Darjeeling, when they were marched for the first eleven days without rest, still rankled at the back of their minds. They were perfectly prepared to cross the Jonsong La, provided they were given one rest day in four working days. Naturally, this was agreed to, but it is a pity that such a situation should have arisen.

Late that afternoon Schneider and Wieland arrived.

Their reconnaissance of the Nepal Gap had been most successful. Not only had they been able to solve the problem of the Gap, but Schneider had made a lone ascent of the unnamed 23,470 feet peak to the north of it. Thus, if Graham's claimed ascent of Kabru is not taken into account, it was the highest actual summit yet reached, for it was slightly higher than Mount Kaufmann in the Alai Pamirs, also climbed by Schneider in 1929, or Trisul, in the Garhwal Himalayas, climbed by Dr. Longstaff in 1907.

The party had first of all ascended the tributary of the Kangchenjunga Glacier enclosed between the Twins and the 23,470 feet peak. They had made no attempt to reach the Gap directly from this glacier as the slopes are extremely steep, and consist for the most part of rotten rocks, but they had ascended a subsidiary glacier falling from the ridge between the Nepal Gap and the 23,470 feet peak. On this they had camped, and thence proceeded with little difficulty to the ridge. On the far side of this, and well to the north-west of the actual Nepal Gap, they had discovered a short, steep snow slope leading downwards towards the Zemu Glacier. They described it as being very similar to the south side of the Jungfraujoch in the Bernese Oberland. Thus, strictly speaking, the problem of the actual Gap remained unsolved, but a practicable way had been discovered over the main chain a little distance to the north-west of it, which is obviously much easier than the direct traverse of the Gap, even although the ridge traversed is a few hundred feet higher than the Gap.

Having made this important discovery, they decided to

attack the 23,470 feet peak. Wieland was unwell, but the indefatigable Schneider climbed it alone, a truly splendid effort. Low down, he had to dodge an ice-fall, that cut across the lower part of the ridge. Above this was a steep snow ridge. The snow was hard and icy, but with crampons scaling it was an easy matter, and he had to cut no steps. The summit was attained without further difficulty, whence he enjoyed a glorious view of distant Everest and Makalu. The name of the 23,470 feet peak suggests itself, and we christened it the Nepal Peak.

That evening we made merry in the camp. By some sleight of hand on the part of Frau Dyhrenfurth a small crate of champagne materialised. My mouth organ emerged from the seclusion forced upon it by cracked and sunburnt lips, and the peace of the Jonsong La was broken by the strains of "John Peel," the rousing chorus of which was rendered by Wood Johnson.

But the great peaks of the Himalayas take defeat hardly. That night I was sleeping peacefully, as a man should sleep after champagne, when I began to dream that I was involved in a railway accident. I could hear the coaches in front of mine telescoping, one after another, with a series of appalling crashes. My own was just about to smash when I awoke trembling with terror. The crashes continued, each one was nearer than the last. With an almost animal-like quickness my mind grasped the danger—boulders were rolling down the slopes on to the camp ! I struggled to get out of my sleeping bag and tent, but it was too late ; the former gripped me lovingly, the flaps of the latter had been securely laced up by Nemu. I could do nothing but lie where I was and hope for the best. Some sort of curious sixth sense, a sense dependent entirely upon sound, told me that one boulder was coming straight for my tent. One side of the tent was occupied by my luggage, including a large tin box. Against this I rolled myself, hoping vaguely that it would break the force of the boulder. Actually, of course, it would have been crushed like an egg-shell beneath the falling lump of granite. For what seemed an eternity I could hear the onrush of the boulder. It was travelling in bounds. One moment, with a crash, it would strike another rock, the next, it would fall with a dull thud into the yielding turf. There came a great thud not more than a few yards away, the next bound would assuredly bring it on top of me. It was a tense moment. Then came a mighty thudding splash, and silence. The boulder had plunged into the drift of *nieves penitentes* not three yards from my tent !

It had been the last to fall. I scrambled out of the tent wondering whether any damage had been done by the other boulders. There were perhaps half a dozen in all. The camp was awake, all save Wood Johnson. Bawling into his tent elicited nothing more than a sleepy " Whaser-marrer ? " Happy indeed the man who can sleep thus, even after champagne.

The next morning I searched for and found my potential assassin. It was a rock about a foot and a half cube. A certain piquancy was added to the situation all unconsciously by Nemu. As he packed my kit, he glanced disparagingly at my tin box and remarked, " Box, him come to pieces, Sahib, you get other box from cook." He was right ; the tin box certainly was on its last legs and on the point of collapsing from the ill usage of the past few weeks. I took his advice and surreptitiously exchanged it for a stronger one owned by the cook.

As this camp was to remain until everything had been transported over the Jonsong La, it should have been transferred to another and less dangerous spot. This would perforce have been on the glacier, which was here rough and moraine covered. That it was not, indicated the callous—one could scarcely call it philosophical—frame of mind into which we had dropped. The result of not moving the camp was evidenced a few days later when Frau Dyhrenfurth, who had been left by Professor Dyhrenfurth in charge, was nearly killed by another and larger fall of rocks. It was curious that these falls of rock should have occurred at precisely the same spot. The slope above the camp is by no means steep, and why two falls should have come down it when there were other and far more favourable slopes for falling rocks is a mystery. It almost seemed as though they had been uprooted and aimed at the camp by some malignant hand. The porters put them down to the Snow Men, and for once I was not inclined to disagree with them.

Explorers of the great Baltoro Glacier in the Karakorams relate that it takes no less than four days to march up the moraine-covered part of the glacier, before the ice is actually trodden. The Jonsong and Kangchenjunga glaciers combined cannot rival the Baltoro in size, yet in approaching the Jonsong La from Kangbachen the traveller marches a full three days on moraine before reaching open ice.

Leaving the camp we climbed up and down over the stony moraine. There is little of beauty about the lower portion of the Jonsong Glacier, but there is a certain impressiveness in the barren grimness of its stony reaches ; it is nothing more than a gigantic refuse bin for the great peaks about it.

The Dhudwallah was a most useful acquisition to the expedition. Without him we should frequently have been at a loss as to the easiest route, and might have wasted much time in the stony labyrinth, but he picked out the way with the skill and aplomb of an Alpine guide, his leathery, wrinkled face with its deep-set hawk-like eyes frequently cracking into a broad grin of conscious importance.

Some distance above the camp was a small glacier lake. High parapets of ice surrounded it from which a frieze of javelin-like icicles were suspended. Miniature icebergs floated on it, and its deep green depths, as placid as a Scottish loch on a calm September morning, reflected the glories of the great peaks around. Presently, as we toiled over the wearying stones, a considerable glacier opened out to the west. This was the one explored by Dr. Kellas, when prospecting the south face of the Jonsong Peak. Half a mile above its junction with the main ice stream of the Jonsong Glacier this glacier thrusts out pinnacles similar to those of the Rongbuk Glacier on Everest. These ice pinnacles are not found on the Kangchenjunga Glacier, and are common only to those parts of the Himalaya exposed to the dry airs of Thibet. There is something attractively fantastic in them ; their queer constructions, their cleanly chiselled walls, minarets and spires suggest a goblin city, the queer phantoms of a cubist's dream, or maybe a halted regiment of the Mountain King.

It was hard going for the porters. The glacier rose gently, but we must have climbed an additional two or three thousand feet up and down these moraine mounds. As we walked we searched for gem stones among the multi-coloured rocks, but all we found were gneissic stones inlaid with small garnets.

At last the most turbulent part of the glacier was passed, and we pitched camp thankfully in a small hollow near the middle of the glacier.

There are really two glaciers here flowing side by side, and sharing a common valley. That on the eastern side of the valley flows from the elevated snow-fields dominated by the Langpo Peak and the Pyramid. That on the western side has its source in the snows of the Jonsong La. Though coming together high up, the two glaciers maintain their individuality for two or three miles before becoming indistinguishable from one another. The Jonsong La branch resembles any ordinary Alpine glacier, but the Langpo branch exhibits a multitude of monstrous ice pinnacles of the same pattern as those to which I have alluded. So vast is the scale of the country hereabouts, that it is not until the mountaineer approaches close to these pinnacles that he is able to appreciate their size. Some of them, as the accompanying illustration shows, are nearly a hundred feet high. Our camp was near them, and Wood Johnson and I practised cutting steps up a minor one. We found the ice hard and tenacious, and it provided Wood Johnson with an excellent first lesson in icemanship.

As the sun sank, the scene became beautiful in the extreme. The foreground was set with the ice pinnacles, the background with Kangchenjunga. During the day the

CAMP TWO, JONSONG LA

latter had sulked behind the clouds, now the clouds were absorbed into the evening and it rose serenely into a deep mauve sky. But it was plain that the bad weather had not left it unscathed, for the upper part of the mountain was powdered in new snow. It was some consolation to think that even had we been able to hack our way up to the North Ridge, and established higher camps, we should most likely have been beaten by the weather on the final push towards the top. Day died amid almost unearthly splendours. The pale ghostly pinnacles were faintly lit by the reflection of Kangchenjunga's sunset flare, and when night had at last cooled the red-hot castings of the peaks, bright-eyed stars glanced down on a world of awful desolation.

We were off early the next morning. After the irritations of the previous day, it was delightful to stroll along the nearly level crest of a medial moraine, which formed the boundary between the two ice streams.

The general condition of the party had greatly improved ; better food, and improved " nerves," had worked wonders on our health. Wood Johnson and I pelted uphill almost as though we were on the fells above Wastdale, and not 2,000 feet higher than the summit of Mont Blanc. Kurz, who had gone on a day in advance of the main party to do some surveying, had pitched his camp where Kellas had pitched his, at the junction of the Langpo and Jonsong glaciers. Passing him, we continued on up the latter glacier, accompanied by the Dhudwallah carrying my ski, building small cairns as we went for the benefit of the porters who were following.

At last, after two and a half days' marching, we trod

snow and ice, where Hoerlin joined us, having come by some mysterious short cut of his own, through the ice-fall which here occupied the centre of the glacier. He and I put on ski, and continued up a snowy corridor contained between the ice-fall and the mountainside. Wood Johnson had not skied before, and he continued on foot with the Dhudwallah. Every few yards there were undulations in the snow, suspiciously like concealed crevasses, and the suggestion was made that those on foot had better rope up. The Dhudwallah, however, greeted this with contempt, and declared there were no " holes." He was right, the undulations were merely due to the melting effects of the sun, or rivulets beneath the snow.

There is no doubt that with a little training the Dhudwallah would make a first-rate guide. As it was, the way he led us up the pass was remarkable in its mountaineering instinct and judgment ; he seemed to know the Jonsong Glacier as well as a Zermatt guide knows the Matterhorn.

Ski were much quicker than foot-slogging, and leaving Hoerlin to make some adjustment to his bindings, I went on ahead to find a suitable camping site. The corridor was the easy and obvious route, but at its upper end, where it debouched on to the unbroken glacier above the ice-fall, it was liable to be swept by ice avalanches from a hanging glacier on the mountainside above. It was only a small hanging glacier, the danger being limited to a few yards, and on ski one would have stood a sporting chance of dodging an avalanche. The dangerous area was traversed in a few seconds, and I was soon sliding over the gently sloping upper snow-field of the glacier.

Camp was pitched in a shallow snow hollow. Above it

rose a steep slope of snow about 2,000 feet high. I saw Schneider fasten his eyes on this slope with that half fanatical, half predatory gleam peculiar to ski-runners. The next instant, unable to withstand temptation, he was off. For half an hour he climbed vigorously, then, pointing his ski straight downhill, he descended like a thunderbolt on the camp.

The Jonsong La was close at hand, and I suggested to Wood Johnson that we might ascend to it on ski, and prospect the way for the morrow.

The shadows were lengthening as we started up the glacier, and the glaring arc lights of day were being dimmed by the stealthy hand of night. In another hour or two they would be switched off altogether, and tropical darkness would fall almost with the suddenness of a blow.

It was the first time that Wood Johnson had donned ski, but he made excellent progress ; surely no one has ever taken their first lesson in ski-ing at 20,000 feet. The glacier led us gently upwards to the foot of a steep little snow slope falling from the pass. Frost had already hardened the snow into a crust, and we found it easier to leave our ski, and climb the slope on foot.

A bitter wind met us on the pass, but we scarcely heeded its onslaught. We were looking down into a new world, a world of yellow, brown and gold. The mountaineer experiences many dramatic views ; there is the view from the summit of the Wetterhorn, with its fascinating and terrible glimpse down to the emerald pastures and doll-like châlets of Grindelwald ; there is that backward glance down the Brenva face of Mont Blanc to the wrinkled surface of the Brenva Glacier curving over towards the heat-hazed meadows of Courmayeur; there is enough drama in the outlook from the Dolomite Vajolet Towers to satiate the most earnest seeker after the sensational. Yet, none of these views impressed me so much as that from the Jonsong La. We had come from a world of ice and snow, we were passing into a world of earth and rock. Our eyes, tired with the unrelenting glare of snow-fields, rested gratefully on the brown terraces and colourful scree of the Lhonak Valley. We even tried to delude ourselves into thinking that it was a warm country we were descending into, but we knew that it was not; these colourful slopes were on the edge of the bleak and inhospitable plateaux of Thibet.

Our soliloquies were cut short by the wind. Fingers and toes were numbing. Furious banners of snow were streaming from the ridges on either hand. We turned. The shadows had stolen across the smooth carpet of the glacier beneath, and were marching up the opposite slopes. Kangchenjunga was yellow and unearthly. Eastward, night's purple band was mounting the sky, sowing the first stars in its wake.

Beating gloved hands together, we ran down the slope to our ski. I wish Wood Johnson could have enjoyed the run down as much as I. Perhaps he did, for ski-ing can be enjoyed equally well by the complete novice or the expert of experts, that is not the least of its charms.

Wood Johnson responded readily to tuition, and some distance down executed a manœuvre which he triumphantly described as a Stemming turn. When the camp was in view I regret to say I left him to his own devices. Perhaps it was selfish, but who could resist the long unbroken slopes, so hard, and yet with their crystalline surface so perfect for ski-ing. I took them straight. The wind roared at me ; a fierce exultation gripped me. I felt as I did on my first solo flight when, with the engine shut off, and the wind crooning in the rigging wires, the old 'bus dived swiftly towards the little row of hangars that came rushing up to meet me. All was the same, only here, in place of hangars, the camp. An aerial dive, a perfect ski-run, there is a close affinity. And so with a long, almost lingering Christiania to a standstill.

The weather was again good next morning. For photography's sake I started before the others, and from the pass was able to snap the party as it crawled wormlike up the glacier beneath. It is only by views containing figures that one is able to give to others any idea of the vast scale of mountain country. My thumb at arm's length before me sufficed to conceal the whole party from view.

A strong cold wind was blowing across the pass, this time from the south. About fifty feet down on the Sikkim side an outcrop of rocks formed a sheltered place. There I remained for nearly two hours basking in the sun, while awaiting the remainder of the party. Below this outcrop the slopes dropped steeply for five hundred feet, with rocks jagging from them here and there. Only in one place, immediately to the right of the outcrop, was there an unbroken run out. As the snow was hard and icy in places, and it was not certain whether a slip or slide might not be attended with unpleasant consequences, it seemed safest to fix a long rope down the steep upper portion for the porters. These seemed to think the descent a huge joke, and when they saw that there was no danger, many let themselves glissade before they had reached the end of the rope, and shot down, loads and all, to the glacier.

The angle of the upper part of the slopes was at least fifty degrees, but apparently only the perpendicular can deter Schneider on ski. The only compliment he paid the slope was by not taking all of it straight, and he descended the first part in a series of miraculous swings before pointing his ski straight at the glacier. Other and less venturesome mortals preferred to put on their ski at the level where Schneider had disdained to make any more swings. It was a glorious run down the glacier, for the snow was of that delightful crystalline consistency commonly found in the Alps in spring. As we descended we slanted across to the left, taking care to give a wide berth to a hanging glacier on a subsidiary ridge of the Jonsong Peak, which is liable to discharge ice avalanches.

The difference of snow level between this, the Sikkim side of the Jonsong La, and the Nepal side is striking. Even taking into account the steepness with which the glacier falls, the snow line is much higher than on the Nepal side and only a few minutes' running was necessary to bring us from snow to a stony waste of moraines.

As usual Nature, which obviously favours ski-runners in this part of the world, had provided a snow-filled corridor between the moraine and the mountainside to the west of the glacier. Down this we loitered, stopping every few minutes on the stones at the side for a siesta in the sun.

Far away now, was the pass with the descending porters strung up on it like a row of pendent black beads. I was reminded strongly of the opening scene in Charlie Chaplin's

PINNACLES OF SOLID ICE—ON THE WAY TO THE JONSONG LA

film *The Gold Rush*, which shows the seekers after wealth toiling in single file up the Chilkoot Pass.

Eastwards of the Jonsong La is a nameless peak of 22,160 feet, and the Langpo Peak, 22,700 feet, which was climbed by Dr. Kellas. It was but one of many great ascents that he made in this district. Looking at it, and later at other peaks that he climbed, one could not but be impressed by his mountaineering judgment and route-finding abilities. Climbing with only native porters as companions, he had to rely solely on an instinct and judgment that seldom, if ever, failed him. When the history of the Golden Age of Himalayan exploration comes to be written, Dr. Kellas's name will take a high place in the select little list of early mountaineers.

The snowy corridor petered out into a stony waste. To the west was a subsidiary glacier, and we traversed across to it, floundering through bog-like patches of snow between the rocks. The snow of this glacier was abominable, whole masses of it frequently collapsing beneath our ski, letting them sink into water-undermined cavities.

The glacier ended in an abrupt nose of ice. Beneath was a little lake, a blue-green gem in a sombre setting. It was an ideal spot for a camp, and Kurz and I returned with the welcome news to the porters who were finding it heavy going in the soft snow.

Our camping place was Arctic in its solitude and beauty. Above us towered the ice nose festooned with giant icicles, and sculptured into all manner of forms. There was the wrinkled face of an old witch, peering sardonically down upon us, and, in bas-relief, three classical figures linked hand in hand. Beneath was a hermit's cave, and above, a little balcony from which the fair-haired snow maidens could gaze rapturously, if not enviously, down upon us, as we munched our dinner of sardines and gherkins. All these things were reflected with faultless accuracy in the green blue depths of the little lake beneath. That evening, when frost stalked out with the shadows, freezing the surface of the lake into a smooth, white floor, the elves and fairies held a midnight ball, while we sophisticated mortals snored in our tents.

We were short of fuel, and it was essential to secure some without delay. The porters had had a trying day traversing the Jonsong La, and were entitled to a rest. We called, therefore, for volunteers, who, for an extra day's pay, would descend the Lhonak Valley and bring up rhododendron wood. Fortunately, sufficient were forthcoming. Also, we had none too much coolie food left, and runners were dispatched with notes to the Maharajah of Sikkim at Gangtok, and the Headman of Lachen, requesting immediate assistance.

Above the camp was a low ridge pushed into the Lhonak Valley by the Jonsong Massif. This rose to a little knob, which formed an ideal belvedere for viewing the head of the Lhonak Valley, its glaciers and surrounding peaks. Seated on the gaunt, granite slabs piled up like a ruined Stonehenge on the summit, we drank in the glories of this new country. There was much to interest and impress us ; the brown upland valley ; the lateral terraces 1,000 feet above the floor of the Lhonak Valley telling of a former Ice Age when a great glacier extended many miles down towards the plains ; the rugged limestone peaks of the Dodang Nyima Range, governed by the graceful summit of the

KANGCHENJUNGA FROM THE JONSONG LA

Dodang Peak, 22,700 feet high; a sea of peaks to the north-west, above which projected two great combers, Chomiomo, 22,430 feet, and Kangchenjau, 22,700 feet, ascended by Dr. Kellas, in 1910 and 1912 respectively. But it was not these distant peaks that delighted our eyes so much as a beautiful snow peak which stands watch and ward over the head of the Lhonak Valley. It is the Weisshorn of the district, possessing as it does all the gracefulness and elegance of the Zermatt peak. The superb sweep of its ridges culminates with mathematical preciseness in a slender spire of snow, and so well designed is it that it deceived us utterly as to its height, and we began to believe that it was actually higher than the Jonsong Peak. Only the upper part of the last named was visible. Its south-east ridge immediately below the summit appeared easy, but could it be reached? Kellas, we knew, had attacked it from the north-west, and we had already learnt enough about him to realise that his judgment was likely to be sound. This problem must wait until the morrow, when we hoped to set off on our attempt.

Below us, two main tributaries of the Lhonak Glacier united to form a great ice stream which stretched far down the valley. This ice stream was, for a mile or two, broken up into similar pinnacles to those met with on the way to the Jonsong La. A weird procession they were, contrasting oddly with the browns and yellows of the scree slopes on either side of the valley.

That denudation as well as glacier ice plays an important part in shaping these valleys was evidenced by a collection of earth pyramids on the northern side of the valley resembling in general characteristics the well-known ones above

Bozen (now called Bolzano) in South Tyrol. They are due to water forming deep runnels in the soft earth of the hill-side. As these runnels become deeper, so do the ridges between them become sharper. Some parts of these ridges are more knit together by stones and harder than others. The soft parts fall, or are worn away, the hard parts remain, forming eventually these quaint pinnacles of earth and stones.

The Jonsong Peak was now within our grasp. But would the weather hold, could we snatch it from the teeth of the monsoon? Westwards, battalions of cumuli cloud were flooding up from the Teesta Valley. Were they the advance guard of the monsoon? Wood Johnson thought they were, and pointed out inky black clouds which floated detached from the main body of cumuli, saying that they were typical monsoon clouds. We had endured one great disappointment, were we to experience another? Time alone could tell.

CHAPTER XVI

THE CONQUEST OF JONSONG PEAK: THE FIRST ASCENT

The day of our little reconnaissance of the summit of the rocky point above the camp had ended in snow squalls, but monsoonish threats came to naught and the following morning, May 30, was calm and sunny. The party that was to make the first attempt on the Jonsong Peak consisted of Schneider, Hoerlin, Wood Johnson and myself. It was decided that the Europeans should go on ahead of the porters and see if there was any possibility of reaching the South-east Ridge via the north face of the mountain. We knew that the ridge was possible if we could gain it, but the north face was cut off from view by a buttress, and it remained to be seen what was round the corner.

Wood Johnson and I were the first away. Crossing the ridge above the camp, we descended the broad snow-field on the other side diagonally towards the Lhonak Glacier. The glacier is split in its upper portion into two streams, one fed by the Jonsong Peak, and the other by the Lhonak Peak and the Dodang Nyima range. A long lower ridge divides the two, bending down from the North-west Ridge of the Jonsong Peak. So far as we could ascertain from his description, Dr. Kellas when attempting the Jonsong Peak had camped low down at, or near the end of this ridge. His second camp had been on the col between the

Jonsong Peak and an unnamed peak next to the Lhonak Peak. This unnamed peak does not appear to advantage when looking up the Lhonak Glacier, for it is farther away than its more impressive neighbour, the Lhonak Peak. Yet, as we learned later, it is a worthy mountain.

There were no crevasses on the snow-field, and we walked down and across it unroped. The rocks of the buttress were easy but disagreeably loose, and we dislodged great masses that thundered down to the glacier amid clouds of sulphurous dust.

All hope of reaching the South-east Ridge was erased from our hearts as we turned the buttress. One glance at the great precipices falling from the ridge armoured and defended with hanging glaciers was sufficient. Farther along, the rock precipices ended, and directly beneath the peak there appeared to be a chance of reaching the South-east Ridge up the 7,000 feet of snow and ice slopes forming the north face of the peak. But it was a very remote possibility, for the steep average angle of the slopes, plus confused masses of unstable ice pinnacles and hanging glaciers strewn indiscriminately over them suggested dangers at least as great as those of Kangchenjunga.

The reader may wonder why we continued considering attacking the South-east Ridge when we knew that Dr. Kellas thought the mountain to be accessible by the North-west Ridge. The answer is that it is the mountaineer's duty to consider every possibility however remote. Following blindly in the steps of his defeated predecessor is not the right attitude of mind in which to attack a great peak in the Himalayas. That was one reason why we had attempted the Nepal face of Kangchenjunga in preference to the better known Sikkim face. As regards the Jonsong Peak another reason must be admitted, and that was the appearance of the North-west Ridge; it looked terribly long. From the col reached by Dr. Kellas, it swept up in ice edges over point after point before merging into the final rock and ice slopes of the peak. Earlier in the expedition we might have gone for it with cheerful *insouciance*, but Kangchenjunga had taught us wisdom. Length alone will forever militate against the ascent of the majority of the greater Himalayan ridges. Yet, Dr. Kellas had seen the peak from a better vantage point than we, for he had approached it directly up the Lhonak Valley and he was too good a mountaineer to waste his time attempting a hopelessly inaccessible route, or one beyond the powers of his expedition. We had already learned to respect his judgment, and the fact that he had tried the North-west Ridge of the Jonsong peak, though he had returned defeated from it, was practically a guarantee of its accessibility.

Scrambling down the slopes of loose boulders, we gained the side moraine of the south branch of the Lhonak Glacier. There we sat down to await Schneider and Hoerlin. They and the porters were not long in coming. The latter were going well. There were only a dozen of them—all picked men—for we hoped to make a rapid push for the top. The porters left at the Base Camp were to relay the remaining loads over the Jonsong La. The men we had were all hard-bitten "Tigers," as tough, hardy and weather-beaten as the Old Guard of Napoleon. They were not merely porters, but genuine mountaineers and adventurers, who enjoyed a tussle with a great mountain as much as we did, and were as keen as we were to get to the top.

The hanging glaciers on the north face of the Jonsong Peak were too obviously unstable to risk passing close beneath them. Fortunately, the broad upper part of the glacier was unbroken enough to enable us to keep in the middle out of range of their ice avalanches. For the most part we trod glacier ice, but here and there stretches of snow covered it. This snow seemed to have been laid down by some diabolical demon. If there were any watery hollows, they were concealed by innocent looking coverlets into which we floundered, sometimes up to the hips. The diabolical demon could seldom have laughed so heartily as he did that day.

The surface of the ice was curiously fretted with little *nieves penitentes*. This could only have been the work of the sun. Many little pinnacles, no more than a few inches high, were capped by stones, forming minute glacier tables. The stones, of course, had protected the ice from the sun, so that when the surrounding ice had melted away, a little stalk had been left on which rested the stone.

As we mounted the glacier, the snow and ice face immediately beneath the peak came into full view, and we saw what we had not seen lower down, that a possible route might be forced up it. But it was a route that would undoubtedly be exposed to unavoidable risks—risks of both snow and ice avalanches. Our last doubts were removed; it only remained for us to follow in the footsteps of Dr. Kellas. First of all we must cross the glacier, thence climb to the crest of the low ridge, where we would make Camp One.

For the first time on the expedition we found ourselves among large crevasses. It is easy enough to get off the Mer de Glace on Mont Blanc to the Mauvais Pas if you know the right way, but if you do not, you are liable to get hung up by crevasses at the edge of the glacier. Such was our position now. We could see the side moraine only fifty yards away, and an easy slanting shelf leading up from it to the crest of the ridge, but that fifty yards was riven and torn into huge crevasses, with knife-like blades of ice between. Europeans could, of course, have forced a way even though it involved some tricky ice work, but it was a different matter for the porters. An easy way must be found by which we could send them up and down between Camp One and the Base Camp unaccompanied by a European. A way was found at last along a little horizontal gully of ice which led out unexpectedly to the moraine. The shelf, as anticipated, offered no difficulty, and soon we had reached the crest of the ridge some five hundred feet above the glacier. There we camped.

The actual crest of the ridge consisted of a hog-backed gently inclined snow-field, but we preferred as a camping site a rocky edge almost flush with the snow.

The ridge was well sheltered from the wind by the main North-west Ridge of the Jonsong Peak, and the evening was warm and calm. Far down the valley the setting sun dwelt on the brown slopes of stones and earth, transforming them into sheets of yellow and gold, or lingered on the crests of the ice pinnacles of the Lhonak Glacier. There was one pinnacle conspicuous among the rest which formed a tapering neck, surmounted by a bird-like head with a cruel beak. As the sun set, and other and lower pinnacles had become cold and livid, one shaft of light, passing through a gap in some distant ridge, lit this pinnacle with a ruddy glare. I almost imagined myself to be looking down at some strange and terrible prehistoric monster steeped in the blood of its victims.

Day perished ; brown changed to violet, violet to purple. The huddle of ice pinnacles became cold and ghostly. Above the world, a vein-like network of cloud tendrils glowed fiercely as though suspended over the blaze of a city's lights. Slowly, they faded, and were lost amid the stars.

On Kangchenjunga we had known no peace of mind, we had awakened in alarm to the roar of ice avalanches, but now we could sleep peacefully.

For the most part the night was a quiet one, with only the groaning and cracking of the glacier beneath to tell of its slow progress. Once came the bellow of an ice avalanche from the Jonsong Peak, like the startled growl of an aroused watch dog.

Morning dawned mistily. Grey clouds roofed in the world ; but the rising sun thinned them, and tore them apart. In its powerful rays they dissolved swiftly into a sky of Italian blue. I was reminded of a Whitsun morning up Langdale; when the turf is silvered with dew, the lambs cry through the low mists, and Pike O'Stickle and Bowfell take to themselves the dawn.

A friendly sun smiled down upon us, as we trudged over the marble-like surface of the snow-field above the camp. We had hoped that the ridge would lead us straight to the col reached by Dr. Kellas, and it was something of a disappointment to find that ahead it looked difficult. The

THE NORTH FACE OF THE JONSONG PEAK—7,000 FEET HIGH—AND CAMP ONE

alternative was to descend to the north branch of the Lhonak Glacier. I volunteered to go on ahead and prospect the ridge. A short scramble up a slope of boulders brought me to a point whence, so far as I could see, the ridge stretched without difficulty for a considerable distance. Seen thus, there seemed every hope that we should be able to follow it all the way and that it would merge eventually into the snow slopes directly beneath the col. Rather prematurely, therefore, I waved on the others. This was a mistake. Only for a short distance was the ridge free from difficulties. Soon it became a conventional Himalayan knife-edge of ice, and writhed downwards evilly into a deep gap. We retreated. Some hard things were said, but they were deserved.

We descended a slope about 200 feet high to the glacier. Soon we were wallowing and floundering in soft snow, the most terrible snow we had ever experienced. The sun had softened a crust formed by an overnight's frost. For a step or two it would bear us, then a whole cake of it would collapse, and we would go knee-deep or even waist-deep into a hole.

But if it was trying or irritating work for the sahibs, it was much worse for heavily laden porters. Even though we stamped out the track, they, with their loads, frequently sank in to a much greater depth. Over the worst part of the glacier, I do not think we progressed more than 300 yards in an hour, and that along the level.

We halted for lunch. The weather was not propitious ; a snowstorm was brewing, and grey clouds brought with them a tide of scurrying snowflakes. The sun reappeared again for a few moments, but its smile was but a transitory one, and soon faded and died behind leaden mists.

Above our luncheon place the snow was less disagreeable, and we climbed thankfully out from the worst part of the glacial snow swamp to the foot of an ice-fall. We had come to regard Himalayan ice-falls with something of disdain. They were usually much easier than they looked, due to the absence of big crevasses. This one gave us no reason to revise our opinion. It was a tame affair, so tame that we did not need to rope until above the steepest portion, and that only for a solitary crevasse with overhanging eaves of snow necessitating an awkward step.

The storm clouds had rolled back, and a benevolent sun illuminated the long snow-field before us, that lifted gently up towards Kellas Col, as we had already learnt to call it. Dominating this snow-field rose a little peak. Sunlight and shadow chased across it, a wilful mist concealed it for a few instants. Without it the world seemed dull and lifeless. Then it reappeared, supremely arrogant, and important. Actually, it was just an insignificant hump, on the great North-west ridge of the Jonsong Peak.

We took off the rope, which we had put on for the one crevasse, and trudged manfully up the soft snow slopes. Ahead, was a sky-line, which we thought must be Kellas Col. We breasted it, only to find more slopes ahead. Time was getting on ; the day had been a hard one, for all concerned. Therefore, we were content to camp on a little platform beneath the humpy little peak. Only the tireless Schneider elected to go on, and prospect the way. For once his prospecting nearly led him into trouble. In the dull light, he was unable to see the slight depression formed by a solitary crevasse, treacherously bridged. He went through up to the waist, and was lucky not to go farther. Although a narrow crevasse, it was a deep one.

We awoke the next morning to hear the unpleasant sound of pattering snow on our tents. Enforced delay was something more than disappointing. We were short of food and fuel. In order to travel light, we had left as much as possible of the former at Camp One, and of the latter we had taken all the Meta solid fuel available at the Base Camp, the remainder had still to come over the Jonsong La. We estimated that if the snowstorm delayed us but one day, we would only have enough Meta to heat two cups of hot tea a day. How long would it last ? Monsoonish opinions alternated with hopes of a clearance, but the snowfall continued without intermission.

Had we known, stern events were afoot. Frau Dyhrenfurth, who had been left in charge of transport organisation, on the Nepal side of the Jonsong La, having carried out her task of sending relays of porters off with the remainder of the loads, had left for the Jonsong La. As luck would have it, the day that she traversed the pass coincided with the snowstorm. Duvanel and Dr. Richter had come over before her, and she had no European companions. She was accompanied, however, by her servant, the Nepali Subadar, and a Subadar Major, who had recently come up from Khunza. In spite of the snowstorm, these last two escorted her to the actual frontier before turning back, another remarkable instance of the courtesy and help with which the Nepalese authorities had greeted us while we were in Nepal.

To traverse a pass 20,200 feet high in a snowstorm

during which we, mere men, were cowering in our tents, was a fine effort, and one which, as regards height alone, has probably only been surpassed by women on two or three previous occasions. Luck had held, and the crossing of the Jonsong La had been successfully accomplished. Unfortunately, it had been marred by one slight accident, and a glissading coolie had come to grief and broken an arm. Disaster had also overtaken some of the more fragile loads. Of the two typewriters on which I was wont to hammer out my dispatches one was no more. The box containing the gramophone records had broken loose from a porter's back, and bounded down the glacier. Only a number of strong and thick records that had been supplied by Eberl had survived, and these were strictly classical. Our souls, and our porters' souls, hungered not for Wagner or Beethoven, but for the bass-voiced gentleman who used to advise us every evening to give ourselves a pat on the back. Now he was lying shattered to fragments at the foot of the Jonsong La.

It was still snowing the next morning, and our spirits sank to zero. We had little enough food and fuel left, and could not afford to play a waiting game. We had to decide definitely whether we would advance, or retreat. The former was scarcely practicable, and the latter seemed inevitable. We were preparing to descend when the snow stopped. A bright light smote through the mist pall ; a tiny patch of blue sky appeared. Miraculously it broadened and an eager sun burst through. The mists rolled back ; a wind from the north-west completed their discomfiture; they had to relinquish their hold on our ridge, and retreat to the Lhonak Valley, where they congregated in

DESCENDING THE JONSONG PEAK BELOW CAMP TWO. THE PEAK IN THE BACKGROUND IS A MINOR BUTTRESS OF THE NORTH-WEST RIDGE

sullen battalions ready for a further assault on the heights.

Nearly two feet of new snow had obliterated our tracks. It would be hard but not dangerous work going on, for so far as we could see there was no fear of the gentle slopes we must climb avalanching.

It was certainly hard work, but not so strenuous as we had anticipated. The new snow was of a more or less uniform depth, and was light and powdery. We climbed roped, for there were several concealed crevasses, two or three of which were only discovered by " trial and error."

From the Lhonak Valley the North-west Ridge had appeared a definite edge all the way from Kellas' Col. In point of fact, for some considerable distance there is no ridge, and what appears to be a ridge from below is merely the edge of a gently sloping snow-field. This snow-field gradually narrows, until at a height of about 21,500 feet it does actually become ridge.

One or two of the porters were feeling the effect of the altitude, and one of them, Nima, unroped himself from the rest. He was cautioned and tied up again. In the absence of an accredited sirdar, Nemu was put in charge. It was interesting to watch the psychological effect of responsibility. As Mr. Samuel Weller would have had it, he seemed to " svell wisibly." His countenance became even more earnest and worried, if such a thing were possible, and he fussed about like an old hen over a brood of chickens, but withal, he made a good sirdar, and one whom the men respected and obeyed.

At the head of the snow-field was a platform, on which we enjoyed lunch and a welcome rest. Immediately below the platform and to the west precipices dropped to a great glacier, which has its source in the snows of the Jonsong Peak. This glacier at first runs in a north-westerly direction before curving round to the west. It is at least fifteen or twenty miles long, and its direction, and the ranges bounding it, are delineated inaccurately on the Government map. Whence do its waters flow? Do they enter the Khunza Valley at Kangbachen, or do they flow northwards into Thibet, and join the headwaters of the Arun River? This was a question that we were unable definitely to solve, but it seems probable that the latter direction is the correct one. This glacier, like the Jonsong Glacier, only consists of bare ice for a few miles. Its lower portion is so moraine covered as to be invisible, but the ice continues for many miles under the stones. As Mr. Freshfield pointed out, many of the early travellers and surveyors utterly misjudged the length of the glaciers in this district owing to their thinking that the glacier ended at the point where the ice was no longer to be seen. In its upper portion this glacier rises in a great ice-fall. Rocky spurs jut out into it, and over these ice avalanches fall periodically with thunderous roars.

Beyond the glacier, we looked over ridge upon ridge of peaks, some easy looking snow mountains, others more difficult, and here and there carnivorous-like fangs of rock, forming summits which appeared hopelessly inaccessible. Our gaze passed far across these turbulent mountains, to where seventy miles away two superb summits stood aloof from the world—Everest and Makalu.

Everest has been described as a dull, if imposing mountain, when seen from the north and not to be compared with Makalu in grandeur or beauty. The latter is certainly a superb peak. Its delicately shaped summit based on two wide shoulders is as perfectly proportioned as the Lhonak Peak. Yet, grand mountain though it is, it somehow lacks the sovereign dignity of the World's highest summit. From our position we saw the North Ridge of Everest in profile, sweeping down in a graceful parabola to the North Col, to the right of which rose the little North Peak. But the most imposing face of the mountain is its southern, or Nepal face. No European has ever stood beneath it. Were he to do so, he would find himself looking up the grandest mountain wall there is. The north-west face of Nanga Parbat rises 22,000 feet from the Indus Valley. It is possible that Everest's southern face does not exceed this height, and it is probably less, but no other mountain can show a face to rival its unbroken general angle, combined with its length. We saw it in profile, and seventy miles away though we were from it, it seemed to drop and drop for thousands of feet, to disappear finally into the flocks of cumuli cloud that browsed about its base.

We could have stopped long gazing upon that view, but our start had been a late one, and the sun was well past its zenith. So far the foot-slogging had been easy, if arduous, of a type Baedeker would class as, " For adults only." Immediately above us, the snow-field rose in steep waves, before narrowing into a sharp snow-ridge. Henceforward the climbing was, " For experts only, with perfectly steady heads." At the foot of the lowest wave was an incipient bergschrund. This was only visible on the right, on the left it was firmly bridged. The wind sweeping the slopes above it had compacted the snow into a hard icy cake. Luckily there was no ice, and a few slashes with the adze end of the axe sufficed to make a step. Above this lower wave, the slope eased off for a few yards ; then came a similar wave but a few feet high, and easily surmounted.

We found ourselves on a level shelf, forming the lower lip of a long snowy trough. Above the trough rose the final wave. We looked at it with sinking hearts. Like the ice wall of Kangchenjunga, it was a brutal, elemental bulge of blue ice. Schneider thought there was a possibility of circumventing it, and quickly traversed along to the left like an old hound nosing out the trail. A minute or two later he returned with the glad news that he had found a way, and the advance was resumed.

At one point the lower lip of the trough we were traversing was split at right-angles by an abysmal cleft. An insecure-looking tongue projected on our side, and from this we stepped gingerly across. At its westward end, the trough and the ice bulge petered out into an ice slope to gain which we had to cross another crevasse. Now came the first real climbing of the day. The ice slope fell away to the right, like the roof of a house, ending in a sheer drop to the glacier we had discovered. Steps, and good steps, had to be cut. A slip on the part of the porters was not to be thought of. Schneider cut the steps, which Hoerlin, Wood Johnson and myself enlarged to the dimensions of buckets for the porters. Nevertheless, we gave the latter a tight rope. The slope was short, not more than 100 feet high ; and soon we stepped on to the crest of the North-west Ridge. There we experienced a disagreeable surprise. For some way the ridge was level, then it rose to an icy point which formed a respectable peak in itself. So far the ridge was reasonably broad, and free from difficulty, but

NEARING CAMP THREE ON THE JONSONG PEAK

beyond the little peak it narrowed to a mere ice-blade of obvious and aggressive difficulty. Between this ridge and the Jonsong Peak was a gently inclined glacier, forming one of the heads of the glacier flowing north-west. Could we but gain this glacier all would be well, for from it's head we could attack the final slopes of the Jonsong Peak.

There were two possibilities of descending to this glacier. One, by following the North-west Ridge to a point where it sank to within reasonable reach of the glacier, and the other, by descending the ice slopes directly beneath us. Both were possible, but to get porters over either route meant an extra day's work, and another camp, and for this we had neither sufficient food nor fuel. The only alternative was to camp where we were on the ridge, and leaving the porters, making a bid for the summit the following day. It would be a very long and strenuous day, and a race against time. Any real difficulty such as steep rock climbing, or step cutting, would defeat us, and enforce retreat if we were to escape being benighted. It was by no means certain that there were no real difficulties on the final 2,000 feet of snow slopes and rocks separating the head of the glacier from the summit. It certainly looked easy enough, but as we knew from bitter experience, apparent easiness in the Himalayas is too often apt to prove a delusion and a snare.

Another factor by no means to be neglected was altitude. We had been going slowly to-day in the soft snow, and that from 19,500 feet to 21,700 feet. We would go more slowly on the morrow. Such was the problem, and like that of the Jonsong La, it was one that luck alone could solve.

The ridge was a poor place to camp upon, and we would

have done better to have descended to the platform below, or to the trough. But every foot of height and minute of time was precious, and we decided, therefore, to stop where we were, even though forced to bear the brunt of the west wind.

It would be difficult to imagine a more superb camping site, and we lounged about in the sun enjoying every minute of the remainder of the day. As we did so, we studied the route to be followed, and after a prolonged argument as to the respective merits of the ridge and the ice slope, the former was adopted as affording the most convenient route to the glacier.

On the peak itself there were two possibilities. One up the crest of the North-west Ridge, which would mostly consist of rock climbing, and the other up snow slopes to the col between the highest point of the peak and a subsidiary summit to the west. The final decision, however, as to which was the better of these two routes would have to be left until we were actually at grips with the mountain, for it was difficult to tell by mere visual examination which was likely to prove the easiest.

From a geological standpoint, the Jonsong Peak is very interesting. It forms the point at which the gneiss of Kangchenjunga, and the limestone of Thibet meet. The upper part of the mountain is composed of stratified limestone, precisely similar to that of Everest, which we hoped would provide as easy climbing as it does on Everest. This limestone is based on gneiss. Where the two meet, there are alternate layers of gneiss and limestone, which run for a considerable distance across the mountainside.

For warmth and companionship's sake we placed our

tents end to end. Hoerlin and Schneider shared one, and Wood Johnson and I the other. The porters were housed in a tent of Polar design, which had been found to withstand the fiercest winds. They had also a little Welzenbach tent, which in shape resembled a triangular slab of cheese, being head-high to a sitting man at one end, and sloping wedge-like to the feet-end.

As the sun set, the west wind rose, and howled with bitter venom across the ridge, blowing fine powdery snow through every chink between the laced-up flaps. Our little camp was bathed in a ruddy glare. So beautiful was the scene that Wood Johnson and I, peering through the gauze-covered ventilation square at the back of our tent, could not forbear to go outside and photograph it. For perhaps a minute I stood in the snow, fumbling with numbed fingers at my camera. The sun was sinking northwards of Everest. One stiletto of cloud spanned the ranges, its hilt reached to Everest, its acute point, so acute that it was hard to tell where it ended, stretched far over Thibet. The hilt was dark, the point afire, as though it was steeped in blood. Although seventy miles away, Everest was as sharp and clear as though it rose from the range across the nearest valley. The North Col and the weary East Ridge up which expeditions had fought their way were clearly distinguishable. As I gazed at the final cone, beneath which high hopes were shattered, I thought of Mallory and Irvine. Their last resting place is surely one to be envied. When all the other peaks were cold and grey, one steadfast cloud banner streamed from it, whilst below, the great mountain drew to itself night's purple folds, like the toga of some imperial Cæsar.

The cold was intense. We had no thermometer, but there were at least fifty degrees of frost. I took two photographs, but my fingers became white and dead. I beat and rubbed them for fully a quarter of an hour inside the tent before the sluggish circulation returned. After cooking a cheerless and limited supper, we gulped down gratefully our one precious cup of hot tea, and wriggled into our sleeping bags.

The night was a wild one. The wind roared across the ridge, its snow-charged gusts flinging themselves on the camp with an insane fury. Once again our little tents held out nobly. Nevertheless, it was not altogether a comfortable feeling knowing that there were precipices on either hand. I thought of Captain G. I. Finch and Mr. Geoffrey Bruce's windy night on Everest, but their experience was a far worse one than ours.

Dawn broke ; the sky was unclouded, and the sun rose unhindered, but the wind continued with unabated violence. We peered out of our tents. A *tourmente* of wind-blown snow was whirling past, and far up in the blue sky to the leeward of the ridge its crystals scintillated in the sun like a myriad elfin spear points. At the Base Camp they would be thinking about breakfast, basking in the sun, maybe. Possibly some observant eye would note a slight fuzziness about the ridges, but little would they realise what it really meant. To start was impossible, for to have faced the blast would have meant frostbite. The peak was within our grasp, yet we must retreat. With our limited supplies of food and fuel, we could not afford to wait another day. From Camp One we had sent back all the porters we could possibly spare. Instructions had been

KELLAS PEAK

sent to the Base Camp to send up food and fuel at the earliest possible moment, but this was scarcely likely to arrive in time. The hard work of the past few days had been wasted. We had resigned ourselves to endure yet another bitter disappointment when with dramatic suddenness, at about 8.30 a.m. the canvas of our tents ceased to roar and smack—the wind had dropped ! For some time we lay listening for its return, but save for a petulant gust or two, it did not return. We ate a hurried breakfast, while our servants thawed our frozen boots—I think Nemu took mine to bed with him—and packed our rucksacks with necessaries.

At 9 a.m. we were off, in two parties, Schneider and Hoerlin on one rope ; Wood Johnson and myself on the other. We were all wearing crampons. Walking easily up the ridge we gained the summit of the ice peak which is about 150 feet above the camp, and nearly 22,000 feet high. This marked the beginning of the difficult section of the ridge.

From the ice peak the ridge descended steeply for some distance, in a series of sweeps to a col above which it rose again to another little peak. The col was only about 200 feet above the glacier, and once it was reached, the descent to the latter should be a comparatively easy matter. There was no possibility of keeping to the crest of the ridge, it was too sharp, whilst enormous cornices festooned with icicles overhanging the Lhonak side had to be avoided. We must traverse well below it on the south, or Jonsong Peak side. Had we not had crampons, the mountain would not have been climbed that day, for without them the steep icy slopes would have involved several hours of step cutting. As it was, steps were seldom necessary although it was tiring work flexing the feet in order to drive the crampon spikes well home. But if crampons made it possible to succeed without step cutting, it was not altogether easy work. The slope was too steep to face outwards, we had to face sideways, and descend like crabs. Below, sharp shark's teeth of rock, projecting viciously from the slope, and a bergschrund awaited a false step.

Schneider and Hoerlin moved for the most part both together, and were soon far ahead. Wood Johnson and I moved for the most part one at a time and were therefore very slow. This slowness was dictated partly by the fact that Wood Johnson had had little previous experience of snow and ice, and was actually wearing crampons for the first time. There was, however, another reason of which I was not aware at the time, he was not feeling fit. It is only fair and just to remark that considering his unfamiliarity with such work he put up a remarkably fine performance. The technique of crampons is not to be learned in a day.

Below the col, the ice was harder and steeper than above, and Schneider found step cutting essential. This enabled us to catch up to some extent, but even so by the time the first party had reached the glacier, we were still a long way behind. Schneider had cut a cunning zig-zag staircase, which led to the one place where the bergschrund could be crossed without much difficulty. After flexing the ankles on the slopes above the col, it was a relief to tread in good honest steps. The upper lip of the bergschrund was steep, but this Schneider had facilitated by hacking out large buckets of steps.

Seated on the glacier, we ate a snack of chocolate. The weather was now perfect, and the sun burned down with a fierce intensity, untempered by a breath of wind. Before us, the glacier sloped gently upwards with scarcely a ripple to mar its smooth surface. Trudging up it, mere dots now, were Hoerlin and Schneider. They were at least an hour ahead of us. We started after them. Almost at once, I noticed that Wood Johnson was going very badly. We had not gone far before he said he was too tired to go on. He said he would sit down in the snow, and wait until I returned. Naturally, I thought that altitude alone was responsible. He was feeling what I felt on the Ramthang Peak, when wearing the expedition boots, only worse. Under the circumstances ; a safe glacier, a windless day, and a broiling sun, I felt no scruples in agreeing to his suggestion that I should go on to the summit. Had I known, however, that he was suffering, not from altitude, but from a definite physical malady, there would have been no question of my going on. I should have returned with him then and there to the camp.

Would it be possible to overtake Schneider and Hoerlin ? They were going very fast. Could I go faster ? I thought I could, for I was feeling very fit. I said good-bye to Wood Johnson with deep regret. It was something more than hard luck for him, and no one was keener than he to do the Jonsong Peak. Yet, he could console himself with the thought that should it be climbed, his share in its conquest would be as great as anyone's, for it was only his able management of the porters, which was every bit as important towards the success of the undertaking as the actual climbing, that had rendered the ascent possible.

Every man possesses his own natural pace on a mountain, and by natural pace I mean the pace at which he is able to conserve the greatest amount of energy. This pace is, of course, apart from the difficulty of the ground, dependent on general bodily and mental condition, combined with the limitations imposed by altitude. At 22,000 feet pace and rhythm are synonymous. Increasing the pace, and breaking the rhythm, results in an output of energy far out of proportion to the time saved. This I discovered to my cost. At low altitudes, this loss of energy is negligible, and there is always a larger store of energy held in reserve than at high altitudes. The men who reach the summit of Everest will be drawing on their last dregs of reserve energy. My attempt to catch up Schneider and Hoerlin failed because by going faster than my natural pace I unfortunately exhausted myself by utilising my reserve energy.

Putting every ounce of energy into it I toiled up the glacier at a speed which would not have been out of place on Mont Blanc. I got within 100 yards of them, as they sat resting prior to leaving the glacier in favour of a steep little couloir leading up into the rocks of the peak. Here I sat down in a state of tired inertness, from which I never fully recovered for the remainder of the day. It was fully half an hour before I could move, and during that time I had the mortification of seeing Schneider and Hoerlin continue on their way. Quite rightly, they could not afford to wait for me. The peak was, after all, the first thing.

I started again to follow them. The spurt had done me little good, for I was now almost as far behind as I had been when I left Wood Johnson, and now I had tired myself to such an extent that I could not go as fast as Schneider and Hoerlin.

If I have described at length the evil effects of hurrying at high altitudes, I have done so to save others who may be tempted to hurry. Rhythm will one day get men to the top of Everest, but hurry, such as a race against time or weather, will defeat them utterly, and perhaps even render them so exhausted as to bring about disaster. It is possible that Mallory and Irvine perished thus, for if Mr. Odell was not mistaken in thinking he saw them, they were so late in starting that their attempt must have been a race against time.

From the head of the glacier, there was no question as to which route should be followed. The apparently easy snow slopes leading up to the col between the two summits of the Jonsong Peak were composed not of snow, but of ice, and ice set at a steeper angle than had appeared from the camp. The rocky North-west Ridge was by far the easiest route.

I plugged up the couloir. At first wide and fan-like, it gradually narrowed. Its western bank was formed by the ice slopes of the glacier falling from the ridge connecting the two summits. The other bank consisted of rocky shelves. On one of these shelves Schneider and Hoerlin had left every article of equipment they could spare. Obviously, they considered that time was of the utmost importance, and that if they were to reach the summit without being benighted on the descent, they must climb to it as lightly laden as possible.

At the ledge, they had left the couloir in favour of the rocky shelves. I preferred to continue up the former, for the rocky shelves were ice glazed here and there. It was not altogether a wise choice, for it was fatiguing work kicking and cutting steps in the hard snow of the couloir, and after climbing it a short distance I left it in preference for the rocks.

A falling stone passed with the vicious buzz of a racing car. I looked up. Schneider and Hoerlin were fully 500 feet higher. They were now on the crest of the ridge and silhouetted on the sky-line. They seemed to be moving quickly. I scrambled to the left out of range of anything they might send down. The mountain was patently rotten—a ruined mass of broken, shattered limestone. I looked at my watch, 3 p.m. My height was about 23,000 feet, approximately 1,500 feet from the top. It would take another three hours, at least, perhaps four hours. To go on meant being benighted. Great mountains have little sympathy for the solitary climber, and the Himalayas none at all. The foolhardiness entailed in going on would be fair neither to my companions, nor to myself. So I sat down, and prepared to enjoy a quiet half-hour.

From my position I could see Wood Johnson seated on the glacier. He had followed me slowly for a short distance, and then returned and stopped near the foot of the ice-slope. Now that there was no question of going on, I felt contented and happy. The day had been something more than a disappointing one, but altitude has the beneficial effect of dulling disappointment in the same way as it dulls ambition, and ambition had sunk beneath the oily surface of lassitude. From my perch I gazed upon a view combining both interest and beauty. All the nearer peaks were below, and I could gaze over the Lhonak and Dodang summits.

Northwards, over the Dodang Nyima range was the brown plateau of Thibet, contrasting oddly with the nearer snowy summits. Little cloud nautilæ sailed gently over its vast expanses, their undersides tinged brown from the reflected ruddiness of the earth. North-west of the Lhonak Peak were rolling snow peaks and snowfields. What a paradise for the ski-runner or mountaineer they would make, for there are many summits between 20,000 and 23,000 feet that are assailable either on ski or foot.

I turned to descend. Schneider and Hoerlin were out of sight now. I could not even hear their voices. Eastwards of every peak and ridge, blue shadows were stealing over the snows, greedily gulping the sunlight ; now and again a chill, little wind puffed across and was gone. Here was a peace such as we had not experienced on Kangchenjunga, a peace unbroken by the grumble of ice avalanches. Quickly I scrambled down the rocks, and descended the couloir until it was possible to glissade safely. It had taken me nearly two hours to ascend to my highest point from the glacier ; I scrambled and glissaded down in a few minutes.

I strolled down the glacier to Wood Johnson. His appearance shocked me. His face was drawn and haggard, and he showed every sign of being a sick man. I was even more shocked to learn that, some time after I had left him, he had had a stomach seizure, and had actually fainted. He recovered consciousness to find himself lying in the snow. I asked him whether he thought he would have the strength to ascend the ice ridge to the camp. He replied that he was game to try.

There were three things that might be done. I could return to camp and bring back porters. This I dismissed instantly as being impractical; the porters would be more of a hindrance than a help on the ice ridge and could never be got back before nightfall. Moreover, they were not used to crampons, and steps would have to be cut the whole way—hours of work. We might remain where we were until Schneider and Hoerlin returned, but they would most likely be back late, possibly after dark, and they would be tired. The sole remaining alternative was for Wood Johnson and myself to start as soon as possible and take things very easily in the hope that Wood Johnson would be able to muster up sufficient strength.

As we stood considering the situation, two minute dots passed slowly up the last snow slope towards the summit of the Jonsong Peak. They traversed to the right and disappeared, but in a few minutes more, reappeared, toiling upwards. At last they stood on the summit, barely distinguishable against the deep blue sky. It was a great moment. Schneider and Hoerlin had accomplished a splendid feat of pluck and endurance. Taking into account the height lost in descending from the camp to the glacier, they had ascended about 3,000 feet in seven hours. Schneider had led magnificently whilst Hoerlin's performance, considering that not long before he had been ill with influenza, told of a splendid constitution.

Wood Johnson's strength must be kept up, and I insisted on him eating some chocolate. This put new life into him, and he decided to make an attempt to get back to camp then and there. It was a journey I shall not easily forget for he was very weak, and every upward step cost him an intense effort. He had reached the stage of not caring what happened to himself, and only the knowledge that he was roped to me, and that by slipping he would involve me, as well as himself, in disaster, prevented his complete collapse. It was one more example of how closely, spiritually as well as physically, two friends can be linked by a mere hempen line. I do not know how long we took to climb the ridge, the time seemed interminable. It was probably about three hours. Slowly, rope length by rope length we progressed. The declining sun flamed and died around us. A vivid furnace with bars of scarlet glared behind Everest ; the tropic night rushed down upon us. The wind rose again, and began to numb our hands and feet.

A wall of mist gathered on the Lhonak side of the ridge. At one point near the crest of the ridge, the nearly horizontal sun thrust each man's shadow against it, in a beautiful Brocken Spectre. As I lifted my ice-axe to plunge it into the icy snow, so did a ghostly figure, surrounded by a brilliant, prismatic halo, gesticulate, with a weird, eerie abandon. Slowly, the sun sank behind the ranges, its spear-like beams radiating far into the green heavens, like the spurts from some monstrous explosion.

The wind pack fell upon us, beating our faces with painful spiculæ of snow and ice. A myriad stars looked down on a scene of intense effort and the snows around us had assumed a cold pallor as of death, as I took in the rope for the last time. We breasted the crest of the little ice peak, and looked down the broad easy snow ridge to the camp. Porters came rushing forth through the gloom to meet and greet us. Only then did Wood Johnson collapse. His effort had been one of which any mountaineer might be proud.

A minute or two later, our servants had pulled off our boots as we sat in our tents. Our feet had lost their feeling, my own had become encased in ice, for during the heat of the day, my boots had leaked, and my feet had become wet. In a trice, Nemu had my stockings off, and started to massage my toes with his horny hands. He proved himself an adept at it, and soon I was groaning under the exquisite torment of returning circulation.

Food and fuel had arrived that day in the shape of a chicken and coolie food, some petrol and a primus stove. How we poured down hot tea, and gnawed the tough chicken! A meal was prepared for Schneider and Hoerlin. It was not until some time after dark that they arrived: they were very tired, but by no means exhausted. When we had all assembled once more, and not until then, a bottle of rum began to circulate steadily between the occupants of the two tents. One day, many years hence, the bottle in which this rum was contained will come out at the end of the glacier beneath, perhaps to provide some future generation of airmen with material for speculation as to what sort of men were those who elected to climb on their flat feet before the helicopteral age.

The wind was blowing hard again the next morning, and our start was delayed, even later than on the previous morning. This was unfortunate as it meant that by the time we got down below Camp Two, the sun had done its worst, and the snow was in vile condition. It was a curious fact that the principal precipitation of snow had been confined between 19,000 and 21,000 feet. Above and below that range of altitude there had been practically no new snow.

It was a trying descent for Wood Johnson. Once more he fainted, but soon recovered. It was a weary wade for him across the level glacier near Camp One, and it was a tired party that floundered through the snowy morass and plugged uphill to Camp One.

At Camp One a surprise awaited us. Professor Dyhrenfurth, Kurz, and Wieland had come up from the Base Camp with the intention also of climbing the Jonsong Peak. Schneider, Hoerlin, and Wood Johnson were to descend to the Base Camp the next day for a rest, after which the first two were to ascend to the Choten Nyima La, the 18,500 feet pass on the frontier of Sikkim and Thibet, whence they hoped to ascend the Dodang Peak, 22,700 feet, the highest point of the limestone Dodang Nyima Range, bounding the northern side of the Lhonak Valley. I should like to have accompanied them, but I naturally preferred to attempt the Jonsong Peak once more, and although feeling in need of a rest, I decided to go back with Professor Dyhrenfurth's party next day.

Some cylinders of oxygen had been brought up from the Base Camp, more as an experiment than anything else, for there was certainly no necessity for oxygen. However, it can be extremely beneficial taken medicinally, as was demonstrated in the case of Wood Johnson. He had arrived practically exhausted at Camp One. As is common with exhausted men, his pulse rate was a high one, 115, but after a few minutes' inhalation of oxygen it was found to be 95, and much of his strength had returned to him. Therefore, I would recommend that even if oxygen is not taken on future Everest expeditions as a help to actual climbing, it should be taken as a revivifier. Also it promotes warmth, and may thus stimulate the circulation, or minimise the effects of frostbite. A dose taken in the morning before the start of a climb should prove a valuable preliminary to a hard day's work.

Plenty of food and fuel were now available, and that evening we did our best to make up for the privations of the last few days.

I cannot close this chapter without reference to the porters. Although on short commons, they had not once grumbled, but had carried out their arduous tasks with uncomplaining cheerfulness and fortitude. As a reward for their work, they were to be given three days' rest at the Base Camp, and a bonus on their pay. All save one of them were ready to descend. Nemu was not going to allow his sahib to return without someone to look after him ; he would accompany me once again up the Jonsong Peak.

CHAPTER XVII

THE CONQUEST OF JONSONG PEAK: THE SECOND ASCENT

The following morning, June 4, dawned mistily. A slight sprinkling of snow had fallen overnight, but this vanished with the first lick of the kindly sun. The weather *felt* good, and the air was fresh, with that magical tang of the hills that presages a brilliant day. The frost crystals on the grey rocks round glittered defiantly, but slowly, insidiously, the sun absorbed them and relegated them to the Infinite. As on the last occasion when we had left Camp One, so with this ; it was easy to imagine that somewhere hidden by the grey shawls of mist was a little llyn or loch, the still green waters of which had yet to be disturbed by the slim brown trout flashing upwards for their breakfast.

Wood Johnson was stronger, yet it was imperative that he should descend to the Base Camp for medical attention. What wretched luck ! Of all of us he was the one who most deserved to reach the summit. Among the porters who had come up from the Base Camp were some of the Bhutias who had previously grumbled at not being equipped to the same extent as the Sherpas. Several of them now took the opportunity of renewing their grievances, and declared it as their intention not to go on. Fortunately, they were prevailed upon to do so. It was unfortunate that Lobsang was still at the Base Camp, for his influence over the porters was great. Recently, he had completed the arduous task of getting the remainder of the loads over the Jonsong La, and it had been arranged that as soon as he had had a rest, he should come up with a support party carrying food.

Our first ascent of the Jonsong Peak had been dependent upon speed and good weather ; now, with the arrival of food and fuel both over the Jonsong La and from Lachen, we could afford to play a waiting game should the necessity arise, not an indefinite waiting game, but one that allowed for two or three days' bad weather.

To avoid having to wade through the glacier morass, we left early before the sun had time to soften the snow. The going was delightful. Of all sounds there is none more pleasant to the ear of the mountaineer than the musical creak of frozen snow beneath the nailed boot in the early morning. It is one that to me, at least, is charged with as much delight as the thud of an ice-axe pick meeting ice or the soft silken swish of a pair of ski parting powdery snow. On our first ascent we had waded for hours across the glacier, and up the ice-fall above, now we strolled, conscious that each upward swing of the leg was bringing us with the minimum of effort towards our goal. The porters seemed to realise this, too, and the importance of gaining as much height as possible before the snow was softened by the sun, for they came on well, their tireless gait telling of perfect training, coupled with a physique which makes them the finest natural mountaineers in the world.

In spite of the last few days of hard work, I felt in good training too, and found myself sufficiently far ahead to be able to lounge for an hour in the sun, on the former site of Camp Two. While doing so, I ate a meditative lunch, washing it down with long pulls from a large, new Thermos flask, which had appeared mysteriously in place of my last one which had been broken on the first ascent. It was my fourth Thermos, for three had been broken, but in every case a new one had appeared in place of the smashed one. I did not think it politic to question Nemu as to the means or methods by which these miracles were accomplished. Naturally of an untidy and careless disposition, I had lost or broken a number of articles, but replacements of these had invariably appeared. Once or twice, it is true, I seemed to detect growls of discontent from other members of the expedition, but it seemed to me tactful not to enquire into them. I preferred to think that Nemu had, in some mysterious manner, discovered the secret of reincarnating the spirits of broken Thermos flasks into newer and better Thermos flasks. In this particular instance the reincarnation had been so successfully accomplished, that I was now the proud possessor of the largest Thermos flask I had yet had. It was, in fact, the twin brother of one that I had seen Hoerlin using. While I was having my lunch, Nemu himself passed, carrying my tent and bedding. As he did so, I noted that his solemn brown eyes rested on the Thermos flask; they seemed to lighten a little, almost twinkle in fact; the creases in his forehead, which gave to him his habitual worried expression, were smoothed for an instant; something—was it a smile?—twitched at the corners of his broad mouth.

So good was the snow, and so easy the going, that Professor Dyhrenfurth decided not to camp at the site of the former Camp Two, but to push on up to Camp Three. In view of the fact that the porters were carrying very heavy loads, that the altitude was not inconsiderable, that the Bhutias had before resented attempts to double march them, and that we had plenty of food and fuel, it would have been wiser to have stopped at Camp Two. At all events, by the time the platform beneath the icy waves, or bulges, below the ridge had been gained, it was obvious that a number of porters would not, or could not, proceed farther that day, and the camp *had* to be pitched.

Kurz suggested that he and I should go on and prospect a way down the ice slopes from the ridge on which we had previously pitched Camp Three to the glacier we must ascend. This was necessary for two reasons. We hoped to make a shorter day of the final ascent by camping at the head of the glacier, for we were anxious to have enough time to carry out topographical, photographic, and cinematographic work from the Jonsong Peak, then, while the ice ridge beyond Camp Three might be a reasonable traverse for Europeans, it was hardly suitable for laden porters. Whichever way we descended to the glacier a secure staircase and fixed ropes would be essential, and while we had enough rope for a direct descent to the glacier we had not enough for the ice ridge.

We ascended by the same route as last time until we came to the commencement of the roof-like ice slope. Across this we cut horizontally to join a steepish snow ridge falling from the main ridge just below the site of Camp Three. There I anchored myself, and payed out a long length of rope as Kurz descended in search of the easiest route to the glacier 500 feet beneath.

The slopes did not belie their appearance; they looked steep and they were steep, probably a good sixty degrees in angle. As I expected, Kurz returned with the news that a

THE LHONAK PEAK FROM THE LHONAK GLACIER

way could be forced down, but that it would entail hours of step-cutting and necessitate fixed ropes for the porters.

The afternoon was drawing on, and the declining sun had lost its white heat and was slowly sinking, a red-hot ball, into the black abysses of night, as we descended to camp. The day had fulfilled its early promise. If only the good weather would hold.

As I gulped my plateful of soup I peered out between the flaps of my tent on the beauties of a mountain sunset. Below in the Lhonak Valley a cold broth of mist was brewing. The glaciers and slopes up which we had passed had been won over to the advancing hordes of night, but above, the beautiful Lhonak Peak stood out like a glowing beacon, as though warning the fatigued and retreating hosts of day of their impending dissolution. Much later, when night had triumphed, and all the peaks about us had pinned its dark cockade on their crests, Everest and Makalu, like two great citadels, stood between night and the fleeing remnants of day. But, finally, they too were lost, and night's hosts bivouacked on the ground they had won round a million starry fires.

But night had allied itself to our old and capricious enemy, the wind. Impetuously, savagely, it smote our tents, and several times I awoke to listen to its futile snarlings and worryings.

On our last ascent, the wind had had the decency to drop by 9 a.m., but on this occasion it evidently considered that such perfunctory politeness was no longer needed, and instead of dropping, it became if anything more violent, and joyfully seizing up the loose snow, hurled it with shrewd aim at the camp.

Eventually, we decided to make a start. I was first away, with the idea I must confess of finding a spot sheltered from the wind on one of the rocky outcrops projecting from the ice slope and lazing away an hour or so. But as I struggled against the buffeting onrushes of bitter wind across the roof-like slope, it seemed to me that I should have been wiser to have remained in my sleeping bag until the last moment. Descending, where Kurz had descended the previous day, I found what I was looking for, a little rock pinnacle with a sunny sheltered alcove on the leeward side, the floor of which was paved by a granite slab obviously intended for a lazy mountaineer. There I sat, smoking cigarette after cigarette. The wind moaned and sobbed above the pinnacle, but I listened to it with the complacent assurance of one immune from its scoldings. The sun was warm, and I leant languidly back. The mountain world floated unsubstantially between half closed eyelids ; the smoke spiral of my cigarette ascended gently, until caught by the wind it was whirled into nothingness ; the peace that is engendered by an ordered digestion and a warm body stole upon me. . . .

I glanced at my watch. Something must have gone wrong with the mainspring. Two hours had passed in a few minutes. Where were the others ? They, too, seemed to have preferred to shelter from the wind, and were probably still in their sleeping bags. More anxious thoughts supervened. In the wind the roof-like slope would be no joke for laden porters ; a slip there . . . I hurried back.

My anxieties were relieved as I turned the corner. No one appeared to have left the camp. The situation was explained when I reached the camp. The long march on the previous day plus the wind had been too much for the porters, and they had refused to start.

The camp was in a peculiarly shelterless position, and even though a day's climbing was lost we could, at least, find a better place for it. Between us and our old camping site on the ridge was the trough mentioned in the last chapter. Although formed by a choked crevasse, the snow was good and solid for the most part, and within an hour after my return we had broken camp and remade it there. At all events, there would have been little object in taking on the porters that day, for their presence during the cutting of steps down the ice slopes to the glacier would have been more dangerous than useful. Professor Dyhrenfurth and Wieland decided to spend the remainder of the day cutting some of these steps ; Kurz and I, meanwhile, dug ourselves in, and built a wall of snow blocks as some protection for the tents against the onslaught of the wind. I felt proud of the work of Nemu and myself, a horse-shoe shaped wall higher than the top of my tent, and I had just stepped back with a sigh of contentment to admire it when I went up to my knees in a crevasse. It was not a particularly dangerous crevasse, but it was unpleasantly near to the door of my tent. Stepping out of one's tent door into a crevasse would be tantamount to stepping out of the door of one of those economically constructed seaside lodging-houses where the unsuspecting visitor steps out of his bedroom, not on to a landing, but straight down the stairs.

The evening meal had been cooked when Professor Dyhrenfurth and Wieland returned. They had done capital work, having cut steps about half-way down the slopes to the glacier.

The building of a snow wall was a cunning move, for shortly after it was completed the wind dropped, a phenomenon which reminded me of what promised to be a wet fortnight in the Isle of Skye, but which, after only two days of rain, had been changed to a dry fortnight by the zeal of two meteorologists, who planted a number of rain gauges round the district.

The atmosphere, if chilly, was calm when we left the next morning. Our camp had been a cold one, and we had started for once unwarmed by the sun, but that kindly orb made full amends for its tardiness on the slopes to the glacier. Indeed, it glared upon us so furiously that we felt our now leather-like face covering (it is scarcely correct to call it skin) regaining that unpleasant drum-like tightness which we knew only too well preceded the disruption of our countenances.

Professor Dyhrenfurth and Wieland had worked out a good route down to the glacier, and a straightforward bout of step-cutting was all that remained to be done. They had descended the same route as Kurz and I for some distance, then leaving it, cut downwards and across to a rib of rocks; descending these as far as practicable, they had started to cut across steep and very hard ice towards a point where the bergschrund looked feasible. Wieland described the ice as being exceptionally tough and hard, a description that I was able to endorse as, held on the rope from the rock rib, I started on the task of continuing the staircase.

Whether a man is acclimatised to altitude or not, cutting in hard ice at nearly 22,000 feet will always be something more than a strenuous exercise. A minute or two's hard work, a few dozen blows, and the wind is *non est.*

Altitude has, metaphorically speaking, given you a straight left in the solar plexus, and you double up gasping for life-giving oxygen. Don't gasp shallowly, but deeply, using your will-power to force the air into the lungs. In the Alps the respiratory organs function automatically, but in the Himalayas they have to be forced to work if they are to give of their best, and the same applies to other parts of the body. It is not a brainless machine, however efficient at a low level, that will get to the highest summits of the Himalayas, but a machine ordered and directed by will-power, and not least, that other something we call the spirit.

The axe hit the ice with a dull thud. Several blows were often necessary to dislodge a chip or flake. A step meant several dozen blows. A few steps, it was enough. I retired and Wieland took my place. Both of us could, of course, have gone on for a long time with intervals of rest, but it was much quicker to take turns, even though it meant retreating each time back along the line of steps to the rocks.

For twenty yards the ice was tough and transparent. Frequently, the pick stuck in it as it might hard glue, and had to be wriggled and coaxed out. Gradually it became more flaky, and easier to cut into. At last came hard snow with a soft ice under-stratum, in which it was safest to cut a step, for the sun would soften the snow by midday. We unroped, and while Wieland and Kurz proceeded to enlarge the steps, drive in pitons, and fix ropes I continued to descend alone in order to discover the easiest way over the bergschrund.

The slope here was in excellent condition, and a couple of good kicks sufficed to make a secure step. In a quarter of an hour or so I had reached the bergschrund. At this point it was perfectly feasible for roped men, but if possible, I wanted to find a place where it could be crossed safely by an unroped man, or two men on one rope, in case we had to send porters back. I accordingly traversed to the left to a point where the moat seemed to be well bridged by a thick tongue of snow. The upper lip of the bergschrund was steep and icy, and I cut two or three large steps in it. Standing on these, I probed the snow tongue with my axe—it seemed safe enough. With the axe pick driven well in, I stepped down cautiously, holding on to the shaft with my left hand. It was fortunate I did so, for with startling suddenness my feet went through the snow tongue into nothingness. My whole weight came on my left arm and ice-axe, and for an instant I swung free across the upper lip of the bergschrund. The next moment I pulled myself back into safety. The wrench upon my left arm and wrist had been considerable, and the twisting effect on the wrist as I oscillated for a moment on the lip had sprained the latter. It was not a bad sprain, but one that reminded me many times during the next week of a nasty moment.

A yard or two to the right the bergschrund, although insecurely bridged, was so narrow that it was possible to jump it, and a few instants later I was gaily glissading down the snow slopes below it to the level floor of the glacier. There I sat down in the sun and watched Kurz and Wieland, followed by Professor Dyhrenfurth and the porters, enlarging the ice steps and fixing ropes. They came straight down, and crossed the snow bridge at which I had first looked, which proved, despite its appearance, to be perfectly safe. Helped by fixed ropes as well as good steps, the

THE ICE SLOPE ON THE JONSONG PEAK

porters soon descended, and the whole party forgathered on the glacier for lunch.

So far, so good. Everything, excluding my sprained wrist, had gone splendidly, but the ice slopes had taken us a long time to descend, and evening was drawing on apace as we trudged up the glacier. We had hoped to make our camp on the glacier at its head, on or below the broad col in the North-west Ridge, but our old enemy, the wind, thought otherwise, and as the day declined, so did it, like an habitué of a night club, gird up its loins and prepare to spend a night of revelry and devilry. But we were now used to its little tantrums, and its blasts elicited nothing more than a conventional curse or two as we approached the col, although, for comfort and warmth's sake, it was essential to find some place more or less sheltered from its venomous gusts.

The crest of the col was defended by two or three crevasses, over which the wind had laid a thin covering of pie-crust-like snow as innocent looking as the sands of Margate, but as treacherous as an elephant trap. Circumventing this, we reached the crest of the col and looked down the great ice face above Camp One. Just beneath us, and to the right, a little shelf ran along under an ice bulwark, below which the ice slopes dropped with appalling steepness for thousands of feet. It was the only break, and the only possible site for a camp where we might reasonably expect some shelter from the wind. We descended to it without difficulty, a shovel was produced, and we started to dig out platforms for our tents in a sloping snow-drift, as near to the protecting ice bulwark as possible.

If we thought to find shelter here from the wind, we had

made a sad mistake, for our relentless opponent poured over the col and descended upon us with a merciless *joie de vivre*. There is something almost human in the way it seeks out every niche and cranny in these Himalayan mountain-sides.

By the time the tents were pitched and the pegs driven firmly and deeply into the snow in expectation of a wild night, the sun was setting. It was invisible to us from our chilly shelf, but its rays lit the snow eddies as they were blown furiously over the ridge above us, until they resembled gossamer-like scarves of spun gold trailed negligently from the white shoulders of the snow maidens.

Wieland and I shared a tent, and after a chilly supper, Wieland, with characteristic enthusiasm, proceeded to indulge in what at first appeared to be some strange and mystic ceremony, but which he condescended to inform me is known as "Determination of Height by means of a Boiling-Point Thermometer."[1] For some reason this necessitated the use of alcohol, but it seemed to me that this alcohol could be more beneficially employed elsewhere. But Science must be served, even at the expense of numbed fingers in a small tent which the wind is doing its best to carry away. Perhaps I should not speak so lightly of sacred things, but I must confess that at the time I was concerned not with the determination of height to three places of decimals, but to having a good night's rest preparatory to a strenuous day. However, to cheer Wieland, I gave a short recital on my mouth organ. Beneath the insidious influence of "She's got Hot Lips," the water boiled in great style

[1] The height determined was 6,620 metres=21,720 feet, 2,624 feet below the summit of the Jonsong Peak.

round the thermometer, and the mercury rose to prodigious heights. Both performances ended in rum, and a sleep such as only rum can induce.

The wind was still blowing when we awoke next morning. My companions were pessimistic, but on the strength of our experiences on the first ascent, I ventured to indulge in a little optimism, and even went so far as to declare that it would drop by 9 a.m. The wind, however, objected to having its fortune foretold in this way, and instead of completely dropping, as it fully intended to do, it compromised with its dignity by only moderating.

Our start was a chilly one. We took with us our servants Lewa, Tsinabo, and Nemu: the name of Wieland's servant I do not remember.

Just before leaving the camp one or two of the party took a cocktail of oxygen to wet their appetite for the thin air of 24,000 feet. Personally, I refused this extraneous aid, as I wanted to convince myself that I was capable, not only of getting to the top of the Jonsong Peak on my own lungs, but of going higher.

The camp was reasonably sheltered, and the morning sun shone brilliantly over a cloudy carpet that covered all but the highest peaks in the east, but on the col above we met the full force of the wind, which seemed to cut into our flesh like a knife in spite of every stitch of spare clothing.

On the first ascent, the little couloir leading up into the rocks had contained good snow, into which steps could be easily kicked, but since then the wind had done its worst and had blown its surface hard and icy and steps were necessary. I led, deriving some measure of warmth by slashing out steps as quickly as the altitude would permit.

We might have saved ourselves twenty minutes' work by wearing crampons, but on such a cold morning they would probably have numbed the feet, and circulation once lost is hard to regain over 22,000 feet.

Arriving on the rock ledge where Hoerlin and Schneider had dumped their kit, we started to climb up the rocks of the face towards the ridge. They were easy enough rocks, yet a slip would have been hard to stop. They reminded me strongly of the photograph taken by Mr. Somervell of Colonel Norton at 28,000 feet on Everest. There, as here, were the same tile-like slabs of limestone, as dark and forbidding as the rock of the Coolin Hills in Skye. Only here the angle was steeper than on Everest, and powdery snow burdened every ledge, sometimes concealing a glaze of ice.

The wind was something more than unpleasant; it roared across the gaunt slabs, licking up the powdery snow, and beating us with its stinging particles. Sometimes advance was impossible, and we crouched in close to the rocks, with bowed heads and turning our backs to its fury. Nevertheless, we made good progress, although we knew that should the wind increase as we gained height, we would not be likely to reach the summit. The porters did not like it. At the best of times they hate wind, and no weapon that a Himalayan peak can produce demoralises them to a greater extent. Soon I noticed that Nemu was going badly. He was finding it hard to keep up with Kurz and myself, and was gradually dropping farther and farther behind. Obviously he was tired, and no wonder considering the work he had done on the expedition, especially since we had left our last Base Camp. In returning with me, instead of descending with the other porters of the first party

WIND ! PORTERS DESCENDING THE JONSONG PEAK

to the Base Camp for a rest, he had shown of what stuff he was made. He was not one to spare himself, and he would, I knew, go on until he dropped if by so doing he could serve his master. I waited on the ledge until he had joined me, then, taking the rucksack he was carrying, which contained food, photographic apparatus, spare gloves, etc., I bade him go back. At first he pretended not to understand. I shouted at him again above the roaring wind that he must do so, and pointed downwards towards the camp. And Nemu went, after one reproachful look, like a faithful hound that has been ordered home for he knows not why. I felt really sorry for him, but the Jonsong Peak is no mountain for a tired or exhausted man.

We had expected to find the wind worse on the ridge itself, but strangely enough, it was not nearly so strong. We could still see it sweeping the slopes below, driving the snow before it like sand. We seemed to have stepped from an area of storm into an area of comparative calm. In fact, once the ridge had been reached, there was no longer any doubt as to our gaining the summit so far as the weather was concerned.

For some distance the ridge formed a sharp snow edge, but Kurz and Tsinabo, who were first, had stamped an excellent trail. Above the snow, the ridge rose steeply for two or three hundred feet, forcing us out on to the western face. Never have I seen more rotten rocks. This part of the peak is nothing more than a festering sore of shale and limestone. There was scarcely a firm hold. The safest method of climbing such rock is to have always three points of attachment. This means that the climber should never trust to one hold only, but distribute his weight between at least three hand-holds and foot-holds. This may sound simple in theory, but it is not so simple in practice. Many accidents have resulted from yielding to the temptation to rely on one seemingly good hold.

For two hundred feet the climbing was steep, and the inadvisability of not using a rope might have been argued. But I think that the rope would have been more dangerous than useful, and Kurz had evidently assured himself that Tsinabo was sufficiently expert at rock climbing to climb without its aid. Tsinabo was certainly climbing in splendid style, and seemed to enjoy the work for its own sake. Both he and Lewa are excellent rock climbers, and with their wonderful strength and agility would probably be capable of leading the most difficult rock climbs in the Alps.

Once or twice I glanced down the great mountainside. It was still in shadow, and looked terribly forbidding, its brutal black-jawed crags at savage variance with the peaceful serenity of the sunlit snow-fields. The peaks that had recently dominated our outlook had sunk beneath us. Even the Lhonak Peak looked formless and insignificant, and our gaze passed over the Dodang Nyima Range into the brown fastnesses of Thibet.

The steep rocks eased off. We found ourselves on a slope of slabs similar to those below. We were now definitely feeling the altitude. Each upward step was an increasing effort. I felt strongly tempted to leave what now seemed an abominably heavy rucksack, but which only weighed about ten pounds, and climb to the top without it. Photographic scruples came to the rescue. Had I not taken the expedition boots to the summit of the Ramthang Peak? And these with crampons had weighed nearly half as much again as my present rucksack. Heartened by this reflection, I toiled on.

The wind had by no means dropped, but it had lost much of its former venom, and the sun was shining with great power. Climbing at high altitudes is a " slow motion " of climbing at low altitudes. Movement is the same, but it is slowed down, and the climber concentrates upon performing every action with the minimum of effort. Thus, the man who is accustomed to climbing neatly and with a minimum expenditure of effort on Alpine peaks will, other things being equal, be a better climber at high altitudes than he who always relies on brute force rather than skill.

Major J. B. L. Noel in his book, *Through Tibet to Everest*, wrote : " Collect an Olympic team of fine young men who represent the manhood of the world, and send them equipped with modern scientific appliances and devices. Let them not attack or assault Everest, but let them *walk up* the mountain and prove its conquest without loss, injury or suffering to themselves. . . . It would be a victory for modern man." These are magnificent sentiments. Unfortunately, however, the Olympic athlete without mountaineering experience would be of little more use on Everest, or any other of the big peaks in the Himalayas, than Falstaff with gout. Mountaineering experience, and in this I include development and training of mental as well as physical powers, is the first essential. How often do young and brilliant batsmen fail when tried out in a Test Match. It is simply lack of experience. The skill is there, but the brain is incapable of utilising it advantageously. Precisely the same applies to Himalayan mountaineering. Everest will be climbed not on a record of super athletism, but on a record of all-round mountaineering experience coupled to a suitable temperament.

The slabs petered out into a long slope of scree stretching up almost to the summit. Easy technically, it was yet trying work, for while the scree would delight the heart of a roadmender, or one of those evilly disposed Urban District Councils that cover up a perfectly good road with small sharp stones, it awakened no such response in our hearts, for it rested upon a frozen sub-stratum, and slipped back at every step. A few steps, a bout of panting while leaning on our ice-axes, then another few steps, was our method of progression.

It is interesting to remember the thoughts that flash through the brain at such a time. My first thought was what an unutterably weary business it was, how "fed up" I was, and what a fool I was toiling up there, when I might have been sitting in the Planters' Club at Darjeeling, admiring the Himalayas through a telescope. I sat down for a rest. And as I sat fatigue magically departed, and I experienced to the full the joys of my wonderful position. But always, at the back of my mind like a cloud, hung the thought that I had to go on. I heaved myself to my feet, and went on. Two steps, and weariness returned, but this time, I was able to counter it. I remember thinking that it would be quite easy if I could discipline my brain to think of the same things as when sitting down for a rest, but such a task the brain seemed incapable of performing. At rest, æsthetic enjoyment had predominated, but it was impossible to experience æsthetic enjoyment when heart and lungs were beating like sledge hammers, legs felt leaden, and knees ached at every upward step.

What the brain did was to compromise with the body, and compromise so effectively that it made me more than half forget that I was toiling up a vile scree slope at a height of over 24,000 feet. It brought a power of mental detachment. Without bidding, a number of trivial thoughts and remembrances flashed through my mind. They are not worth repeating, even to a psycho-analyst, and not many of those are likely to read this book. They were quite trivial, quite ordinary, some of them absurd, so that I wanted to laugh, and lose the wind I was so carefully trying to husband. Then, quite suddenly, the little devils of weariness returned with redoubled force. I halted, but when I glanced back I was surprised to find how far I had climbed from my last halting-place.

I have mentioned these things because they are of interest to all who appreciate the real power of mind over body. I think the men who will eventually reach the summit of Mount Everest will not be of the type accustomed to set teeth and "bullock" forwards unthinkingly, they will be men capable of detaching their minds from the physical work which their bodies are performing. Nowhere else is the power of the mind over the body demonstrated to a greater extent than at high altitudes. It is not sufficient for the mind deliberately to force the body into action, it must humour it, even delude it into thinking that it is not working so hard as it really is.

So far I have only mentioned the conscious control of mind over body. I have not mentioned the subconscious control, yet that is what really counts, for when all else has failed, and the conscious mind and the body are united in one desire to quit, it is this subconscious " something " that will drive a worn-out body beyond the ultimate limits of endurance.

The final slope was snow. Below it was a little outcrop of rocks on which we rested for a few minutes. Kurz and Tsinabo were first away. The summit was not more than a hundred feet above the rocks. After the stones, it was a relief to kick steps into firm snow. The worst thing about the stones was that rhythmical movement was impossible, but now, in spite of the height I found myself going much more easily than I had lower down.

The slope steepened into a little lip a few feet high, forming the sky-line. Kurz and Tsinabo climbed over it and disappeared. There came a thin faint shout. I followed. Even in the hard work of those moments there was borne upon me an intense feeling of excitement. On the stones there had been merely weariness, but now weariness was forgotten. I had no longer consciously or subconsciously to force myself to go on, I *wanted* to. To see over that snowy lip was my one dominant idea. Something wonderful was the other side. As a small boy I had often longed to climb a hill behind the house where I lived. I was certain that a new and wonderful world lay the other side. One day I did climb it, to see—factory chimneys. The feeling now was much the same, only I knew that whatever I should see it would not be factory chimneys.

My legs levered me up, my head rose over the lip, my eyes peered across a flat tabletop of snow and stones to meet vast pillars of cloud, blue depths, silver heights—Kangchenjunga and Jannu. The next moment my gloved hands were grasping those of Kurz and Tsinabo. The ascent of 2,624 feet from the camp had taken a little over five hours, an average uphill speed of 500 feet an hour. This is fast going, especially taking into account the fact that the ascent had been by no means a walk, whilst we had been delayed a little by the wind on the lower portion of the climb. The wind had now dropped considerably, but what there was shortened a stay that will live in my memory.

A savage mountain world surrounded us ; our gaze passed at a glance over inconceivable distances, resting on mountains and glaciers unknown to man, seeking languidly the infinitude of vast horizons in a subconscious attempt to escape from a nearer and an unvarying world of rock, snow, and ice. The atmosphere was wonderfully clear. Over the brown Thibetan plateau to the north-east rose two huge snowy peaks. Only their snow-covered upper parts were visible, their bases were beneath the horizon. We were 24,344 feet, the Thibetan plateau is about 12,000 feet, yet the lower half of these mountains was below the horizon. How far were they away, and what was their height ? Their distance was so great that the tip of the little finger held out at arm's length would have covered them both.

I have seen Monte Viso from the summit of the Piz Bernina, a distance of about 180 miles as the crow flies, and these peaks were much farther. In direction, I should place them as being approximately in the same line as Lhasa. Lhasa is about 220 miles distant from the Jonsong Peak, so that it is probable that they were some 50 miles or more beyond Lhasa. On the other hand, 150 miles away, and slightly to the south of this last line are the peaks of Nangkartse Dz, but I am positive that they cannot have been these. One hundred and fifty miles is no excessive distance to see in the clear air of Thibet. If these peaks were actually to the north-east of Lhasa, what could they have been? The only definite statement I can make is that a considerable portion of their height was concealed by the horizon, a horizon consisting not of a high intervening range, but of the rolling hills and minor ranges common to this part of Thibet. Anyway, I will not commit myself to any positive statements as to their distance or height or exact direction, for we had no means of determining them. They looked immense mountains even at that great distance, and dominated everything.

Westwards, and much nearer, were Everest and Makalu. From our lower camps we had seen them between gaps in the nearer ridges, and though these latter had not detracted from their magnificence, it was not so easy to appreciate their sovereignty over all other peaks. Seen from the summit of the Jonsong Peak, one realised to the full that Everest is indeed the "Goddess Mother of the World."

The whole country to the south-east was covered by the cloudy pall of the monsoon, above which the highest peaks stood out like a fairy archipelago. For the first time we saw Kangchenjunga without being misled by foreshortening. Had Mr. Freshfield seen it from the same vantage point, I doubt very much whether he would have held out any hopes whatever as to the possibility of climbing it from the Nepal side. Of course, looking at this side as we were from directly in front of it, we were liable to be deceived in the opposite extreme. Edward Whymper never dreamed of climbing the Matterhorn by the east face until he had seen it in profile, for looked at from Zermatt, or the Riffel, it looks fearfully steep. The same applies, no doubt, to some extent to our view of Kangchenjunga from the Jonsong Peak, yet I am convinced that the impressions gained from what we saw were more accurate ones than those gained when viewing the mountain from Pangperma or the Jonsong Glacier.

For one thing, the terraces which had appeared flat, or gently sloping, were now seen to be set at a much steeper angle than we had supposed, whilst in many places they consisted, not of snow-covered glacier, but of bare ice. Furthermore, we saw the summit pyramid in its true proportions. It is not easy to climb, and is likely to prove much harder than the final pyramid of Everest. The Everest pyramid is about 800 feet high, that of Kangchenjunga about 1,500 feet high. It will not be possible for climbers, who may one day try to storm it, to keep to the crest of the North Ridge above the highest terrace, for this rises directly above the terrace in a Λ-shaped cut-off. They will be forced out on to the face on the western side of the ridge, where they are likely to experience little gullies and chimneys filled with incoherent, powdery snow and smooth granite slabs.

Because we failed, I have no wish to pour cold water on the aspirations of others, but let those who attempt the same route as the Munich expedition remember that the difficulties are *not* over when the upper and easier portion of the ice ridge is reached. Only the hardest of the *technical* difficulties are behind, the *real* difficulties, altitude, powdery snow, wind, and rocks are to come, and they will tax the climber to the uttermost limits of his powers.

Only with the aid of exceptional and superlative good fortune can he hope to conquer them, and Kangchenjunga is not a mountain that bestows good fortune on those that woo it.

We could see that the monsoon had already broken on Kangchenjunga and the country to the south. Indeed, we heard later that during the time that we were attacking the Jonsong Peak, rain poured for days on end at Darjeeling. It was difficult to believe that the sunny billows of cloud over which we gazed were in reality rain clouds, which were deluging the lower valleys. We were lucky to see Kangchenjunga, for it was smothered in new snow, and it was evident that the monsoon had already wreaked some of its fury on the great mountain. Even as we watched, we could see battalion after battalion of cloud marching up from the south endeavouring to encircle Kangchenjunga, and pour up the Jonsong Glacier. And the north wind was losing. Sullenly, doggedly, it was fighting a rearguard action. In a few days it would have been beaten back to its fortress keep, Thibet. There it would hold the monsoon, which would beat impotently on the ranges bounding the brown plateaux of that barren land.

The advancing tide of the monsoon was slowly creeping towards us ; its streams were pouring up the Teesta Valley to the east, and the Arun Valley to the west, slowly outflanking the dry corners of North-east Nepal and North-west Sikkim. One could say definitely that two or three days' marching down the Lhonak Valley would bring one into the monsoon area. It was an interesting spectacle, and one which meteorologists would have given much to see.

Here and there above the cloudy carpet to the south, huge columns and towers of cumuli-nimbus projected far into the clear blue sky like scattered trees rising from a vast snow-covered prairie. One or two of them were drawn out at their crests like anvils by upper air currents, a typical thunder formation. Occasionally, bits would become detached, and swim placidly up into the blue heaven like Zeppelins. The mountaineer who sees these long fish-bellied, smooth-looking clouds in the Alps, knows that almost invariably they precede bad weather. Here they preceded more than a mere storm, they were the forerunner of the south-west monsoon, the rains of which bring life to the sun-scorched plains of India.

To the cartoonist, who is frequently led by some strange reasoning process to associate mountain tops with politics, there is only one type of mountain top. It is shaped like a dunce's hat, and its summit is a mathematical point, on which is seated, a trifle uncomfortably, a mountaineer, who usually takes the form of some striped-trousered politician, yodelling blithely some political profundity or sentiment. If there are other, and more fearful mountain tops, they are assuredly those that emanate from the fertile brain of Mr. Heath Robinson. His are too sharp even to sit upon, and are usually tenanted by a stout gentleman with a silk hat and spats, who, balancing upon one leg, operates some fearful and wonderful magnetic mechanism which draws more stout gentlemen to the top. Exactly how they are to crowd together on the top is never explained.

There was nothing so thrilling about the summit of the Jonsong Peak. It was, in fact, tame and dull, consisting as it did of a long drift of snow and a bed of loose stones.

The stones were all of the same size and were evidently intended as a reserve dump for the Borough Engineer, whose job it is to repair the ravages of climbing parties on the scree slopes below. We were even able to promenade up and down, while indulging in that vigorous arm exercise practised by the drivers of taxi-cabs. In this way we preserved some semblance of warmth in face of the wind, which cut across the summit, jabbing us cruelly with its icy stilettos. But even arm exercises and promenading cannot be carried out as vigorously at 24,000 feet as at sea level, and soon we decided that we had had enough, and after taking a number of photographs, and swinging our vision along that marvellous panorama in a vain attempt to capture some of its beauties, we turned to go.

What a difference there is in the Himalayas between ascending and descending. On the ascent, the last little bit above the rocky outcrop had seemed by no means inconsiderable. Now, we strode down it like giants. How wearying the slope of scree had been to ascend, how ridiculously easy to descend. The mountains that had sunk below the horizon seemed almost to shoot up at us as we rattled down.

In a minute or two we were off the scree, and scrambling down the slopes. There we met Professor Dyhrenfurth and Lewa. We had taken only a few minutes from the top, it would take them over another hour at least to get there, and perhaps longer, for as I shouted a greeting, I perceived at the same instant that Professor Dyhrenfurth was wearing the expedition boots. In what spirit of selflessness had he done this ? Was it in the same spirit that a scientifically minded friend of mine once declared that it was easier to climb a mountain with the climbing boots carried in the rucksack than on the feet? He urged me to ascend the precipitous slopes of Box Hill in this manner, first with boots, then without boots altogether, and then carrying the boots in the rucksack, while he timed my efforts with a stop-watch. In view of the broken bottles distributed there every week-end by motorists, I am happy to say that for some reason this experiment never materialised. Perhaps, therefore, it was something of the same spirit of scientific enquiry which led Professor Dyhrenfurth to don the expedition boots. Knowing that they weighed eight and a half pounds, and that they had to be carried through a height of 2,624 feet, should provide a basis for a pretty calculation in horse-power and foot-pounds.

I discovered what I had been looking for, a sheltered place out of the wind, where I could enjoy the view to the full. It was only 300 or 400 feet beneath the summit, and the panorama extended from Everest to Chomolhari, 23,930 feet, the holy peak of Eastern Thibet. On the summit æsthetic appreciation of the view had been numbed by the wind, now I could even take off my boots, and toast chilled feet in the sun. As I laid my boots carefully on a rock beside me, I could not help shuddering at the thought of accidentally knocking them down the mountainside. Once I had been with a friend on a long walk in the country. It was a hot day, and we had sat down on a river bank to dip our feet into the cold waters of a mountain torrent. We were many miles from the nearest village, and my friend remarked on the fact, and said what a terrible thing it would be to lose a boot. He had hardly said so when one of his boots was snatched, as if by magic, from his hand

and dropped into the mountain torrent. He never saw it again. Fortunately, however, we were able to discover lying under a hedge an aged and enormous boot which had apparently been discarded, after many years' wear, by a fastidious tramp. I have not forgotten my friend's remarks on his return to civilisation, or the size of his blisters when at length he did get there. To lose a boot on a Himalayan peak would be a much more serious business, and the man who did so would stand a good chance of losing his foot from frostbite, if he got down at all. I put my boots on very, very carefully.

From my vantage point I looked down to the long, unknown glacier which flows in a north-westerly direction from the Jonsong Peak. It is at least 15 miles long, but even from this height, it was not possible to tell which river received its waters. In this corner of the Himalayas there are many peaks accessible to ordinary mountaineering parties, and it is certain that a party making the Lhonak Valley its headquarters could scale a dozen or more fine peaks in the course of a comparatively short holiday. Naturally, ambitious minded man is more anxious to climb the greater peaks of the Himalayas, but one cannot help thinking that he is beginning at the wrong end, and that by neglecting the many fine mountains of 20,000 to 23,000 feet, he is denying himself the real pleasures of mountaineering. For instance, north-westwards of the Lhonak Peak there are a number of fine snow mountains, all of which can be climbed, whilst in the north-east corner of Nepal itself are dozens upon dozens of accessible mountains.

Kurz had gone on down, but presently I was joined by

UNEXPLORED COUNTRY TO NORTH-WEST OF JONSONG PEAK. A VIEW FROM THE SUMMIT

Wieland, whose servant had deserted him at about the same place from which Nemu had returned. Together we continued the descent, rattling down the rocks at an almost Alpine rate. With the approach of evening the wind began to rise once more, and by the time we had reached the lower slopes it was snarling at us with ever increasing ferocity. But, as we glissaded down the couloir and trod once more the friendly glacier, we could forgive it its spitefulness, for taking all in all, it had been a wonderful day and the fates had been kind to us.

We stood for a few moments on the col above the camp, bathed in the radiance of the reddening sun. Its gleams lit the steel heads of our trusty ice-axes, and our shadows were thrown blue and spider-like across the wind-rippled snow. Our eyes sought the long ridge we had descended for Professor Dyhrenfurth and Lewa. There was no sign of them ; obviously they would be late, but should they be benighted, the moon would aid them on their descent.

Darkness fell ; the wind steadily increased as we lay in our sleeping bags. Driven snow lashed the tent Wieland and I were sharing. At 8 p.m., there was still no sign of Professor Dyhrenfurth. We looked outside ; the air was full of snowy spindrift. Above the camp the wind was roaring over the col in a deep symposium of sound, like the bass note of a huge organ. Our anxiety increased. Ought we to get together a rescue party ? Even supposing we did, what could we do on such a night ? It was nearly nine o'clock when we heard a whistle. An ice-sheeted figure sank down in the snow outside—Professor Dyhrenfurth.

He was very tired, and no wonder, for not content with

having climbed the highest summit of the Jonsong Peak, his geological enthusiasm had caused him to traverse the ridge to the lower summit. He told us that the descent had been a terrible one. He had expected moonlight, but the moon had not risen sufficiently high to light the western face of the ridge. The wind had harried them continuously, and in the driving clouds of snow raised by it, the way had been hard to find. Lewa had done simply magnificently.

It had been a great effort for a man of forty-four years of age, especially in view of having climbed in the expedition boots. The boots had triumphantly vindicated themselves on the descent, for in spite of the wind and the cold, Professor Dyhrenfurth did not have frostbite. On the other hand, Lewa was wearing only ordinary boots, and he also had no frostbite. It is perhaps doubtful whether the party would have been benighted had Professor Dyhrenfurth not worn the expedition boots.

The wind had done its worst, and we awoke to a morning of perfect calm. Leisurely we prepared for the descent, basking in the sunlight the while. We left at 9 a.m. and strolled down the glacier. If only we had known that the weather would hold like this, we should have postponed the climb, for no snow streamers were being drawn from the mountain tops, and the Jonsong Peak rose calm and untroubled into the blue.

Up the ice slope we went, releasing the fixed ropes as we did so, and down the other side to our former camp. There we were greeted by Lobsang and several tins of Christmas pudding. Personally, I found the presence of the former more acceptable than the latter, for if there is one thing more calculated to disarrange the digestion at a high altitude, it is tinned Christmas pudding. So far as I remember there was only one member of the expedition who ever seemed to appreciate it, and that was Schneider, but even he used to find it necessary to help it down with salad dressing and Worcester sauce.

Had the weather turned bad, the advent of Lobsang and his men with the Christmas puddings might have enabled us to have stuck it out, but I shudder to think of what life without exercise in a small tent would have been like on a diet of Christmas puddings. Full of Christmas pudding I glissaded with great velocity down the snow slopes.

The day ended in a struggle and a wade through the inevitable glacier morass which, despite the passage of many porters and the ploughing out of a deep track, seemed to be worse than ever. After camping on snow for four nights it was pleasant to get back on to the stony ridge where Camp One was pitched. Seated on a granite slab, I watched the last of the porters swinging down the snow slopes. The sun was setting in a transparent bank of mist, and its rays lighted the ice crust already formed by Jack Frost until the snow gleamed like beaten silver.

Slowly the last man came trudging in with his heavy load, yet as he sank gratefully on to his haunches, and slipped out of his head-band, that cheery grin that knows no tiredness broke over his countenance. As he passed one ragged sleeve over his sweat-bedewed brow, his eyes swept upwards to the Jonsong Peak, and the grin was replaced almost by a look of awe. Was it possible that he had been up there near that great summit, glowing in the declining sun with the sahibs, so near to the gods?

The following morning we packed up. After leaving two cairns that the porters had built ornamented with prayer flags, and a number of empty oxygen cylinders, we set off for the Base Camp. With the arrival of all the loads over the Jonsong La the Base Camp had been shifted to the end of the Lhonak Glacier. It was better, therefore, to descend to the northern branch of the glacier instead of the southern up which we had approached Camp One. Easy snow slopes led us to the crest of a steep declivity some three hundred feet high, consisting of ice overlaid with soft snow. Had it been a little longer it would have been dangerous from avalanches. As it was, those detached by glissading porters were not large enough to harm anyone.

Nemu was the last down. Not for him the wild glissade, with load bumping one way and its owner the other. He followed Wieland, who thoughtfully cut steps for such porters who had to descend carefully on account of fragile loads. It was not until nearly half way down that he permitted himself to slide, using my tin box as a toboggan, descending with dignity and decorum.

Below these slopes were rocks, between which meandered a little rivulet fringed with flowers and mosses. They were the first flowers I had seen since I had left the Base Camp, and I greeted them gratefully. What would mountains or mountaineering be without its contrasts between the little things and the great things? These flowers were as important to me as the Jonsong Peak, and perhaps even greater, for they were synonymous with the small and homely things of life, and these are the things which the mountaineer turns to with rejoicing and gratitude. Only by knowing the ugly can we adore the beautiful, and only

THE LAST PORTER RETURNS TO CAMP ON THE JONSONG PEAK

by seeing the small can we appreciate the great. I remained behind to sit down and dream for a few moments among the flowers.

We followed the side moraine of the glacier. Lower down we encountered some of the most lovely ice scenery upon which I have ever gazed. There was a little glacier lake bounded on three sides by walls of ice. Sun, evaporation and melting had sculptured these walls into fantastic forms. There was the Gothic, with its flying buttresses and daring minarets, the Roman, with its superb solidity, and not least, the Victorian, for many of the pillars ornamenting these walls bore a striking resemblance to those that flank the doorways of the more respectable houses in Kensington. In fact had M. Karel Capek seen one stretch of this ice wall he would most likely have compared it to the frozen respectability of Westbourne Grove.

Apart from these things, there was in one corner a fine organ of ice with keyboard and pipes complete, and even as we passed there seemed to come from it a deeply resonant note—no doubt due to the movement of the glacier.

After this the way became duller. The glacier was moraine covered, and included among the moraines were many stones of singular beauty, mostly from the reddish-veined limestone of the Dodang Nyima range. I appropriated several as paper weights.

Traversing the junction of the east and west branches of the glacier was a tiresome business. Up and down we went over enormous moraine mounds, and soon any joy we might have had at descending to the Base Camp had completely disappeared. The trudge became weary and uninteresting, although brightened once or twice by little clusters of Eidelweiss. We passed the pinnacled portion of the glacier, where I noticed that the beak-like structure which I had seen from Camp One was still preserved.

Near the snout of the glacier Professor Dyhrenfurth and I left the main party in order to have a look at the curious earth pyramids which we had previously noted. They are indeed weird structures, and appeared so unstable that we did not linger beneath them longer than was necessary. This peregrination brought us opposite to the Base Camp, but on the wrong side of the glacier torrent. Fortunately, the latter here divides into a number of smaller streams. We waded across these, but the last stream, a deep and swift-torrent, daunted us. We shouted lustily. Our shouts were heard, and grinning porters soon arrived to carry us pick-a-back across. Not the least humorous spectacle of the expedition was the arrival of the leader at the Base Camp, clad in his pants.

Wood Johnson was much better, and that night, before turning in, he and I strolled away from the camp. The soft turf muffled our tread. How pleasant it was to feel it again and scent its elusive fragrance. The moon was rising. Her soft rays illuminated the great terminal moraine of the Lhonak Glacier and the weird earth pinnacles. Almost, we fancied ourselves looking up at a titanic cinder heap, ejected from some mountain hell.

Up and down we walked, yarning over the events of the past fortnight, and when at last we turned in the moon rode high in the heavens and the great peaks around stood radiant against the stars.

CHAPTER XVIII

THE RETURN TO DARJEELING

We had arrived back at the Base Camp on June 10. The following day was necessarily a rest day, and we devoted it to lounging about the camp, writing letters to home, or making desperate endeavours to fill in many blank pages of our diaries.

For some time I dutifully hammered away at a dispatch on the portable typewriter, but soon I gave even that up, and sitting in the sun on the warm springy turf allowed my mind to wander back over the events of the past fortnight. From May 29 to June 12 there had been for me only one rest day, and that was on June 1 when we had lain in our tents unable to move owing to a snowstorm. Kangchenjunga had been too nerve-wracking for enjoyment, but though we had had some tough and trying times on the Jonsong Peak we had enjoyed them, too ; we had not been merely avalanche fodder, we had climbed free from nerve-strain and anxiety, and life had been very good. Staying on in the Lhonak Valley as Professor Dyhrenfurth wanted to do might result in some useful exploration and geological work, but to me at least the thought of a hot bath submerged every other consideration. I looked at my hands ; they were brown and wrinkled with the sun and wind, the hands of an old man. My fingers explored my face, pulling on the red beard sprouting therefrom with a feeling, not of pride at its luxuriant growth, but of loathing.

Hoerlin had been the only one to escape a beard, and had been known as Pallas (Pallas Athene). Dr. Richter had weighed us that morning. The work of the past twelve weeks had told, and we had all lost a stone or more each, Professor Dyhrenfurth as much as twenty-two pounds.

By courtesy of *The Times*

That afternoon Schneider and Hoerlin returned from the Dodang Nyima Range. They had added yet another success to their splendid climbing achievements by ascending the Dodang Peak, 22,700 feet. With characteristic modesty they had little to say about it, beyond the fact that the climbing had been of a most difficult nature. They had cut steps for many hours in the toughest ice they had ever encountered, and the picks of their ice-axes bore striking witness to the toughness, for they were bent round out of alignment. First of all they had descended to the Choten Nyima La, across which runs the Thibetan frontier ; thence they had climbed the Dodang Peak. It had cost them nearly a day to work through a difficult ice-fall, and on the final climb they had only just escaped being benighted, so difficult had been the work.

Wood Johnson, who was much better, was anxious to return to his tea estate, as his leave was nearly up. Frau Dyhrenfurth, Dr. Richter, Duvanel and myself decided to accompany him, leaving the remainder of the party to attempt the ascent of the Lhonak Peak, and afterwards cross over one of the passes into the Zemu Valley in order to view the great eastern precipices of Kangchenjunga and the ice ridge attempted by the Munich expedition. Whether or not they would be able to do this before the arrival of the monsoon was, however, doubtful. It needed only a glance down the valley to see the clouds flooding steadily up from the Teesta Valley, and it was practically certain that the latter part of their programme, at least, would be spoilt by the rains, as the Zemu Valley receives them earlier than the head of the Lhonak Valley.

One march from the Base Camp down the Lhonak Valley was a yak-grazing ground, and a runner was sent down ordering yaks to be sent up for our luggage. Perhaps it was memories of Wood Johnson's adventure with the Khunza yak that led Duvanel to object strongly to having his exposed films and cinematograph apparatus yak-borne down the valley. However, while even a Lhonak yak might have objected to the yakmanship of Wood Johnson, it apparently did not mind carrying Duvanel's films, and the matter was thus amicably settled. As a matter of fact, I noticed no desire on the part of Wood Johnson to "yak it" down the valley.

June 12 was another beautiful day, and Europeans, porters and yaks started off in great fettle. Frau Dyhrenfurth was left behind, typing Professor Dyhrenfurth's letters and articles, and was to follow with her servant later.

A mile or two down the valley we turned for one last look at the beauties we were leaving. The huge snout of the Lhonak Glacier was thrust down the valley like some tremendous earthwork of the gods. Far above rose the Jonsong Peak, serene and peaceful. Had we really stood on that remote summit, so far above the world? Dominating the head of the Lhonak Glacier stood the Lhonak Peak, rising in perfect symmetry and superb simplicity. Northwards, was the brown reef of mountains separating us from Thibet. Silently we stood gazing at the Jonsong Peak. It had taken and given some hard knocks. We had conquered it, but conquered not its spirit, it had merely suffered us. The true mountaineer does not regard a vanquished summit with contempt, but rather with increased respect. Kangchenjunga is terrible, it is difficult to think of it in any other way. It is a giant, with all a giant's meaningless passions and illogical rages. The Jonsong Peak is a more tolerant mountain. In stature it cannot rival Kangchenjunga, therefore, it is more sober, less blatant. After being cast out from the precincts of Kangchenjunga, we had approached it with humility, and it had welcomed us.

One last regretful glance at brown valley, silver peak and

YAKS AT THE JONSONG BASE CAMP

gentian sky. We turned. Soon a corner had hidden peaks and glacier from view.

For some distance we strolled over turf and over the shoulders of rolling hills that put me in mind of the South Downs. We were well content with life ; so too were the porters. Even the " Thundering Herd " of yaks seemed to sense the gaiety of the occasion, and increased their normal speed of two miles to nearly two and a half miles per hour.

We were short of coolie food, but word had been sent down to Lachen, and we were expecting to meet some loads. Unfortunately, they were sent on the other side of the glacier torrent, and it was only with considerable difficulty that a sack of coolie food was slung across on a rope, for it was impossible to ford the torrent.

We passed the end of the valley leading up towards the range running south from the Langpo Peak. Looking up it we were rewarded with a fine view of the Tent Peak, with a plume of monsoon clouds tearing its summit.

The grass, at first dry and green, became greener and more luscious. Brooks of clear, cool water babbled down the hillside to join the turgid mountain torrent that followed the valley. Little flowers grew beside them, many of which were familiar Alpine friends, and for the first time since leaving Kangbachen we came upon dwarf rhododendrons. The broad valley narrowed abruptly into a steeper defile. Just before it did so there was situated a little group of huts, marked on the map as Tancha.

A stiff wind was blowing down the valley, and we took good care to pitch our tents to the windward of the filthy hovels in which dwelt the yakherds and their families. This portion of the Lhonak Valley reminded me of a valley in the Red Coolins of Skye, only here the ground was not bog-like, there was no misty drizzle, and neither bannock cakes nor whiskey were to be purchased at the yakherds' huts. For the rest there were the same bare slopes, and colourful reddish rocks and broken crags, similar to those of the Red Coolins. At eventide when the sun gilded the hillcrests, I almost felt that I had only to walk to the crest of one of them to see the landlocked waters of the sea lochs, and the dim, blue isles of the Hebrides. The darkness fell more swiftly than it does over the Hebrides. Here was no lingering twilight, no gradual merging of blue and violet, violet and purple, but a sudden and brutal switch over from light to darkness.

We began to feel anxious as to the whereabouts of Frau Dyhrenfurth, but presently we espied two figures in the gloom, and went out to greet her. She had been kept longer than had been anticipated by her typing duties, and it was not until long after we had left that she was able to leave the Base Camp, together with her servant, a youth of sixteen, named Kipa. She had forded the torrent under the impression that we had gone down the same route as that followed by the men carrying coolie food, and she had had to cross back. Kipa, who had carried her, had been nearly carried away and drowned by the swiftly running waters. As it was she was very wet, and anyone with a less tough constitution might well have caught a severe chill.

My estimate as to the distance from the Base Camp at which we might expect to meet the monsoon rains was not far out, for we had not marched more than a mile or so down the valley the following morning when we ran into a depressing drizzle and damp mists. Wood Johnson revelled in it, for being a North-countryman it naturally reminded him of the purlieus of Manchester and Wasdale Head. I fear that for my part I found it merely depressing. It soon cleared up, however, and as we descended to a flat plain marked on the map as Langpo, the sun peered out again.

We were now on the north bank of the river, having forded it with some difficulty below Tancha. We began to encounter a number of side streams flowing from the main watershed of the Himalayas to the north, along which runs the Thibetan frontier. Sometimes, it was no easy matter fording these, but the porters were used to such work, and carrying us pick-a-back, picked their way sure-footedly through the rapids.

One of these streams, the Chaka Chu, flows down the valley at the head of which is the Nakpo La Pass on the frontier of Sikkim and Thibet. It is a pass probably not often used, but we came across an old man with his son and a yak. The yak was laden with an extraordinary variety of objects. Had Lewis Carroll seen it he might have mounted his White Knight on a yak instead of the more conventional war-horse. If the White Knight had been so mounted, he would not have needed to fall off, he would have been thrown off, and that frequently.

Tucking up their dirty robes, the old man and his son strove to coax the yak across the stream. First of all the son pulled on the bridle, while the old man shoved behind ; then the old man pulled on the bridle while the son shoved behind. These proceedings seemed merely to bore the yak, and it turned its brown eyes upon the two in the same pitying way that Wood Johnson's yak had regarded him. At last, after many efforts to budge the yak had failed, the old man and his son halted, too exhausted even for profanity. As they did so, the yak gave them one contemptuous glance, and with stately tread, crossed the stream of its own accord.

A little distance beyond this stream we camped. Though our height was only 14,000 feet, wet snow was falling heavily and the climate had degenerated into a rawness similar to that of a November day in England. For the first time on the expedition we felt really chilly. Up high we had experienced occasional numbness and had narrowly escaped frostbite on two or three occasions, but though one might numb, one did not shiver. In order to experience a really unpleasant form of cold, it is unnecessary to leave Great Britain. Towards evening the sun broke through for a short time, but the snow instead of evaporating was resolved into a wet slush.

The next morning saw us tramping along a path of muddiness reminiscent of a clay valley in Surrey. Wood Johnson rejoiced in it, for it reminded him once more of Manchester. We were now in a delightful country "between the pinewoods and the snow," the alps of Kangchenjunga. I would that I were a botanist, and it was indeed unfortunate one was not included in the party. The whole hillside was covered in dwarf rhododendrons in full bloom; there were clumps of gorgeous blue poppies, and everywhere dwarf pines, to say nothing of many flowering mosses and rock flowers, some of which were familiar and some were not.

The valley narrowed almost to a gorge. We ate our lunch near some great drifts of avalanche snow. Everything pointed to the fact that the rainfall and snowfall are far greater in the lower part of the Lhonak Valley than in the upper. The snow line was definitely lower, and the drifts still left on the hillside suggested a heavy winter snowfall.

As we had only been able to take yaks to our last camping place, word had previously been sent to Lachen for local coolies to carry our loads. We met some twenty-five of them both men and women. They had come up from Lachen the same day, and expected to reach our last camping site ere nightfall, a prodigious piece of walking. These Lachen people are remarkably handsome, with finely chiselled features and smooth, clear skins. Like most of the peoples who dwell in these upper valleys of Sikkim and Nepal they had emigrated from the bleak plateaux of Thibet to the more fertile valleys south of the main Himalayan watershed.

Shortly after passing them, we entered the gorge of the Zemu Chu.[1] We were on the north-eastern bank of the stream, and it was essential to cross to the south-west bank in order to reach the camping place at Yaktang at the junction of the Zemu and Lhonak valleys.[2] Former travellers have mentioned a huge boulder resting in the torrent bed, by utilising which it is possible to cross the torrent. This may be possible at normal times, but certainly not during the rains. A party of our own men, under the charge of Tikeram, who had been sent on ahead some days previously, and aided by the Lachen men had, however, constructed a bridge from pine trunks to which cross

[1] Chu equals River.

[2] The nomenclature is here somewhat confusing. The Zemu Chu is not the stream from the Zemu Glacier, but the lower portion of the Lambo Chu which flows down the Lhonak Valley.

pieces were lashed with yak-hair rope. Though primitive in appearance, it was strong enough for its purpose, and well worth the fifteen rupees charge for the yak-hair rope by the Head Man of Lachen. We crossed it gingerly, one by one, for to have fallen into the boiling torrent beneath would have meant certain death.

We were now down to the level of giant rhododendrons and coniferous trees. Beyond our home-made bridge the way had been prepared and a track hacked through the snaky tangle of rhododendrons. Had it not been prepared, we could not possibly have got to Yaktang that day. The gorge was a wild gloomy place, and its gloominess was enhanced by a low roof of cloud. We felt imprisoned. I found myself longing for the upland breezy slopes of the Lhonak Valley, for there is something terribly depressing about these great gorges that carry the melted snow waters of the Himalayas to the plains.

The gorge opened suddenly out, dropping at the same time fully 1,000 feet to Yaktang. Down the pitch thus formed the swollen torrent of the Zemu Chu roared in a tremendous cataract. What a place for a hydro-electric station! A million or more horse power which could easily be harnessed are going to waste.

We found ourselves once more in the region of deciduous trees, and for the first time since we had left Yoksam a tropical forest enclosed us. Wild strawberries were growing everywhere, but they were watery and tasteless. The path became muddier and muddier. Wood Johnson and I were far ahead of the others, and we hurried on.

At the junction of the Zemu and Lhonak valleys there is a flat open space, where is situated the shepherd's hut

A HOMEMADE BRIDGE OVER THE LHONAK RIVER

dignified by the title of Yaktang. Here we found the assistant cook, comfortably ensconced before a roaring fire, and proceeded to arouse him to a sense of his duties. It was found that he had in his possession a large tin of strawberries : these, together with a tin of condensed milk, were opened and engulfed—there is no better word to express our hunger and greed—by Wood Johnson and myself. A day or two after this episode, Frau Dyhrenfurth, when checking her list of stores, announced with joy that so far as she could remember there was still a tin of strawberries unopened and uneaten. The cook was told to produce them. He could not, neither, fortunately, could he speak English or German. His jabber in Nepali was, however, translated by Wood Johnson to the effect that the cook regretted it, but the strawberries had been eaten. A more literal translation would, however, have been to the effect that Wood Johnson and I had eaten the strawberries and he, the cook, did not see why he should be blamed. Now, I fear, the " Memsahib " will know the disgraceful truth as to the fate of that tin of strawberries.

It was a dismal night, but despite the rain we preferred to camp on the wet grass outside the hut rather than on the years' old layers of offal comprising the floor of the hut. We had hoped to obtain a view of Siniolchum, but the monsoon had now this part of the Himalayas in its grip, and we marched down the valley squelching through glutinous mud under a leaden sky. We reached Lachen before midday, and for the first time for over two months entered the door of a civilised dwelling.

At Lachen there are two lady missionaries, one of whom, Miss Konquist, a Swedish lady, has been there for thirty years. Their good work is evidenced by the neatness and cleanliness of the village, and the industry of its inhabitants. The latter had been taught weaving, and I brought back with me to England a handsome rug, dyed in natural colours from the flowers of the Teesta Valley, and a quantity of cloth, as superior in quality as the finest Harris homespun. The fact that anyone should spend thirty years in such a remote corner of the world bears testimony to the charm of Lachen. It is indeed a beautiful little place, nestling on a shelf of the Teesta Valley, 8,000 feet above sea level, amid charming woodlands, dells and glades where many varieties of fruit and vegetables, including the homely apple tree, flourish.

We were invited to tea at the Mission House. Surely it was never before invaded by such a set of blackguardly looking ruffians. I exclude, of course, the "Memsahib," whose appearance went far to redeem that of her bewhiskered companions. It was strange to be sitting in a drawing room again, balancing a cup of tea in one hand, and biting elegantly at a piece of bread and butter held in the other. I fear our bites were neither elegant nor few, and the excellent cakes and scones provided disappeared at almost an indecent speed.

From Lachen to Gangtok is four marches. The weather was kind to us for the first two marches, and we were able to enjoy the scenery and flora of one of the loveliest valleys in the Himalayas, the great valley of the Teesta River. Owing to landships, it was impossible to take ponies more than a few miles beyond Tsuntang, one march from Lachen. The rains had begun, so the missionaries told us, at Lachen eleven days ago, when we had been enjoying fine weather on the Jonsong Peak. They must have been very heavy indeed, amounting to a cloudburst, for between Tsuntang and Singhik the path had been obliterated in many places by landslides, which in some cases had swept broad tracks through the dense forests. We had expected to find many leeches, but curiously enough, we encountered hardly any, although in some places it was necessary to keep a sharp look-out.

Singhik bungalow is in a delightful situation, and admirably placed for a stay of several days for botanists who like to browse among the varied flora of this part of the Teesta Valley, but after my own experience there, I think I should prefer to give it a miss in the future.

In order to finish a dispatch to *The Times*, which was to be telegraphed from Gangtok, I sat up until after midnight writing. The job done, I took up the candle by the light of which I had been writing, and started off to the room I was sharing with Wood Johnson. In order to get there I had to walk along the verandah. I had hardly passed out of the sitting-room door on to the latter, when suddenly I received a heavy blow on the neck almost sufficient to stun me. Thinking I was being attacked by some robber or other evil disposed person, I let out a yell, and dropping the candle turned round to face my attacker. There was no one there, the verandah was deserted ! Then came a horrid thought, above the verandah the roof was supported by rafters ; perhaps a snake hanging from one of these had struck the blow ! I put my hand to my neck, but there was no blood, neither was it bruised or sore, though the blow had seemed a heavy one. I took up the candle, relit it, and passing along the verandah, entered the bedroom. My yell had been sufficient to wake Wood Johnson, but not to get him out of bed—*that* would require nothing short of an earthquake, or some other natural cataclysm. The obvious explanation was a bat, owl, or some other nocturnal rover, yet, one of these could scarcely have felt like a human fist. There would, in addition, have been the beat of wings. Probably it was due to a lack of a suitable explanation but my sleep was a disturbed one. I dreamt that I was trying to escape from something malignant and horrible. Then the ground I was standing on began to rock in the grip of an earthquake. I awoke to find myself standing on the unfortunate Wood Johnson trying to climb out of the window. Altogether, it was a somewhat disturbed night.

Between Singhik and Dikchu the weather during the day was no longer able to contain itself, and broke wrathfully in what novelists writing of the tropics usually describe as " ropes of rain." I did not see anything that resembled " ropes of rain," and it will probably give a better idea to the scientifically minded reader of the rainfall to say that it probably fell at the rate of about one inch per hour.

The bungalow at Dikchu is in a bad situation, and is only 2,000 feet above sea level, near the Teesta River, and in the middle of dense jungle. It is well within the malarial area, and as I have before remarked Teesta malaria is one of the most virulent forms of malaria known. Also, the moist heat was unpleasant after the clear cold air we had been used to. Lightning flamed through the jungle canopy, and the rain roared down so loudly as almost to drown the crash of thunder. We had no mosquito nets, and we were badly bitten during the night. It was probably here that Dr. Richter and Kurz got a touch of malaria.

The weather rained itself out during the night, and we climbed up to the Penlong La in fine weather, save for a desultory shower or two. Near the pass we were met by servants of the Maharajah of Sikkim with the Maharajah's own racing ponies. It was a kindly thought and the ponies fairly flew along guided by the familiar Chu ! Chu ! which is successful above all exclamations in this part of the world in galvanising ponies and yaks into activity.

The first thing that encountered our gaze as we entered the dak-bungalow at Gangtok was a bottle of whiskey standing like a Serjeant-Major before a row of tins containing various delicacies, a gift of the Maharajah's. We were greeted also by Mr. Dudley, the Maharajah's secretary, and his wife, whose hospitality we are never likely to forget.

Gangtok is something like Darjeeling on a smaller scale. There are the same terraced roads, and platforms for houses cut in the hillsides. The following morning we called upon the Maharajah and the Maharanee, and were shown round a temple that was being constructed in the Palace grounds. The interior was being painted by expert native artists. Though there appeared to be little in the nature of any preliminary plans or drawings, the work was being executed with extraordinary accuracy as regards spacing and attention to detail. The wonderful designs were Chinese in their conception, and were presumably intended to represent incidents in the life of Buddha and the beliefs of Buddhism. But in one corner was a squatting figure with a cruel countenance and sardonic grin, which we were told was the God of Kangchenjunga. Before we left I mentioned the little incident at Singhik to the Maharajah who told me that people avoid the bungalow as far as possible and even double march in preference to spending a night there. Possibly, however, he only told me this out of politeness to my story !

That evening the Maharajah entertained us to dinner. I fear that we were hardly dressed for the part, but any slight diffidence we may have felt regarding our beards and clothes was soon forgotten under the influence of an excellent dinner, including one or two strange Chinese dishes with which we were not familiar. Indeed, I found myself relating to the Maharanee, who speaks excellent English, my best stories, which were translated into Thibetan for the benefit of a stout gentleman who sat on my other side, who, I gathered, was the Holiest Lama of Sikkim. That evening his holiness was not proof against certain Welsh stories into which I endeavoured to impart as much as possible of that accent for which the leader of another great Himalayan expedition is renowned. It was a convivial evening. Among other things we were told that once a year a great dinner is given by the Maharajah to the Lamas of the Sikkim Monasteries, and that it is considered an insult to the hospitality of the Maharajah if the Lamas are able to leave the Palace on their own legs. I can well believe that they never do.

The following morning we said good-bye to Gangtok, and to Mr. and Mrs. Dudley with regret. We had hoped to be able to travel in motor-cars all the way to Darjeeling, but owing to floods and the main road bridge being down at Tsingtang we walked and rode. Riding proved something more than exciting, for our ponies had been trained as racing ponies, and one and all hated to see another pony in front of them. Their mouths were like iron, and at times it was impossible to hold them in. I shall not easily forget mine bolting at a point where the road was narrow and turned a sharp corner, below which sheer cliffs two or three hundred feet high fell to the torrent beneath. For a non-horseman like myself it was a relief to cross the temporary bridge at Tsingtang to find a little fleet of docile " baby " cars waiting to take us over the last stage of some forty miles to Darjeeling.

We stopped at Gielle Tea Estate, where we were hospitably received by Mr. McKean, Wood Johnson's Manager. Darkness and rain were falling as the gallant little cars, laden to overflowing, toiled up the steep hills to Darjeeling. A little later the fashionably dressed habitués of the ballroom at the Mount Everest Hotel were startled by the appearance of a number of ill favoured tramps, the entrance of whom was greeted by the band with what some described as " Die Wache am Rhein " and others as " The Star-spangled Banner " or was it the Frothblowers' Anthem ?

Three days later we took leave of Wood Johnson and many hospitable friends at Darjeeling, and motored down to Siliguri. Our servants and porters said good-bye to us as we got into our cars and each of them slipped little cotton scarves over our shoulders as a mark of esteem. I shall always remember the grip of Nemu's horny hand.

Two glimpses with which we were rewarded on that journey are memorable. The first glimpse occurred as we came out of the monsoon mists which were enwrapping Darjeeling and the hills round with a grey shroud, to see the Plain of Bengal stretched out below us in the sunlight.

For three months we had seen nothing but hills, mountains and valleys, now we looked upon one of those vast fertile plains which had been vouchsafed by Nature for the use of man. Far into the dim blue distances it stretched, with its dark green forest blurs, and the silver thread of the great Teesta River, no longer turbulent, but calm and serene, bearing the melted snows of the Himalayas to the ocean. To appreciate life to its full, you must sample its contrasts. We had toiled amid the snows, our cheeks had felt their harsh coldness, had been scorched by their burning suns, and lashed by their bitter blizzards. Now the soft warm air of the plain came up to meet us. Tropical forests enclosed us, and above the purr of the car we could hear the *chanson* of innumerable insects.

The second view was later when we had left the hills, and were passing along the flat straight road near Siliguri. The last gleams of sunset were fading from earth and sky, the insect chorus had died away, and no sound came from the hushed forests on either hand. Before us stretched the plain, behind us rose the Himalayas. A range of towering cumuli clouds rested on the foothills, their crests sharply outlined against a saffron sky. Grand, solid, immovable, they rose, seemingly as eternal as the great mountain range over which they stood watch and ward.

CHAPTER XIX

LESSONS OF THE EXPEDITION

Before the War little was known of the peculiar mountaineering problems presented by the greatest peaks of the Himalayas. Peaks of 22,000 feet and 23,000 feet had been conquered by such pioneers as Dr. Longstaff and Dr. Kellas, the Duke of the Abruzzi had reached a height of 24,000 feet in a bold but unsuccessful attempt on the Bride Peak in the Karakorams, and two of the giants, Kangchenjunga and Nanga Parbat, had been also vainly attempted. In the light of subsequent experience, however, these attempts can only be regarded as tentative, if valuable, reconnaissances into altitudes formerly deemed impossible of access. The lack of knowledge as to the special equipment, and the elaborate camping and transport organisation necessary, and the absence of real information of the effect of altitude on the bodily functions made attempts on the greater peaks in those days foredoomed to failure.

After the War, however, a new era of mountaineering was inaugurated by the three assaults on Mount Everest, in which Colonel Norton and Mr. Somervell, by reaching a height of 28,000 feet, showed that man's body is capable of acclimatising itself to pressures of air as low as those into which Everest thrusts its crest. Curiously enough, Everest is the only great Himalayan peak which can definitely be said to be accessible to mountaineers. Other great peaks may defy all comers for many generations, and among these I would number Kangchenjunga.

Our attack on Kangchenjunga from the Nepal side was largely based on Mr. Douglas Freshfield's analysis of the most likely lines of attack in his book "Round Kangchenjunga." Photographs of Kangchenjunga from the Kangchenjunga Glacier appear to indicate a mountain face of reasonable angle. Actually, they give an entirely false impression of this huge face. Distortion and foreshortening misrepresent the scale and steepness of the rock and ice slopes, while in place of the rocky shelves, which Mr. Freshfield thought might form the head of the Eastern Tributary of the Kangchenjunga Glacier leading easily upwards to the col in the North Ridge separating Kangchenjunga from the Twins, there is instead a rock and ice slope 4,000 feet high set at an impossible angle.

Considering that, with the exception of Colonel Tobin and Wood Johnson, not one of the party had had previous Himalayan experience, the project of approaching the Base Camp site through Nepal by way of two high passes, the Kang La (16,373 feet), and the Mirgin La (14,853 feet), was ambitious. Had we known what difficulties confronted us, in particular the lateness of the winter and consequent lowness of the snow-line, we should certainly have preferred the alternative route by way of the Teesta and Lhonak valleys and the 20,200 feet pass of the Jonsong La. The Jonsong La would have been much less difficult in spite of its height, and, as we proved later, we could have worked our transport in relays of trustworthy porters.

There are two types of Himalayan expeditions, the large expedition with its correspondingly elaborate bandobast, and the small expedition burdened only with a light transport. The present expedition was probably the largest climbing expedition that has ever visited the Himalayas, and in its transport was unwieldy and top-heavy. The chief advantage that a small expedition has over a large one is that it can live more on the country. Had it not been for the generous help of the Maharajah of Nepal our expedition would have been impossible, as not enough supplies could have been obtained from the sparsely populated valleys through which the expedition passed. The large expedition has, of course, several advantages over the small expedition. In the case of illness there is a reserve of climbers to carry on with the work, and the climbing party can be split up into two or more groups, one group undertaking the work of establishing high camps, leaving the others free to rest before their attempt on the summit.

But provided its members keep fit the small expedition has other advantages besides those of easier provisioning. It is mobile, it needs comparatively few porters, and it can take its pick from first-rate men, thus making its plans secure and free from labour troubles. The ascent of the Jonsong Peak proved that four men backed up by good porters are capable of overcoming a great peak. The greater giants of the Himalayas, such as Everest and Kangchenjunga, demand the large expedition, if only on grounds of health, for altitude will surely weed out the climbing party, leaving perhaps from eight or ten men not more than two or three fit to make the final attempt on the summit.

Himalayan mountaineering only resembles Alpine mountaineering so far as the actual technique of climbing is concerned. In scale, snow and weather conditions, route finding, and general organisation, it is so different that only by experience can the Alpine-trained mountaineer learn safely to tackle its manifold problems—and this experience is gained all too frequently at the cost of valuable lives.

Kangchenjunga is not merely a mountain built on a greater scale than an Alpine peak. It is a mountain that is a law unto itself. Its northern and western faces are among the most desperately dangerous mountainsides in the world. Had we realised how dangerous the western side of Kangchenjunga was we should have abandoned any attempt on it at the outset. But, not unnaturally, it was some time before we were able to accustom ourselves to conditions entirely different from those which any of us had previously experienced, and it was not until the mountain discharged an avalanche upon us of almost cataclysmic dimensions did we realise how utterly different was the work compared to that of the Alps. This, at least, was a bitter lesson, for it cost the life of Chettan, a porter of almost unparalleled Himalayan experience.

In the Alps the risk of being overwhelmed by an avalanche is sometimes taken, but such a risk is usually incurred only for a few minutes when passing beneath a hanging glacier or under unstable ice pinnacles in an ice face. On Kangchenjunga the risk lasts as long as the party is on the mountain. Communications must be maintained, and parties go to and fro between camps. Thus, one short stretch of ground exposed to avalanches may have to be traversed not once, but many times, and the probability of accident is greatly increased. Himalayan porters do not appreciate danger, they place implicit trust in their sahibs, whom they are prepared to follow anywhere. Thus the sahib incurs a grave responsibility by risking the lives of his porters and cannot afford to betray such magnificent confidence.

Ice avalanches are Kangchenjunga's deadliest weapon. Ice walls, forming the edge of hanging glaciers 1,000 feet thick and running for miles across the face of the mountain bar approach. These hanging glaciers are in a constant state of downward movement. They break off in masses weighing millions of tons, which fall for thousands of feet down the granite precipices.

The avalanche that on May 9 ended our attempt to reach the North Ridge of Kangchenjunga covered about a square mile of snowfield with débris several feet thick, which weighed at a rough estimate about 1,000,000 tons. Other and greater avalanches fell later, in particular one that completely swept the route between Lower and Upper Camp Two, and, not content with this, the site of Lower Camp Two, fortunately evacuated a few days before, nearly a mile from the foot of the mountain face. It is difficult to appreciate the scale of such monstrous falls, and I shall always remember the period spent on Kangchenjunga as the most continually nerve-racking that I have ever experienced. In several of the camps one never felt secure, although everything possible was done to pitch them in protected sites. It is easy to be wise after the event, but even such a great mountaineer as Mummery was deceived by the " scale of things " and perished on Nanga Parbat, together with his two Gurkha followers.

The second attempt on Kangchenjunga by the North-west Ridge a week later taught lessons of a different kind.

Owing to scale and deceptive foreshortening, the difficulty of this route was under-estimated, for its length alone militated against any attempt. Yet an attempt *was* made more as a forlorn hope than anything else and, as we expected, failed. Even if the knife edges of ice and rock, carved and split into icy towers, had proved practicable to the expert climbers of the expedition, the impossibility of establishing camps on the crest and of getting up laden porters would have made it a hopeless proposition. To tackle routes of advanced Alpine difficulty on such peaks as Kangchenjunga is a mere waste of time.

Curiously enough, we seldom met with dangerous snow conditions and saw only a few snow avalanches. Generally speaking, conditions were similar to those of the Alps during late winter and early spring. Most of the party were expert winter mountaineers and ski runners, so that the danger of being involved in a snow avalanche was slight. As regards weather, Kangchenjunga is great enough to make its own local conditions and these are not favourable to the mountaineer. Sudden storms of wind and snow are liable to strike with but little warning. Wind, in particular, will ever be the climber's bitter enemy, and on the upper ridges blows for days on end with paralysing intensity. Porters will face most things but wind demoralises them completely. Perhaps in its fury they recognise the wrath of the gods.

Himalayan ice is frequently unusually tough, and cutting steps in it is a more gruelling task than in the Alps. This toughness or plasticity is probably due to rapid evaporation, combined with a great range of temperature, varying from an almost tropical sun heat during the day to zero temperature at night. It is this capacity for bending that is partly due to the size of ice avalanches. Where Alpine ice would break away in small quantities at a time, Himalayan ice does not fall until large overhanging masses of it are no longer able to resist the tug of gravity.[1] The ice ridge encountered on the Ramthang Peak afforded an interesting example of this peculiar tenaciousness. Though appearing to be precariously poised on the crest of the ridge, it was found possible to traverse edges and masses of ice that could not exist in Alpine ridges. It is undoubtedly this quality of elasticity and tenaciousness that results in the extraordinary ice ridges of many Himalayan peaks such as Siniolchum and the Wedge Peak.

Will Kangchenjunga be climbed? The answer is, Yes, but most likely not in this generation and not by present-day mountaineering methods. The only route offering any hope would appear to be that attempted in 1929 by the Munich Expedition. But the difficulties are likely to be so great on the final rock pyramid that, taken together with the effects of altitude and the inevitable wind, it is doubtful whether they can be overcome.

In an analysis of the Munich Expedition as compared with the Everest Expedition in the *Himalayan Journal*, Colonel E. F. Norton compares the respective dangers and difficulties. Progress on Everest was more than twice as fast as that on Kangchenjunga, yet, whereas on Everest a height of 28,000 feet was reached, on Kangchenjunga but 24,400 feet was reached after five and a half weeks of gruelling work before bad weather enforced retreat. The Bavarians considered that they had overcome the principal

[1] See Appendix: "Glaciology: Snow Conditions and Avalanches."

difficulties. Such, however, is far from the case. These difficulties had scarcely begun. Altitude and its effects only begin to be really serious over 24,000 feet, and being on the sheltered side of the mountain they had not yet begun to experience that terrible west wind which sweeps the upper part of the North Ridge with such merciless severity. And last, but not least, is the final pyramid—a rock pile rivalling the upper part of the Matterhorn in its steepness and technical difficulty.

Present day oxygen apparatus is too heavy for such climbing as is offered by Kangchenjunga, and it is the conviction of the present expedition that only by some medical means which will artificially acclimatise the climber so that he is able to put forth the same effort at 25,000 feet as he would at sea level, or at least on Mont Blanc, will the upper part of Kangchenjunga be justifiably assailable. The present expedition were lucky to escape from an avalanche ; the Munich Expedition were luckier still to escape with no loss of life after being overtaken by a snowstorm of great severity.

After we had abandoned the attack on Kangchenjunga, having been driven back by ice avalanches from the North Ridge, and by the sheer difficulty of the route from the North-west Ridge, we decided to cross the 20,200 feet Jonsong La. We were able to get over this pass by the efforts of Frau Dyhrenfurth and Wood Johnson, together with invaluable help in the shape of coolies from the Nepalese authorities. The number of loads far exceeded the number of porters available, so the transport had to operate in relays. Everything worked perfectly, but luck was with us. The season was well advanced and the monsoon imminent. Had the weather broken, the expedition might have found itself in a serious predicament with some of its loads on one side and some on the other side of the pass, and faced, in addition, with a possible desertion *en masse* of the coolies. The move proved weatherwise, for shortly afterwards the monsoon broke on Kangchenjunga, covering it with new snow, while the district at the head of the Lhonak Valley remained untouched by bad weather.

In its topographical and geological work the expedition has added considerably to the previously little known country at the head of the Lhonak Valley and in North-eastern Nepal. The western and north-western glaciers of Kangchenjunga were thoroughly explored, while Schneider and Wieland found a practicable route over the Nepal Gap, thereby making a new pass between Sikkim and Nepal and solving a problem that had interested mountaineers for many years. The Dodang Nyima Range, separating the Lhonak Valley from Thibet, was also explored by Schneider and Hoerlin, who ascended its highest point, the 22,700 feet Dodang Peak, and traversed the Choten Nyima La.

Some idea of how little is known of the district to the west of the watershed at the head of the Lhonak Valley may be gained from the fact that a glacier was observed at least fifteen miles long not marked in any map. When political prejudices and difficulties have been overcome, this district of Northern and North-eastern Nepal will offer an interesting field for the explorer and mountaineer. Geologically, the district is extremely interesting, as it forms the junction of the Thibetan limestone with the granite of which Kangchenjunga and its satellites are composed. Fossils were discovered in the limestone Dodang Nyima range at a height of about 20,000 feet.

There is indisputable evidence of a former ice age in the huge terraces of the Lhonak Valley. The topographical data collected by Kurz and the geological work of Professor Dyhrenfurth have yet to be analysed and classified. Much valuable information will be at the disposal of the topographical and geological survey authorities. The meteorology of the district is remarkable. The difference of precipitation between that of Kangchenjunga and that of the Lhonak Valley is great, and the monsoon conditions quite different. Observations and photographs were made which should prove of interest in determining the approach and extent of the monsoon on this part of the Himalaya.

In addition to Duvanel's fine cinematograph work, Professor Dyhrenfurth took the highest film yet taken from the summit of the Jonsong Peak. Probably nowhere else does the actinic value of the light vary so much as in the Himalayas, and the photographers of the expedition had much difficulty in judging the correct exposure. In the lower regions, though the sunlight is brilliant, its yellow quality demands an aperture as great as f.8. and an exposure of 1/25 second. On the snowfields, however, the ultra-violet rays demand an aperture as small as f.22. and an exposure of 1/50 second.

Much forethought was given to equipping the expedition. To guard against cold and frostbite, thick tricot suits were supplied. But these, together with the special high climbing boots, were found to be unnecessarily heavy, and to impede active movement on difficult ground. The climbing boots, weighing 6½ lbs. the pair and containing over sixty nails each, proved extremely fatiguing, and most members climbed for preference in their ordinary Alpine boots. Incidentally, such a large number of nails is unsuitable in the Himalayas, as they conduct cold to the feet. On Everest comparatively light boots, sparsely nailed, proved effective, so long as they were large enough to hold several pairs of socks. Heavy clothing does not necessarily spell warmth, and several layers of light clothing is preferable to one layer of heavy clothing. The writer found that three or four light Shetland sweaters, weighing but a few ounces each, beneath a light water-proof jacket, withstood the coldest winds. No member suffered frostbite.

The feeding of climbers at high altitudes is a very real problem. A mountaineer climbs on his stomach even more than a soldier crawls on his. Altitude impairs the power of the stomach to assimilate food, and the strongest constitution may be laid low by gastritis and other "tummy troubles." The appetite must be kept up and the palate titillated if rapid deterioration of strength is to be prevented. At heights of over 20,000 feet light sugary foods were found most suitable, such as jams, biscuits, chocolate, sugar, tinned fish and fruit, and condensed milk. A little alcohol is a great aid to the digestion. Hot rum taken at bedtime is the best of all drinks to promote the sleep that is as essential as good feeding to the hardworked and mentally stressed mountaineer.

Owing to transport difficulties, the climbers during the early stages of the attempt on Kangchenjunga had to subsist on yak flesh and other mostly unsuitable foods. As a result a marked deterioration soon became evident, and it is practically certain that much of the subsequent illness that weakened the party was due to this. Later, with the arrival of good food, there was a rapid pick-up, and towards the end of the expedition on the Jonsong Peak the climbers, though reduced by a stone or more in weight, were putting forth their best efforts.

The general health of the expedition was well cared for by Dr. Richter. Attempts to combat the deleterious effects of altitude were made by blood-letting, to relieve blood pressure, as it was considered that the high blood pressure relative to the low pressure of the atmosphere is responsible for headaches and mountain sickness.

Only two members, Professor Dyhrenfurth and Duvanel, submitted to having 200 cubic centimetres of blood withdrawn, and as they were both subsequently taken ill, Professor Dyhrenfurth within a few days, and Duvanel later, it is doubtful whether any good resulted from the experiment. More successful was the special liver preparation invented by Dr. Richter. This took the form of a pill, nine of which had to be swallowed daily. It is believed to have assisted the special formation of the essential hæmoglobin corpuscles, which enable the climber to acclimatise to altitude. As on Everest, it was possible to form but few conclusions from physical tests made before the expedition. The capacity to hold the breath for a long period, or to blow up mercury to great heights has little or no bearing on the subsequent fitness of the climber on the mountain, where only genuine stamina, physique, and will-power avail.

A certain amount of oxygen should always be taken by a Himalayan expedition, if only for medicinal purposes. When Wood Johnson returned ill to camp on the Jonsong

Peak, an inhalation of oxygen reduced the pulse rate from 115 to 95 in a few minutes. If oxygen could be continuously used on the upper part of a peak, its effects would be good, but used intermittently it serves only to stimulate the body for a short time, while the subsequent reaction is severe. The weight of the apparatus prohibits prolonged use and by tiring the climber neutralises the effect of the oxygen. The experience of the last Everest Expedition makes it clear that, provided the actual climbing offers no great physical difficulty, the highest summits of the earth can be reached without oxygen. The secret of high climbing is slow acclimatisation, and this is best effected by living for several weeks as comfortably as possible at a height of about 20,000 feet. At this height the appetite is unimpaired and sound sleep possible. A future Kangchenjunga or Everest expedition would do well to send its climbing party a month or so in advance of the date fixed for the attempt, build a substantial wooden hut, and make small expeditions to moderate altitudes, and thus acclimatise to their task.

Himalayan mountaineering is mental as well as physical. Nowhere is the control, conscious and subconscious, of mind over matter better demonstrated than at great altitudes, and the reaction of the body to the processes of the mind is marked. The man who dislikes the work is more likely to become ill than the man who enjoys it, and, though the greatest mountaineering enthusiast is likely to crock, the finest physique is useless without a proper mental complement. The men who will force their way to the summits of Everest and Kangchenjunga will be men capable of disciplining their minds as well as their bodies, genuine philosophers at heart, who experience in mountaineering something far greater and finer than the mere physical joys of struggling with an inanimate opponent.

Apart from the difficulties of the country and the weather, some mistakes were made at the outset. Expeditions starting from Darjeeling should give long notice of their intended date of departure, in order that coolies may have time to come in from remote villages. Unfortunately, this was not done, and it was found necessary to recruit many coolies entirely unsuitable to the work. The best porters are Sherpas and Bhutias, and while in carrying power and endurance there is little to choose between these hardy races, the Sherpa is the better mountaineer on really difficult ground. Of those at Darjeeling, many are "rickshaw wallahs," and such was their keenness to join the expedition, that they were prepared to throw up easy and profitable work at the beginning of the season to face dangers and hardships of the nature of which they were fully aware.

To Colonel Tobin, the transport officer, who was in charge of the third party, fell the responsible task of getting the transport to the Base Camp. It is safe to say that without him and the two other British transport officers the expedition would have failed.

Owing to permission to enter Nepal coming at the last moment, a complete reorganisation had to be made. Apart from the difficulties of the route, which included two snow clad passes, numerous problems had to be solved, of which shortage of reliable porters, shortage of boots, shortage of snow goggles, and the uncertainty of obtaining even a limited number of local porters on the route were the most important. Most of these difficulties were foreseen and emphasised by Colonel Tobin before the start, but it was not easy to obviate, or even minimise them, and the leader decided to take the responsibility of facing all the risks involved.

The first party with Wood Johnson as transport officer left on April 6, with two hundred and twenty porters, the second party with about one hundred and sixty porters under the charge of Hannah left the following day, and Colonel Tobin, chief transport officer left with eighty mule loads on April 12. Between April 7 and April 12, twenty-five other porters started with loads that had arrived late in Darjeeling.

Darjeeling had been so denuded of porters, that the only method of transporting the remaining porter loads was on mules. These loads would, of course, have to be transferred to porters for porterage over the Kang La, and it was arranged that as soon as the first two parties were over the Kang La, one hundred and fifty porters with a good sirdar should return to Dzongri. The farthest point to which mules could be taken was the bridge between Tingling and Yoksam. Colonel Tobin actually hoped that he would be able to get his loads to Dzongri by April 17 or 18, carried by local porters and the porters sent back. It was also understood that a European member of the expedition would remain at Khunza until the third party reached that place. Khunza was the most important point on the route, being the junction of the lines of supply from Darjeeling and Nepal.

If this part of the scheme had been carried out, the loads of the first two parties would have been worked from Tseram to the Base Camp with two hundred porters.

It was anticipated that supplies and equipment would thus reach the Base Camp sufficient for the work of fifteen days or more on Kangchenjunga. Had this plan been carried out the first two parties, with about three hundred loads, would have arrived at the Base Camp by about May 3. The first two hundred loads would, of course, have reached the Base Camp by about April 23. This was sufficient to start climbing operations, and it was arranged that one hundred and twenty to two hundred and fifty porters would then be available to return to Tseram for the remaining loads.

Unforeseen circumstances prevented this plan from being carried out, with the result that it was not until May 3 that any of these men returned to Tseram. Meanwhile, Colonel Tobin had succeeded in working his loads by means of a few locally raised porters to Dzongri by April 20, but these men refused to work beyond that place. After a delay, twenty men were obtained from Yoksam and Tingling, which are three and four marches respectively below Dzongri, and these agreed to lift the Dzongri loads up to the snow-line on the Kang La, but no farther. This was completed by April 28, and on that date in very foul weather Colonel Tobin crossed the Kang La with the intention of raising porters in Nepal, as it seemed that there was no prospect of getting any Darjeeling porters for an indefinite time.

He reached Tseram on April 29, with only two of the nine men he had started with fit for anything. Of the remainder, two had deserted *en route*, two had left their loads in the snow, and three were snow-blind. On April 30, seventeen coolies from Khunza arrived. They included six women and five small boys, and they were despatched to the Kang La, but were driven back by the heavy snow and the strong winds. On the second occasion, they had to carry back four of the boys, but at the third attempt they were more successful.

Colonel Tobin sustained a fall on the Kang La. This, combined with the great physical and mental strain that he had been undergoing, made him unfit to go farther in the quest of transport. However, on May 3, seventy porters and a temporary sirdar arrived, and the clearing forward of the Kang La dump began in earnest, although the sirdar, Phuri, died on the pass.

By May 8, many of the loads began to reach Khunza, and by May 11 they were arriving at the Base Camp. Further batches of porters meanwhile became available. Messrs. Wood Johnson and Hannah were sent down the line to assist, for the food situation began to cause great anxiety. Indeed, the climbers had been on rather short commons. However, by the last named date, the situation had improved, and more local porters were being procured.

But the absence of a responsible sirdar, and the presence of certain disaffected coolies had resulted in looting on the Kang La, and on the upper route, so that many of the boxes reached the Base Camp depleted. The expedition was able to carry on, though at one time it was feared that a temporary withdrawal would be imposed on it.

The situation was greatly eased by the arrival of supplies ordered by the Maharajah of Nepal himself. Colonel Tobin gave over to Hannah at Tseram on May 12, and started back to Darjeeling down the Yalung Valley and through Nepal. By that date the Kang La dump was well on its way to the Base Camp. It was actually cleared by May 15.

There are many lessons to be learnt from the above story, and it may be remarked that it was fortunate that the expedition, though faced with a serious situation, had only a temporary set-back.

Colonel Tobin made some interesting commentaries. He said that an expedition requiring an enormous quantity of stores and equipment should arrange for its transportation a long time beforehand. Food packed in zinc cases which have to be cut open are superior to easily opened boxes fastened with nails or insecure padlocks. For an expedition on such a large scale, it would be advisable to arrange a series of food and equipment dumps the previous autumn season. Other members of the expedition should understand the supplies and transportation arrangements. Actually, the arrangements for an attack on Kangchenjunga via the Zemu route had been put on paper, but owing to the eleventh hour change of route, the scheme of operations was not so carefully worked out, with the result that a serious situation nearly occurred.

It should have been realised at Khunza that it was an important point, and that the presence there of a European, at least until supplies were assured, was imperative. Bauer, the leader of the Bavarian Expedition in 1929, with a less vital line of communication, kept one of his members halfway between his Base Camp and Lachen arranging operations. Hard luck on the individual, no doubt, but each member of an expedition must remember that he is one of a team, and should have his definite job allotted. Large batches of coolies must be in charge of a reliable sirdar. Failure to arrange this was not only the cause of bad work, but also of desertion and looting.

Until the expedition is concentrated, those engaged on transportation, at least, must be kept apprised of the local situation, as well as of the general position to ensure intelligent co-operation which is essential. Moreover, the work behind is dull, and men engaged on it are liable to become apathetic unless they are told what is going on at the front.

An ample supply of good boots is necessary. Owing to the excessive number of coolies requiring these they were not available. On another occasion it would be better to issue these in Darjeeling, and risk the small loss due to desertion. Shortage of goggles was also due to so many coolies not being allowed for.

After Colonel Tobin had returned to Darjeeling, the responsibility for transport devolved entirely upon Wood Johnson. Though theoretically a climbing member of the expedition, he undertook the arduous task of looking after the porters and arranging for supplies of food. No man should have been expected to shoulder the responsibility and do the work he did as well as climb, but it was entirely due to his efficient organisation that the expedition was able to carry out its programme, and it was entirely due too, to his unselfish and disinterested work on behalf of the expedition that he subsequently broke down on the Jonsong Peak.

Nor must Frau Dyhrenfurth be forgotten. There were those who had said she would be little better than a passenger on the expedition. Her management of stores and supervising of communications, especially those over the

Jonsong La, were invaluable to the expedition, and could not in its efficiency have been excelled by one well versed in the peculiar problems of commissariat in the Himalayas. And lastly, must be mentioned Naik Tikeram Thapa, who served as a valuable connecting link at Khunza and Lachen in the supply and dispatch of stores, added to which he supervised the porters' pay roll.

Did we make a mistake in attempting Kangchenjunga before the monsoon? Only time can tell. Heavy snowstorms appear more probable after the moonsoon, and the Bavarian party narrowly escaped disaster from a snowfall of seven feet, while Mr. Freshfield was considerably hampered in his plans by a fall of similar severity. On the other hand, these two parties experienced little or no wind, and wind is the greatest enemy of the Himalayan mountaineer. The present expedition had to withstand fierce winds, which according to porters were as bad as or worse than those on Everest. Nothing is more demoralising or lowers the vitality more than wind at a great altitude. The danger of being overtaken by a heavy snowfall, plus the increasing cold with the approach of winter after the monsoon, is more than counterbalanced by the winds before the monsoon. On the whole, therefore, another party attacking Kangchenjunga will do better to go out after the monsoon.

No general summary of the work of the expedition, and the lessons learned from it, would be complete that left out reference to the porters, without whom the expedition would have been impossible. It is absolutely essential that any Himalayan expedition should include transport officers who speak the language of the porters and understand them. The expedition was fortunate in having

Colonel Tobin, who is well acquainted with local conditions, whilst Mr. Wood Johnson, by reason of tea-planting experience, speaks fluent Nepali, and thoroughly understands the child-like temperament of the splendid men to whom the expedition owes so much.

The work of the chief Sirdar, Lobsang, was invaluable, and was equal in intelligence and trustworthiness to that of a sahib. Less spectacular, but also useful, was that of Naspati and Gyaljen, who were engaged with Colonel Tobin on the transport. Among those who did so well—and they are but a few among many equally good—must be mentioned the names of Nemu, Lewa, Sonam, Tsinabo, Ondi, Narsang, Kipa, Nima and, not least, Tencheddar, the cook, who, if frequently reviled, certainly did his best to propitiate rebellious palates. May but a short time elapse before I see again their broad, homely faces, with their infectious grins, and share once more with them the thrills and delights of mountaineering on the great peaks of the Himalayas.

APPENDIX I

GLACIOLOGY: SNOW CONDITIONS AND AVALANCHES

The most striking property possessed by Himalayan glacier ice as found in the Kangchenjunga district is its plasticity. This results in several striking differences in the general characteristics of glaciers as compared to Alpine glaciers, which at first sight strike the Alpine mountaineer as curious.

Why should Himalayan ice be more plastic than Alpine ice? The answer is temperature range. Unfortunately, we did not measure the direct heat of the sun at mid-day on the snow-fields of Kangchenjunga, but it is considerably greater than that of an Alpine sun, for it shines almost directly overhead and to the climbers at least its rays seemed often to beat down with paralysing intensity. The air temperature is, however, at or below freezing-point as a rule even at mid-day. At night the temperature may drop to -30° F. or more below zero. Thus the temperature range between mid-day and midnight is enormous, probably over 200° F. It will be seen from this that *ordinary* climatic conditions in the High Himalayas resemble a combination of winter and summer Alpine conditions, the night temperatures being comparable to Alpine winter night temperatures, and the sun temperatures during the day being far in excess of sun temperatures in the Alps at midsummer.

The exact physical process that occurs in snow and ice

as a result of continual temperature fluctuations is a matter for physicists. Of its effects, I can only quote from my own observations. Let us consider exactly what happens to snow that is changed by pressure and temperature range into ice. First of all the snow is compacted and consolidated by the pressure of more snow falling on top of it; it becomes at first brittle flaky ice, and then is changed by increasing pressure into harder and tougher ice. In the Alps pure ice is formed by pressure considerably below the surface of a snow-field. As the temperature of the ice once it has been covered by newly fallen snow, is more or less constant, it is only affected by pressure, and the effect of pressure is not the same as that of temperature range. Alpine ice is formed almost entirely by pressure and temperature range does not enter into its formation to nearly the same extent as it does in the Himalayas.

In the Himalayas, owing to a far greater temperature range, snow is changed into pure ice nearer the surface than it is in the Alps. Pressure, of course, enters into it, but it is not principally pressure that forms Himalayan ice, but pressure assisted considerably by temperature range. Thus, instead of a flaky intermediate stage, snow is converted almost straight away into ice, and ice tougher and more glue-like than that found in most Alpine districts. Mountaineers who have climbed on the Brenva face of Mont Blanc declare the ice there to be exceptionally tough. I can vouch for this, for during the three ascents I have made of that face, I encountered ice so tough that many more strokes than usual were required to cut steps in it. Dr. Claude Wilson described it in the *Alpine Journal* as " Steep slippery ice, of a hardness unknown to us before, and with a curious quality unique in our experience, born probably of great cold and enormous pressure—a quality of viscosity which gave the impression of cutting into something which would not chip, but whose particles clung together like stiff tar . . . almost as hard as marble and tough as rubber."

Now, there is probably no mountain face in the Alps that experiences a fiercer sun, and lower night temperatures, and the temperature range is probably greater than on any other peak in the Alps.

There is one more factor which enters into the question, evaporation. It is difficult to see how this can affect the formation of ice, but it probably results in the disappearance of the brittle surface ice, leaving only the tougher ice.

The toughness of Himalayan ice leads to conditions of interest and vital importance to the mountaineer. The main ice streams of Himalayan glaciers have usually a convenient corridor on either side, between the ice and the mountainside, which offers a convenient line of least resistance. Such corridors are seldom found in the Alps, owing to the fact that the ice being more brittle, breaks away at the side, filling any intermediate space that may be formed between the glacier and the mountainside.

Still more interesting is the scarcity of crevasses. Even in a steep ice-fall where the ice is hummocked and pinnacled, there are few actual crevasses. This again is due to the plasticity and bending capacity of the ice. Like glue, it prefers to bend over an inequality in the ground rather than split into crevasses. Pressure may raise its surface into mounds, knobs and even pinnacles, but it cannot break the ice as it does in the Alps. We frequently observed ice pinnacles bent over like candles in a heat wave, and it is not until the bending becomes so great and an enormous stress is exerted on the base of the pinnacle that the ice is fractured and the pinnacles collapsed.

This quality of bending is no doubt partly responsible for the enormous avalanches that fall from the hanging glaciers of Kangchenjunga. As we learnt to our cost, these hanging glaciers are very much " alive " and the speed of their downward movement is, owing to the huge annual snowfall, considerably greater than that of similar hanging glaciers in the Alps. Also, these hanging glaciers are frequently of enormous thickness, and walls of ice 600 to 1,000 feet high decorate the sides of Kangchenjunga. Were hanging glaciers of this size in the Alps, there would be great avalanches, but they would not be nearly so great as those that occur on Kangchenjunga. The reason is this : were these hanging glaciers in the Alps, the ice, owing to its brittleness, would break away more often, and there would be many avalanches, but none of a magnitude comparable to those that fall from Kangchenjunga. On Kangchenjunga the ice walls bend farther over the edge of precipices before breaking off, and when at last the ice is no longer able to withstand the internal stresses set up by unstable equilibrium, it cracks, and a huge avalanche occurs.

Thus, it is not so much the size of a hanging glacier, but physical reasons that result in avalanches of almost cataclysmic dimensions which sweep far across the level glaciers beneath. Until the Alpine-trained mountaineer learns to appreciate this fact, he will not be safe in the Himalayas.

That the quality of ice is affected by climatic conditions is borne out by the different formations and structures it exhibits. The ice scenery at the head of the Jonsong Glacier and the Lhonak Valley is very different from that of Kangchenjunga. The Lhonak Glacier is in its lower portion broken up into pinnacles, similar to those of the Everest glaciers. It is not so easy to find an explanation for these pinnacles, but in view of the fact that the districts where they occur get a comparatively small precipitation of snow and a drier climate it seems probable that evaporation is the cause and that they are formed in a similar manner to *nieves penitentes*.[1]

As regards movement of the glaciers, it was unfortunate that we took no observations of it. The downward movement of the hanging glaciers is very rapid and that of the main ice streams must be rapid too. I am, however, no glaciologist, and have only touched on one subject which interested me especially. There are many other equally interesting points to be investigated in connection with the glaciers of the Kangchenjunga district, and of these the most interesting is the determination of their present rate of movement, and what relation this bears to the precipitation of snow.

Evaporation plays a very important part in determining the size of Himalayan glaciers. I have already had occasion to mention the surprising smallness of the glacier streams ; apart from the rainy seasons, or periods of rapid melting they are usually little larger than Alpine streams. This is due to the fact that the rate of evaporation is far greater in the Himalayas than in the Alps. As we frequently observed,

[1] See page 318.

the surface drainage of a glacier is negligible, and the familiar streams and *moulins* such as are common on Alpine glaciers are almost entirely absent. Evaporation is the only reasonable explanation, and if the rate of evaporation in the Himalayas was the same as that in the Alps, it is certain that their glaciers would be very much larger than they are.

Perhaps I should make it clear that when I speak of evaporation, I do not necessarily mean that the snow or ice is melted first, and then evaporated, but that evaporation also takes place at temperatures below freezing-point. Such evaporation is probably due to the direct rays of the sun, and not to air temperature, which at high altitudes is usually below freezing.

Evaporation also plays an important part in determining snow conditions. It clears off new snow from rocks with extraordinary rapidity, so much so that even after a heavy snowfall, a rock mountain may be in climbing condition within twenty-four hours. Snow slopes sheltered from the sun should, however, be suspected of avalanches for a day or two. Owing to this partial clearance of snow by evaporation, the mountaineer may be led into thinking that because one portion of a mountain is safe, the mountain is safe everywhere else. But this by no means follows, and each slope and couloir must be studied on its merits. In this respect Himalayan mountaineering involves a closer study of snowcraft than Alpine mountaineering.

On account of the great temperature range, Himalayan snow varies between powdery snow such as may be found in the Alps in mid-winter, and the slushy, or wet crystalline snow found on an Alpine snow-field on a hot summer's afternoon. In fact, it is safe to say that almost every variety of snow may be experienced in the space of twelve hours. On this account a man cannot climb safely in the Himalayas until he has learnt to appreciate the rapidly changing conditions, and in snowcraft at least experience of winter mountaineering in the Alps is invaluable. A party of purely summer trained Alpine mountaineers, however skilled they might be in mountain craft and summer snow conditions, would be by no means safe in the Himalayas, where conditions more closely approximate to Alpine winter snow conditions. At least one avalanche disaster in the past could have been avoided if the party had been experienced winter mountaineers.

Heavy snowfalls on Kangchenjunga are usually accompanied by wind, and it is tolerably certain that wind slabs are formed on the leeward sides of ridges. The gravest objection to the proposed alternative route to avoid the steep portion of the North Ridge would have been danger from this particular form of avalanche, for so much snow is always blowing from the North Ridge that it probably compacts into wind slabs on the east or leeward side of the ridge. The same danger applies to Everest, and after a heavy snowfall from the west, the danger of wind slab avalanches will exist on the slopes leading to the North Col. After a heavy night's snowfall the mountaineer must expect to find wind slab, or powdery snow avalanche conditions in the early morning, but after the sun has been at work for an hour or two wet snow avalanches must be expected.

APPENDIX II

THE WEATHER OF KANGCHENJUNGA

"Mountains make their own weather." No better example of this truism is afforded by the weather which is made by Kangchenjunga. As has been pointed out elsewhere in this book, the mountaineer has only two short seasons in which to attack Kangchenjunga, before and after the monsoon. Both are short seasons, and neither of them can be called a summer season in an Alpine sense, they are merely two springs. Both are pitifully short, and the total time available for attacking Kangchenjunga is no longer than four or five weeks, and even this is liable to be interrupted by local bad weather.

Standing as Kangchenjunga does, an isolated mountain group rising straight out of deep, humid, tropical valleys, local bad weather is only to be expected. Weather data is only to be gathered by experience, and so few parties have visited Kangchenjunga that it is not possible yet to say definitely whether it is better to attempt the mountain before or after the monsoon.

Wind will always be the greatest enemy of those who attempt it before the monsoon. I do not remember a day on which snow was not being blown off the mountain by westerly winds. The Munich Expedition experienced but little wind, but they were on the sheltered side of the mountain, and the wind blows almost invariably between south and west, and west and north. On the other hand, every day after the monsoon is bringing the winter nearer. The Munich party, who were overtaken by a snowfall of seven feet towards the end of their attempt of Kangchenjunga in October, considered that they were exceptionally unlucky, but others who know the mountain considered them exceptionally lucky not to have had it before! We had no heavy snowfalls but we experienced plenty of wind. That is the problem future expeditions will have to solve—whether they are prepared to endure winds before the monsoon, or risk a heavy snowfall after the monsoon.

Passing through the lower tropical valleys we had, to begin with, heavy rainstorms in early April. As we approached the Base Camp we came out of this area, or level of rain, and experienced only small snowstorms, depositing but a few inches of snow at a time. It would appear that at a certain level, about 15,000 feet, the dry westerly winds prevent the rain clouds in the lower valleys from rising higher. Above this level, local snowstorms are liable to occur, but they are definitely local, and the area covered by them is small, whereas the area covered by a rainstorm in the lower valleys may be very great. But sometimes the bad weather which pours up the local valleys is so intense that it is able to force its vanguard of storm clouds up the glaciers of Kangchenjunga. This is particularly noticeable in the case of two of the main bad weather avenues which we saw, the Kangchenjunga Glacier and the Zemu Glacier, but it is probable that there is even worse weather at the heads of the Yalung and Talung glaciers which stretch from the south side of the mountain.

When ascending towards the Jonsong La it was interesting to note the bad weather seething up from Khunza. It was able to deposit snow on our Base Camp, but the clouds were unable to penetrate farther up the glaciers owing to the strong Thibetan winds pouring over the ranges to the north-west, and in particular over the Jonsong La.

The difference of climate experienced within a few miles when ascending from the Base Camp to the Jonsong La was striking. As we turned the corner of Pangperma we left the moisture laden airs for drier airs, and that this was so was shown by the glaciers themselves. Only once on Kangchenjunga did we hear thunder, and that was when climbing the North-west Ridge. It came from the south, in the direction of the Yalung Valley, and it was far below us. Whether thunder-storms ever attack the upper part of Kangchenjunga is doubtful. It is probable that they never rise to a greater altitude than about 20,000 feet, although we remarked cumuli nimbus clouds, the summits of which were well above 25,000 feet.

From the Jonsong Peak it was interesting to watch the monsoon clouds flooding up the Teesta and Arun valleys in an attempt to outflank and surround us. But they never got far over the main watershed of the Himalayas into Thibet before they were dissolved by the dry winds, although sometimes the plateaux of Thibet generated their own little clouds and storms.

What is the cause of the relentless north-west wind which makes climbing so unpleasant in this part of the world? I think it is simply the colder air of the Thibetan plateaux circulating into the warmer valleys south of the watershed. On the Jonsong Peak the strongest winds were at night, and they usually dropped by 9 a.m. This is possibly due to the fact that at night there is a greater variation of temperature between the lower valleys south of the watershed and the Thibetan plateaux than during the daytime. At night the temperature may drop to thirty or forty degrees below zero Fahrenheit, a total drop of possibly sixty or seventy degrees Fahrenheit. In the tropical valleys there is nothing like such a great temperature range, and by temperature range it must be understood that I mean the temperature of the air. Thus the circulation caused by the cold air rushing in to fill in spaces left by the rising of the hot air (and also compensating for its shrinkage when the temperature falls in the evening) is far more violent.

So dry was the head of the Lhonak Valley, that we scarcely expected it to get the monsoon, but it did, although much later than Kangchenjunga and the south. Dr. Kellas has proved that it is possible to climb on the peaks of Northern Sikkim during the monsoon.

The lowest temperatures we had were not on Kangchenjunga, but on the Jonsong Peak. It was a pity that we had no maximum and minimum thermometer. No party should go into the Himalayas without one, for interesting data should be obtained if its readings are studied on a mountain group such as Kangchenjunga. Another useful instrument would be a wet and dry bulb thermometer. With these two simple pieces of apparatus, combined with a boiling point thermometer and an aneroid, some valuable observations of weather could be made.

INDEX